Shakespeare in Perspective
Volume Two

SHAKESPEARE
IN PERSPECTIVE
Volume Two

Edited by Roger Sales

ARIEL BOOKS
BRITISH BROADCASTING CORPORATION

REFERENCE NUMBERS
A reference number follows each Shakespearean quotation in this book, all of which are taken from the BBC edition of the plays. The first digit refers to the relevant act in the play, the second to the scene and the final digits are the line numbers, eg 1.3.81–7 Act 1. Scene 3. Lines 81 to 87

First published 1985
Published by the British Broadcasting Corporation
35 Marylebone High Street, London WIM 4AA

Printed in England by Mackays of Chatham Ltd, Kent
Typeset in Ehrhardt by Phoenix Photosetting, Chatham, Kent

ISBN 0 563 21070 2

CONTENTS

INTRODUCTION
Roger Sales

The television and radio talks collected together here were given as curtain raisers to the plays transmitted in the last three series of the BBC TV Shakespeare. They were intended to provide informative, entertaining programme notes. The television talks, called *Shakespeare in Perspective*, were given by well-known writers and broadcasters who approached the plays both as period pieces and in terms of their relevance for a modern television audience. The radio talks, called *Prefaces to Shakespeare*, were given by a distinguished company of actors and actresses, who had a professional knowledge of the play that they introduced as well as more personal feelings towards it. So, instead of being offered impersonal programme notes, viewers and listeners had the privilege of being taken on a brisk, unpretentious guided tour by somebody who was not just knowledgeable about Shakespeare but also excited and enthusiastic about him. Our guides spoke from the heart as well as the head. Although they quite often considered other reactions as a way of clarifying their own, they were not interested in bland summaries of received wisdom. They had to engage and hold an audience and so dealt, refreshingly and engagingly, with their own opinions and feelings. The talks were informed but informal. Hearts and prejudices were worn, as they should be, on the sleeve.

It would be foolish to pretend that nothing has been lost in transferring these talks to the printed page. The radio programmes were written largely for the ear. The guide's own voice was an integral part of the experience, as were some of the equally distinctive voices on the recordings that were used. Similarly, there is no way that the harmony between the visual and the verbal that occurred in the television programmes can be recaptured, even with illustrations. These programmes were, in Shakespeare's own words, meant 'to glad your ear, and please your eye'.

Nevertheless, although they were certainly richer in performance, they can still be read for pleasure and profit. There are, for
instance, important gains to balance out the inevitable losses. The
programmes raised general issues as well as particular curtains.
They are therefore collected together here not as a conventional
tie-in, but rather because they tie together to form an exciting and
often unconventional introduction to Shakespeare. They can still
be used as one-off programme notes, but taken as a whole they
offer more sustained perspectives on Shakespeare which challenge some traditional assumptions and approaches. There is, for
example, a very strong emphasis throughout on the need to free
Shakespeare from the classroom or study and put him back in the
theatre where he belongs. We are actively encouraged to think in
terms of production and performance. As Dennis Potter reminds
us, drama can never be just words on a page. For those bored by
deskbound criticisms, these talks can offer an appreciation
straight from the boards. Plays which are usually written off as
'mouldy tales' or worse, are shown to possess such vital theatrical
ingredients as pace and suspense. Ensemble pieces such as *Love's
Labour's Lost* and *The Merry Wives of Windsor*, it is suggested,
come right off the page on stage. Some of the entrances and exits
in *The Comedy of Errors* have to be seen to be believed.

We are not just introduced to particular plays. There are, for
instance, plenty of general insights to the actor's craft. Patrick
Stewart discusses the problems of standing and delivering early
Shakespearean verse, as well as the difficulties of pacing through a
demanding role. Pace and pacing are important considerations
throughout this volume. Ian Hogg offers a detailed impression of
the mental preparation he undergoes before even rehearsing a
part. We can also piece together a general view of twentieth-
century stage history, as the actors and actresses tell us about
some of the famous productions in which they have appeared.
Frances de la Tour gives us a behind-the-scenes account of one of
the most sensational post-war Shakespearean productions, Peter
Brook's discovery of the dark side of the moon in his *A Midsummer
Night's Dream*. The relativity, and thus the excitement, of theatrical interpretation is also brought home to us through references to
the rediscovery of Richard III's comic qualities, or to recent
attempts to rescue Goneril and Regan from pantomime
stereotyping. We are given a good sense of the way in which
particular plays, as well as particular parts, can be rescued and
rehabilitated. As Norman Rodway and others show, plays which

were struck out of the repertoire because their black comedy and violence once seemed offensive have been successfully revived precisely because these qualities strike a chord with modern audiences. Although these talks do not deal specifically with Shakespeare's life, the incidental details and speculations can, once again, be pieced together to form a biographical outline. The debates over Shakespeare's authorship of particular plays are, for instance, dealt with quite fully in a number of the talks. We are told, then, about acting techniques, stage histories and Shakespeare's life. We learn, above all, that the play itself is the most important thing. That may seem rather a simple conclusion to reach, until it is remembered that more complex approaches can, consciously or unconsciously, place unnecessary barriers between interpretation and performance.

Although the radio talks have important points to make about Shakespeare's England, this approach becomes more of a focal point in the television ones. Shakespeare can, of course, be dragged kicking and screaming into the twentieth century. He does not become our contemporary, however, just because his characters are crammed into jackboots or pinstripes or both. It is only when we appreciate his relationship to his own contemporaries that we are in a position to begin talking about him as our contemporary as well. As the title suggests, the *Shakespeare in Perspective* programmes operated this kind of double focus. Michael Wood only begins to suggest the modern parallels to the *Henry VI* plays after offering us a detailed account of Elizabethan attitudes to kingship, education, and law and order. Victor Poole, the producer of all the *Perspective* programmes, wanted to demystify Shakespeare and so chose presenters who could offer personal appreciations rather than impersonal criticisms. He felt that writers, or those who worked creatively in the same areas as Shakespeare had, would respond to this challenge. Thus the programmes can offer not just a general interplay between the modern and the Shakespearean, but also the more specialised perspectives of modern writers on the greatest writer ever. Both the radio and the television talks stress the importance of a creative, imaginative and appreciative set of responses towards Shakespeare. They complement each other in the sense that, while the controlling perspective may be broadly similar, the actors and writers inevitably concentrate on different aspects of Shakespeare's work. This is entirely appropriate since Shakespeare was a professional actor as well as being a professional writer.

The initial emphasis on Shakespeare's relationship to his own contemporaries means that, taken together, these television talks contain a mine of historical detail and speculation about Elizabethan and Jacobean England. We find out about court and country, war and peace, myth and propaganda, religion and superstition, learning and living. The presenters take care to suggest some of the important ways in which Shakespeare's world, and world-view, differed from our own. Frank Kermode is quite right to remind us, in a different context, that the overall effect of certain plays depends upon a process of defamiliarisation. Given the range and depth of Shakespeare's achievement, however, there are also plays which can become more accessible when related to the familiar and the everyday. Jilly Cooper is quick to spot the merry wives of Windsor out shopping in the hypermarket. Shakespeare's Comedies obviously do not just mock Tudor. Anthony Clare invites some of Shakespeare's characters to take a seat in the psychiatrist's chair and Julian Symons relates *Macbeth* to twentieth-century criminal psychology. Both Sir David Hunt and General Sir John Hackett find that their own experiences during the Second World War help them to form opinions on Shakespeare's treatment of war. It is important to doorstop the past to find out about Shakespeare's England, but that does not rule out the strong possibility of finding parts of it on your own doorstep. Jonathan Miller used a Renaissance palace in Urbino as the basis for some of the visual images in his production of *Othello*, whereas Jane Howell found that an adventure playground in Fulham provided her with a controlling perspective for her productions of the *Henry VI* plays and *Richard III*. Shakespeare's plays are not necessarily set in a far-away country, nor are they concerned exclusively with the lives of people about whom we know nothing.

A number of the radio and television presenters suggest that we can trip over Shakespeare on the doorstep by relating the plays to modern forms of entertainment. Sara Kestelman indicates that *Macbeth* has attracted film directors such as Polanski and Kurosawa precisely because of its own cinematic flow, rhythm and pace. Even Orson Welles's more flawed adaptation manages to retain, almost despite itself, this emphasis on speed. Rosemary Anne Sisson makes a connection between the 'bustle' of the Elizabethan stage and caper movies. Amanda Redman wonders whether the dumb shows in *Pericles* might not be the Jacobean equivalents of montage sequences, whereas Roger Rees spots links between *The Comedy of Errors* and classic film comedy.

Prunella Scales points to some of the similarities between *The Merry Wives of Windsor* and modern television situation comedies. Roy Hudd, in the most sustained treatment of connections between Shakespearean and modern entertainment, shows why it is essential to bring our own experiences of variety and light entertainment to bear on a play like *The Comedy of Errors*, which is bursting with double-acts, stand-up routines and running gags. He concludes by stressing that comedy 'is a living tradition, not to be dissected, but to be acted and enjoyed on the small screen as well as in the theatre'. Shakespeare needs to be related to Elizabethan and Jacobean theatrical traditions, but these in turn can be related to more universal ones.

The English and Roman History plays tend to evoke visual images from a whole range of 'room at the top', 'power game' and 'main chance' films and television series. They can also be related to some of the classic gangster movies. The plays are about the 'survival of the slickest', to appropriate A. P. Rossiter's telling phrase, or what Sir Peter Parker describes as the 'unacceptable face of feudalism'. They are stuffed with wheelers and dealers who try to pour their oily rhetoric over troubled political waters. The feuds between the Yorkists and the Lancastrians are remarkably similar to the essentially dynastic struggles that form the basis of most television soap operas. Jane Howell takes such a comparison one stage further by noticing the way in which the Histories often rely upon the basic storytelling devices of the serial or continuous series such as cliffhanger endings. If academic criticism has tended to emphasise the traditional at the expense of the living, it has also never really been seated comfortably with Shakespeare the storyteller. *Titus Andronicus*, Roman horror show and Elizabethan video nasty, can be tied too exclusively to Elizabethan traditions of revenge. Yet, anybody who has seen films like *The Godfather* with its code of 'my family right or right', or indeed has been fed on a diet of spaghetti westerns, knows what revenge drama is all about. Anybody who has sat on the edge of their seat in anticipation, or fear, during modern melodramas is in a good condition to appreciate Shakespeare the storyteller.

All this is not to underestimate the very real difficulties presented by Shakespearean language for a modern audience. It is riddled with riddles and layered, or folded, with meanings. Its silken terms are never precise as the silver tongue is also a slippery one. Kenneth Branagh suggests that actors and directors have two alternatives: either to play this language of rhetorical airs and stylistic graces 'to the hilt', or else to slow it down so that a modern audience can understand it. It is a difficult choice to make for plays like *Love's Labour's Lost* and *Much Ado About Nothing* where the main themes are style, literally in a word. Indeed, the Elizabethans did not really have a choice between presenting language as spectacle or meaning. Such distinctions were alien to a world where wit was wisdom, mirth was matter, show was substance, facility was rarely facile and true words were invariably spoken in jest. There is thus a strong case for playing the Comedies 'to the hilt' since they are very much plays on words. If the fast-talking characters really do shoot their lines, then at least a modern audience will be able to recover some of the exuberance and pace of Elizabethan comedy. For, as Emma Tennant points out, these plays revel in their emancipation from Latinate and other traditional influences. The London apprentices set fire to the language schools in and around the Strand in 1593. Shakespeare also put a match under them in *Love's Labour Lost*, but at least he could claim that something unique rose from the ashes.

Unlike Ben Jonson, Shakespeare did not set great store by the 'penned' or printed word. His plays were only published individually for copyright reasons and he never bothered to bring out an edition of his complete dramatic works. Thus it is not surprising that the spoken word is usually allowed to triumph over the written one in his plays. In *Love's Labour's Lost*, for instance, written articles are broken, 'penned' proclamations are ignored and letters go astray. Bookworms like Holofernes are continually upstaged. The King of Navarre wants to believe that words inscribed on a tombstone will provide the most permanent record, or 'register', of events, but Shakespeare suggests that the moment of verbal facility in the theatre is in fact truer and more substantial. The spoken word is God. The swordplay of the verbal duels, which is often so sharp that the participants cut themselves, is invariably presented as being mightier than the pen. Shakespeare's language does not need to be slowed down, or even modernised, but rather played 'to the hilt' as performance and spectacle. Drama is words on a stage rather than a page.

The directors, designers and costume experts involved in the television productions did not want to treat Shakespeare as a museum piece, to be looked at but not touched. Even when they decided to 'pictorialise' a play through a study of Renaissance art, the emphasis was on a creative interplay, or perspective, between plays and paintings. The task was to visualise rather than merely intellectualise the plays. Shakespeare himself reminded his audiences at the Globe, bare boards bare to the sky, of the need to give their imaginations full rein, or play, to fill out some of the empty spaces. Some critics have taken this as a cue to suggest that film and television adaptations ought to confine themselves to these bare boards, although it seems to me that this view actually confines Shakespeare to the glass case in the museum. He becomes part of a tradition, but not a living one. The processes of creative, imaginative interplay are arguably truer to the the spirit of the plays. Just as the presenters of the *Perspective* programmes used a variety of locations to suggest, but not define, mood and atmosphere, so the productions themselves have reflected a concern for visual landscapes. There is no play, and therefore no Shakespeare, unless actors, production teams and audiences respond to the challenge and bring their own perspectives to bear upon it. The BBC TV Shakespeare has created a new audience for the plays as well as allowing enthusiasts of longer standing, in theatre queues and elsewhere, to develop their interest. The project as a whole, including the programmes that are now collected together in the two volumes of *Shakespeare in Perspective*, has posed important questions about the nature of the perspectives of actor, director and audience and the relationships between them. There may be more questions than answers, although the fundamental point to emerge is that each of these perspectives needs to be an active and creative one. The plays themselves, and the radio and television programmes which introduce them, all suggest that the best context for an appreciation of Shakespeare's work is provided by the creative, performing and visual arts in all their diversity.

Shakespeare's Comedies and Romances often seem to have more in common with opera and ballet than with forms of naturalistic theatre. Perhaps this is why there are no hard and fast distinctions nowadays between the Shakespearean and the operatic director. Operatic delivery, patterned movement and stylised settings were dominant features in some of the productions. Yet I suspect that the hardest single point for a modern audience to appreciate about Shakespeare is that his artistic vision could encompass both grand opera and soap opera and all stations in between. It is a unique blend of what we have been conditioned to label the sophisticated and the popular: classical mythology and fairy tales, courtly literature and melodrama, spectacle and slapstick, ballet and pantomime, cabaret and circus, operatic arias and nursery rhymes, sublime and bawdy, poetic and grotesque. Television may well be the ideal medium through which to try to reawaken and recreate such an all-embracing cultural perspective. The 'traffic' of Shakespeare's stage has a number of similarities with the 'flow' of television. This is not to lose sight of the fact that some of Shakespeare's plays were specifically written for private, or coterie, audiences. Sir Roy Strong, for instance, gives us a vivid account of the first night of *A Midsummer Night's Dream*, which he suggests took place to celebrate an aristocratic wedding. Yet it has to be remembered that such plays also found their way into the public repertoire and that is ultimately where they had to stand or fall. Although the seating or viewing arrangements within the Elizabethan and Jacobean public theatres tended to reinforce social gradation and distinction, there is still a very important sense in which they were also truly national theatres entertaining a wide range of people with a wide range of cultural forms. The historical moment of Shakespeare can never be recreated nor should we ever attempt to do so. Such a traditional reconstruction provides no substitute for the real thing, which is to present Shakespeare as part of a living tradition. As television has inherited some, but by no means all, of the characteristics of the Elizabethan public theatres, it is uniquely placed to present Shakespeare in terms of a tradition 'to be acted and enjoyed'. The inspired decision to schedule some of the Comedies as part a Christmas season of entertainment may have been appropriately Elizabethan in its conception, but it was also modern in both its execution and reception.

The message of the radio talks to students, teachers and the general reader is to leave the critical tracts in the classroom or study and to make tracks for the theatre, cinema or television screen. The suggestion is that Shakespeare's plays should not be read as novels. The hope is that an awareness of, and an appreciation for, production and performance can enhance one's appreciation and understanding. The message of the television programmes is that everybody ought to write their own *Perspective* programmes. This means making imaginative, creative voyages of discovery to castles and country houses, art galleries and museums, but it also means trying to relate the plays to personal experiences, environments and forms of entertainment. The message from both media is that these voyages of discovery should be ones of self-discovery as well. The contributors to this volume offer you their travellers' tales to excite your curiosity and fire your enthusiasm for your own very different journey.

Editorial Policy

My editorial policy, which has been carried out in consultation with the contributors, may be summarised under six headings:

1 I have made some changes to the original scripts to achieve a uniform house style. The radio scripts took their quotations from a wide variety of editions, whereas I have standardised things by using the BBC TV editions throughout. A reference number follows each of the Shakespearean quotations. The first digit refers to the relevant act in the play, the second to the scene and the final digits are the line numbers. For instance, 1.3.81–7 refers to Act 1, Scene 3, lines 81 to 87. As can be seen from the editions, there are a number of differences between the full text and the text as transmitted. I have usually preferred to go back to the full text but have, on a few occasions, retained the edited transmission version. In all cases, however, the reference numbers are to the full text.

2 All the scripts appear in essay form, without production details or shot lists. This seemed the most appropriate form for the radio scripts, although it occasionally proved to be something of a compromise as far as some of the television ones were concerned as some of the explicit visual sign-posting had to be omitted. I and the contributors themselves have made a limited number of stylistic changes to make the scripts more accessible on the printed page, but they have not been altered more fundamentally.

3 I decided not to include illustrations as I felt that the book could not possibly hope to emulate the television programmes. It would have been too difficult, not to say invidious, to decide what to illustrate and what to leave to the reader's

imagination. We might have ended up with a copiously illustrated volume as it usually turns out to be a case of all or nothing. There are, however, enough good picture books on Shakespeare's life and times. The producers of both the radio and television programmes felt that a reasonably priced, simply laid-out edition of talks by a distinguished repertory company of household names could make a more positive contribution to the way in which Shakespeare is approached in schools and colleges, without losing its appeal for the general reader. This view was confirmed by the success of Volume One.

4 I often asked the contributors to consider either omitting altogether, or else shortening, one or two of the quotations from the plays. The radio programmes sometimes contained some very long quotations, which I felt were more effective over the air than on the printed page. The quotations in the television programmes tended to be shorter, but there were still occasions when they seemed either too action-packed, or just too character-packed, to work on the printed page.

5 I have placed the scripts according to the series for which they were originally intended rather than in transmission order. The order within each series does, however, correspond with transmission. The *Perspectives* are placed before the *Prefaces*, as they were in Volume One. There was certainly a case for making an exception to this rule as far as the *Henry VI* plays were concerned: Michael Wood dealt with them individually in three television programmes, whereas Brewster Mason offered an overview of them in one radio talk. I nevertheless decided to go for uniformity, although the reader perhaps ought to start with the overview.

6 As mentioned in the Introduction, the *Perspectives* and the *Prefaces* complement each other. There were a few occasions when they overlapped more directly, but there were strong reasons for retaining such passages. Here and elsewhere I was very conscious of the fact that all the contributors had been asked by the BBC for a personal view on Shakespeare. The scripts have therefore been published with only a limited number of changes designed to make them more accessible.

OTHELLO
Susan Hill

Susan Hill is a novelist and radio playwright. Her publications include I'm the King of the Castle *and* The Bird of Prey. *She made this programme on location at Saltwood Castle.*

It seems to me that this play is, in a way, only about two characters, Iago and Othello. There are of course other characters and they are very important to the plot. Nevertheless, they are less fully treated and they seem very subordinate to the central pair. It's a play about contrasts, particularly the contrast between the two men. It's about other contrasts too. There is the contrast between the black man and the other men who surround him who are not black. There is the contrast between Othello's love for Desdemona which is a passionate, romantic, devoted love which has come upon him suddenly and which turns to its opposite: hatred, jealousy and murderous passion. There is a contrast between the way Iago and Othello treat their wives. But the basic contrast is between the essential characters of these two men.

The effect on us in the theatre of watching three hours of *Othello* is claustrophobic and rather terrifying because there is absolutely no relief. If you think about it, nothing much happens other than the central action. There is no comic relief as there almost always is in Shakespeare. There is admittedly one clown, but his appearance is not very notable – or funny – and he is quite often cut out in performance. There is no music – not entirely true as there is one very poignant, bitter, sad song from Desdemona on the evening of her death, but that could hardly be counted as musical relief. There are no references to supernatural forces as Shakespeare usually has. There are no sub-plots at all. At the beginning of the play we are led to expect that there will be a sub-plot. We are, after all, told that the Turks are about to invade Cyprus and that Othello is going out to command the Venetian forces against them. What happens when he gets to Cyprus? That whole episode is brushed aside and we are left with no rest, no let-up, no relief at all.

Othello does not really know himself. He knows a little about himself and he could claim, perhaps, to know more, but basically he is ignorant of whole areas of his personality. But Iago is full of self-knowledge. He knows himself through and through. This is how he declares himself to us:

> I hate the Moor;
> And it is thought abroad that 'twixt my sheets
> 'Has done my office. I know not if't be true;
> Yet I, for mere suspicion in that kind,
> Will do as if for surety. He holds me well;
> The better shall my purpose work on him.
> Cassio's a proper man. Let me see now:
> To get his place, and to plume up my will
> In double knavery. How? How? Let's see:
> After some time to abuse Othello's ear
> That he is too familiar with his wife.
> He hath a person and a smooth dispose
> To be suspected – fram'd to make women false.
> The Moor is of a free and open nature
> That thinks men honest that but seem to be so;
> And will as tenderly be led by th' nose
> As asses are.
> I ha't – it is engender'd. Hell and night
> Must bring this monstrous birth to the world's light.

1.3.380–98

Iago's evil intent and his cold, calculating wickedness is contrasted with another kind of badness. It is more understandable and forgivable, but badness all the same. I feel that there must have been something within Othello for the evil cunning of Iago to call forth. Othello is bad out of self ignorance. He is unsophisticated and unknowing in the ways of the world. His badness is impetuous and hotheaded, whereas Iago's is totally understandable and totally unforgivable. A lot of people have seen Othello as the good figure duped by the evil one, but I don't see it like that. In my eyes, Othello is guilty of much.

Othello is a black man. He is a black man in a predominantly white society. This, then, is a play about racial matters. It would be temptingly easy to think that we can translate *Othello* into immediate contemporary terms. I don't think we should because sixteenth and seventeenth century Venice, or Shakespeare's England, were simply not the same as our present day multi-racial society. They were not Brixton or Bradford. Things have changed. But one thing has not changed and that is human nature. The basic human fear and mistrust of the person who is different from ourselves is still exactly the same. Othello is a figure of some considerable importance in the Venice of the play. He is a soldier, a general, and is honoured and respected as such. The Venetians do not treat him quite as one of them, of course. They regard him rather indulgently as a romantic adventurer and an exotic foreigner. He tells stirring tales of his early days:

> Her father lov'd me, oft invited me;
> Still question'd me the story of my life
> From year to year – the battles, sieges, fortunes,
> That I have pass'd.
> I ran it through, even from my boyish days
> To th' very moment that he bade me tell it;
> Wherein I spake of most disastrous chances,
> Of moving accidents by flood and field;
> Of hairbreadth scapes i' th' imminent deadly breach;
> Of being taken by the insolent foe
> And sold to slavery; of my redemption thence,
> And portance in my travel's history;
> . . . .

1.3.128–39

Desdemona is every man's ideal of what a young girl should be. She is innocent, charming, shy and obedient. She has rejected all kinds of suitable young men. But Othello dares to marry her. Everything changes at that point. He is immediately the outcast and referred to as 'the black man'. Once it becomes known in public that Othello has dared to marry Desdemona, then all the latent racist prejudices emerge in the language of the play. The language referring to this black man becomes extremely offensive. He is referred as as 'this old black ram' and as a 'Barbary horse'. He has a 'sooty bosom' and is called a 'thick lips'. This is extreme and intense. Othello has done what no black man should dare to do. So much so that people wonder how this charming, innocent young girl could possibly have fallen for this black man. Surely, they say, the attraction is not natural, normal, and innocent. Surely, they say, the black man must have used some form of witchcraft upon her. Othello explains it differently:

> My story being done,
> She gave me for my pains a world of sighs;
> She swore, in faith, 'twas strange, 'twas passing strange;
> 'Twas pitiful, 'twas wondrous pitiful.
> She wish'd she had not heard it; yet she wish'd

That heaven had made her such a man. She thank'd me;
And bade me, if I had a friend that lov'd her,
I should but teach him how to tell my story,
And that would woo her. Upon this hint I spake;
She lov'd me for the dangers I had pass'd;
And I lov'd her that she did pity them.
This only is the witchcraft I have us'd.   1.3.158–69

Now all writers have obsessions, themes to which they keep
returning again and again in their work. Shakespeare did this as
much as anyone. One of his principal obsessive themes is the
difference between being and seeming, between the appearance
of things and the reality of them. This comes up again and again in
his work, but it is one of the dominant themes in *Othello*. What
kind of a man does Othello seem to be? As a strong man of action,
he is a man in control of the destinies of other men. In private life
he is a passionate lover and a new husband completely devoted to
his bride. He certainly seems to be a man quite incapable of ever
feeling anything but the deepest, most trusting love for her. But
appearance and reality don't match. This is not the whole story.
Othello may still be a soldier and a leader of men, but he is not in
control of himself. He turns out to fall the moment he is tempted
by Iago:

OTHELLO: What dost thou say, Iago?
IAGO: Did Michael Cassio, when you woo'd my lady,
    Know of your love?
OTHELLO: He did, from first to last. Why dost thou ask?
IAGO: But for a satisfaction of my thought-
    No further harm.
OTHELLO: Why of thy thought, Iago?
IAGO: I did not think he had been acquainted with her.
OTHELLO: O, yes; and went between us very often.
IAGO: Indeed!
OTHELLO: Indeed? Ay, indeed. Discern'st thou aught in that?
    Is he not honest?
IAGO: Honest, my lord?
OTHELLO: Honest? Ay, honest.
IAGO: My lord, for aught I know.
OTHELLO: What dost thou think?
IAGO: Think, my lord?
OTHELLO: Think, my lord! By heaven, he echoes me,
    As if there were some monster in his thought
    Too hideous to be shown.   3.3.94–112

How does Desdemona seem to be? To her father, Brabantio, she has always seemed to be an innocent, trustworthy and good girl. She has been shy and nervous of men, an obedient and dutiful daughter. Yet she runs off with Othello, the very man least likely to be her husband. Her distracted father says to other fathers 'trust not your daughters' minds/By what you see them act'. He says to Othello

> Look to her, Moor, if thou hast eyes to see:
> She has deceiv'd her father, and may thee.
>
> 1.3.292-3

But it is when we come to the character of Iago that we reach the absolute nub of this conflict between being and seeming. How does Iago seem to be? He seems to be loyal, straightforward and good. An 'honest' man, that is what they all say about Iago. That word 'honest' is used no less than forty-two times in the course of the play and that is a very considerable repetition. But, as Iago reveals to us in his soliloquies and asides to the audience, he is far from an honest man and not to be trusted. This great theme of being and seeming is not only dramatised by Shakespeare in the course of the play, it is discussed very many times. People actually talk about whether you can tell if a man is as he seems to be:

> OTHELLO: If thou dost love me,
>   Show me thy thought.
> IAGO: My lord, you know I love you.
> OTHELLO: I think thou dost;
>   And for I know thou art full of love and honesty,
>   And weigh'st thy words before thou giv'st them breath,
>   Therefore these stops of thine affright me the more;
>   For such things in a false disloyal knave
>   Are tricks of custom; but in a man that's just
>   They are close delations, working from the heart
>   That passion cannot rule.
> IAGO: For Michael Cassio,
>   I dare presume I think that he is honest.
> OTHELLO: I think so too.
> IAGO: Men should be that they seem;
>   Or those that be not, would they might seem none!
> OTHELLO: Certain, men should be what they seem.
>
> 3.3.119-32

Othello is a tragedy. Now we often use the word tragedy in connection with plays of Shakespeare. What exactly do we mean by a tragedy? Is it simply a sad play with a lot of bodies at the end? No, there is more to it than that. Chaucer meant something quite specific by tragedy. He meant what he called 'a falling from high estate', a story about the downfall of a great man, and that is certainly true of Othello. But I think there is a particularly Shakespearean concept of tragedy. One of Shakespeare's great themes is the voyage of self-discovery, the quest in man for self-knowledge. I think that a play of his is a comedy when the hero finds out the truth about himself in time to right some wrongs and to profit by his self-knowledge. But a play is a tragedy when the hero finds out the truth too late to do anything about the misdeeds and wrong that have been done out of his lack of self-knowledge. Othello is insanely jealous and it is this that blinds him to the truth within himself. It might seem that what brings about his downfall is a rather silly device that would not deceive a child, a plot about a handkerchief. In fact Othello will believe anything at this point, he is so credulous. If he stopped to think, he would realise that, when Iago tells him that he has shared a bed with Cassio and heard him sleep-talk about Desdemona, there has not been time for this to happen. But at this point Othello is out of his mind and he can't think about time schemes:

IAGO: I lay with Cassio lately,
    And, being troubled with a raging tooth,
    I could not sleep.
    There are a kind of men so loose of soul
    That in their sleeps will mutter their affairs:
    One of this kind is Cassio.
    In sleep I heard him say 'Sweet Desdemona,
    Let us be wary, let us hide our loves',
    And then, sir, would he gripe and wring my hand,
    Cry 'O sweet creature!' then kiss me hard,
    As if he pluck'd up kisses by the roots,
    That grew upon my lips – then laid his leg
    Over my thigh – and sigh'd, and kiss'd, and then
    Cried 'Cursed fate that gave thee to the Moor!'
OTHELLO: O monstrous! monstrous!
IAGO: Nay, this was but his dream.
OTHELLO: But this denoted a foregone conclusion.
IAGO: 'Tis a shrewd doubt, though it be but a dream,
    And this may help to thicken other proofs
    That do demonstrate thinly.
OTHELLO: I'll tear her all to pieces.   3.3.417–35

Othello has been driven insane, first by extreme love and then by extreme, passionate jealousy. I believe that once you admit that sort of extreme, passionate, total love, you also admit the obverse. You admit the possibility of feeling passionate, murderous hatred and jealousy. Why does this happen to Othello? How does he allow it to happen to himself? It is quite simply inexperience. He is a middle-aged man who has never known or loved a woman. He has never really admitted to himself any personal, intimate emotions. So when he falls in love, he falls completely, totally and utterly. He says that he is not a jealous man and has never known the feeling of jealousy. The moment he does admit jealousy, then he is jealous to an extreme of murderous passion.

Truly *Othello* is a black play. The word 'black' suffuses the whole text. But at the black heart of it is the black heart of the evil Iago. The climax of all the blackness and evil in the play is the deathbed scene where Othello murders Desdemona. This is where we see the downfall of whatever nobility Othello had. This is where we see quite how successfully Iago has brought him down to his own level of evil. The most chilling thing about this scene for me is the deliberate and calculating way that Othello goes about the murder:

DESDEMONA: Who's there? Othello?
OTHELLO: Ay, Desdemona.
DESDEMONA: Will you come to bed, my lord?
OTHELLO: Have you pray'd to-night, Desdemona?
DESDEMONA: Ay, my lord.
OTHELLO: If you bethink yourself of any crime
    Unreconcil'd as yet to heaven and grace,
    Solicit for it straight.
DESDEMONA: Alack, my lord,
    What may you mean by that?
OTHELLO: Well, do it, and be brief; I will walk by.
    I would not kill thy unprepared spirit;
    No, heaven forfend! – I would not kill thy soul.
DESDEMONA: Talk you of killing?
OTHELLO: Ay, I do.
DESDEMONA: Then Heaven
    Have mercy on me!
OTHELLO: Amen, with all my heart!

5.2.23–37

This is a play about the relationships between men and women. It is private emotion, the love of his wife, that eventually brings about

23

Othello's downfall. But it seems to me that there is not one truly good, equal and mature relationship between a man and a woman in the course of the play. Desdemona falls in love with Othello's own romatic account of himself. She almost falls in love with his heroic past as he relates it. He idolises her and falls in love with her devotion to him. What about the marriage between Iago and Emilia? Iago treats his wife very badly indeed in public and in private. He despises her, but does not want anyone else to value her as he is a pathologically jealous man. When Emilia finds out the truth about her husband, then she betrays him with no hesitation at all. When she does that he murders her. In other words, the pattern of their relationship has followed that of Othello's and Desdemona's and it is ended in murder. I've called this a black play, black to the heart. Is there then no goodness or light in it at all? There is goodness in the characters of Desdemona and Emilia. Desdemona is good, pure and innocent. She makes a good death. But Emilia's is a different sort of goodness. It's a fierce goodness. She is entirely loyal to Desdemona and her goodness leads to her own self-sacrifice and death. The goodness of these two women seems to me to be really the only ray of hope in the course of the whole play.

I have to confess that I don't very much enjoy *Othello* as a play. I would not want to go and watch it every night of the week because it is much too harrowing and too intense. But it is a play about human beings and I do find it endlessly interesting and absorbing because of that. The human relationships and emotions that it describes seem to me very immediate, very timeless. They are also very contemporary.

OTHELLO

Bob Peck

Bob Peck is a member of the Royal Shakespeare Company. Besides Iago in Othello, *his other parts have included the title roles in* Macbeth *and in Edward Bond's* Lear.

*O*thello is one of Shakespeare's best known and most popular plays. It contains Iago, the most theatrically attractive villain ever portrayed except perhaps for Richard III, Othello himself, the most exotic tragic hero and Desdemona, a tragic heroine of beauty, innocence, will and intelligence. The play moves with enormous speed. It starts in the middle of the night at a moment of national and domestic crisis. Event then cascades upon event: journeys, storms, riots, skirmishes all leading to the climactic bedroom scene. Running through these events is the struggle of a loving relationship to survive in an alien environment, which is poisoned by racial prejudice and the machinations of an uncompassionate fiend of supreme cunning, energy, opportunism and invention.

The fascination of the play for most people centres on the struggle between Othello, the black or Moorish General and his evil lieutenant Iago, who persuades him by deception to believe in his wife's adultery and to kill her. It is a struggle between equals. The controversial element in the play is the way in which an inter-racial marriage is used to force an audience, whose own prejudices are put into the mouth and actions of a very seductive and persuasive villain, to adopt a moral attitude towards its events. There are at least three reasons why modern audiences, or potential audiences, tend to view the play with some suspicion. First, because it is by Shakespeare and they think that this means an archaic setting and language, which are totally irrelevant to contemporary needs or interests. I would claim that Shakespearean language, given the right help and work, can be rendered intelligibly as modern language without any loss of poetry, retaining a greater density of thought than our everyday speech. Secondly, we tend to be embarrassed by the idea of a white actor playing a noble black man in authority in an alien society, particularly as he then has to portray an apparent return to barbarism. I believe that a good actor can overcome these problems. Thirdly, inter-racial marriage is still a very sensitive subject in our modern, 'mixed' society, even though we might like to pretend that an old play has nothing to teach our educated, liberal society. I think that recent events in this country indicate that we are in as great, if not greater, need of insight and understanding on the nature of racialism than ever before.

Othello, the Moor of Venice shares its location with *The Merchant of Venice*, another racially orientated play. England, like Venice, was an expanding, trading nation using naval and military means to maintain political and economic power and peace abroad at the time that these plays were written. Racial prejudice is not really the central issue in either play. It is rather used as a kind of dramatic lever to throw the real issues into focus. These concern the wider question of the ability of all loving relationships to survive in a hostile, gain-seeking world. Both plays are therefore about not only the fate of individuals, but also about the way in which society can either accommodate or reject these individuals and their relationships. The Venetian Senate is in session at the beginning of the play because part of their trading empire is under threat from the Turkish fleet. They send for Othello, their most respected and efficient General. He has secretly married Desde-mona, the daughter of one of the Senators, without prior consent or warning that very same night. The national crisis and this domestic marriage, which are linked together in the person of Othello, cause a series of chain reactions. The first one of these opens the play. Iago has been conning gold and jewels from Roderigo, a wealthy but gullible young suitor for the hand of Desdemona, by persuading him that she was open to advances and by professing to act as a go-between for him. Desdemona's sudden marriage betrays Iago's double-cross and Roderigo demands an explanation. The situation ought to be desperate for Iago as he is in danger of being revealed not just as a liar and thief, but also as somebody who is untrustworthy enough to abuse his position of privilege within the army as the General's Ancient or Ensign. Yet he turns the crisis to his own advantage, thinking and acting with great speed on his feet, by deflecting Roderigo's anger from himself on to Othello. He turns the scene into a sort of obscene game by wakening Desdemona's father, Brabantio, and presenting the marriage in a totally vile light to him. Brabantio reacts with extraordinary vehemence and refuses to believe that his daughter participated willingly in the marriage. He therefore accuses Othello of abduction:

> O thou foul thief, where hast thou stow'd my daughter?
> Damn'd as thou art, thou hast enchanted her;
> For I'll refer me to all things of sense,
> If she in chains of magic were not bound,
> Whether a maid so tender, fair, and happy,
> So opposite to marriage that she shunn'd
> The wealthy curled darlings of our nation,
> Would ever have, to incur a general mock,
> Run from her guardage to the sooty bosom
> Of such a thing as thou – to fear, not to delight.
> Judge me the world, if 'tis not gross in sense
> That thou has practis'd on her with foul charms,
> Abus'd her delicate youth with drugs or minerals
> That weakens motion.

1.2.62–75

The Senate is at first totally sympathetic towards Brabantio's indignation and loathing, but in the face of commercial and military requirements accept the marriage and dismiss his objections and personal distress. The Duke's advice to him is to make the best of a bad job. Brabantio nevertheless remains adamant, so Desdemona is placed in the unhappy position of having neither a father nor a husband to turn to since Othello is being called away to deal with the Turks. She solves this dilemma by deciding to go with her new husband to the wars in Cyprus. She joins him in the 'unhoused free condition' of the itinerant mercenary soldier, instead of retiring into a conventional Venetian marriage.

Shakespeare now prepares to shift the entire action of the play to the island of Cyprus. By a strange miracle, the whole of Othello's military party in their several ships survive the storm and arrive safely at their destination whilst the Turkish fleet founders in the same storm and is thus no longer a threat to the island's security. The crisis in Cyprus is resolved by the weather, which makes Othello appear to be in league with the elements. It is just another chapter to add to the stories of miraculous escapes and the air of mystery and magic which surrounds him. The fun is only just beginning for, once everybody has arrived safely, Iago is able to start his systematic destruction of Othello, Desdemona and all those around him. The five or six main characters are now thrown together in the confining atmosphere of a foreign garrison. They have no outside points of reference, so their isolation increases their inter-action. They become, as it were, components of a chemical experiment in the crucible of the play; the catalyst being, of course, Iago. Iago's attacks are against society in general, with its hypocrisy and phoney codes of morality and behaviour, as well as against individuals. The group on the island is in fact a microcosm of Venetian society and the seeds of its destruction were sown back in Venice.

I imagine that the play was written at a time when the company that Shakespeare was writing for had been reduced in numbers. Although it is a very domestic play with a relatively small cast, you still get the feeling when it is performed of enormous events taking place because of the isolation of the main characters. There is also a great compression of time. According to one timescale, the play deals with events that all take place within thirty three hours. There must, however, be a contradiction between such a dramatically compressed timescale and a more literal one in which the events would have to take place over three or four weeks given the distances travelled and the nature of the events themselves. It would take more than thirty three hours, for instance, for a message to travel from Cyprus to Italy and back again. This double timescale of the domestic and the literal is an artistic device which lends an enormous urgency to the play. The compression of time means that it keeps moving forward at great speed.

The speed at which Iago thinks adds to this sense of urgency. He sets people up, making the situation work for him as he rapidly plants and cultivates the seeds of suspicion in Othello's mind:

IAGO: My noble lord!
OTHELLO: What dost thou say, Iago?
IAGO: Did Michael Cassio, when you woo'd my lady,
    Know of your love?
OTHELLO: He did, from first to last. Why dost thou ask?
IAGO: But for a satisfaction of my thought –
    No further harm.
OTHELLO: Why of thy thought, Iago?
IAGO: I did not think he had been acquainted with her.
OTHELLO: O, yes; and went between us very often.
IAGO: Indeed!
OTHELLO: Indeed? Ay, indeed. Discern'st thou aught in that?
    Is he not honest?
IAGO: Honest, my lord?
OTHELLO: Honest? Ay, honest.
IAGO: My lord, for aught I know.

OTHELLO: What dost thou think?

IAGO: Think, my lord?

OTHELLO: Think, my lord! By heaven, he echoes me,
    As if there were some monster in his thought
    Too hideous to be shown. Thou dost mean something:
    I heard thee say but now thou lik'st not that,
    When Cassio left my wife. What didst not like?
    And when I told thee he was of my counsel
    In my whole course of wooing, thou criedst 'Indeed!'
    And didst contract and purse thy brow together,
    As if thou then hadst shut up in thy brain
    Some horrible conceit. If thou dost love me,
    Show me thy thought.   3.3.94–120

The whole play is of course an artefact. Yet a great deal of the job of the actor playing Iago seems to me to lie in creating the illusion that he is always thinking on his feet. He should appear to be improvising around a general strategy.

Iago is a very enjoyable role to play and the ambition of many actors. You can still abuse the part. For instance, Iago addresses audiences directly, but should he be allowed to win them over? I found that there was a temptation in early performances to allow Iago to use these speeches to demonstrate a contempt for Othello. Yet, if you reduce Othello's authority like this, then you also undercut the danger and thus the drama of the situation. I learnt quickly that such an approach was destructive to both the characters. It gives rise to the temptation in the audience to get up and shout to Othello 'Why can't you see what's going on? Why are you being so blind, so gullible and so easily deceived?' Rather like a trapeze artist, if the actor playing Iago starts to make things look glib, facile or easy, instead of demonstrating how dangerous and difficult his tricks are, the dramatic tension slips. Othello then starts to look like just a gullible fool because he is being so easily duped. But if the presence of danger is maintained, Iago's achievement becomes greater whilst Othello's authority and intelligence are not undermined. The danger also has to be there because Iago thrills in playing with fire and living dangerously. He only seems to feel alive in the presence of permanent danger. He is therefore on a permanent 'high' in the presence of Othello. He should be shown as being in constant danger of losing not only his job and place in society, but his own life as well. The moments when Othello physically threatens him should be electric. His moment of physical triumph over Othello is almost a sexually orgasmic experience. It is a turning point in both the play and their relationship when Othello falls down in a fit as a result of being goaded by Desdemona's supposed lasciviousness with Cassio:

OTHELLO: Hath he said anything?

IAGO: He hath, my lord; but be you well assur'd,
No more than he'll unswear.

OTHELLO: What hath he said?

IAGO: Faith, that he did – I know not what he did.

OTHELLO: What? what?

IAGO: Lie-

OTHELLO: With her?

IAGO: With her, on her; what you will.

OTHELLO: Lie with her- lie on her? we say lie on her when they belie her. Lie with her. Zounds, that's fulsome. Handkerchief- confessions – handkerchief! To confess, and be hang'd for his labour – first, to be hang'd, and then to confess. I tremble at it. Nature would not invest herself in such shadowing passion without some instruction. It is not words that shakes me thus – pish! – noses, ears, and lips. Is't possible? Confess! Handkerchief! O devil!

(Falls in a trance)

IAGO: Work on,
My medicine, work. Thus credulous fools are caught;
And many worthy and chaste dames even thus,
All guiltless, meet reproach.

4.1.29–47

Othello's resolve to kill Desdemona is constant from now on and so Iago can step back from the action and let Othello take over.

Othello is fairly passive in the early stages of the play. His authority is created largely by the way in which people respond to him or talk of him. He has enormous personal charisma, but this is based on his own calmness. He deals with Brabantio's railings against him with quiet dignity and confidence. He describes with modesty how his relationship with Desdemona developed:

Her father lov'd me, oft invited me;
Still question'd me the story of my life
From year to year – the battles, sieges, fortunes,
That I have pass'd.
I ran it through, even from my boyish days
To th' very moment that he bade me tell it;
Wherein I spake of most disastrous chances,
Of moving accidents by flood and field;

Of hairbreadth scapes i' th' imminent deadly breach;
Of being taken by the insolent foe
And sold to slavery; of my redemption thence,
And portance in my travel's history;
Wherein of antres vast and deserts idle,
Rough quarries, rocks, and hills whose heads touch heaven,
It was my hint to speak – such was the process;
And of the Cannibals that each other eat,
The Anthropophagi, and men whose heads
Do grow beneath their shoulders. This to hear
Would Desdemona seriously incline; . . .

1.3.128–46

There is something mesmerising, magical and mysterious about the relationship and he seems to cultivate these qualities consciously. He is an intensely private man, who lives by the highest moral standards. He has developed his skills as a leader and has made himself into a general of such stature that he has become indispensable to the Venetian state. He has finally been accepted into this society, working his way from being an alien to the guest of one of the most respected senior members of the city.

Othello has succeeded where Iago, who was already a member of Venetian society, has failed. Iago is not really a soldier at all, but a conman who is skilled at dodging the line. He has a lot of experience of the military machine, but when it comes to a brawl he lets everyone else do the fighting. He is what is called a grafter. He has managed to achieve a certain rank, yet can get no further because Othello does not quite trust him. The next stepping stone for Iago should be a lieutenancy, but this is given to Cassio instead. Why does Iago behave as he does? What motivates him? He seems to me to be a man whose life of deception and fraud is so repugnant to him that he can't bear to see virtue, compassion, love or anything of positive moral good in others. He has a moral conscience, although he refuses to answer to it. We gather from his wife Emilia that he has been unfaithful to her. His own infidelity leads him to suspect it in others. He demonstrates some paranoia on this issue:

That Cassio loves her, I do well believe it;
That she loves him, 'tis apt and of great credit.
The Moor, howbeit that I endure him not,
Is of a constant, loving, noble nature;
And I dare think he'll prove to Desdemona
A most dear husband. Now I do love her too;

Not out of absolute lust, though peradventure
I stand accountant for as great a sin,
But partly led to diet my revenge,
For that I do suspect the lustful Moor
Hath leap'd into my seat; the thought whereof
Doth like a poisonous mineral gnaw my inwards;
And nothing can nor shall content my soul
Till I am even'd with him, wife for wife;
Or failing so, yet that I put the Moor
At least into a jealousy so strong
That judgement cannot cure.

2.1.280–96

Iago is probably confused as to his own sexuality. He lusts after Desdemona, but has he not repressed feeling for Cassio and Othello as well? Yet Iago is not just motivated by racial prejudice, or career ambitions or even sexual jealousy. His whole existence, and the amoral standards on which it is based, are threatened, which is why his hatred is so white-hot. His ambition for a lieutenancy is little more than an excuse for this hatred, as well as providing a trumped-up reason for Roderigo to believe in his loyalty.

The richness of Othello's relationship with Desdemona contrasts with the paucity of Iago's own relationship with his wife, Emilia. Her loyalty to him is almost as extraordinary as Desdemona's faith in her husband. Iago not only takes Emilia's loyalty for granted, he also uses it to lend authority to his trustworthiness. He may be blunt and rather crude, but his married status makes him acceptable to people. He becomes an 'honest fellow' who is above suspicion, rather like the Yorkshire Ripper. He also uses Emilia's closeness to Desdemona to secure a handkerchief, which is the one piece of physical evidence he needs to convince Othello of his wife's adultery. When this handkerchief later becomes of major importance to Desdemona, Emilia can't afford to betray her husband. If she admits to herself that he could do something really evil with the handkerchief, then she could be calling her whole marriage and life into question. She would rather believe that it is going to be used for something harmless and therefore keeps her own counsel. She has nothing left to live for, when she finally realises what Iago has been up to. By then her mistress Desdemona is dead and her reputation, once Iago is revealed for what he is, is that she is somebody who is prepared to harbour a monster.

Iago is undeniably attractive. He excites our admiration with the totality of his ruthlessness, together with his enormous energy and resourcefulness. The extraordinary depth of his understanding of his fellows, which amounts to a virtual omniscience, is probably his most admirable quality. These qualities are, however, the tools that he uses to strike at other people's weaknesses. The pace gets faster and faster, reaching a climax when, with breathtaking speed and skill, he kills Roderigo, wounds Cassio and yet appears in the same scene as the saviour of the situation, lamenting everything and despatching everybody left and right. He basically manipulates everybody throughout the play by using their own thoughts. It is as though he does not exist in the play at all except in the minds and imaginations of the other characters. This idea extends even into the physical actions, for when Othello stabs him he does not die. The sword seems to run through him as through a phantom. Othello's demand for an explanation is just as unsuccessful:

> OTHELLO: Will you, I pray, demand that demi-devil
> Why he hath thus ensnar'd my soul and body?
> IAGO: Demand me nothing. What you know, you know
> From this time forth I never will speak word.

> 5.2.304–7

Such an explanation is in the end left to the audience, who have to examine their consciences and ask where their allegiances lie. Shakespeare seems to indict not only the characters, but the whole society represented in the play and the audience as well. Actors and audience have both been party to the whole proceeding, so we are all involved in the guilt and responsibility for it.

TROILUS AND CRESSIDA
Sir David Hunt

Sir David Hunt's academic career as a classical archaeologist was interrupted by the Second World War, during which he served in North Africa. He then became a diplomat. He won BBC TV's Mastermind in 1977. Some of this programme was made on location at the British Museum.

Troilus and Cressida is a play about a war between the Greeks and Trojans. It is based on a poem by the Greek poet, Homer. Troy was a city on the coast of Asia Minor in what is now Turkey, which was supposedly besieged by the Greeks for ten years. Why did Shakespeare go right back to the Greeks for a story of war? Greek civilisation was in many ways even more remote to the Elizabethans than it is to us today, as many of the famous monuments were unknown heaps of ruins in Shakespeare's time. The answer is that Greek heroic literature was highly valued in Elizabethan England. War was one of the constant pursuits of the Greeks. They gloried in it. Scenes of fighting, idealised in the heroic style, were considered thoroughly suitable to adorn both sacred temples and royal monuments. Shakespeare found such heroic images of war in the tale of the siege of Troy. It was one of the greatest war stories of all times with characters whose names were immortalised by Homer's *Iliad*.

Although the story of the Trojan war in general and Troilus and Cressida in particular was a thoroughly popular theme in Shakespeare's time, it is not as well-known today. So I had better give you an outline of Shakespeare's treatment of this story, particularly as *Troilus and Cressida* is not so frequently acted as some of the other plays. The time is the seventh year of the siege of Troy by the Greeks. This long campaign has settled into a routine with small skirmishes and parleys, but with no great battles or decisive events. The war drags on and both the Greeks and Trojans begin to think about ending it. There is a debate in Troy about sending back Helen, whose abduction from Greece was the original cause of the war. Troilus is in love with Cressida. He confesses this to Cressida's uncle, Pandarus, who brings the two of them together at his house. They each discover that they are as keen as the other.

To the sound of their own amorous twitterings and Pandarus's bawdy comments, they pass off stage to the bedroom, there to spend just one night together like poor Romeo and Juliet:

TROILUS: It is your uncle.

CRESSIDA: A pestilence on him! Now will he be mocking.
I shall have such a life!

PANDARUS: How now, how now! How go maidenheads? Here,
you maid! Where's my cousin Cressid?

CRESSIDA: Go hang yourself, you naughty mocking uncle.
You bring me to do, and then you flout me too.

PANDARUS: To do what? to do what? Let her say what. What
have I brought you to do?

CRESSIDA: Come, come, beshrew your heart! You'll ne'er be
good,
Nor suffer others.

PANDARUS: Ha, ha! Alas, poor wretch! a poor capocchia! hast
not slept tonight? Would he not, a naughty man, let it sleep? A
bugbear take him!

4.2.21–33

After their night together, Cressida is handed over to the Greeks in exchange for a Trojan prisoner. No sooner has she arrived in the Greek camp than she makes it quite plain that she is incapable of constancy. She takes Diomed for her lover and gives him the very same love token that Troilus had given her. This betrayal is witnessed by Troilus himself in the most effective scene in the play:

CRESSIDA: O all you gods! O pretty, pretty pledge!
Thy master now lies thinking on his bed
Of thee and me, and sighs, and takes my glove,
And gives memorial dainty kisses to it,
As I kiss thee. Nay, do not snatch it from me;
He that takes that doth take my heart withal.

DIOMEDES: I had your heart before; this follows it.

TROILUS: I did swear patience.

CRESSIDA: You shall not have it, Diomed; faith, you shall not;
I'll give you something else.

DIOMEDES: I will have this. Whose was it?

CRESSIDA: It is no matter.

DIOMEDES: Come, tell me whose it was.

CRESSIDA: 'Twas one's that lov'd me better than you will.
But, now you have it, take it.

5.2.76–89

The war drags on. Hector, the best man on either side, is treacherously and unheroically murdered by Achilles. Troilus's love has been betrayed and he finds his ideas of chivalry now exposed as folly. And still the war goes on, pointlessly and bloodily. There is no climax, no music at the close, no hero's funeral as in *Hamlet*. There is only a railing, bawdy epilogue by Pandarus.

Let me interpolate a point here which would not have been necessary in 1603. Your sympathies are supposed to be with the Trojans. The Renaissance was far more interested in Latin than in Greek and all the Roman writers were strongly in favour of Troy because that was where their ancestor, Aeneas, was supposed to have come from. Shakespeare was also influenced by medieval ideas and for the men of the middle ages the British too were descended from the Trojans through their mythical ancestor, Brutus, who was supposed to be the grandson of Aeneas. London is often called Troynovaunt, or New Troy, in medieval romances. If we are talking about sympathies, Troy was admittedly in the wrong because of the rape of Helen by Paris. But I think that the first audiences were meant to think of the two sides like someone said about the Roundheads and Cavaliers in the English Civil War – the Greeks were right but repulsive, the Trojans were wrong but romantic.

This leads me to another sense in which *Troilus and Cressida* is a Greek play: the audience knows the whole story beforehand. The Greeks also knew perfectly well what was going to happen on the stage during, for example, *The Oresteia*. The attraction was therefore not the plot itself, but the way in which it was handled by the writer. Both the intellectuals and the man in the street in Elizabethan England knew all about Troilus and Cressida. 'As true as Troilus' and 'As false as Cressida' were proverbs. The lovers had been sung about by the poets, as well as being the subject of popular ballads. The name of Shakespeare on a playbill was a tremendous attraction both to the general public and the highbrows. He had just scored a triumph with *Hamlet*, the most popular of all his plays. So the first audiences for *Troilus and Cressida* would have known the story and been primarily concerned with Shakespeare's treatment of it.

Troilus and Cressida is about war, honour and time, but the greatest of these is war. When I first read it in the 1930s, I was not much taken with it. There's plenty of poetry and eloquence, pathos too, though rather drily expressed and never over-emphasised. But I did not think much of the battle scenes. In 1940, when I was in the army, I picked up a copy of the play on local leave in Alexandria and carried it with me to and fro in the Western Desert for the next couple of years. I must admit to a certain personal identification here because we in the Middle East in those days were as far from home as the Greeks were at Troy. What's more, we were told officially that we could not get home leave for at least seven years, which seemed quite as long as the siege of Troy. The play struck home like a series of hammer blows in these circumstances. There was also the thought in our minds that loved ones far away might be falling for the same temptations as Cressida did, but the central thought was how well Shakespeare depicted the nature of war and how it dominates human behaviour.

I can show that this is not a merely personal view by tracing the play's stage history. It was very rarely played between its first production and the end of the nineteenth century, but the twentieth century has seen far more revivals than all the other centuries before it. A number of them have been in modern dress, with the generals in uniforms with red tabs and Diomed looking like a smart young GI Ops. It is evidently a play which speaks to our times, to our terrible, warlike twentieth century. There were plenty of wars in Shakespeare's time too. Alfred Duff Cooper, later Lord Norwich wrote a short essay called *Sergeant Shakespeare* in which he argued that Shakespeare had served as an NCO in the army under Leicester in the Low Countries. I don't think that I believe this and I am not sure that Duff Cooper did either. He does nevertheless show that in Shakespeare's earlier plays there is a whole series of portraits of admirable, honourable soldiers. He also shows that there are a mass of military metaphors even in the romantic plays. It is quite clear from these early plays that Shakespeare thought highly of soldiers and NCOs, but not so well of generals and most bitterly of war itself. The leading Greek generals are savagely caricatured, especially the blustering Ajax and the murderously unchivalrous Achilles. The best men are on the Trojan side: Troilus, Aeneas and Hector. Like Homer, Shakespeare takes the death of Hector as his climax:

> ACHILLES: Look, Hector, how the sun begins to set;
>   How ugly night comes breathing at his heels;
>   Even with the vail and dark'ning of the sun,
>   To close the day up, Hector's life is done.
> HECTOR: I am unarm'd; forego this vantage, Greek.
> ACHILLES: Strike, fellows, strike; this is the man I seek.
>   So, Ilion, fall thou next! Come, Troy, sink down;

Here lies thy heart, thy sinews, and thy bone.
On, Myrmidons, and cry you all amain
'Achilles hath the mighty Hector slain'.

5.8.5–14

Neither Shakespeare nor Homer goes on to the end of the story which, in a play or poem about a siege, you would naturally expect to be the capture of the city. They did not need to, however, because everyone knew that Troy was sacked in the end. They both rest on the assumption that, with the death of Hector, its fate is sealed. Yet both know that many more brave men will be killed first and that the miserable war will still drag on.

Honour is another important theme in the play. The Trojans in particular profess themselves devoted to it. Shakespeare takes throughout the line which he puts in the mouth of Falstaff on the battlefield of Shrewsbury: 'What is honour? A word'. The good men and the honourable men end sadly like Hector. The bad men, such as Paris and Achilles, live on and enjoy themselves. The women come off worst. Helen is cruelly debunked, although Shakespeare might have made her a sympathetic character like Cleopatra. Cressida's lack of honour is the main motive of the play.

The theme of time had preoccupied Shakespeare ever since the *Henry IV* plays. There is nothing in *Troilus and Cressida* quite comparable with Hotspur's dying speech at Shrewsbury:

O, Harry, thou hast robb'd me of my youth!
I better brook the loss of brittle life
Than those proud titles thou hast won of me:
They wound my thoughts worse than thy sword my flesh;
But thoughts, the slaves of life, and life, time's fool,
And time, that takes survey of all the world,
Must have a stop.

5.4.77–83

There is nevertheless a recurring insistence in *Troilus and Cressida* on the way in which the passage of time erodes reputations. Ulysses tells Achilles that

Time hath, my lord, a wallet at his back,
Wherein he puts alms for oblivion,
A great-siz'd monster of ingratitudes.
Those scraps are good deeds past, which are devour'd
As fast as they are made, forgot as soon
As done.

3.3.145–50

Strangely, there is only one point in the play where Shakespeare gives Cressida some lines to speak which rise to real eloquence. It is when she is swearing to be faithful to Troilus and she too, who elsewhere is represented as the light-headed creature of the moment, here takes up the theme of time. She begins with sombre variations on the thoughts suggested by its destructive effect on greatness and ends with a collection of proverbial instances of treachery:

> If I be false, or swerve a hair from truth,
> When time is old and hath forgot itself,
> When waterdrops have worn the stones of Troy,
> And blind oblivion swallow'd cities up,
> And mighty states characterless are grated
> To dusty nothing – yet let memory
> From false to false, among false maids in love,
> Upbraid my falsehood when th' have said 'As false
> As air, as water, wind, or sandy earth,
> As fox to lamb, or wolf to heifer's calf,
> Pard to the hind, or stepdame to her son' –
> Yea, let them say, to stick the heart of falsehood,
> 'As false as Cressid'.   3.2.179–92

The last line, the climax to which she builds up, is full of that tragic irony that gives special flavour to the work of the Greek dramatists; for 'as false as Cressida' did become a proverb.

Shakespeare's last words in this play are a bawdy epilogue by Pandarus devoted to the venereal diseases which he prophesies for himself and for his audience. He has an opposite number on the Greek side in Thersites, whose railings against all the Greek leaders are even coarser and more savage:

> Here's Agamemnon, an honest fellow enough, and one that loves quails, but he has not so much brain as ear-wax; and the goodly transformation of Jupiter there, his brother, the bull, the primitive statue and oblique memorial of cuckolds, a thrifty shoeing-horn in a chain, hanging at his brother's leg – to what form but that he is, should wit larded with malice, and malice forced with wit, turn him to? To an ass, were nothing: he is both ass and ox. To an ox, were nothing: he is both ox and ass. To be a dog, a mule, a cat, a fitchew, a toad, a lizard, an owl, a puttock, or a herring without a roe, I would not care; but to be Menelaus, I would conspire against destiny.

>   5.1.48–60

Some people may find these railings quite in contemporary taste. They were in a style that was coming into fashion on the Jacobean stage. As C. S. Lewis says, it is startling how often writers of this period will launch into moral diatribes of the most uncompromising ferocity: 'nothing was more saleable, more *comme il faut*, than the censorious'. Such railing is usually not so noticeable in Shakespeare as in other dramatists of this period, but he gave full rein to it in this bitter play.

We can see at once the contrast between Shakespeare's thoughts on honour and heroism and the classical ones by looking at such Greek monuments as the tomb of a Lycian prince re-erected in the British Museum and known as the Nereid Monument. It makes the confident assertions that war is glorious, that it is the pre-eminent means by which honour is won and that its celebration defeats time. The heirs of the man commemorated by this monument thought that they would immortalise his great deeds. Perhaps he gave detailed instructions himself. And what was the result of all their care and thought? His name is unknown, his battles are forgotten, his city has vanished and his monument lay for 2,000 years a heap of stones on a hillside where Turkish shepherds grazed their flocks.

There is one strong impression left on me by the play which I hesitate to express because it seems paradoxical. I catch a note of something Greek in the tone in which Shakespeare represents the battles between the Greeks and the Trojans. I believe that Shakespeare knew more Greek than the pedantic Ben Jonson allowed him. I suspect that he could read *The Iliad*. He certainly caught its tone: today we triumph and tomorrow we are killed in battle and our women dragged into captivity. The heroic age may go on, but an inch beneath the bright surface of Homer's verse there is despair and pointlessness. This is expressed in the ruthlessly poignant line spoken by Achilles to Priam in the last book of *The Iliad*: 'You too, old man, I hear were once happy'. Achilles goes on to talk about himself: 'And here I sit in Troy, afflicting you and your children'. He is not defending Greece or gaining glory, but just carrying on with the war because that is how things happen. As Goethe said, the lesson of *The Iliad* is that on this earth we must enact Hell.

TROILUS AND CRESSIDA

Norman Rodway

Norman Rodway played Thersites in the Royal Shakespeare Company's 1968 production of Troilus and Cressida. *His other Shakespearean parts have included Hotspur in* I Henry IV *(and in Orson Welles's* Chimes at Midnight*) and the title role in* Richard III. *In the BBC TV Shakespeare he has played Apemantus in* Timon of Athens, *Gloucester in* King Lear *and Cleon in* Pericles.

I can think of no group of people more addicted to time-consuming games than actors. Walk into any rehearsal room and you are sure to find somebody hunched in a corner grappling with a crossword. I remember once, on location in the Pyrenees, sitting with a group of half a dozen other actors, all of us made up and waiting, now happily reconciled to the fact that we were not going to be used that day, while the director, panic-stricken and behind schedule, was shooting battle scenes with crowds of extras. We decided to pass the time by each of us making a list, putting the plays of Shakespeare in our individual order of preference. I found it difficult to decide on an outright winner but settled in the end for a photo-finish between *King Lear*, *Henry IV Part Two* and *Troilus and Cressida*. But two others had actually put *Troilus and Cressida* last of all! It has, of course, always been regarded as one on the 'problem plays', but why should some people react violently against it and others, like me, find it completely fascinating? I've had the good luck to be in it twice, playing Thersites in the 1968–9 Royal Shakespeare Company production and, more recently, playing Ulysses in a Radio Three production. I have also seen it a number of times and the hair never fails to bristle on the back of my neck from the opening lines of the Prologue. And yet, during that game of preferences, a colleague protested to me that he found the play so loathesome that he'd never agree to appear in it.

Well, ever since it was written, reaction has been extreme. Take a few comments from illustrious people over the years. John Dryden, introducing his own watered-down version, called

Shakespeare's play 'a heap of Rubbish'. Sir Walter Raleigh, the literary critic, declared that it was 'the despair of all critics who seek in it for unity and purpose of meaning'. George Bernard Shaw produced this rather back-handed compliment:

> Shakespeare made exactly one attempt, in *Troilus and Cressida*, to hold the mirror up to nature and he probably nearly ruined himself by it. At all events he never did it again.

On the other hand, Goethe enigmatically confided that anyone who wanted to know Shakespeare's 'unfettered spirit' had to read *Troilus and Cressida*. Algernon Swinburne sums up these conflicting views:

> This wonderful play, one of the most admirable among all the works of Shakespeare's immeasurable and unfathomable intelligence, as it must always hold its natural high place amongst the most admired, will always in all probability be also, and as naturally, the least beloved of all.

So what is all the fuss about? Why this polarisation of attitudes? I'll start with the plot. What we have are two stories of love and war, one general and one specific, each illustrating and reflecting the other; the particular star-crossed passion of Troilus and Cressida framed in the larger context of the Trojan war. The setting is the siege of Troy by the Greek armies led by Agamemnon. When the play begins, the siege is already seven years old and the apparent reason for the war is to get back the Greek King's wife, Helen, who had been abducted by the Trojans and is now living with a Trojan prince, Paris. The great epic heroes are lined up on both sides. For the Greeks – Achilles, Agamemnon, Ajax and Ulysses. On the Trojan side – Paris, Hector, Priam, Aeneas and, of course, Troilus. Against this setting there is the love story itself. Troilus desires Cressida, the daughter of a Trojan priest, and she desires him. They are brought together for a night of love by her uncle, Pandarus, but it is a short-lived affair because on the following day she is handed over to the Greeks in return for a Trojan prisoner and immediately betrays Troilus with one of the Greek generals.

Now that is the story in a nutshell, but why was it that Shakespeare wanted to turn this particular story into a play? His audiences would certainly have been familiar with Chaucer's long poem *Troilus and Criseyde* or Robert Henryson's *Testament of Cresseid*. So did he just want to present a piece of ancient history to an Elizabethan audience? No, I think that there is much more to it than that. I suspect that he had also been looking into Chapman's

Homer, particularly the episode of the wrath of Achilles, and the inspiration of the fusing of the two stories together unleashed in him an outpouring of his most disturbed and disturbing doubts about accepted values and ideas on the nature of love, war, heroism, honour, fame, beauty, truth, politics and even time itself. The iconoclast, the challenger of other people's cherished beliefs, had found in the Homeric ideal the absolutely perfect sacred cow on which to vent his scepticism. Here is the opening of the Prologue which sets the scene:

> In Troy, there lies the scene. From isles of Greece
> The princes orgillous, their high blood chaf'd,
> Have to the port of Athens sent their ships
> Fraught with the ministers and instruments
> Of cruel war. Sixty and nine that wore
> Their crownets regal from th' Athenian bay
> Put forth toward Phrygia; and their vow is made
> To ransack Troy, within whose strong immures
> The ravish'd Helen, Menelaus' queen,
> With wanton Paris sleeps – and that's the quarrel.

                                                    I–IO

What you might literally call mock-heroic, isn't it? Troy conjures up that most romantic and famous city in classical mythology. Yet all those high sounding words and phrases like 'orgillous' and 'their high blood chaf'd' are suddenly undercut by those last two lines:

> The ravish'd Helen, Menelaus' queen,
> With wanton Paris sleeps – and that's the quarrel.

Yes! That's the quarrel! Somebody is sleeping with somebody else's wife and that's what it's all about. The war has been going on for seven years and nobody quite understands it anymore. Nobody is any closer to winning and, as we meet the participants, we see their frustration, confusion and self-doubt. Vietnam many centuries BC perhaps?

Forgetting the two lovers Troilus and Cressida themselves for a moment, let's look a little more closely at Shakespeare's attitude to the broad theme of war itself. There are two magnificent set scenes in which he gives us first the Greek point of view and then the Trojan, as each side discusses the rights and wrongs of this interminable war and assesses the situation. The attitudes and atmosphere of the two camps are quite distinct. The Greeks are war-weary, cynical, pragmatic and destructive. The Trojans are romantic, self-deluding, blind and self-destructive. Let's take the Greek council of war first. You find that the whole of the Greek top brass is split into various camps. There is no order and the whole place is in total chaos. It is a scene which always reminds me of Stanley Kubrick's film *The Paths of Glory*, where the generals strut about mouthing platitudes. The council of war consists of Agamemnon, Nestor, Ulysses and Menelaus, for whose sake the war is being fought, but who significantly makes no contribution whatever. Agamemnon kicks off by trying to rally flagging spirits, mouthing platitudes about things not being as bad as they seem. Nestor enlarges on this theme with typical examples of politicians' double talk: nothing is easy, troubles are sent to try us and certainly nobody will reduce inflation overnight! Then Ulysses speaks for the first time and cuts through all the shilly-shallying with an impassioned speech about the necessity of preserving order and degree, which, if it was updated, would not be out of place at a party rally in Brighton or Blackpool:

Take but degree away, untune that string,
And hark what discord follows! Each thing melts
In mere oppugnancy: the bounded waters
Should lift their bosoms higher than the shores,
And make a sop of all this solid globe;
Strength should be lord of imbecility,
And the rude son should strike his father dead;
Force should be right; or, rather, right and wrong –
Between whose endless jar justice resides –
Should lose their names, and so should justice too.
Then everything includes itself in power,
Power into will, will into appetite;
And appetite, an universal wolf,
So doubly seconded with will and power
Must make perforce an universal prey,
And last eat up himself. Great Agamemnon,
This chaos, when degree is suffocate,
Follows the choking.
And this neglection of degree it is
That by a pace goes backward, with a purpose
It hath to climb. The general's disdain'd
By him one step below, he by the next,
That next by him beneath; so ever step,
Exampl'd by the first pace that is sick
Of his superior, grows to an envious fever

Of pale and bloodless emulation.
And 'tis this fever that keeps Troy on foot,
Not her own sinews. To end a tale of length,
Troy in our weakness stands, not in her strength.

1.3.109–37

In response to this withering analysis, Agamemnon sardonically asks 'The nature of the sickness found, Ulysses,/ What is the remedy'? We then learn bit by bit of the totally chaotic situation existing in the Greek ranks. Their chief champion, Achilles, the great hero of antiquity, has opted out of the whole situation. He sits sulking in his tent with his close friend Patroclus and undermines the authority of the generals by mimicking them and sending up the whole meaningless deadlock sky-high. But before Ulysses has fully answered Agamemnon's question, they are interrupted by the arrival of Aeneas from Troy bearing an heroic challenge from Hector. This event is seen by Ulysses as an opportunity for some political manoeuvering. Don't offer the challenge to Achilles, he suggests, but devise a means whereby the huge, beefy but dim-witted Ajax can be nominated as Greek champion, thus arousing Achilles to jealousy and perhaps getting him back into the front line. The whole tone of this scene, which shows the frustration, self-justification and even desperation of the Greeks, resonates with parallels to current states of political impotence which you can all provide for yourselves.

Later on we meet the Trojans at their council of war. How are they faring? Priam, their King, starts with the desolate, ever-repeated question:

After so many hours, lives, speeches, spent,
Thus once again says Nestor from the Greeks:
'Deliver Helen, and all damage else –
As honour, loss of time, travail, expense,
Wounds, friends, and what else dear that is consum'd
In hot digestion of this cormorant war –
Shall be struck off'. Hector, what say you to't?

2.2.1–7

Hector argues simply and logically that Helen ought to be given back:

Let Helen go.
Since the first sword was drawn about this question,
Every tithe soul 'mongst many thousand dismes
Hath been as dear as Helen – I mean, of ours.
If we have lost so many tenths of ours

45

> To guard a thing not ours, nor worth to us,
> Had it our name, the value of one ten,
> What merit's in that reason which denies
> The yielding of her up?
>
> 2.2.17–25

This simple question provokes an irrational outburst from Troilus which is followed by a cut and thrust exchange about the nature of values: whether they are objective or subjective. But then, just as the Greek council was interrupted by Aeneas, so this Trojan one is disrupted by the ranting prophetess Cassandra; the voice of unilateral disarmament perhaps?

> Cry, Troyans, cry. Practise your eyes with tears.
> Troy must not be, nor goodly Ilion stand;
> Our firebrand brother, Paris, burns us all.
>
> 2.2.108–10

But Cassandra is removed and her visions of doom are summarily ignored and dismissed. 'Pay no attention to our sister: after all, she's mad!'. Paris then joins the argument to plead his case as the perpetrator of the rape of Helen:

> What treason were it to the ransack'd queen,
> Disgrace to your great worths, and shame to me,
> Now to deliver her possession up
> On terms of base compulsion! Can it be
> That so degenerate a strain as this
> Should once set footing in your generous bosoms?
>
> 2.2.150–5

Hector gives everybody a fair hearing, but goes on to illustrate how their arguments are irrelevant and off the mark:

> If Helen, then, be wife to Sparta's king –
> As it is known she is – these moral laws
> Of nature and of nations speak aloud
> To have her back return'd. Thus to persist
> In doing wrong extenuates not wrong,
> But makes it much more heavy. Hector's opinion
> Is this, in way of truth.
>
> 2.2.183–89

Then, to our astonishment, he does a complete volte-face and ends up agreeing with Troilus and Paris that Helen should not be given back. You can see the ambivalence of Shakespeare's attitude to these classical heroes who stride the stage so confidently in

Homer. What strikes me is the huge gap between people's accurate analysis of a situation and the way in which they actually behave.

The behaviour of these Homeric heroes in these two council scenes is disturbing enough, but Shakespeare has another card up his sleeve. He provides his own kind of war correspondent to comment unequivocally on the state of the play. Thersites, a shadowy, fringe figure in *The Iliad* and described in Shakespeare's cast list as 'a deformed and scurrilous Greek', is brought from time to time to the centre of the stage to deliver his sardonic and nihilistic comments on the whole sorry mess. Here are some of Thersites's views. On the war itself:

> All the argument is a whore and a cuckold – a good quarrel to draw emulous factions and bleed to death upon. Now the dry serpigo on the subject, and war and lechery confound all.
>
> 2.3.69–71

He claims that Ajax 'wears his wit in his belly and his guts in his head'. Later on, he says that he would 'rather be a tick in a sheep than such a valiant ignorance' as Achilles. Agamemnon and his brother Menelaus do not escape unscathed:

> Here's Agamemnon, an honest fellow enough, and one that loves quails, but he has not so much brain as ear-wax; and the goodly transformation of Jupiter there, his brother, the bull, the primitive statue and oblique memorial of cuckolds, a thrifty shoeing-horn in a chain, hanging at his brother's leg – to what form but that he is, should wit larded with malice, and malice forced with wit, turn him to? To an ass, were nothing: he is both ass and ox. To an ox, were nothing: he is both ox and ass. To be a dog, a mule, a cat, a fitchew, a toad, a lizard, an owl, a puttock, or a herring without a roe, I would not care; but to be Menelaus, I would conspire against destiny.
>
> 5.1.48–60

He is just as scathing about Ulysses, Nestor and their political machinations:

> the policy of those crafty swearing rascals – that stale old mouse-eaten dry cheese, Nestor, and that same dog-fox, Ulysses – is not prov'd worth a blackberry.
>
> 5.4.8–10

So much for politics!

It is, perhaps, a further comment on the complexity and

uniqueness of *Troilus and Cressida* that I have been able to go on for so long without saying very much about the pair who give the play its title. Their love story is framed within the wider context of the other corrupted and tainted love affair which is the cause of the war. We do get one actual glimpse of Helen. The face that launched a thousand ships is addressed colloquially as Nell. Her conversation is full of sexual double-entendres and innuendoes. So much so, that even the sniggering and voyeuristic Pandarus is forced to pause for a moment and consider:

> Is this the generation of love: hot blood, hot thoughts, and hot deeds? Why, they are vipers. Is love a generation of vipers?

> 3.1.125–7

The love of Troilus and Cressida is as sincere and passionate as that of Romeo and Juliet. But within the diseased atmosphere of the world they inhabit, it will have no chance and will in fact be mercilessly snuffed out. Their first meeting, state-managed by Pandarus, is light years removed from the high lyricism of the balcony scene in *Romeo and Juliet*. Many actresses will tell you that Cressida is Shakespeare's most rewarding part for a woman. She is certainly very modern: witty, astute, basically honest, ironic and self-sufficient. When she is confused she admits it and she generally reacts according to how she is treated. Troilus is by contrast a self-questioning romantic, who is possessed of a mind as tormented as Hamlet's in his quest for absolutes. They are both children of war. How could they be otherwise? Their love scene, presided over by Uncle Pandarus, is riddled with self-doubt, changes of gear and wariness, but it culminates in a declaration of undying fidelity:

> TROILUS: True swains in love shall in the world to come
>   Approve their truth by Troilus, when their rhymes,
>   Full of protest, of oath, and big compare,
>   Want similes, truth tir'd with iteration –
>   As true as steel, as plantage to the moon,
>   As sun to day, as turtle to her mate,
>   As iron to adamant, as earth to th' centre –
>   Yet, after all comparisons of truth,
>   As truth's authentic author to be cited,
>   'As true as Troilus' shall crown up the verse
>   And sanctify the numbers.
> CRESSIDA: Prophet may you be!
>   If I be false, or swerve a hair from truth,
>   When time is old and hath forgot itself,

When waterdrops have worn the stones of Troy,
And blind oblivion swallow'd cities up,
And mighty states charactless are grated
To dusty nothing – yet let memory
From false to false, among false maids in love,
Upbraid my falsehood when th' have said 'As false
As air, as water, wind, or sandy earth,
As fox to lamb, or wolf to heifer's calf,
Pard to the hind, or stepdame to her son' –
Yea, let them say, to stick the heart of falsehood,
'As false as Cressid'.

3.2.169–92

Pandarus then shows them to a bedchamber but, inevitably, reality in the shape of the war intervenes the next morning. Political manoeuvring dictates that Cressida must be exchanged for an important Trojan who has been taken prisoner by the Greeks. The lovers are distraught and Troilus begins to ask Cressida to remember their vows of the previous night. Of course I will, she says, why do you go on about it? Diomed arrives to escort her to the Greek camp and at once makes veiled advances. The inevitable happens. Cressida is received by the Greeks as a whore and behaves as one. In a viciously cruel scene Troilus is forced to watch her seduction by Diomed under the deadpan but sadistic eye of Ulysses and, of course, inevitably with Thersites as a cackling observer:

How the devil luxury, with his fat rump and potato finger tickles these together! Fry, lechery, fry!

5.2.55–6

In one of Shakespeare's most convoluted and complex speeches, Troilus tries to reconcile the divisions between his Cressida and Diomed's Cressida. He then returns to Troy with nothing to sustain him but hate. Patroclus is killed in battle the next day, which arouses Achilles to fury and, totally independent of the stratagems of Ulysses and Nestor, he returns to the fray, but, out of practice and scant of breath, breaks off his single combat with Hector and then having gathered his thugs around him, finds Hector unarmed and murders him. The Greek generals are left to reflect that, although through no device of theirs, the end of the war may at last be in sight. Troilus is left with the satisfaction of cursing Pandarus and thinking about revenge. At the end of the play Pandarus himself turns to us and promises at the time of his death to bequeath us his diseases.

49

An uncompromising play then; not really a tragedy I suppose as there is no catharsis, although one critic has observed that its less contrived ending may in fact be truer to life. But the play's bleakness is relieved by flashes of human decency and compassion. It is also packed with astonishing language and peopled by as rich and varied a collection of characters as you could wish for. As I mentioned at the beginning, the play has never been universally popular. It is, in fact, very hard to trace a stage history for it during the nineteenth century. Of course, one can see why its anti-heroism, saturation in sex, and images and metaphors of disease would not have appealed to the Victorians. It is only as we have got into this century that it seems to speak to us more and more strongly and so, over the last thirty years or so, there have been quite a number of productions. I can assure you too that the play still arouses strong passions. When I played Thersites at Stratford in 1968, I was made up to suggest tertiary syphilis and wore a codpiece representing a war mask, with a huge rope phallus for a tongue, with which I could do some pretty indecent things! I gathered the greatest collection of hate mail you can imagine. People crossed the street when they saw me coming and one person refused to serve me in a shop. An American impresario declared that 'they would never stand for this in LA. Besides, even if they did, it could only strengthen the anti-Vietnam lobby'! But as the Prologue says:

> Like or find fault; do as your pleasures are;
> Now good or bad, 'tis but the chance of war.

30–1

Certainly, I think that you will be astounded at the play's modernity and relevance and you might even reflect that it could very well be broadcast under the banner of 'A Play For Today'.

A MIDSUMMER NIGHT'S DREAM

Sir Roy Strong

Sir Roy Strong is Director and Secretary of the Victoria and Albert Museum. He is a leading authority on Renaissance culture, whose many publications include Portraits of Elizabeth I, Splendour at Court *and* The Renaissance Garden in England. *He made this programme on location at Hatfield House.*

The first night of *A Midsummer Night's Dream* must have been a great aristocratic marriage to which Queen Elizabeth the First came. It took place some time in the middle of the 1590s in some huge house of the nobility. We can't be sure which one it was, but none better, I think, to evoke the mood of *The Dream* and Elizabeth Tudor than Hatfield. She lived as a princess in Hatfield Old Palace. She was first hailed as Queen beneath the spreading branches of its ancient oaks. The new house that now dominates the landscape was built by her last great minister, Robert Cecil. The fact that it was built a few years after her death is irrelevant. It is saturated with her. Its gardens, architecture and interior decoration were conceived as a setting fit to receive a monarch. Shakespeare's play assumes such a setting and such an audience.

A Midsummer Night's Dream was first played in a Great Hall, like the one at Hatfield. It was the final event of a long day which began in the nearby church with the wedding and after continued in the great house with the wedding breakfast which would have lasted several hours. Then the Great Hall was cleared and set for the play. The audience would have ranged itself in the form of a horseshoe, facing the screens which led to the kitchen. The screen itself would have provided enough entrances and exits for the actors and the gallery at the other end of the hall would have housed the musicians of the household. Perhaps across the floor there would have been scattered pieces of scenery and props. The audience would have been ranked in strict order of precedence: guests, household, in-laws and the happy couple. But the focal point of the great occasion, the Queen and her entourage, would have been the last to arrive and they would have seated themselves at the far end on a dais beneath a canopy. This is one of Shakespeare's plays for an occasion and the occasion would have dictated most of its contents and certainly stretched our playwright's ingenuity to its full. It would have to be a comedy, it would have to be about lovers and of course there would have to be a happy ending. It also needed good, broad, low comedy of a type that would have been acceptable from the Queen to the lowliest serving boy. Shakespeare had a bonus in that a great household would have had marvellous musicians far superior to those available in the playhouse. This would have enabled him to introduce music and dancing on a scale to rival the masques at Court and he knew that he would have to close his play with some stunning visual effect, in which the powers of Heaven were called upon to rain down blessings upon the happy bride and groom. Most important of all, of course, he would have had to make the binding link of the whole event the guest of honour, the Queen.

Shakespeare begins his play by introducing us to the first ingredient – the lovers, four of them. Hermia is in love with Lysander, but her father disapproves of the marriage and they therefore decide to elope. Number three, Demetrius, is also in love with Hermia and number four, Helena, is in love with Demetrius. Helena wishes she had Hermia's beauty so that she could capture Demetrius for herself:

HERMIA: God speed fair Helena! Wither away?
HELENA: Call you me fair? That fair again unsay.
    Demetrius loves your fair. O happy fair!
    Your eyes are lode-stars and your tongue's sweet air
    More tuneable than lark to shepherd's ear,
    When wheat is green, when hawthorn buds appear.
    Sickness is catching; O, were favour so,
    Yours would I catch, fair Hermia, ere I go!
    My ear should catch your voice, my eye your eye,
    My tongue should catch your tongue's sweet melody.
    Were the world mine, Demetrius being bated,
    The rest I'd give to be to you translated.
    O, teach me how you look, and with what art
    You sway the motion of Demetrius' heart!
HERMIA: I frown upon him, yet he loves me still.
HELENA: O that your frowns would teach my smiles such skill!
HERMIA: I give him curses, yet he gives me love.

HELENA: O that my prayers could such affection move!

HERMIA: The more I hate, the more he follows me.

HELENA: The more I love, the more he hateth me.

HERMIA: His folly, Helena, is no fault of mine.

HELENA: None, but your beauty; would that fault were mine!

HERMIA: Take comfort: he no more shall see my face;
   Lysander and myself will fly this place.   1.1.180–203

The lovers are cardboard characters, silly and headstrong, no more than convenient vehicles whereby to send up the conventional love etiquette of the day.

The low humour is very different with more deeply felt, loving caricatures of the mechanicals, or craftsmen, of the age: a weaver, a bellows-mender, a joiner, a tinker and a tailor. They are the sort of people everyone in the audience would have known. Shakespeare brings them in because they have decided to stage a play on the subject of Pyramus and Thisbe, of all things, in honour of the wedding. The wedding, in their instance, is that of Duke Theseus and his bride, Hippolyta, but like everything else in *The Dream* it can also be read as referring to the marriage festivities of the moment:

QUINCE: Flute, you must take Thisby on you.

FLUTE: What is Thisby? A wand'ring knight?

QUINCE: It is the lady that Pyramus must love.

FLUTE: Nay, faith, let not me play a woman; I have a beard coming.

QUINCE: That's all one; you shall play it in a mask, and you may speak as small as you will.

BOTTOM: An I may hide my face, let me play Thisby too. I'll speak in a monstrous little voice: 'Thisne, Thisne!' 'Ah Pyramus, my lover dear! Thy Thisby dear, and lady dear!'

QUINCE: No, no, you must play Pyramus; and Flute, you Thisby.

BOTTOM: Well, proceed.

QUINCE: Robin Starveling, the tailor.

STARVELING: Here, Peter Quince.

QUINCE: You, Pyramus' father; myself, Thisby's father. Snug, the joiner, you, the lion's part. And, I hope, here is a play fitted.

                                                    1.2.37–57

Elizabeth would have laughed at the antics of the rude mechanicals and smiled at the star-crossed lovers. Now in her early sixties, she presided over the occasion as the living embodiment of the age

53

to which she had given her name and created. Almost supernatural powers were accorded her, as the peace which she had brought her country was about to enter its fourth decade. Her programme was always the same, more successful because of its very success. It was peace and plenty, the reconciliation of warring parties, the maintenance of justice and of an ordered and balanced government. The Ermine Portrait at Hatfield is a typical visual instance of this programme. In her right hand she holds the olive of peace. On the table at her side lies the Sword of Justice, while a little ermine nestles on her left arm to remind us as an emblem of purity that she reigns as a Virgin Queen. Shakespeare's play reflects and fits neatly into this perennial pattern of royal eulogy. *The Dream* belongs to a whole series of courtly entertainments in which rivalry and altercation are resolved in and by the presence of the Queen.

So the First Act sets the scene of tangled comedy as both lovers and mechanicals make their way to the woods outside Athens, which are peopled by the third ingredient of the play, the fairies. The fairies are, of course, very hard for us to take today. We have outlived belief in them and, in any case, they have been ruined by the romantic ballet. We can hardly see them in any other way except as wraith-like creatures in billowy tutus, floating around to Mendelssohn's music. Elizabeth the First would never have recognised these as her fairies. Hers were spirit creatures ruling over the realm of Nature. Their appearance was always a compliment to her peaceful rule and, as such, they were part of the stock-in-trade of Court entertainments. The greatest epic of the Elizabethan age had appeared only about five years before, Edmund Spenser's *The Faerie Queene*, which used as its central pivot the realm of 'faery'. Shakespeare would have known this. Fairies pertained to the crown, but as usual he came upon this motif at a slightly different angle. They have fallen out amongst themselves. Oberon, the fairy King, and his consort, Titania, have quarrelled about which of them should have charge of a changeling. Titania has him at the moment. Oberon therefore summons his lieutenant Puck and sends him to seek out the juice of a certain plant. This he places on the eyes of the fairy Queen so that, on awakening, she should fall in love with the first object that she sees. Partly by luck and partly by arrangement, that object turns out to be Bottom, on whose head Oberon's magic has placed an ass's head:

TITANIA: Thou art as wise as thou art beautiful.

BOTTOM: No so, neither; but if I had wit enough to get out of this wood, I have enough to serve mine own turn.

TITANIA: Out of this wood do not desire to go;
    Thou shalt remain here whether thou wilt or no.
    I am a spirit of no common rate;
    The summer still doth tend upon my state;
    And I do love thee; therefore, go with me.   3.1.135–42

So Shakespeare redoubles the discord in the wood and cleverly mingles the layers of character in his plot. The class-conscious audience would have relished this scene in which a queen embraces a weaver, or worse still an ass notorious for his sexual prowess and promiscuity.

Shakespeare has, however, a trump card to play. He needs to draw together all the ingredients in his play with some compliment to the Queen. There is a magical moment when the fairy King turns to Elizabeth and pays tribute to her in her island kingdom of England. He evokes Cupid drawing his bow and aiming a fiery arrow at her, which is extinguished and misses and falls instead upon a flower, the heartsease, the love-in-idleness or the pansy. This, like the Tudor rose or eglantine, is the royal flower used in tribute to the Queen and in one brilliant, inventive stroke Shakespeare has made it the chief agent of his play. The Queen would have loved it:

OBERON: My gentle Puck, come hither. Thou rememb'rest
    Since once I sat upon a promontory,
    And heard a mermaid on a dolphin's back
    Uttering such dulcet and harmonious breath
    That the rude sea grew civil at her song,
    And certain stars shot madly from their spheres
    To hear the sea-maid's music.
PUCK: I remember.
OBERON: That very time I saw, but thou couldst not,
    Flying between the cold moon and the earth
    Cupid, all arm'd; a certain aim he took
    At a fair vestal, throned by the west,
    And loos'd his love-shaft smartly from his bow,
    As it should pierce a hundred thousand hearts;
    But I might see young Cupid's fiery shaft
    Quench'd in the chaste beams of the wat'ry moon;
    And the imperial vot'ress passed on,
    In maiden meditation, fancy-free.
    Yet mark'd I where the bolt of Cupid fell.
    It fell upon a little western flower,
    Before milk-white, now purple with love's wound,

And maidens call it Love-in-idleness.
Fetch me that flow'r, the herb I showed thee once.
The juice of it on sleeping eyelids laid
Will make or man or woman madly dote
Upon the next live creature that it sees.
Fetch me this herb, and be thou here again
Ere the leviathan can swim a league.
PUCK: I'll put a girdle round about the earth
In forty minutes.

2.1.148–76

So discord is deliberately accelerated before it is resolved.

Enfolding darkness becomes less the setting for a dream than a nightmare as the relationships of the characters in the plot twist and turn and chop and change. We began the play with Hermia and Lysander in love, with Demetrius also in love with Hermia and with Helena left out in the cold, jilted. In the wood we go through all the permutations that could befall such a quartet. Initially Oberon tries to put things right by the magic juice of the love-in-idleness flower, but Puck of course puts the juice into the eyes of the wrong person. The order now reverses. Lysander now pursues Helena, Helena pursues Demetrius, Demetrius pursues Hermia and Hermia is still pursuing Lysander. The result is total chaos and high comedy:

HELENA: You do advance your cunning more and more.
When truth kills truth, O devilish-holy fray!
These vows are Hermia's. Will you give her o'er?
Weigh oath with oath, and you will nothing weigh:
Your vows to her and me, put in two scales,
Will even weigh; and both as light as tales.
LYSANDER: I had no judgment when to her I swore.
HELENA: Nor none, in my mind, now you give her o'er.
LYSANDER: Demetrius loves her, and he loves not you.
DEMETRIUS: O Helen, goddess, nymph, perfect, divine!
To what, my love, shall I compare thine eyne?
Crystal is muddy. O, how ripe in show
Thy lips, those kissing cherries, tempting grow!
That pure congealed white, high Taurus' snow,
Fann'd with the eastern wind, turns to a crow
When thou hold'st up thy hand. O, let me kiss
This princess of pure white, this seal of bliss!
HELENA: O spite! O hell! I see you all are bent
To set against me for your merriment.

3.2.128–46

It is essentially Elizabethan. Like the meandering paths of a maze or the patterns of a knot garden, there is coherence and ultimate order in the end. The audience is taken through discord in order to see concord restored. It is pure ritual. In these resolutions Elizabethan society was reaffirming itself in its belief in an ordered cosmos. *The Dream*, with its elaborate point and counterpoint, disharmony leading to harmony, is a typical product of Renaissance thought and art, which was eternally with tuning earth to heaven. So in the end Titania inevitably sees Bottom as he really is. The lovers pair off with mutual forgiving under the aegis of Theseus and Hippolyta. In the stillness of dawn, the fairy King and Queen give expression to this restoration of harmony in the purest of Renaissance terms. They dance, mirroring in their movements the stars in the sky and the world's order:

> OBERON: Sound, music. Come, my Queen, take hands with me,
> And rock the ground whereon those sleepers be.
> Now thou and I are new in amity,
> And will to-morrow midnight solemnly
> Dance in Duke Theseus' house triumphantly,
> And bless it to all fair prosperity.
> There shall the pairs of faithful lovers be
> Wedded, with Theseus, all in jollity.
> PUCK: Fairy King, attend and mark;
> I do hear the morning lark.
> OBERON: Then, my Queen, in silence sad,
> Trip we after night's shade.
> We the globe can encompass soon,
> Swifter than the wand'ring moon.
> TITANIA: Come, my lord; and in our flight,
> Tell me how it came this night
> That I sleeping here was found
> With these mortals on the ground.

4.1.82–99

The Dream is a moonlit play. It opens with Hippolyta telling Theseus that in four days' time 'the moon, like to a silver bow/ New-bent in heaven, shall behold the night/Of our solemnities'. Oberon and Titania meet by moonlight. The luminous, mysterious beams of the moon flood the play from beginning to end, and rightly so because in one aspect it is Queen Elizabeth the First in one of her most famous roles, that of the Virgin Moon Goddess celebrated by Ben Jonson as 'Queen and huntress, chaste and fair' and by Sir Walter Raleigh as 'Cynthia, Lady of the Sea'. It is also alluded to in the famous Rainbow Portrait at Hatfield through the crescent moon-shaped jewel that sits on top of her fantastic headdress. This is how every educated Elizabethan would have read the play beneath the surface comedy. It was an age that revelled in hidden and secret layers of meaning. Every image, whether in word or picture yielded several layers of interpretation that added all the more to the richness and to the enjoyment. The Rainbow Portrait is close in mood to the play. Besides the moon in her headdress, she wears other emblems of her rule. A golden cloak covered with eyes and ears, for as a wise ruler she sees and hears everything in her kingdom. On her left sleeve there is embroidered the Serpent of Wisdom, for the Queen is wise not only in affairs of the heart but in high, celestial matters. On her sleeves and on her bodice are embroidered spring flowers, including the pivot of our play the pansy, or the love-in-idleness. And in her right hand she holds the rainbow, symbol of peace after storms, of Elizabethan the reconciler: a role in *The Dream* that was shortly to reach its conclusion in the Great Hall over which she would preside as the couples paired off, both those in reality and those in the play.

As the festivities reach a finale, yet more layers are revealed. The Court looks on to a Court as Gloriana's Court looks on to that of Theseus and Hippolyta. Both are celebrating marriages and both do so with a play. It is the old trick of a play within a play, although in the case of that given by the Mechanicals absolutely everything goes wrong. Is Shakespeare modestly suggesting that this is how his audience would have regarded his contribution? I have often wondered. *The Dream* closes with the arrival of the third, or fairy, Court. Suddenly the party is over. Oberon and Titania appear with a train of fairies bearing lanterns and torches. It is a stunning visual climax to the whole evening as their costumes catch the light and glitter and shimmer by the torches as they dance and sing. I like to think that their dances formed the letters of the bride and bridegroom's name. We don't know, but it was a stunning climax to the whole evening. Mr Shakespeare had certainly amused. Once more the trumpets would have sounded, and once more the procession of the Queen and the great ones reformed and made its way to the riverside to take barge for Whitehall or Greenwich. A nervous host and hostess would have taken to their beds exhausted. Tomorrow would come the reckoning.

A MIDSUMMER NIGHT'S DREAM

Frances de la Tour

Frances de la Tour played Helena in Peter Brook's production of A Midsummer Night's Dream. *She has also played Rosalind in* As You Like It *and Stephanie in* Duet for One.

I know a bank where the wild thyme blows,
Where oxslips and the nodding violet grows,
Quite over-canopied with luscious woodbine,
With sweet musk-roses, and with eglantine;
There sleeps Titania sometime of the night,
Lull'd in these flowers with dances and delight;
And there the snake throws her enamell'd skin,
Weed wide enough to wrap a fairy in;
And with the juice of this I'll streak her eyes,
And make her full of hateful fantasies.
Take thou some of it, and seek through this grove:
A sweet Athenian lady is in love
With a disdainful youth; anoint his eyes;
But do it when the next thing he espies
May be the lady.   2.1.249–63

To me *A Midsummer Night's Dream* is a nightmare journey into love and out of love. It's about passion and the pain of passion, rejected love and unrequited love. It's also about the coming together of different groups of people from different strata of life and how they are affected by love in much the same way. Both the working men, or the Mechanicals, who put on the play for the aristocracy, and the aristocrats themselves, that is the court of Theseus and Hippolyta, respond to love in the same way. So do the Fairies. The parts of Theseus and Hippolyta are usually doubled by the actors who play Oberon and Titania, the King and Queen of the Fairies, to emphasise the similarities. Theseus and Hippolyta thus become the alter-egos of Oberon and Titania. Puck, the chief fairy, makes the impossible possible, like magic. He creates the conditions for unrequited love to become requited, but occasionally gets it all wrong. This is because his particular brand of magic is not always magical but often downright mischievous. The wrong person gets the magic potion and so falls in love with the wrong partner. These 'accidents' are the driving force of the play and amongst them is the accident of the two young men, Demetrius and Lysander, both falling in love with Helena. She always wanted Demetrius's love. It was indeed a case of unrequited love, but when she gets it she doesn't quite trust it. Rightly so, because one minute he is pushing her aside and then the next he adores her. The other deliberate 'accident', if you can call it that, is the way in which Titania, Queen of the Fairies, falls in love with a creature half-man, half-ass. Magic indeed!

Before we go any further into the plot, let's look at the three different groups of characters who are separate to begin with and then come together. As the play opens we see Theseus, the Duke of Athens, arranging the celebrations for his forthcoming marriage to Hippolyta. The light, happy atmosphere is suddenly dashed by a heavy-handed, unhappy father, Egeus, who comes to petition the Duke. A marriage celebration rapidly turns into a trial scene. Hermia wants to marry Lysander, but her father, Egeus, wants her to marry Demetrius. This is odd because there is no difference in status between Demetrius and Lysander. As Lysander says, 'I've got all the qualifications that Demetrius has so why shouldn't I marry her, particularly as she happens to love me!' But, as Theseus proclaims

> To you your father should be as a god;
> One that compos'd your beauties; yea, and one
> To whom you are but as a form in wax,
> By him imprinted, and within his power
> To leave the figure, or disfigure it.

I.I.47-51

In other words, you are just a replica of your father, which is enough to give anyone an identity complex. According to Theseus, Hermia must either marry Demetrius, or die by law or become a nun. A curious set of options! The tragedy of love is established right here at the beginning of the play. There is nothing funny about love which is forbidden by society.

The lovers are then left alone. It becomes like *Romeo and Juliet* – 'what shall we do? We love each other so much'. Then Lysander says 'I've got an aunt in the country so let's elope and live with her'. Hermia's friend, Helena, comes in just as they are about to set off into the woods beyond the city. She learns of their plans and wishes them well. Then she is left alone reflecting 'how happy some o'er other some can be'. She feels alone and rejected, but thinks that at least Hermia and Demetrius have got each other and are together. She goes on to contemplate love and the arbitrary nature of attraction:

And as he errs, doting on Hermia's eyes,
So I, admiring of his qualities.
Things base and vile, holding no quantity,
Love can transpose to form and dignity.
Love looks not with the eyes, but with the mind;
And therefore is wing'd Cupid painted blind.
Nor hath Love's mind of any judgment taste;
Wings and no eyes figure unheedy haste.
And therefore is Love said to be a child,
Because in choice he is so oft beguil'd.   1.1.230–9

Helena sees herself as plain and ugly, but then reflects that in Athens 'I am thought as fair as she', referring to her rival, Hermia. So I think that it is quite wrong that Helena should be played as a plain girl. It comes out later that she is gawky and tall, but there is nothing to suggest that she is plain. It is because Demetrius does not love her that she feels herself to be plain. So already we have got an interesting string of relationships. Helena is chasing Demetrius who is chasing Hermia who is chasing Lysander, who for the moment reciprocates by chasing Hermia.

Then the second group, the Mechanicals, come in to the woods. Bottom the weaver, Quince the carpenter, Flute, Snout, Snug and Starveling are the working men from the pit of Shakespeare's theatre. They are held up and sent up before their very eyes, no doubt with their approval. They want to put on a play about unrequited love for the Duke. It is a tragedy where both lovers come to an untimely end. In the privacy of the forest the Mechanicals are planning this play which draws them into the realms of what it is like to love and be loved. It sets up another angle on love. I think that this is the first time you really laugh because it is not part of the Mechanicals' make-up to express love in that heroic, lordly way. As they are workers, the contrast between who they are and what they are doing makes it funny.

Helena then comes into the woods at full pelt chasing Demetrius, who is hell bent on catching up with the runaway lovers to claim back Hermia. It is a horrible scene of rejection and, because it is so desperate, it is very funny. Hermia is so adamant about her love and pursues Demetrius so determinedly that he feels forced to be really foul to her because she is well beyond taking any gentle hints:

> DEMETRIUS: Do I entice you? Do I speak you fair?
> Or, rather, do I not in plainest truth
> Tell you I do not nor I cannot love you?
> HELENA: And even for that do I love you the more.
> I am your spaniel; and, Demetrius,
> The more you beat me, I will fawn on you.
> Use me but as your spaniel, spurn me, strike me,
> Neglect me, lose me; only give me leave,
> Unworthy as I am, to follow you.
> What worser place can I beg in your love,
> And yet a place of high respect with me,
> Than to be used as you use your dog?
> DEMETRIUS: Tempt not too much the hatred of my spirit;
> For I am sick when I do look on thee.
> HELENA: And I am sick when I look not on you.
> DEMETRIUS: You do impeach your modesty too much
> To leave the city and commit yourself
> Into the hands of one that loves you not;
> To trust the opportunity of night,
> And the ill counsel of a desert place,
> With the rich worth of your virginity.

2.1.199–219

You might wonder why she loves him. I think it becomes a challenge, a crusade, to get the person you've convinced yourself you love.

Oberon, King of the Fairies, hears all this and decides to change Demetrius's mind for him. We have already seen the main characters from this third group. Titania is having a bitter quarrel with Oberon about the way she has been treated by him and whether one of them has been unfaithful is in doubt. Jealousy is growing up over a small boy whom Titania has adopted and whom Oberon wants as his henchman. Oberon is not only determined to help the lovers, but also to do something to Titania to get his own back. He will make her fall in love with the first living creature that she sees when she wakes up from a sleep that Puck will put her into with the help of a magic potion. As it happens, the Mechanicals have now come back into the forest to rehearse their play and one of them, Bottom, becomes Puck's victim. Titania wakes up after having been given the potion by Puck and falls in love with Bottom, who has been turned into an ass:

TITANIA: Thou art as wise as thou art beautiful.
BOTTOM: Not so, neither; but if I had wit enough to get out of
    this wood, I have enough to serve mine own turn.
TITANIA: Out of this wood do not desire to go;
Thou shalt remain here whether thou wilt or no.
I am a spirit of no common rate;
The summer still doth tend upon my state;
And I do love thee; therefore, go with me.
I'll give thee fairies to attend on thee;
And they shall fetch thee jewels from the deep,
And sing, while thou on pressed flowers dost sleep;
And I will purge thy mortal grossness so
That thou shalt like an airy spirit go.

                             3.1.135–47

This of course makes an ass of Titania and, because Bottom is an ass, it is very sexual and potent. They go off together to Mendelssohn's Wedding March.

Worse complications set in when Puck sprinkles Lysander with the potion in mistakes for Demetrius. One man sleeping under a tree looks much like another after all. To Hermia's amazement, Lysander spurns her and falls madly for this tall, elegant creature who used to be so plain. There is plenty of the potion to go round so Puck tries to put things right by giving Demetrius the dose he should have had. But Demetrius now sees Helena in a totally new light and pursues her accordingly. This is a joke in the worst possible taste for Helena because to be told that you are loved by somebody you know doesn't love you is the worst mockery. She shouts and screams 'who do you think you're kidding, calling me fair?'. She is trying to get away from him whilst he is trying to get at her. I think that this love potion contains a high portion of sex because it's all to do with grabbing hold of people and having them. Both men now adore Helena. She can't believe it and doesn't believe, and thinking that Hermia is in on the act, she is having to fight them all. Hermia also can't believe what is going on and gets angry and turns against Helena. Two women fighting provides a very strong situation and I think that it should be done for real. They are about to kill each other:

LYSANDER: Be certain, nothing truer; 'tis no jest
    That I do hate thee and love Helena.
HERMIA: O me! you juggler! you cankerblossom!
    You thief of love! What! Have you come by night,
    And stol'n my love's heart from him?

HELENA: Fine, i'faith!
    Have you no modesty, no maiden shame,
    No touch of bashfulness? What! Will you tear
    Impatient answers from my gentle tongue?
    Fie, fie! you counterfeit, you puppet you!
HERMIA: 'Puppet!' why so? Ay, that way goes the game.
    Now I perceive that she hath made compare
    Between our statures; she hath urg'd her height;
    And with her personage, her tall personage,
    Her height, forsooth, she hath prevail'd with him.
    And are you grown so high in his esteem
    Because I am so dwarfish and so low?
    How low am I, thou painted maypole? Speak.
    How low am I? I am not yet so low
    But that my nails can reach unto thine eyes.   3.2.280–98

The men are trying to stop the women and in the process almost kill each other. Helena eventually manages to run away as she is very frightened of Hermia, who may be a 'dwarf' and a midget but is still dangerous. Eventually Hermia is left completely alone and she simply says 'I am amaz'd, and know not what to say'. A wonderful line after this great fight. It's like Eric Morecambe saying to Ernie Wise 'there's no answer to that!'. And all the time it is getting towards night. I remember in the Peter Brook production we sang, or rather we wailed, our despair. We fell asleep, lost, tired and confused, very close to each other but quite alone.

Then Puck has to come back because Oberon is angry with him for having got it all mixed up. He has in fact changed the lines of communication with one fell stroke. So he has to come back and undo his damage with yet more potion. He makes the lovers all normal again and then they all wake up. This scene is very short and very moving. Theseus is there with Hippolyta saying 'we're very pleased we have found you, as we were all very worried, especially Hermia's father. We realise now how much you do love each other'. It is now quite clear that Demetrius does love Helena, even though he has not got Puck's potion in his system any more. But there is this extraordinary anti-climax of finding the person you really love and wondering if it is really what you want. Was it really a dream, or a nightmare, or did it really happen? And if it wasn't a dream then how come we're all standing here with everyone's blessing? I don't think that it is like a happy reunion but I think that there is something very magical about it nevertheless.

I remember Peter Brook once asked us in rehearsal about the

'secret play'. We all sat around rather pompously in a circle saying Love, Hate, Determination and Passion. We went through all sorts of abstractions like that, but he walked out of the rehearsal room. He was so distressed and appalled with us that he decided to leave us for about two days to think about it. I think that I found out about the 'secret play' two years later during the tour of the production. The actor playing Puck and I were arguing about who was going to get the best laugh on a particular occasion, which really wasn't what it was all about but showed how much we had gone off the rails! I said that 'this scene is about me anyway', but the actor playing Puck said 'no, no, you've got it all wrong, it's about me'. I said 'look, the whole play is about me, about Helena, she is the catalyst of the whole play'. He said 'oh, no, Puck is'! It dawned on me then that the 'secret play' was about each character thinking that the play was about them, which transferred itself into each actor thinking that the play was about them. But when Peter Brook asked his question, I couldn't say that it was about Helena. Who else was I playing but Helena? Why should I think that it was about Oberon or Puck? We just didn't dare to say that it was about our character in search of their love. Yet if we had all answered the same way, we would have realised that it was about all of us as individuals but inextricably connected. This is reflected in the play within a play where we see a mirror-image of ourselves.

There was a story going around that various mums were asking for their money back in the interval because they thought that they were going to see a fairy story with a lot of fun and romping about. Yet our particular production found things, or underlined things, that one wouldn't normally look for in this play. It stuck in peoples' minds as the one with a plain white set, the notorious white box. But it was, and is, a misconception to say that it was a production about a white box, metal trees, spinning plates and trapezes, as those were simply our tools that we used to build the play. I now know that Peter Brook had already decided with his designers, before the cast met, on a white set because he wanted it to be a very open production. He wanted to get rid of false mystery because there was enough mystery in the play. It was totally unnecessary to create fog, trees, shadow and soft lights, as the real magic takes place before your eyes. So what was the clearest way we could show that? The main way was through the text, which was very often treated as an intruder in other productions. We were very exposed in that white box with the bright lights bouncing off the set. I remember sitting there in the middle of this brightness simply trying to speak the text. Fortunately most people thought that they had never heard the story told so well, on or off the trapezes. Although the white box was there, that production could not have been that production without that particular group of people. When it was recast it wasn't the same production. The new cast had not, after all, been through the same journey. So what I am saying is that it was a group of people who came together and who together tried to find the play. Every play has to have a conception and there is no 'right' or 'wrong'. But to have a conventional setting only because you don't want to put it in a white box is a betrayal of yourself and the play. You put it in a conventional setting because you believe it to mean something to you that way. In other words you've got to have a concept and Brook's concept was an open space in which a story would unfold.

The other thing about the white box is that it translates the play into a setting that the audience can accept more readily. We are detached from magic and fairies. We know about them but don't sympathise with them. The white box had elements of pyschodrama. It was something we could tune into more easily now. It was bare, naked and real. But it was theatre nevertheless: larger than life, more frightening, magical and improbable than ordinary life. Theatre is life magnified. So, just because the play is being televised, it should not be made smaller than it is. Love, suicide and revenge are very strong feelings and the text itself is big. It is the opposite of ordinary: poetic and very large in conception. Magic is especially not that commonplace. The only way to express these powerful feelings is through the text. It is not to try to make it modern or realistic by scratching your head whilst speaking or whatever you do. You have to make it that much clearer by observing the rhythm and the speech and taking care not to over-colour or simplify them. The more you adhere to the rhythm the easier the text becomes to speak. When it becomes easy it becomes natural and when it becomes natural it becomes real. Rhythm, verse metre and rhyming couplets are the only means by which these Shakespearean characters express their feelings.

What has happened to the characters at the end? I don't mean in terms of plot. They have obviously all made a journey and come through the 'dream', so how are they different? Well, for a start, I think that the lovers have grown up. They were like children and are now faced with the reality of having to see things through. It is all very well chasing someone you love, but you have to come to terms with being stuck with them. The Duke gives the lovers his blessing, which means that they can marry and have children. But then what do you do? There's no more forest to run through and nobody else for you to chase or to chase you. It's all over. This is a problem that confronts every marriage, as the audience will recognise. I think that it needs to be shown as an ambiguous feeling: what do you do after you have conquered? Only grown-ups know about this, but since so many of us have not grown up we are still in pursuit of children's fantasies and magic. We all know that it is a game and we all know when the game becomes reality. I think that there is an element of this in the 'waking-up scene', as we called it. Sometimes when we did it it was so quiet that you could hear a pin drop, other times we used to hear people crying. I remember that in America at the end of the play we used to shake hands with the audience and there was a lady crying in the front row. One of the actors bent down and asked her why she was crying and she replied 'it's all over and, even if I come again, it won't be the same. It's just all over'.

Coming to the end of what I can only describe as a rather biased approach to *A Midsummer Night's Dream*, I just want to underline what I have said about the play within the play as performed by the Mechanicals encapsulating the whole play. It reflects back on everything that has happened and the 'secret play' is exposed. Theseus decides that everybody has had enough before the Epilogue. Despite the fun and tittering from the audience, notably the lovers, I think he feels that it has been rather painful for everybody including himself and Hippolyta. Although *A Midsummer Night's Dream* is a comedy, I think Shakespeare knew that it would affect people. Yet it won't be at all effective if it is not done very seriously. All the comedy has to have that urgency and desperation. Nothing is funnier than desperation put in a comic form. It is like all those classic situations where everything goes wrong and you try desperately to put it right. It won't be funny if it is half-energised, half-determined and half-desperate. It needs a kind of energy level that comes out of real life wanting of something. Your heart beats and your pulse races and this should happen throughout. I think that you lose the play if it is made lighter. The audience sits back and thinks that it has been let off the hook and indeed it has. I would like to end by quoting a few lines from Peter Brook's *The Empty Space*:

> Once, the theatre could begin as magic, magic at the sacred festival, or magic as the footlights came up. Today it is the other way round, we must open our empty hands and show that there is nothing up our empty sleeves, only then can we begin.

1 HENRY VI

Michael Wood

Michael Wood is a presenter of a wide variety of television programmes: history, cinema and travel. His own series include In Search of the Dark Ages *and* In Search of the Trojan War. *He has also contributed individual programmes to both* The Great Railway Journeys of the World *and* River Journeys *series. He made this programme on location at Westminster Abbey, Kenilworth Castle and the King Edward VI School, Stratford-upon-Avon.*

Shakespeare's three plays on *King Henry VI* begin at Westminster Abbey with the funeral of King Henry V, the victor of Agincourt and paragon of English chivalry. With Henry's death, Shakespeare inaugurates a historical trilogy which spans fifty years of war, revolution and the death of kings. Although only a young man, Shakespeare was already interested in those great questions which would preoccupy his maturity. What does the course of history have to tell us? Does it have a meaning and definite direction? Is it intelligible or merely an eternally repeated cycle of blood, cruel and meaningless, no more rational than a storm? And what of man himself? Is he innately good, or no more just than Nature itself? These are questions which Shakespeare would return to throughout his career, but here he tackles them for the first time.

Shakespeare was born into one of the most literate societies which had yet existed in human history. His plays presuppose a high degree of public interest in historical and moral issues. From the start he was writing intellectually demanding entertainments. Shakespeare went to school in the 1570s, probably at Stratford's Tudor Grammar School. Elizabethan grammar school children spent far longer hours at school than we do today, from before six in the morning till after five at night with only a gap for lunch. They committed to memory a truly vast amount of historical, philosophical, literary and grammatical material. I suspect it would be far beyond us today. We rely so much on mass retrieval systems on videotape and mass reproduced books that for us memory plays an increasingly tiny part. Shakespeare's age was one beginning to be fascinated by the past and voraciously gobbling up the remains of the Classical culture which was becoming available in print all over Europe. It is important to understand this because the man who wrote *Henry VI* was not an untutored country genius. He was a highly intelligent man who had gone through the excellent Tudor grammar school education and had done seven or eight years of Latin. The modern Tudor history books which dealt with the Wars of the Roses, which Shakespeare read as background for these plays, were not part of the school curriculum itself, but the stories about this period were known to every Tudor grammar school boy.

Part One of Henry VI deals with the childhood and youth of the King. Henry himself hardly appears in it at all and then only towards the end. Shakespeare takes us through the gradual eclipse of English chivalry in France, the death of their ageing heroes and the loss of their empire. He also shows us the origins of those corrosive, dynastic quarrels, known as the Wars of the Roses, which were to bring Henry down. At the beginning of the play after bickering over the coffin of the great Henry V, the English nobles receive news of the first of a series of terrible disasters in France:

> BEDFORD: Henry the Fifth, thy ghost I invocate:
> Prosper this realm, keep it from civil broils,
> Combat with adverse planets in the heavens.
> A far more glorious star thy soul will make
> Than Julius Caesar or bright –
> MESSENGER: My honourable lords, health to you all!
> Sad tidings bring I to you out of France,
> Of loss, of slaughter, and discomfiture:
> Guienne, Champagne, Rheims, Orleans,
> Paris, Guysors, Poictiers, are all quite lost.
> BEDFORD: What say'st thou, man, before dead Henry's corse?
> Speak softly, or the loss of those great towns
> Will make him burst his lead and rise from death.

> 1.1.52–64

Although virtually ignored ever since, Part One of *Henry VI* was something of a box office smash in Elizabethan times. It took record receipts and caused even the acid pen of Thomas Nashe to remark of Talbot, the hero of the play:

> how it would have joyed brave *Talbot* (the terror of the French) to think that he should triumph again on the stage and that his

bones should be new-embalmed with the tears of ten thousand spectators who imagine they behold him fresh bleeding.

To understand why the play was so successful we need to understand both what the Elizabethans saw in it and what Shakespeare wanted them to see. This will in turn help us to discover what there is in it for us today. First of all, there were several important Tudor works on history and government which Shakespeare read very carefully before writing the plays. His chief historical sources, which he quarried extensively, were the Chronicles of Raphael Holinshed and Edward Hall. The frontispiece of Hall's *The Union of the Two Noble and Illustre Families of Lancaster and York* depicts the way in which the Tudor dynasty finally reconciled the claims of the Yorkists and Lancastrians. It was through such books that Shakespeare imbibed the Tudor version of history as propaganda: Richard III was presented as an out-and-out Machiavellian villain whilst Henry VI became saintly and other-worldly. This was propaganda because the Tudors had overthrown the Yorkist dynasty of Richard III by violence and therefore needed to justify themselves. Like modern states who use propaganda, they were frightened of the consequences of their actions. Their fears were very real ones. The Catholics plotted invasion and civil war, as well as attempts on Queen Elizabeth's life. She had had to execute her chief rival, the Catholic Mary, Queen of Scots, and only a couple of years before the play was written the Spanish Armada had attempted to conquer England on behalf of the Catholic cause. So the Wars of the Roses provided a grave warning about what might happen if there was a failure of rulership or a disputed succession.

Shakespeare's experience of drama was probably already very diverse before he even left school and perhaps that explains why at the start of his professional career he was able to kick off with such an ambitious scheme as the *Henry VI* plays. Travelling players came to Stratford virtually every year during the period that Shakespeare grew up. They were received by the Mayor and Corporation in the Guildhall, which was in fact underneath the schoolroom, and they performed their plays there as well. So it is a fair bet that William Shakespeare saw his first plays in that very room. He may also have trodden the boards for the first time there because Tudor grammar schools did do school plays. But for plays of the scope of the *Henry VI* trilogy, the medieval mystery plays were probably more influential. These great cycles which told the whole history of creation were still being performed at Coventry, Shakespeare's nearest big city, until he was fifteen. He must surely have seen them. He may also have been influenced by the royal pageants. In the age of Elizabeth I there was a remarkable revival of old-fashioned chivalry centring on the cult of the Virgin Queen, in which the English monarchy itself became an object of dramatisation. Each year on 17 November, the anniversary of her accession, Elizabeth presided over a series of spectacular pageants. Her nobles, dressed up in the Elizabethan fancy-dress version of medieval costume, jousted and broke their lances for her as well as reciting romantic tales to compliment their Queen. It was a deliberate hark-back to the age of chivalry. There were other spectacular royal pageants throughout the year in different places in her realm. The most famous took place at Kenilworth in 1575. It is interesting from our point of view because it seems that young Master Shakespeare got the day off from school to come and see it, along with thousands of other people from Warwickshire, since he described it years later in *A Midsummer Night's Dream*. On that day in 1575 Elizabeth saw a pageant with good and bad knights, gods and goddesses, ladies of the lake and so on. Feudalism was extinct as a social structure, but the Elizabethans in their time of stress in between the medieval and modern worlds seemed to need to recreate it imaginatively in order that the emotional fervour of those feudal bonds could be directed towards their national Queen. Shakespeare had this background to go on when he dealt with the age of chivalry, although his books told him that the real age of chivalry was cruel, brutal and without honour. These plays about Henry VI scrutinise the mythology of chivalry.

The main action of this play takes place in France. The English had been prosecuting their claims to France in savage wars since the time of Henry V and Agincourt. The Elizabethans saw nothing wrong in this, as they believed that foreign aggression and national unity were linked. It is national disunity which probably loses the English their empire in *Henry VI*. As Nashe has already shown us, the English hero or star as far as the Elizabethan audience was concerned is Talbot. He is a seeker after glory, chivalrous but unquestioningly brutal. He outlines this code of morality after Salisbury, the English commander, has been fatally wounded before Orleans:

Now I have paid my vow unto his soul;
For every drop of blood was drawn from him
There hath at least five Frenchmen died to-night.
And that hereafter ages may behold
What ruin happened in revenge of him,

Within their chiefest temple I'll erect
A tomb, wherein his corpse shall be interr'd;
Upon the which, that every one may read,
Shall be engrav'd the sack of Orleans,
The treacherous manner of his mournful death,
And what a terror he had been to France.   2.2.7–17

Shakespeare continued to portray such men throughout his career, culminating in his treatment of Coriolanus. He is not sympathetic towards them and, to be sure, a man who boasts that five Frenchmen have died for every drop of Salisbury's blood is a man who really needs watching. One nation's soldier-hero is often the other side's murderer, so to the French Talbot is no more than a brute who 'by tyranny these many years/ wasted our country'. Although the play is about the English at war, Shakespeare creates a surprising ambivalence which will grow as the cycle of doom works itself out through the trilogy. He doubtless read in his schoolbooks like Erasmus's *Proverbs* that war is 'sweet only to those who have never experienced it' and that men like Talbot are 'a plague on mankind no less than a great flood or a burning drought whereby a great part of living creatures is scorched up'. The perspective begins to shift to this point with the death of Talbot, which occurs in one of those typically Shakespearean scenes where the man of action is pushed into a corner by the force of history and realises that he does not control his destiny and that he too must suffer. This is the scene which had the groundlings in tears in 1591:

SERVANT: O my dear lord, lo where your son is borne!
TALBOT: Thou antic Death, which laugh'st us here to scorn,
   Anon, from thy insulting tyranny,
   Coupled in bonds of perpetuity,
   Two Talbots, winged through the lither sky,
   In thy despite shall scape mortality.
   O thou whose wounds become hard-favoured Death,
   Speak to thy father ere thou yield thy breath!
   Brave Death by speaking, whether he will or no;
   Imagine him a Frenchman and thy foe.
   Poor boy! he smiles, methinks, as who should say,
   Had Death been French, then Death had died today.
   Come, come, and lay him in his father's arms.
   My spirit can no longer bear these harms.
   Soldiers, adieu! I have what I would have,
   Now my old arms are young John Talbot's grave.
(*Dies*)   4.7.17–32

The massacre and ruin caused by the English in France starts to be viewed in a different light by them after Talbot's death. Gloucester calls for a stop to the effusion of Christian blood. Henry himself calls this strife between Christian nations impious and unnatural. The most important expression of these sentiments comes from Joan of Arc, who is now the French heroine and prophetess, as she attempts successfully to win over the Duke of Burgundy, who is an English ally, to the French cause:

> Look on thy country, look on fertile France,
> And see the cities and the towns defac'd
> By wasting ruin of the cruel foe;
> As looks the mother of her lowly babe
> When death doth close his tender dying eyes,
> See, see the pining malady of France
> Behold the wounds, the most unnatural wounds,
> Which thou thyself hast given her woeful breast.
> O, turn thy edged sword another way;
> Strike those that hurt, and hurt not those that help!
> One drop of blood drawn from thy country's bosom
> Should grieve thee more than streams of foreign gore.
> Return thee therefore with a flood of tears,
> And wash away thy country's stained spots.

3·3·44–57

We are obviously meant to feel the awfulness of what the English are doing in France, which is ironic because at the very moment these lines were being delivered on the London stage an English army under the Earl of Essex was besieging Rouen to aid the Protestant cause in Europe. Any overt criticism of English imperialism in France would therefore have received rather a frosty reception. Shakespeare's portrayal of Joan of Arc must have been influenced by this. He trod a delicate line in between the French view of her as a divinely inspired prophetess and the English one that she was a witch, although in the final analysis he did not present her as a heroine who conquers in a just war. He gave her a speech which gains her human sympathy during her condemnation scene, but then threw in Holinshed's story that she was pregnant by a French noble and could not therefore be a holy woman. We are left with images from Hall and Holinshed of Joan as a witch, minister of Hell and enchantress. This Joan is a pathetic, misguided victim of war, who is pursued by fiends rather than by divine voices. Her condemnation scene, which almost verges on black comedy, leaves nobody with any honour:

> WARWICK: And hark ye, sirs; because she is a maid,
>   Spare for no fagots, let there be enow.
>   Place barrels of pitch upon the fatal stake,
>   That so her torture may be shortened.
> PUCELLE: Will nothing turn your unrelenting hearts?
>   Then, Joan, discover thine infirmity
>   That warranteth by law to be thy privilege:
>   I am with child, ye bloody homicides;
>   Murder not then the fruit within my womb,
>   Although ye hale me to a violent death.
> YORK: Now heaven forfend! The holy maid with child!
> WARWICK: The greatest miracle that e'er ye wrought:
>   Is all your strict preciseness come to this?

                                                5.4.55–67

Henry VI Part One is not a great play as it has many of the faults of youth. But even this early in his career Shakespeare has understood that, in the re-enactment of history, there is a kind of ritual for the national audience who watch it. He has also realised that history itself is an elemental force which is capable of generating tragedy and crushing all before it. Shakespeare the playwright or craftsman has also hit on the right way of staging history. It does not help to imagine him as the balding bard of all those statues, looking serene and stolid. Try instead to think of him as a young blade, who was daring, ambitious and keen to experiment. His plays come close on the end of a long tradition of medieval drama, which enables him to draw on a great reservoir of shared belief and symbolism. Yet these plays are typical of the new Protestant civilisation of Elizabethan England in that they interpret history in terms of man's role and personal responsibility. Literally and figuratively, God is no longer centre of the stage.

2 HENRY VI

Michael Wood

This programme was made on location at the Bodleian Library, Oxford, Knole and The King Edward VI School.

This play traces Henry's unhappy and incompetent involvement in the adult world, culminating in the outbreak of civil war between aristocratic factions which we call the Wars of the Roses. We also move from the European stage of Part One back to England.

The memory of Humphrey, Duke of Gloucester as a politic and wise man of government was still current in Shakespeare's time. This is why he almost becomes the tragic hero of the play. Shakespeare's source in the first place was, as usual, Holinshed's Chronicle, in which Humphrey is described as the 'noble Duke who was an upright and politic governor, bending all his endeavours to the advancement of the commonwealth'. He goes on to say that, if anybody wanted to know more about Duke Humphrey, 'I refer the readers unto Master Foxe's Book of Actes and Monuments'. Foxe's book, which we know as the *Book of Martyrs*, was the great work on the Tudor persecution of the Catholics. A fascinating insight into the way in which Shakespeare used his sources is provided by the fact that he obviously acted upon Holinshed's hint. His portrayal of Humphrey was influenced by Foxe's more detailed account of him:

> duke Humphrey had not only a head, to discern and disserver truth from forged and feigned hypocrisy, but study also, and diligence likewise, was in him, to reform that which was amiss. And thus much, hitherto, for the noble Prowess and Virtues, joined with the like ornaments of knowledge and literature, shining in this princely duke: for which as he was both loved of the poor commons, and well spoken of, of all men, and no less deserving the same, being called the 'good' duke of Gloucester; . . . .

He possesses all the essential attributes of government: bending his endeavours to the good of the commonwealth, discerning truth from hypocrisy and being willing to reform what is amiss. Qualities which are as necessary in our own day as they were in Shakespeare's. In short, it is Duke Humphrey who is the upright man on whom the health of the body politic depends. He, not the King, matches up to Sir Thomas Elyot's ideal of the just governor. He is the man who governs 'according to the rule of moderation and reason in contrast to those moved more by sensuality than by reason or any inclination to humanity'.

In the opening scene of the play Duke Humphrey launches an embittered attack on the marriage treaty between Henry and Margaret of Anjou, which will surrender Anjou and Maine to the French:

> Brave peers of England, pillars of the state,
> To you Duke Humphrey must unload his grief –
> Your grief, the common grief of all the land.
> What! did my brother Henry spend his youth,
> His valour, coin, and people, in the wars?
> Did he so often lodge in open field,
> In winter's cold and summer's parching heat,
> To conquer France, his true inheritance?
> Have you yourselves, Somerset, Buckingham,
> Brave York, Salisbury, and victorious Warwick,
> Receiv'd deep scars in France and Normandy?
> Or hath mine uncle Beaufort and myself,
> With all the learned Council of the realm,
> Studied so long, sat in the Council House
> Early and late, debating to and fro
> How France and Frenchmen might be kept in awe?
> And shall these labours and these honours die?

I.I.70–90

The morality of these English conquests is not at issue. The question is Humphrey's fitness to speak for the English. We soon learn that his enemies are going to be too strong for him and he gradually becomes morose and ill-tempered as the tide goes against him. He becomes unreasonable in the universal dissolution.

The main action of the play shows how this man, the Protector of the commonwealth, is plotted against and murdered without Henry lifting a hand to save him. The commonwealth is plunged into civil war as a result. In the end in a horrible parody of justice, rather like a modern show trial, Humphrey is condemned in front of Henry by Queen Margaret and her paramour, Suffolk. They are joined by Cardinal Beaufort and Richard, Duke of York. His enemies are moved by sensuality, hatred and ambition. They have already all but openly decided that he must die:

> GLOUCESTER: Ay, all of you have laid your heads together –
> Myself had notice of your conventicles –
> And all to make away my guiltless life.
> I shall not want false witness to condemn me
> Nor store of treasons to augment my guilt.
> The ancient proverb will be well effected:
> 'A staff is quickly found to beat a dog'.
> CARDINAL: My liege, his railing is intolerable.
> BUCKINGHAM: He'll wrest the sense, and hold us here all day.
> Lord Cardinal, he is your prisoner.
> CARDINAL: Sirs, take away the Duke, and guard him sure.
> GLOUCESTER: Ah, thus King Henry throws away his crutch
> Before his legs be firm to bear his body!
> Thus is the shepherd beaten from thy side,
> And wolves are gnarling who shall gnaw thee first.
> Ah, that my fear were false! ah, that it were!
> For, good King Henry, thy decay I fear.   (*Exit, guarded*)
> KING: My lords, what to your wisdoms seemeth best
> Do or undo, as if ourself were here.

> 3.1.165–196

Humphrey is led away to certain death and with his passing we, the audience, know that Henry has cut himself off irrevocably from the moderation of reason.

We know that Tudor schoolboys had to stand up in class and make orations defending the kingship of Henry VI and attacking that of Richard III, which suggests that the stories of the Wars of the Roses were common currency in Elizabethan England. The Elizabethans were obsessed by these civil wars as they were haunted by the fear that the Tudor line would give out, throwing the crown back into the arena to be contested for by factions. They believed, in other words, that the Wars of the Roses might be fought all over again and that they would be infinitely more bitter because the conflict would be between Catholics and Protestants. Speeches such as this one by York therefore provided a chilling reminder of the possible shape of things to come:

> A day will come when York shall claim his own;
> And therefore I will take the Nevils' parts,

And make a show of love to proud Duke Humphrey,
And when I spy advantage, claim the crown,
For that's the golden mark I seek to hit.
Nor shall proud Lancaster usurp my right,
Nor hold the sceptre in his childish fist,
Nor wear the diadem upon his head,
Whose church-like humours fits not for a crown.
Then, York, be still awhile, till time do serve;
Watch thou and wake, when others be asleep,
To pry into the secrets of the state;
Till Henry, surfeiting in joys of love
With his new bride and England's dear bought queen,
And Humphrey with the peers be fall'n at jars;
Then will I raise aloft the milk-white rose,
With whose sweet smell the air shall be perfum'd,
And in my standard bear the arms of York,
To grapple with the house of Lancaster;
And force perforce I'll make him yield the crown,
Whose bookish rule hath pull'd fair England down.

I.I.234–54

The play shows us a naïve, weak but moral man crumbling under both the force of history and the corruption of politics until he comes to something like a tragic end. This was the Tudor view of Henry VI, which Shakespeare found in Holinshed, Hall and his other staple sources. Hall described Henry as being more suited to the priesthood than to kingship:

> of a meek spirit, and of a simple wit, preferring peace before war, rest before business, honesty before profit, and quietness before labour. And to the intent, that all men might perceive, there could be none more Chaste, more Meek, more Holy, nor a better Creature. . . . He gaped not for honour, nor thirsted for riches, but studied only for the health of his soul: the saving whereof, he esteemed to be the greatest wisdom, and the loss thereof, the extremest follie that could be.

This myth, for myth it is, was created by the Tudors to blacken Henry's Yorkist opponents, whom they themselves had supplanted. Shakespeare dramatises the myth:

WARWICK: It is reported, mighty sovereign,
That good Duke Humphrey traitorously is murd'red
By Suffolk and the Cardinal Beaufort's means.
The commons, like an angry hive of bees

That want their leader, scatter up and down
And care not who they sting in his revenge.
Myself have calm'd their spleenful mutiny
Until they hear the order of his death.
KING: That he is dead, good Warwick, 'tis too true;
But how he died God knows, not Henry.
Enter his chamber, view his breathless corpse,
And comment then upon his sudden death.
WARWICK: That shall I do, my liege. Stay, Salisbury,
With the rude multitude till I return.
KING: O Thou that judgest all things, stay my thoughts –
My thoughts that labour to persuade my soul
Some violent hands were laid on Humphrey's life!
If my suspect be false, forgive me, God;
For judgment only doth belong to Thee.

3.2.122–40

The Tudor view of Henry VI sounds too good to be true and it is. Modern studies have in fact shown that, once he took over personal power, he failed to maintain justice, abused his wide powers of patronage and was partial towards corrupt and powerful kinsmen whilst mistrustful of the men he really should have put his faith in. He may have been naïve, but he was also certainly partisan and vicious. Like most medieval kings, he behaved like a spoilt child.

The climax of the play is reached in the orchards of Kent. A shattering popular revolt shows us most clearly the consequences of Henry's failure of rulership. This rising is led by a war veteran called Jack Cade, who is backed by the disenchanted commons of Kent. Shakespeare's portrayal of the poor, or commons, as individuals is more often than not highly sympathetic. It is rarely so, however, when they gather together as a body and act to a political end. In this he was a man of his time, for the Elizabethans were horrified, although fascinated, by the spectre of popular revolt. This was probably because they lived in such constant fear and expectation of a revolt by the many-headed monster. Shakespeare blackens Cade in no uncertain terms, throwing out Hall's description of him as a 'certain youngman of a goodly nature, and a pregnant wit'. Shakespeare also shows no knowledge of, or interest in, the true grievances of the revolt of 1450. He is content to follow Hall's less flattering description of Cade and his followers as being the dupes of the Yorkist party. As far as he is concerned they are rebels without a cause. For both Shakespeare and Hall, they are the enemies of the commonwealth:

These persuasions, with many other fair promises of liberty (which the common people more affect and desire rather than reasonable obedience, and due conformity) so animated the Kentish people, that they with their Captain above named, in good order of battle (not in great number) came to the plain of Blackheath.

These rebels are presented as haters not merely of justice and knowledge, but also of the power, wealth and privilege of the aristocracy. These days we are apt to think of Shakespeare's time as being a kind of Golden Age of Merrie England. There was in fact quite a background of class hostility then, which meant that a playwright had to be careful when he dealt with a theme like popular rebellion for fear of incurring the wrath, or at least the red pen, of the censor, the Master of Revels. The pamphleteer Thomas Nashe remarks on the disdainful attitude of the commons towards the English upper class and a Scottish observer at the same time commented on the bitter and mistrustful attitude of the English commons towards the gentry and nobility. These feelings were reciprocated. Only the landed class were allowed to bear arms and at the time of the Armada emergency there was considerable anxiety when military training was extended to the whole population. It was argued that, once servants and workers were trained as soldiers, social rank and position might be turned upside down. Thus Cade's rebellion could also represent the shape of things to come for an Elizabethan audience:

CADE: Away, burn all the records of the realm. My mouth shall be the Parliament of England.

HOLLAND: Then we are like to have biting statutes, unless his teeth be pull'd out.

CADE: And henceforward all things shall be in common.

MESSENGER: My lord, a prize, a prize! Here's the Lord Say, which sold the towns in France; he that made us pay one and twenty fifteens, and one shilling to the pound, the last subsidy.

CADE: Well, he shall be beheaded for it ten times.

4.7.13–22

The sinister buffoonery of this scene is a minor masterpiece of black comedy. It is, however, more than just buffoonery, for the Lord Say has replaced Humphrey, Duke of Gloucester, as the pillar of goodness and reason. Cade's treatment of him has an ominously modern ring. In our news bulletins these days we are used to totalitarian regimes of both the Right and Left who attack literacy and learning. It was enough to be known to be able to write your name to be condemned to death in Cambodia.

Shakespeare got this and other ideas not just from accounts of Cade's rebellion, but also from Holinshed's description of the great Peasants' Revolt of 1381 when Wat Tyler and his rebels determined that they would do away with everybody who understood the law in order that things might be shared in common. They made teachers of children in grammar schools swear not to practice their art and it was dangerous to be known as one who was learned. Shakespeare draws on this material for his portrayal of Cade's rebellion:

> CADE: How now! Who's there?
> WEAVER: The clerk of Chatham. He can write and read and cast accompt.
> CADE: O monstrous!
> WEAVER: We took him setting of boys' copies.
> CADE: I am sorry for't; the man is a proper man, of mine honour; unless I find him guilty, he shall not die. Come hither, sirrah, I must examine thee. What is thy name?
> CLERK: Emmanuel.
> CADE: Dost thou use to write thy name, or hast thou a mark to thyself, like an honest plain-dealing man?
> CLERK: Sir, I thank God, I have been so well brought up that I can write my name.
> ALL: He hath confess'd. Away with him! He's a villain and a traitor.
> CADE: Away with him, I say! Hang him with his pen and inkhorn about his neck.

4.2.80–105

So Shakespeare is not giving us a historically accurate account of the Cade rebellion. That is not his purpose at all. What he is doing is to show us what happens when greed and sheer hatred take over and justice is kicked out of the window. This is the pass to which the English have come through the incompetence of Henry's government and the rottenness of his advisers. To Shakespeare, as to most educated Elizabethans, it was axiomatic, as Sir Thomas Elyot had written, that the commonwealth depended on men of understanding and knowledge. He also believed that the public weal is governed by the rule and moderation of reason rather than by the Jack Cades of this world.

The play ends with the outbreak of the Wars of the Roses as

Richard, Duke of York, challenges Henry outright for the throne on the basis of his own descent and Henry's incompetent government. So those great lords whom we first met in Part One taking sides in the rose garden can now vent their lust for blood and power and their mindless militarism in open warfare. I think that *Henry VI Part Two* is the most interesting play in the trilogy, but like the others it has been ignored until modern times. The revivals in the 1950s and 1960s seem to have struck a chord. It is as if an audience that has grown up with the Second World War and all the vicissitudes of the post-war world has found it easier to accept the cruelty, violence and cynicism of Shakespeare's characters. Many of them may be cardboard ones compared with Hamlet, but their situations are true to life. We can accept the death or murder of most of the protagonists because, like the Elizabethans, we recognise that the repetition of cruelties is part of the mechanism of history itself. Every age will find in Shakespeare what it wants to find. Genteel critics in the eighteenth and nineteenth centuries, who had a faith in progress, found these plays so shocking and crude that they could not believe that Shakespeare had written them. We at least know better than them that Shakespeare is always true to life.

3 HENRY VI
Michael Wood

This programme was made on location at Saxton Parish Church, the Battlefield at Towton and The King Edward VI School.

Shakespeare now takes us into the very worst fighting of the Wars of the Roses and presents us with the final breakdown of Henry's government, his gradual detachment from the world and his final deposition and death. The play begins with a definitive spectacle of royal crisis. Henry is confronted at Parliament in London by his kinsman, Richard Plantagenet, Duke of York, who claims the throne on the basis of the illegal deposition of his ancestor, Richard II, by Henry's ancestor, Henry IV. York's claim is strengthened by Henry's incompetent rule. It is a scene that must have sent shivers down the spine of an Elizabethan audience as Henry, admittedly the Lord's annointed, is exposed as king-worthy in no other way:

> KING HENRY; Think'st thou that I will leave my kingly throne,
>   Wherein my grandsire and my father sat?
>   No; first shall war unpeople this my realm;
>   Ay, and their colours, often borne in France,
>   And now in England to our heart's great sorrow,
>   Shall be my winding-sheet. Why faint you, lords?
>   My title's good, and better far than his.
> WARWICK: Prove it, Henry, and thou shalt be King.
> KING HENRY: Henry the Fourth by conquest got the crown.
> YORK: 'Twas by rebellion against his king.
> KING HENRY: I know not what to say; my title's weak. –
>   Tell me, may not a king adopt an heir?
> YORK: What then?
> KING HENRY: An if he may, then am I lawful King;
>   For Richard, in the view of many lords,
>   Resign'd the crown to Henry the Fourth,
>   Whose heir my father was, and I am his.

I.I.124–40

The upshot of this bitter debate is recounted by Edward Hall:

> After long arguments, it was agreed by the Three Estates for so much as King Henry had been taken as King by the space of thirty-eight years and more, that he should enjoy the name and title of King and have possession of the realm during his life natural and that if he either died or resigned, then the said crown and authority royal should immediately be devoluted to the Duke of York if he then lived or to the next heir of his line.

In other words, Henry was disinheriting his own son in favour of the Duke of York and his heirs and so restoring the line of Richard II.

Every educated Elizabethan probably knew this story backwards. It was one of those stories which they knew from childhood from having to stand up and recite it at their desks in school. No Elizabethan would have missed the contemporary relevance of this story. A society could not tolerate two kings any more than Elizabeth could tolerate two queens. Shakespeare follows his sources very closely here and, like a good Tudor, he accepts Hall's statement that when Richard II resigned he did so willingly. The important point was that he conceded his kingdom without constraint. This meant that Yorkists were striking against the Lord's annointed and would have to pay:

> QUEEN MARGARET: A crown for York! – and, lords, bow low to him.
> Hold you his hands whilst I do set it on
>   (*Putting a paper crown on his head*)
> Ay, marry, sir, now looks he like a king!
> Ay, this is he that took King Henry's chair,
> And this is he was his adopted heir.
> But how is it that great Plantagenet
> Is crown'd so soon and broke his solemn oath?
> As I bethink me, you should not be King
> Till our King Henry had shook hands with death.
> And will you pale your head in Henry's glory,
> And rob his temples of the diadem,
> Now in his life, against your holy oath?
> O, 'tis a fault too too unpardonable!
> Off with the crown and with the crown his head;
> And, whilst we breathe, take time to do him dead.

1.4.94–108

In this dreadful moment, crowned with paper in mockery, York is at once a player king, a king of fools and, in an unmistakable visual allusion to the Mystery plays, a Christ-like King of Sorrows. The whole scene is terribly cruel. All human feeling has gone from Margaret and there is only hatred left. It is a truly horrible scene, which is only made bearable by the very formal control on Shakespeare's part and by one masterly, typically Shakespearean touch, Northumberland's human response to the grief of his enemy:

> Had he been slaughter-man to all my kin,
> I should not for my life but weep with him,
> To see how inly sorrow gripes his soul.   1.4.169–71

Natural feeling and the capacity to be moved are as essential in a ruler as in a private citizen, but Margaret and Clifford have lost them together with all moderation of reason, to use Sir Thomas Elyot's phrase. They are no longer moved by humanity but by a violent and excessive sensuality.

After York's death, the action moves swiftly on to the great set-piece of the play, which is the Battle of Towton. It was remembered in the sixteenth century as the bloodiest and most frightful battle in memory. According to Edward Hall, it was fought 'in a manner unnatural' as father fought against son and brother against brother. This battle represented civil war incarnate for the Tudors. It was fought between the two villages of Saxton and Towton ten miles south of York on Palm Sunday 1461, a 100 years before Shakespeare was born. The Lancastrians lined themselves up along a ridge expecting an attack from the south. The Yorkists, who were lined up on the opposite ridge, attacked them in a dense blizzard. This battle, says Edward Hall, remained in doubt for ten hours. It was only decided in the growing gloom towards evening when Yorkist reinforcements arrived on the eastern side of the battlefield and the Lancastrians were then broken and driven westwards into the river valley of the Cock Beck. The bluffs above the river were too precipitous to allow an ordered retreat. When the defeated Lancastrians plunged into the river valley, they found it flooded by the spring snows and, as darkness fell, a terrible slaughter of the fugitives occurred by the river. The remains of the defeated army tried to cross over the bodies of their dead comrades. The River Wharfe itself, into which the Cock flows, was said to have run with blood for three days.

Shakespeare extracts all the fratricidal horror out of Edward Hall's account of this battle. He constructs a series of mini scenes to dramatise the bankruptcy of the politicians. First of all King Henry, who was not actually present at the battle but sitting in a warm room in York, is given a famous soliloquy in which he compares the burdens of kingship with what he imagines to be the carefree idyll of the peasant:

> O God! methinks it were a happy life
> To be no better than a homely swain;
> To sit upon a hill, as I do now,
> To carve out dials quaintly, point by point,
> Thereby to see the minutes how they run –
> How many makes the hour full complete,
> How many hours brings about the day,
> How many days will finish up the year,
> How many years a mortal man may live.
> When this is known, then to divide the times –
> So many hours must I tend my flock;
> So many hours must I take my rest;
> So many hours must I contemplate;
> So many hours must I sport myself;
> So many days my ewes have been with young;
> So many weeks ere the poor fools will ean;
> So many years ere I shall shear the fleece:
> So minutes, hours, days, months, and years,
> Pass'd over to the end they were created,
> Would bring white hairs unto a quiet grave.
> Ah, what a life were this! how sweet! how lovely!
> Gives not the hawthorn bush a sweeter shade
> To shepherds looking on their silly sheep,
> Than doth a rich embroider'd canopy
> To kings that fear their subjects' treachery?
> O yes, it doth; a thousand-fold it doth.

2.5.21–46

This speech seems an anachronism in a trilogy full of noise, conflict and action. Coming in the middle of a battle, its delicate, lyrical feeling gives the audience their only real chance to contemplate the causes of all this mayhem. It is also Henry's only real opportunity to indulge to the full his nostalgic longing to escape the burdens of kingship.

The King's reverie is immediately broken by the most shocking confirmation of what his withdrawal from the world has meant for his people:

SON: From London by the King was I press'd forth;
    My father, being the Earl of Warwick's man,
    Came on the part of York, press'd by his master
    And I, who at his hands receiv'd my life,
    Have by my hands of life bereaved him.
    Pardon me, God, I knew not what I did.
    And pardon, father, for I knew not thee.
    My tears shall wipe away these bloody marks;
    And no more words till they have flow'd their fill.
KING HENRY: O piteous spectacle! O bloody times!
    Whiles lions war and battle for their dens,
    Poor harmless lambs abide their enmity.
    Weep, wretched man; I'll aid thee tear for tear;
    And let our hearts and eyes, like civil war,
    Be blind with tears and break o'ercharg'd with grief.   2.5.64–78

This scene is even more formal than what has gone before. It is almost a speaking tableau, which merely asks us to contemplate the complete breakdown of civilisation. Reason and justice have gone astray and now even the bonds of nature themselves are loosed.

During the historical battle of Towton, the people of the nearby village of Saxton locked themselves up inside their church and submitted themselves to the protection of their God. This provides an image of that all-embracing, religious view of the world which medieval man accepted unquestioningly. That world had been swept away when Shakespeare came to re-tell the story by the Protestant Reformation which inaugurated the new, secular, capitalist world of the Tudors. But the Tudors still hankered after an ideological unity of the kind that they had thrown away in rejecting the Catholic church. The most effective symbol that they found to substitute for that was the person of the monarch. And so it came to be believed that the life of even a wicked or ineffective ruler was sacred, a doctrine that was preached from the pulpit and appears in a number of Shakespeare's plays. The allegiance which had previously gone to the Catholic church increasingly started to focus upon the figure of the national secular monarch, who was dressed up in the doctrine of the Divine Right of Kings. An Elizabethan audience would therefore probably have found the scene in which Henry sits on a molehill and wishes he could be a shepherd an odious and uncomely perversion of the natural order of things, as Sir Thomas Elyot would have said. He argued that just as a ploughman would make an unmeet administrator, so it was much more unfitting that a king should wish to be a homely swain. Yet Shakespeare's Henry and the real man are worlds apart. There is a gap not merely of time, but of mentality and imagination caused by the Reformation. Shakespeare's portrayal depends on the Tudor propaganda of Henry as a man of extraordinary sanctity, whose shrine wrought miracles and cures for the pilgrims it drew from all over Britain. He was a Christ-like figure who was prayed for in churches throughout the land. Although his kingdom was deemed to be not of this world, he still became a fitting subject for Tudor speculations on the Divine Right of Kings.

This was the myth that lay behind Shakespeare's portrayal. The real Henry was something rather different. There is, surprisingly enough, no evidence from Henry's own life to support this view of him as a blameless ascetic. His great ceremonial courts were, for instance, far more extravagant than his predecessors'. There is also no evidence to suggest that he was inordinately devoted to prayer and meditation. As for his own behaviour, the local court records of the time show that even the man in the street thought him unsuited to be a king and, as grandson of a usurper, possibly even without title. The educated men who knew him found him to be capricious, unforgiving and likely to ignore the need for justice and mercy. The two portrayals of Henry could hardly be further apart, but it is the Tudor portrait, through Shakespeare, which has lodged so firmly in the popular imagination today. Henry is almost a kind of anti-hero for today's audiences, who wins our sympathy because he is a politician who finds the brutal realities of the world too painful to bear.

Henry flees his kingdom after his defeat at the Battle of Towton and York's son, Edward, is crowned Edward IV. Act Three ends with Henry's exile in Scotland, but not without a reminder that, if God appoints kings to be his vicars on earth, then the curse that has dogged the Plantagenets since the deposition of Richard II still has longer to run. The disguised Henry is recognised in a forest in the north of England by two gamekeepers who have overheard him talking about the fall of kings:

> SECOND KEEPER: Say, what art thou that talk'st of kings and
> queens?
> KING HENRY: More than I seem, and less than I was born to:
> A man at least, for less I should not be;
> And men may talk of kings, and why not I?
> SECOND KEEPER: Ay, but thou talk'st as if thou wert a king.
> KING HENRY: Why, so I am – in mind; and that's enough.
> SECOND KEEPER: But, if thou be a king, where is thy crown?

KING HENRY: My crown is in my heart, not on my head;
  Not deck'd with diamonds and Indian stones,
  Not to be seen. My crown is call'd content;
  A crown it is that seldom kings enjoy.
SECOND KEEPER: Well, if you be a king crown'd with content,
  Your crown content and you must be contented
  To go along with us; for as we think,
  You are the king King Edward hath depos'd;
  And we his subjects, sworn in all allegiance,
  Will apprehend you as his enemy.

3.1.55–71

The last two acts of the play are a violent hurly-burly in which the characters are constant only in their treachery and lust for power. Finally, Henry is defeated at Tewkesbury, his only son and heir murdered and then he himself is done to death in the Tower. The chain of blood has now crossed five generations. The trilogy ends with the voluptuary Edward IV back in power, but no doubt his boastful self-satisfaction was a source of irony to an Elizabethan audience who knew that soon enough Henry Tudor would over-throw the Yorkists and establish the dynasty of which Elizabeth I was the descendant.

Shakespeare, barely out of his mid-twenties, had already con-ceived, written and staged a cycle of dramas unmatched in scope since the trilogies of the ancient Greek dramatists. Fifty years of history are crammed into ten hours of drama. In conclusion, what are we to make of it all? Is it just a racy stage show telling the story of the background of the Tudor triumph from the point of view of the ruling dynasty? Or is it just a show that was aimed at the Elizabethan box office? I have tried to demonstrate that Shake-speare's reading of history was important in the writing of these plays. Like most great artists, he had probably done the bulk of all the reading that he would ever do by the time he had reached his mid-twenties. The history that he read told him, on the face of it, that history is a continuous chain of violence, a succession of great men and kings who climb over each other or kill each other to get to the throne. These books also provided him with models for action: cowardly and heroic, just and unjust, cruel and kind. I think that what the young Shakespeare learned from his education was, like Sir Thomas Elyot, a respect for the moderating power of reason and justice in society. He knew that when reason and justice go overboard society becomes divided in itself and cruelty, greed and brute force win over. He also, perhaps, believed like the

Greeks that crime breeds crime and evil produces more evil, but I don't think that he believed in political or historical ideals. There is always a contradiction between morals and action in his fictional world. Political and religious idealists think that morals and action can and should be the same. Great artists are at once more realistic and more pessimistic and they make their art by articulating that contradiction. They know that the whole of human history shows that men and women are not perfectable and that the contradiction between morality and action is human fate. This idea lies at the basis of Shakespeare's great tragedies but, in a crude way, the germ of it is there in his early history plays on Henry VI's reign. They are only the start of that astonishing career, but in them there is much to prepare us for the future masterpieces of the world's greatest dramatist.

1, 2 AND 3 HENRY VI

Brewster Mason

Brewster Mason played the Earl of Warwick in the Royal Shakespeare Company's productions of The Wars of the Roses *between 1963 and 1965. His other Shakespearean roles have included the title part in* Othello *and Falstaff in both* The Merry Wives of Windsor *and in the two parts of* Henry IV.

It has always seemed to me strangely ironic that such delicate things as roses were plucked as symbols by the two opposing sides in the Wars of the Roses, which were surely the bitterest and bloodiest family feuds in history. Shakespeare's *Henry VI* is a dramatic treatise on this ruthless conflict. The trilogy is generally considered to be Shakespeare's first work as it seems to have been written and performed by the summer of 1592. If this is so, then it was a magnificent way to launch a career with plays so staggering in their scope and ambition. You only have to think of the technical problems of research, selection and dramatic construction involved in drawing together the events of half a century from 1422 to 1471 to appreciate the achievement. There has been a lot of speculation as to derivation of plots, historical accuracy, time sequences and co-authorship, as indeed there has been with most of Shakespeare's work. The authorship question in particular has exercised many a scholarly mind over the years. Did Shakespeare write the plays on his own, or did he borrow, to put it kindly, and adapt other peoples' work? Modern scholars are inclined to be less doubtful about Shakespeare's talented theatrical debut than some of their predecessors. Much of this academic speculation is both stimulating and fascinating, but in the end it is difficult to deny the control of one guiding hand in the long saga.

I played the role of the Earl of Warwick in the 1964 production by Peter Hall and John Barton at Stratford. It was only when I began to study the plays that I realised what a vast canvas they cover and indeed what a high degree of competence they demand from the cast and director. Make no mistake, they are difficult to do. I found the whole experience fascinating, partly because up to that point I had always been more than a little confused by the complicated military and political aspects of this period of English history. Yet when one sees the plays come to life, or off the page as actors term it, then the stage lights up and there is the compelling sight of a wonderful parade of characters. One has to be careful not to have one's head cut off in reality in the full sweep of performance amidst the smoke with all those alarums and excursions, swords and banners. There is also lots of blood, sweat and tears, as there is no escaping from the semblance of reality. Talking of sweat, I can tell you that the armour is not made of cardboard. Mine weighed seventy-six pounds and I also had to carry an authentic copy of Warwick's sword which reposes at Warwick Castle. So you can see that actors have quite mundane problems to deal with, apart from agonising over the soul of the play.

I can't possibly give you a synopsis of the whole plot, but let me give you some idea of how it is put together and what to expect. The Chorus's epilogue to *Henry V*, which was actually written some years later, provides a simple introduction to the main theme of the *Henry VI* trilogy:

> Thus far, with rough and all-unable pen,
> Our bending author hath pursu'd the story,
> In little room confining mighty men,
> Mangling by starts the full course of their glory.
> Small time, but, in that small, most greatly lived
> This star of England. Fortune made his sword;
> By which the world's best garden he achieved,
> And of it left his son imperial lord.
> Henry the Sixth, in infant bands crown'd king
> Of France and England, did this king succeed;
> Whose state so many had the managing
> That they lost France and made his England bleed;
> Which oft our stage hath shown; and, for their sake,
> In your fair minds let this acceptance take.

I–14

This is very much the theme taken up in the opening sequence of *Henry VI*. We see the funeral procession of Henry V and immediately get the sense of a great vacuum created by his death. The power and charisma of Henry V had seemed to unite the country in the successful cause of the conquest of France. But his son is a mere child and straightaway the court is fragmented by rivalry and dissent, in particular between the young King's two uncles, Humphrey Duke of Gloucester and the Bishop of Winchester:

WINCHESTER: He was a king bless'd of the King of kings;
 Unto the French the dreadful judgment-day
 So dreadful will not be as was his sight.
 The battles of the Lord of Hosts he fought;
 The Church's prayers made him so prosperous.
GLOUCESTER: The Church! Where is it? Had not churchmen
 pray'd
 His thread of life had not so soon decay'd.
 None do you like but an effeminate prince,
 Whom like a school-boy you may overawe.
WINCHESTER: Gloucester, whate'er we like, thou art Protector
 And lookest to command the Prince and realm.
 Thy wife is proud; she holdeth thee in awe
 More than God or religious churchmen may.
GLOUCESTER: Name not religion, for thou lov'st the flesh;
 And ne'er throughout the year to church thou go'st,
 Except it be to pray against thy foes.

I.I.28–43

A messenger charges in with bad news from France as the family
quarrels over the coffin:

 Sad tidings bring I to you out of France,
 Of loss, of slaughter, and discomfiture:
 Guienne, Champagne, Rheims, Orleans,
 Paris, Guysors, Poictiers, are all quite lost.

I.I.58–61

This is an interesting bit of compression as a matter of fact as these
losses actually took place over a good few years. They were not the
overnight disaster suggested here, but the point that the politicians are quarrelling whilst the French empire is slipping away is
made more effectively by presenting them as such.

 This scene sets the stage for Part One. A great deal of this play
is taken up with the struggle of the valiant Talbot to hold onto the
French territories in the latter stages of the Hundred Years War.
His foe is the Dauphin, whose right-hand woman Joan La Pucelle
is better known to us as Joan of Arc. She is portrayed here along
very traditional lines as an enchantress and whore, or rather she is
spoken about in these terms but not shown as such. The wars go to
and fro in a bewildering sequence of victory and defeat. They take
on at times a curious knockabout quality, as in the scene where
Talbot and Joan shout insults at one another across the
battlements. Talbot is finally defeated and killed at Bordeaux

through the failure of support and re-inforcement. Shakespeare suggests that it would not have happened, but for the petty differences between the nobles in command of the English forces.

So the main political theme which dominates all the plays is interspersed with all the blood and smoke of the French wars. It is initiated in a symbolic scene in Temple Garden, where members of the contending royal lines argue about the case for succession. We see Richard Plantagenet, later Duke of York, and his very distant cousin the Duke of Somerset, who is a member of the Lancastrian line. Warwick and Suffolk are also present. Although Warwick later supports the Yorkist cause, he does not quite know what to think at this moment:

SOMERSET: Judge you, my Lord of Warwick, then, between us.
WARWICK: Between two hawks, which flies the higher pitch;
    Between two dogs, which hath the deeper mouth;
    Between two blades, which bears the better temper;
    Between two horses, which doth bear him best;
    Between two girls, which hath the merriest eye –
    I have perhaps some shallow spirit of judgment;
    But in these nice sharp quillets of the law,
    Good faith, I am no wiser than a daw.
PLANTAGENET: Tut, tut, here is a mannerly forbearance:
    The truth appears so naked on my side
    That any purblind eye may find it out.
SOMERSET: And on my side it is so well apparell'd,
    So clear, so shining, and so evident,
    That it will glimmer through a blind man's eye.
PLANTAGENET: Since you are tongue-tied and so loath to speak,
    In dumb significants proclaim your thoughts.
    Let him that is a true-born gentleman
    And stands upon the honour of his birth,
    If he supposes that I have pleaded truth,
    From off this brier pluck a white rose with me.
SOMERSET: Let him that is no coward nor no flatterer,
    But dare maintain the party of the truth,
    Pluck a red rose from off this thorn with me.
WARWICK: I love no colours; and, without all colour
    Of base insinuating flattery,
    I pluck this white rose with Plantagenet.

2.4.10–36

The merits of the argument are difficult to judge at this point, but in the following scene Richard comes to his dying uncle Edmund

Mortimer, Earl of March. The old man explains to him the legal foundation of the Yorkist case, so it is worth spending a moment considering what it was. The Houses of York and Lancaster were derived from two lines of descent from Edward III. Edward was succeeded by his grandson Richard II. Richard, who had no children, was deposed in 1399 and at that point the crown went to Henry IV and then it passed directly to his son, Henry V, and his grandson, Henry VI. Henry IV claimed the throne through descent from John of Gaunt, Duke of Lancaster, who was the fourth son of Edward III. The Yorkists, on the other hand, could claim descent through Edward's third son, Lionel, Duke of Clarence, as a result of Anne Mortimer's marriage into the family. She became the mother of Richard Plantagenet, the Duke of York who appears in the play. So the essence of the Yorkist case was that when Henry IV took the throne the line of succession had gone down a wrong turning and should therefore be restored to those in the rightful line of descent. This is certainly what the dying Mortimer tells Richard Plantagenet. Mortimer himself, the natural successor in the Yorkist line, has spent nearly ten years in prison. When he dies, that right is inherited by Richard. The emotion of the moment isn't lost on him:

> In prison hast thou spent a pilgrimage,
> And like a hermit overpass'd thy days.
> Well, I will lock his counsel in my breast;
> And what I do imagine, let that rest.
> Keepers, convey him hence; and I myself
> Will see his burial better than his life.
> Here dies the dusky torch of Mortimer,
> Chok'd with ambition of the meaner sort;
> And for those wrongs, those bitter injuries,
> Which Somerset hath offer'd to my house,
> I doubt not but with honour to redress;
> And therefore haste I to the Parliament,
> Either to be restored to my blood,
> Or make my ill th' advantage of my good.

2.5.116–29

And finally, towards the end of this First Part, we meet Margaret of Anjou, the future bride of Henry VI and surely one of the toughest consorts in history. We learn of the Duke of Suffolk's plan to introduce her to the King, now a young man, in a somewhat devious way to advance his own career:

Thus Suffolk hath prevail'd; and thus he goes,
As did the youthful Paris once to Greece,
With hope to find the like event in love
But prosper better than the Troyan did.
Margaret shall now be Queen, and rule the King;
But I will rule both her, the King, and realm.

5.5.103–8

This is the main theme of the plot, which Shakespeare weaves through the trilogy in a masterly way. This political conflict grows throughout the plays, until in Part Three it takes over totally as the final slaughter is played out. The bold pattern is studded with fine points of detail, which are tellingly inserted at many points in the play. These details may seem to be gratuitous, but they provide a human touch to history. It is rather like looking through pictures of a public event in a scrapbook and suddenly noticing a little old lady in the bottom corner. Sometimes the detailed scenes provide a commentary on the main action, often introducing us to a wider range of characters. We move from master to servant, general to soldier, nobility to common herd. For example, when Winchester and Gloucester quarrel we see their servants brawling in the streets as well. There is a whole pageant of minor characters, who take the stage, make their point and disappear. Behind it all is Shakespeare's preoccupation with the power of kinship and family pride, as well as with the importance of honour, valour and duty. He seems to find it puzzling that men can slaughter one another with unquestioning enthusiasm and loyalty.

Part Two opens with the arrival of Margaret of Anjou in London for her marriage with Henry. This is part of a plan by the Duke of Suffolk to increase his own influence at court. Henry is quite delighted with his bride, but Gloucester is concerned about the unfavourable marriage contract. The scheming Suffolk has agreed to give up the conquered provinces of Anjou and Maine to Margaret's father even though there is no corresponding dowry from Margaret herself. Henry agrees to these terms, much to Gloucester's indignation, and from this point Margaret begins to take over. We see it first in a sequence which is often overlooked, the female rivalry between her and Gloucester's wife, Eleanor. Eleanor is ambitious, but believes her husband to be too weak and ineffectual. She feels that, given a bit of effort on his part, she could be Queen. Margaret's rejoinder to Suffolk in the following scene is to complain that Henry is still Gloucester's pupil. The removal of the Gloucesters turns out to be quite simple. Eleanor is involved in plotting and witchcraft and her husband, guilty by association, is removed from the Regency. He is later murdered by Suffolk. The early part of the play can be seen in terms of the removal of Gloucester, the emergence of Margaret as the power behind the throne and the divided reactions of Henry himself.

Henry's position is under constant assault from this point on in the play. Richard of York unfolds his plan to leave for Ireland to enlist soldiers, whilst employing a headstrong Kentishman, Jack Cade, to stir up rebellion amongst the people at home. A lot of the play is now devoted to a portrait of Cade's rebellion in which the actions of the common people are dealt with. Shakespeare shows how a braggart like Cade can persuade a mob into action by the use of apt phrases. Then as now a forceful delivery is much more important than an understanding of the facts:

CADE: Be brave, then, for your captain is brave, and vows reformation. There shall be in England seven halfpenny loaves sold for a penny; the three-hoop'd pot shall have ten hoops; and I will make it felony to drink small beer. All the realm shall be in common, and in Cheapside shall my palfrey go to grass. And when I am king – as king I will be –

ALL: God save your Majesty!

CADE: I thank you, good people – there shall be no money; all shall eat and drink on my score, and I will apparel them all in one livery, that they may agree like brothers and worship me their lord.

DICK: The first thing we do, let's kill all the lawyers.

CADE: Nay, that I mean to do. Is not this a lamentable thing, that of the skin of an innocent lamb should be made parchment? That parchment, being scribbled o'er, should undo a man? Some say the bee stings; but I say 'tis the bee's wax; for I did but seal once to a thing, and I was never mine own man since.

4.2.61–79

Cade's rebellion was put down by Henry, but then Richard's Irish army bears down upon him. Part Two ends with the Yorkist victory at the Battle of St Albans and Henry's flight back to London.

Part Three covers the long period from the Battle of St Albans to the last decisive battle of the Wars of the Roses at Tewkesbury. At the start of the play Henry agrees that Richard of York shall succeed him, but asks that he may be allowed to reign during his lifetime. York agrees to this, but Margaret dissociates herself from the decision and prepares to pursue the war. York is captured and then murdered by Margaret and Clifford. His three sons, Edward, George and Richard, rejoin the battle and succeed in deposing Henry in favour of Edward, who becomes Edward IV. There is a further period of turmoil when the new King offends Warwick by an ill-judged marriage. Warwick defects from the Yorkists to Margaret and helps to re-instate Henry. That is not the end of it, for Edward escapes from captivity and gathers his allies. Warwick is slain at Barnet and the Lancastrian power is finally broken at the Battle of Tewkesbury in 1471. Margaret is captured and her son is murdered in front of her by Edward and his brothers. One of these brothers, Richard of Gloucester, hastes away to London to murder Henry in the Tower.

Those are the very barest of bones of this great saga. You have to see it before you can realise how richly it is written and the scope it affords the actors. But what of the King himself? Shakespeare's starting point for many of his characters, as well as the events, was the Chronicles of Hall and Holinshed. Hall was quite precise about Henry. He tells us that he had a beautiful face.

> in the which continually was resident the bounty of mind with which he was inwardly endowed. He did abhor of his own nature all the vices, as well as of the body as of the soul; and from his very infancy he was of honest conversation and pure integrity; no knower of evil, and a keeper of all goodness; a despiser of all things which were wont to cause the minds of moral men to slide. Besides this, patience was so radicate in his heart that of all the injuries to him committed (which were no small number) he never asked vengeance nor punishment.

This is precisely the view that Shakespeare takes. He presents Henry as being neither a fool nor a weakling nor a moral coward, even though his critics within the plays look upon him as unassertive, bookish and feeble. He is basically ill-equipped to deal with the powerful and ruthless barons who surround him. He is very ably supported first by Gloucester, who makes the decisions in a way that removes the incentive or necessity for him to govern, and then by Margaret, even though she clearly despises him. She has no compunction about doing all the dirty work as she must win at all costs. Henry does not have the killer instinct and so cannot and will not involve himself in this way. You may notice that he is never the first to speak, but rather the patient listener appealing for moderation and reason. He strives hard to reconcile his spiritual convictions with his temporal duty. When asked how he is going to respond to Cade's rebellion, he replies:

I'll send some holy bishop to entreat;
For God forbid so many simple souls
Should perish by the sword! And I myself,
Rather than bloody war shall cut them short,
Will parley with Jack Cade their general.

4.4.9–13

As his great soliloquy in Part Three illustrates, he is in the wrong place at the wrong time:

O God! methinks it were a happy life
To be no better than a homely swain;
To sit upon a hill, as I do now,
To carve out dials quaintly, point by point,
Thereby to see the minutes how they run –
How many makes the hour full complete,
How many hours brings about the day,
How many days will finish up the year,
How many years a mortal man may live.

2.5.21–9

RICHARD III
Rosemary Anne Sisson

Rosemary Anne Sisson writes for both television and the cinema. She contributed to The Six Wives of Henry VIII, *as well as to the* Elizabeth R *series. She was one of the main writers for* Upstairs, Downstairs *and has also adapted* The Irish RM *for television. Her films include an adaptation of* The Wind in the Willows. *She made this programme on location at the Maddermarket Theatre in Norwich.*

I think that people sometimes forget that Shakespeare, like every other playwright, started writing his plays in his study and in his head. You have a notion of the story you want to tell and of the characters who will travel from your head onto the page. The notion then becomes a compulsion and at last you have to sit down and write. The exciting thing about *Richard III* is that we know exactly where Shakespeare got that notion. He had just written three plays about Henry VI and *Richard III* was the obvious sequel.

I know all about sequels because that is how I came to write my first play. I had been to Stratford in 1951 to see the History plays, which were played in a permanent set modelled on Shakespeare's Globe Theatre. They had a stunning cast which included Michael Redgrave, Barbara Jefford, Anthony Quayle and Alan Badel. Robert Hardy played several small parts – and there was also a very promising young actor called Richard Burton playing Henry V. I fell desperately in love with him, and when Henry became engaged to the charming young French princess at the end of the play – well, it was like watching *Crossroads* – I just had to know what happened next. So I went and looked it up in Holinshed's Histories, the very book where Shakespeare found his *Richard III*. The title page of the copy in my library is missing, and the binding is new, but it is the very book, and for all I know, it could be the very copy that Shakespeare used. I discovered that Henry V died very soon after the marriage, and that his little widow, Katherine de Valois, fell in love with a handsome young Welsh soldier called Owen Tudor. Their love story was a tragic one, but from their secret marriage came the first Tudor king, Henry VII. So I wrote my first play, *The Queen and the Welshman*, the play which Shake-speare didn't write. And, what's more, I wrote it in Shakespearean blank verse. The management sent it back very smartly and so I took the hint and re-wrote it in prose.

People often ask me if I write regular hours every day and I always say 'No, I can't, because until the characters talk to me, I can't write.' Richard III first talked to Shakespeare at the end of *3 Henry VI*:

> Then, since the heavens have shap'd my body so,
> Let hell make crook'd my mind to answer it.
> I have no brother, I am like no brother;
> And this word 'love', which greybeards call divine,
> Be resident in men like one another,
> And not in me! I am myself alone.

5.6.78–83

'I am myself alone'. When Richard spoke those words in Shake-speare's mind, he staked his claim to be the hero of Shakespeare's next play. He was alive and kicking and ready to go, not just as a supporting character in someone else's play but as the leading character in his own. Shakespeare could very well have sat down and hacked out the play of *Richard III* on the spot, but by a great piece of good fortune, he didn't.

The plague hit London and everybody cleared out. The theatres were closed and Shakespeare either went on tour or home to Stratford. I think he probably went to Stratford because he took time out to write poetry, which was the thing he really cared about at the time. He wrote two long poems, *Venus and Adonis* and *The Rape of Lucrece*, and got them both printed under his own name and dedicated to his patron, the Earl of Southamp-ton. And all this time, *Richard III* was quietly ticking away in his mind like a splendid time bomb. Then the plague ended, and he returned to London.

His poems had given him status as a literary figure and not just a hack, and he was working with his own repertory company, the Chamberlain's Men, with Richard Burbage, the Laurence Olivier of the time, as its leading actor. There is a time in a writer's life when his feet are set on the path to success. This was Shake-speare's moment and I swear that, as he rode back from Stratford or walked through the streets of London, the first speech of *Richard III* was all there in his mind just waiting to be written:

> Now is the winter of our discontent
> Made glorious summer by this sun of York;

And all the clouds that lour'd upon our house
In the deep bosom of the ocean buried.
Now are our brows bound with victorious wreaths;
Our bruised arms hung up for monuments;
Our stern alarums chang'd to merry meetings,
Our dreadful marches to delightful measures.
Grim-visag'd war hath smooth'd his wrinkled front,
And now, instead of mounting barbed steeds
To fright the souls of fearful adversaries,
He capers nimbly in a lady's chamber
To the lascivious pleasing of a lute.

I.I.I–13

What a moment that must have been for Shakespeare when his
Richard stepped out on the stage and spoke that opening speech!
At the dress rehearsal of my first play, I remember sitting in the
stalls and trembling from head to foot and clean through to the
walls of my stomach, not with fright but with sheer excitement.
When you have written something good, you feel it quite literally
in your guts and I am sure that Shakespeare felt it when he heard
that first speech and even more when the audience reacted to it:

And therefore, since I cannot prove a lover
To entertain these fair well-spoken days,
I am determined to prove a villain
And hate the idle pleasures of these days.
Plots have I laid, inductions dangerous,
By drunken prophecies, libels, and dreams,
To set my brother Clarence and the King
In deadly hate the one against the other;
. . . .

I.I.28–35

But Shakespeare had a long way to go before then. He was still in
his study, with that first speech in his head, and Holinshed in his
hand, and that mysterious compulsion driving him on. But he was
a working playwright – and the working playwright, as soon as he
begins to write, sees the play in his mind's eye on the stage.

The theatre for which Shakespeare wrote his plays had an open
platform, an Inner Stage which could be closed off with a curtain,
and an Upper Stage, which was a sort of balcony. It was marvellous for quick-flowing action, with one scene following straight
upon another. But there was very little scenery – just the odd
banner or throne. The attention of the audience had to be fixed,
not by French windows or ingenious transformations, but by the
words and characters – and above all, by the hero.

But in writing *Richard III*, Shakespeare didn't have a hero. He had a villain. Sir Thomas More wrote a rather uncomplimentary history of Richard III. Holinshed used that as source material and that was what Shakespeare drew on when he came to write his play. If you consider that Shakespeare was writing during the reign of Elizabeth I, whose grandfather took the throne from Richard, you realise that he could not really start meddling with the accepted version of history. If he had made Richard the hero and Henry VII the villain, it would have been just like writing a play about John F. Kennedy and Richard Nixon at the time of Watergate, and making Nixon the hero, except that Shakespeare would not just have been blasted by the drama critics, but hanged, drawn and quartered. I am not sure that he even wanted to. We all tend to believe the truths of our time. So there was Shakespeare with a villain as his hero. The natural sequel to Henry V would have been a play about Henry VII, but Shakespeare was hooked on Richard. This was the play he had to write. So how does he make his audience care about an accepted villain? It was Sir Thomas More who gave him the first clue. He said that Richard was 'of a ready, pregnant and quick wit, wily to feign and apt to dissemble'. That was all Shakespeare needed. When you write a play, you speak through the mouths of your characters and, to do that, you have to enter into their hearts and minds. You have to become their interpreter and apologist. You think as they do. So I can imagine Shakespeare saying 'Well, Richard really had to kill his brother Clarence. He was becoming such a nuisance.' And then, Shakespeare would have said, Buckingham really had to go. He was like a greedy politician, always exacting a price for loyalty and throwing in a touch of blackmail.

This was why Shakespeare's incomparable dramatic instinct, even at this early stage in his career, made him allow Richard to take the audience into his confidence. Other playwrights had used the soliloquy before him, but always in a very heavy-handed, ham-ish way – sort of twirling their moustaches. It was Shakespeare whose Richard III first beckoned the audience into his mind and plans and feelings:

HASTINGS: The King is sickly, weak, and melancholy,
    And his physicians fear him mightily.
RICHARD: Now, by Saint John, that news is bad indeed.
    O, he hath kept an evil diet long
    And overmuch consum'd his royal person!
    'Tis very grievous to be thought upon.
    Where is he? In his bed?

HASTINGS: He is.
RICHARD: Go you before, and I will follow you.
   He cannot live, I hope, and must not die
   Till George be pack'd with posthorse up to heaven.
   I'll in to urge his hatred more to Clarence
   With lies well steel'd with weighty arguments;
   And, if I fail not in my deep intent,
   Clarence hath not another day to live;
   Which done, God take King Edward to his mercy,
   And leave the world for me to bustle in!

I.I.136–52

'Bustle in' is a splendid expression. It makes Richard sound like a busy, interesting sort of man. And then, we can always forgive an amusing villain. It reminds me of those caper films where people are planning to rob a bank. You know you should not want them to get away with it, but you do. Richard is the ingenious conman, and we can't help wanting him to beat those gullible fools.

But now Shakespeare was faced with a new problem: Richard has to woo Lady Anne, the widow of Henry VI's son. It was to be one of those dynastic marriages, since she was the daughter of the Earl of Warwick, and Richard needed to bind Warwick to his cause. The problem was that, as Richard was generally held to be responsible for the death of her husband, the audience would surely be revolted by the idea of her marrying her husband's murderer. It could only work if she found Richard absolutely irresistible. But how could this be when the audience also had to believe that Richard was evil and deformed? Shakespeare had just written two stunning love poems, and he would soon be writing *Romeo and Juliet*. The fascination of his early plays is that it is in them that we see Shakespeare discovering what he could do. In the wooing of Lady Anne, Shakespeare discovered himself to be a master of love scenes:

RICHARD: Nay, do not pause; for I did kill King Henry –
   But 'twas thy beauty that provoked me.
   Nay, now dispatch; 'twas I that stabb'd young Edward –
   But 'twas thy heavenly face that set me on.
   Take up the sword again, or take up me.
ANNE: Arise, dissembler; though I wish thy death,
   I will not be thy executioner.
RICHARD: Then bid me kill myself, and I will do it.
ANNE: I have already.
RICHARD: That was in thy rage.

Speak it again, and even with the word
This hand, which for thy love did kill thy love,
Shall for thy love kill a far truer love;
To both their deaths shalt thou be accessary.

ANNE: I would I knew thy heart.

RICHARD: 'Tis figur'd in my tongue.

ANNE: I fear me both are false.

RICHARD: Then never was man true.

ANNE: Well, well, put up your sword.

RICHARD: Say, then, my peace is made.

ANNE: That shalt thou know hereafter.

RICHARD: But shall I live in hope?

ANNE: All men, I hope, live so.

RICHARD: Vouchsafe to wear this ring.

ANNE: To take is not to give.

RICHARD: Look how my ring encompasseth thy finger,
    Even so thy breast encloseth my poor heart;
    Wear both of them, for both of them are thine.

1.2.179–205

This is great stuff. Every man in the audience thinks 'You clever devil!' and every woman thinks 'Oh dear, I couldn't resist him either'. And then Richard plays to the gallery, laughs at himself and says he must be handsomer than he thought. We can always forgive a man who laughs at himself and it is even rather touching if he laughs at himself for being physically deformed. And then again, one has to admit that to many women the notion of reforming a repentant sinner sounds a lot more fun than marrying a virtuous bore.

So there is Richard with the audience just where Shakespeare wants it to be, in the palm of his hand. Ah, but wait a minute. Even the most specious and amusing rogue ceases to be appealing once we know that he has murdered his two young nephews in cold blood, and that's what Shakespeare has to deal with next. It was one thing to knock off various political enemies and fellow-conspirators, but this was different.

I suppose there is no historical enigma more hotly argued than the question of whether or not Richard killed the Little Princes in the Tower. If Richard didn't give the order for their murder, then Henry VII did – and if you ask me which of them did it, I must say, for all sorts of reasons, I believe it was Richard. I'd say that, when it came to killing, Richard did what had to be done, but that Henry was as parsimonious in this particular as in everything else.

But it's not just the characters of the two men. There is circumstantial evidence as well. When Richard claimed the throne, he said it was because his nephews were illegitimate. The subsequent rumour that he had murdered them was circulating long before Henry Tudor landed. If the boys were still alive, why didn't Richard produce them? It was the sort of thing that was always being done. All he had to do was to haul them out of the Tower some fine Feast Day, show them to the multitude and say, 'Here they are, the little bastards!' It was so simple, and would have silenced the rumours once and for all. But he never did it. As for Henry, once he'd won the Battle of Bosworth, he didn't have to bother about the Little Princes. Richard had declared them illegitimate, and if they had been still alive, he would have done the same with them as with the other Yorkist survivors, the Earl of Warwick and the Earl of Lincoln – kept them in prison, produced them now and then when necessary, and then, when they became too much of a focus of rebellion, very rationally and legally had them executed. But, in fact, it never happened because the boys had already vanished, and were never heard of again.

The argument is, in any event, irrelevant to Shakespeare's play. He had to believe that Richard was guilty, and I'm sure that he did. His problem was to continue to engage the interest of the audience in his leading character, while never for a moment suggesting that Richard was the good guy and Henry VII was the bad guy. Ironically enough, the passage in Holinshed which most powerfully argues Richard's guilt also gives Shakespeare the clue of how to deal with it. Holinshed based his account on Sir Thomas More's history of Richard III: 'I have heard by credible report of such as were secret with his Chamberlain that after this abominable deed done, he never had a quiet mind.'

Thomas More was writing while many people who remembered those days were still alive. It sends a shiver down one's back, doesn't it, to know that he had actually spoken with people who were intimately acquainted with Richard's chamberlain? And Shakespeare is writing for an audience whose grandfathers might have fought in the Battle of Bosworth. Years later, Shakespeare will write that psychological masterpiece, *Macbeth*. But this is where he learned it, here in *Richard III*, when the cold-blooded joker of the first scenes of the play gives way to the man haunted by guilt, and in torment of mind.

Whether Richard actually killed his nephews or not, once he took the title of King from young Edward V he became a usurper in the eyes of many people and his path was set for Bosworth

Field. The Battle of Bosworth had to be the climax of the play. It was a very exciting one as everything was in the balance until the last moment, when Richard galloped across the field to confront his enemy face to face, in one tremendous gamble which failed. But how could Shakespeare tell that story? He did not have rolling hills, great banners, horses, cannons or flights of arrows. All he had was twenty feet of bare board. But there was a way. According to Holinshed, Richard had a 'dreadful and terrible dream' the night before the battle. 'It was' he says 'no dream, but a punction and prick of his sinful conscience.' That was enough for Shakespeare. Instead of trying to dramatise the whole battle, he began with the night before. He pitched the tents of the two protagonists on either side of the stage and made it psychological warfare. On one side there is Henry sleeping soundly so as to emerge merry, bright and victorious, whilst on the other side is Richard, suddenly the underdog suffering from bad dreams and struggling with a sense of impending defeat. But, even more ingenious, Shakespeare took Holinshed's dream of devils and turned them into the ghosts of those whom Richard had murdered and who now joined the battle against him:

> GHOST OF KING HENRY: When I was mortal, my annointed body
>   By thee was punched full of deadly holes.
>   Think on the Tower and me. Despair, and die.
>   (To RICHMOND) Virtuous and holy, be thou conqueror!
>   Harry, that prophesied thou shouldst be King,
>   Doth comfort thee in thy sleep. Live and flourish!

> 5.3.124–38

Now it is all plain sailing. Even his worst enemies agreed about Richard's courage. Shakespeare found in Holinshed the fine oration which each leader makes to his troops – and Richard's is a particularly effective one. Shakespeare even takes a chance, and lets Richard describe Henry as 'a milksop'. (In Holinshed, it's 'a Welsh milksop', but maybe Shakespeare decided that would be chancing his arm too far. After all, he's talking about Queen Elizabeth's grandfather!) The young, untried Henry fought bravely in the moment of crisis when he came face to face with Richard, which must have been a great relief to his followers, and which gives a natural nobility to the end of the play.

But here's a funny thing! Holinshed reported in his account of the battle that Richard's followers, when they realised the field was lost, brought him 'a swift and a light horse to convey him away', but that Richard still refused to flee. Shakespeare remembered this, but changed it by giving Richard the initiative. So the most famous words in the whole play, 'A horse! A horse! my kingdom for a horse!' were Shakespeare's own invention.

When we write a play, we're trying to be God, to create people, or if they already exist, to breathe new life into them. Did Shakespeare create a monster instead of a man? Perhaps he did. But he created the Richard he saw, ruthlessly ambitious, with a wicked, sardonic sense of humour, heartless and yet tormented, a dark and haunting man. For good or ill, Shakespeare's Richard III lives for ever.

RICHARD III
Edward Woodward

Edward Woodward played the title role in Richard
III *at the Ludlow Festival in 1982. His other Shakespearean parts have included Mercutio in* Romeo
and Juliet, *Laertes in* Hamlet *and Claudio in*
Much Ado About Nothing. *He also played the title
role in the television series* Callan.

What happens in the tragedy of *Richard III* must have been very
real to Elizabethan audiences. It was written around about 1590
and tells of the rise to the throne of Richard, Duke of Gloucester,
and his eventual death on the battlefield at Bosworth. These
events happened roughly a century earlier. Now, to Elizabethan
audiences, the effect must have been rather like us going to the
theatre today to see a play about the closing years of Queen
Victoria's reign in which somebody, in order to get to the throne,
murders the Queen and some of her family. He also does away
with a few members of the House of Lords who stood in his way to
the throne and a few more who helped to put him there. It would
be really tremendous stuff. The grandparents of the people in the
audience would have actually remembered the events. Similarly,
the grandparents of an Elizabethan audience would have known
all about Richard.

Shakespeare's Richard of Gloucester is one of the greatest
villains in literature, although it is another matter whether the real
Richard was so evil. Shakespeare's story goes rather like this.
Richard of Gloucester, the younger of the two brothers of King
Edward IV, is a man of appalling ambition. He is fourth in
succession to the throne and we follow him through his bitter
political infighting to attain the crown. He already has a couple of
murders at least on his hands before the play starts. He begins the
play by arranging for his brother George, the Duke of Clarence, to
be murdered. He then disposes of his wife, Anne, and the two
Princes in the Tower. He goes on to destroy a number of other
members of the Court as well. It is all quite confusing, although
what is certain is that *Richard III* is probably the most exciting of
Shakespeare's plays and has always been one of the most popular.

I gather that Richard used to be played as a black villain throughout the play, until Laurence Olivier's definitive performance. One of the great things that Olivier brought to the part was an outrageous sense of comedy. He made us all, certainly made me, realise that the play is arguably the greatest black comedy of all time. Richard constantly turns to the audience and tells them what he has just done and what he is about to do. Then when he has accomplished it, he turns to the audience again and says 'aren't I clever?'. He makes the full ramifications of his villainy very clear to the audience because he revels in it. He is in fact an enormously witty and tremendously charming man. He also has the largest ego I have ever seen and a tremendous determination to succeed, which eventually turns itself into a paranoia.

The play for me is very much split into two phases. When Richard realises that the crown is within his grasp, he changes very rapidly and dramatically. The end of the first phase comes therefore when Richard and Buckingham's crew persuade the citizens of London to make him King of England. One of the young Princes in the Tower, Edward, is the uncrowned King, but Richard allows Buckingham to persuade the citizens that the Lord Protector would make a better king than a young boy. Richard is a completely different man when he becomes King. All the laughter and comedy is gone. He is now pure villainy from beginning to end. He has to start killing off his friends, as he has already murdered most of his enemies. The most dramatic turnaround is his total dismissal of Buckingham, who had wheeled and dealed for him throughout the play. He placed ideas in Buckingham's mind and then allowed his friend to carry them out. His dismissal of Buckingham at the beginning of the second phase is his first major blunder. The rest of the play is almost all about military confrontations. Richmond lands and moves quickly towards Richard's forces. Richard panics as he has not got very many people at this time on his side. Those whom he has not killed off have gone over to the other side. The great denouement of the play, and one of the saddest parts of it, is when he is going into battle against Richmond. He realises that he may not live, so it is possible that everything he has dreamed of and everything he has villainously worked towards will come to nothing. This premonition is accompanied by a series of dreams in which all the people whom he has killed appear to him. He goes into battle pretty certain that he is not going to survive, yet the greatness of the man himself comes out in his rallying cry to his soldiers. Not once does he let anybody see his true feelings. His army is finally destroyed and he himself dies in a final one-to-one combat with Richmond. His body is thrown to the ground and the crown is snatched up to be given to Richmond, who becomes King Henry VII, the first of the Tudor Kings. There is a strange footnote to Shakespeare's play. It is known that Richard's body was stripped naked, thrown over a horse and taken into Leicester to be buried in an unhallowed grave. If you go to Leicester today, you will see a superb statue of Richard. It is odd that one of the few things known about the real Richard is the manner of his death.

The opening soliloquy to *Richard III* is possibly one of the greatest pieces of blank verse in Shakespeare. I was brought up at school like an awful lot of people in my generation being forced to read rather than act Shakespeare. It was only when I started playing Shakespeare that I realised just how great a writer he was. The opening soliloquy gives an actor a terrible problem because he comes on to the stage shaking in his shoes, having spent months learning what is about the second longest part in Shakespeare. He walks on to this empty stage and, lo and behold, has to start on this massive soliloquy. I can tell you from personal experience that, once you have done the soliloquy, there is nothing else in the play that is quite as frightening:

> Now is the winter of our discontent
> Made glorious summer by this sun of York;
> And all the clouds that lour'd upon our house
> In the deep bosom of the ocean buried.
>
> I.I.I–4

This refers to the Wars of the Roses which everybody, except Richard, hopes have come to an end. If he has anything to do with it, the horrible deeds of the Yorkists and Lancastrians will not be easily buried:

> Now are our brows bound with victorious wreaths;
> Our bruised arms hung up for monuments;
> Our stern alarums chang'd to merry meetings,
> Our dreadful marches to delightful measures.
> Grim-visag'd war hath smooth'd his wrinkled front,
> And now, instead of mounting barbed steeds
> To fright the souls of fearful adversaries,
> He capers nimbly in a lady's chamber
> To the lascivious pleasing of a lute.
>
> I.I.4–13

Richard is obviously a great general and, like an awful lot of professional soldiers, yearns for the 'stern alarums', 'dreadful

marches' and the other excitements of war. I find the next passage
fascinating because Richard was a hunchback with a withered arm
and gammy leg. He tells the audience right at the beginning of the
play that 'I know that you know that I know that you know'. He is
already ahead of them:

> But I – that am not shap'd for sportive tricks,
> Nor made to court an amorous looking-glass –
> I – that am rudely stamp'd, and want love's majesty
> To strut before a wanton ambling nymph –
> I – that am curtail'd of this fair proportion,
> Cheated of feature by dissembling nature,
> Deform'd, unfinish'd, sent before my time
> Into this breathing world scare half made up,
> And that so lamely and unfashionable
> That dogs bark at me as I halt by them –
> Why, I, in this weak piping time of peace,
> Have no delight to pass away the time,
> Unless to spy my shadow in the sun
> And descant on mine own deformity.

1.1.14–27

He is saying 'look at me, I'm nasty, deformed and ugly' and then
he proceeds to make this deformity an excuse for all the evil that
follows:

> And therefore, since I cannot prove a lover
> To entertain these fair well-spoken days,
> I am determined to prove a villain
> And hate the idle pleasures of these days.

1.1.28–31

He then starts to tell the audience what he has done and what he is
about to do:

> Plots have I laid, inductions dangerous,
> By drunken prophecies, libels, and dreams,
> To set my brother Clarence and the King
> In deadly hate the one against the other;
> And if King Edward be as true and just
> As I am subtle, false, and treacherous,
> This day should Clarence closely be mew'd up –
> About a prophecy which says that G
> Of Edward's heirs the murderer shall be.

1.1.32–40

One has to remember that the Elizabethans believed in ghoulies, ghosties and things that go bump in the night. They believed in prophecies and the supernatural, which were hangovers not just from the medieval past but also from the days of paganism before Christianity itself. It was therefore not strange for an Elizabethan audience to be told that dukes and royal brothers should believe in prophecies. The play starts off in a very clear way because Richard tells us exactly what he is going to do. The immediate past is also laid out for the audience and the present is very clearly stated.

Richard disposes of people right, left and centre, but Shakespeare makes his deeds totally credible even for today's audiences. One of the most extraordinary scenes in the play, which comes very early on, is the wooing of Lady Anne. Now Richard has already killed her husband, Edward, Prince of Wales, as well as her father-in-law, Henry VI. Yet he decides that it is politic to marry her to get that side of the family behind him. But how do you set about wooing a lady who thinks you are disgusting, evil and vile? Richard not only woos her, but wins her all within the space of one scene. He does it by enormous charm and loads and loads of crocodile tears. She strikes him and spits at him, but he turns all this to his own advantage. He ends up by begging her to go further and actually kill him:

> I never sued to friend nor enemy;
> My tongue could never learn sweet smoothing word;
> But, now thy beauty is propos'd my fee,
> My proud heart sues, and prompts my tongue to speak.
> Teach not thy lip such scorn; for it was made
> For kissing, lady, not for such contempt.
> If thy revengeful heart cannot forgive,
> Lo here I lend thee this sharp-pointed sword;
> Which if thou please to hide in this true breast
> And let the soul forth that adoreth thee,
> I lay it naked to the deadly stroke,
> And humbly beg the death upon my knee.
> Nay, do not pause; for I did kill King Henry –
> But 'twas thy beauty that provoked me.
> Nay, now dispatch; 'twas I that stabb'd young Edward –
> But 'twas thy heavenly face that set me on.
> Take up the sword again, or take up me.

>   1.2.167–83

When Lady Anne refuses to take up the sword and become his 'executioner', Richard knows that he has got her. He has even persuaded her that he killed her husband and father-in-law out of love for her. When she leaves she has, to all intents and purposes, accepted his offer of marriage. Richard then characteristically turns straight to the audience:

> Was ever woman in this humour woo'd?
> Was ever woman in this humour won?
> I'll have her; but I will not keep her long.
> What! I that kill'd her husband and his father –
> To take her in her heart's extremest hate,
> With curses in her mouth, tears in her eyes,
> The bleeding witness of my hatred by;
> Having God, her conscience, and these bars against me,
> And I no friends to back my suit at all
> But the plain devil and dissembling looks,
> And yet to win her, all the world to nothing!
>
> I.2.227–37

Richard takes the audience with him by taking them into his confidence like this in the first phase of the play. The Elizabethan theatre thrived on audience participation. The audiences shouted a lot, unlike today's fairly respectful ones. There were things being sold whilst the play was going on. Some people sat on the stage itself during a performance and, like everybody else, came and went for most of the time. Any actor playing Richard has to remember that the Elizabethans were actively involved with a play. Richard talks to the audience almost more, I think, than any other character in Shakespeare. He takes the audience with him on his journey, partly by pointing the finger of fun at most of the other characters on the stage. Yet, as suggested, he treats the audience in a very off-hand manner when he becomes King. I think that he only ever speaks directly to them once, whereas in the first phase of the play he never stops talking to them.

Richard has the whole play to show his strengths and weaknesses and the ins and outs of his labyrinthine mind. Richmond has very little time in which to do this, yet it is still a marvellous part because it has some of the most beautiful blank verse in the play. He has to be equal in strength to Richard in the final struggle between good and evil. Shakespeare gives the goodie certain ways of saying things and the baddie other ways of saying the same things. Richmond rallies his troops with these words:

> For what is he they follow? Truly, gentlemen,
> A bloody tyrant and a homicide;

One rais'd in blood, and one in blood establish'd;
One that made means to come by what he hath,
And slaughtered those that were the means to help him;
A base foul stone, made precious by the foil
Of England's chair, where he is falsely set;
One that hath ever been God's enemy.
Then if you fight against God's enemy,
God will in justice ward you as his soldiers;
If you do sweat to put a tyrant down,
You sleep in peace, the tyrant being slain;
. . . .

5.3.245–56

It is stirring stuff, although Richmond talks quietly and gently to his audience. By contrast, Richard shouts a political diatribe at his audience to try to whip them up into a welter of blood:

Remember whom you are to cope withal –
A sort of vagabonds, rascals, and runaways,
A scum of Britaines, and base lackey peasants,
Whom their o'er-cloyed country vomits forth
To desperate adventures and assur'd destruction.
You sleeping safe, they bring to you unrest;
You having lands, and bless'd with beauteous wives,
They would restrain the one, distain the other.
And who doth lead them but a paltry fellow,
A milk-sop, one that never in his life
Felt so much cold as over shoes in snow?
Let's whip these stragglers o'er the seas again;
Lash hence these over-weening rags of France,
These famish'd beggars, weary of their lives;
Who, but for dreaming on this fond exploit,
For want of means, poor rats, had hang'd themselves.
If we be conquered, let men conquer us,
And not these bastard Britaines, whom our fathers
Have in their own land beaten, bobb'd, and thump'd,
And, in record, left them the heirs of shame.
Shall these enjoy our lands? Lie with our wives,
Ravish our daughters?

5.3.315–37

This is also stirring stuff, but it is also rather like that well-worn statement that was reiterated many times during the 1914–18 war. When somebody doubted that the war was a good idea, they were always asked what they would do if a German raped their sister. The answer was, and always is and always will be, that nobody wants their sisters or their daughters raped. Yet Richard is using a good argument in a bad cause. Shakespeare lays out the differences between the goodies and baddies in these two speeches in the classic tradition of the Western film. The most important thing to remember about this play is that it is a very exciting and understandable one.

KING LEAR
Frank Kermode

Frank Kermode was King Edward VII Professor of English Literature at Cambridge from 1974 to 1982. He is a leading authority on Renaissance literature and has published widely on Shakespeare and his contemporaries. He made this programme on location at Bodiam Castle.

A castle provides shelter. But it's also a source of power and a symbol of dignity. Suppose that shelter, power and dignity are all illusions. Take the castle away and the king is deprived of them all. It's the same with those other symbols of his invulnerability, his crown and his royal robes. Take them away and he's a naked thing. As we say, naked as the day he was born and naked as he will die.

King Lear is the most terrible of Shakespeare's tragedies and yet it begins like a folk tale. An irritable old king decides to divide his kingdom between his three daughters, but he makes them take part first in a competition to show which of them loves him most. The two elder daughters, who are flashy types, find no difficulty in this performance, but the younger daughter won't play at all:

LEAR: What can you say to draw
    A third more opulent than your sisters? Speak.
CORDELIA: Nothing, my lord.
LEAR: Nothing!
CORDELIA: Nothing.
LEAR: Nothing will come of nothing. Speak again.
CORDELIA: Unhappy that I am, I cannot heave
    My heart into my mouth. I love your Majesty
    According to my bond; no more nor less.
LEAR: How, how, Cordelia! Mend your speech a little,
    Lest you may mar your fortunes.
CORDELIA: Good my lord,
    You have begot me, bred me, lov'd me; I
    Return those duties back as are right fit,
    Obey you, love you, and most honour you.
    Why have my sisters husbands, if they say
    They love you all? Haply, when I shall wed,

>   That lord whose hand must take my plight shall carry
>   Half my love with him, half my care and duty.
>   Sure I shall never marry like my sisters,
>   To love my father all.
>   LEAR: But goes thy heart with this?
>   CORDELIA: Ay, my good lord.

1.1.84–104

So the furious old man disinherits his favourite daughter and leaves all his lands and his power to the other two, preserving to himself only the external trappings of kingship. He plans to divide his time between the houses, or castles, of the two wicked daughters. But soon he finds that they don't want him or his followers. He becomes homeless, wandering without shelter in bleak weather. He takes refuge in a hovel where he meets a naked madman. Eventually, he's reunited with the daughter who really loves him, but by that time he too is mad. He barely has time to recognise her before she dies and then he dies too. The survivors agree that he is better dead:

>   KENT: Vex not his ghost. O, let him pass! He hates him
>   That would upon the rack of this tough world
>   Stretch him out longer.
>   EDGAR: He is gone indeed.

5.3.313–5

With this story Shakespeare interweaves another, again about a father and his children. A bastard son, Edmund, plots against his legitimate elder brother. The good son, Edgar, is forced to flee. He adopts various disguises, including that of a naked madman, the one that Lear encounters in the hovel. Meanwhile, the bastard son stops at nothing. He makes love to both the wicked daughters of the king but, worse than that, he makes no attempt to intervene when a horrible punishment is inflicted on his father, the Earl of Gloucester. For the Earl of Gloucester has his eyes torn out.

So the fairy story turns into a horror story, an account of cruelty and protracted suffering. Now, it would be monstrous to suggest that it is the story of a foolish old man being paid out for his follies. That is not what tragedy is about. Perhaps it is about making us look steadily, if only for a moment, at certain things that we prefer not to look at. Death, for instance, or the way the world works, which is never the way we want it to work. Lear abandons his responsibilities and thinks that he can retain the name and all the additions of a king. He's wrong. He's not wicked. But he then begins the descent into privation, without shelter, without clothes, without the sanctions of a human society, even without ordinary human language. The play is full of strange gabble. There is the Court Fool, traditionally a mixture of craziness and shrewdness, sometimes impudent, sometimes obscene. There is Lear himself, raving sometimes, sometimes fantasticating. And there is Edgar as Poor Tom, imitating the patter of a naked Bedlam lunatic:

EDGAR: Away! the foul fiend follows me.
　　Through the sharp hawthorn blows the cold wind.
　　Humh! go to thy cold bed and warm thee.
LEAR: Didst thou give all to thy daughters? And art thou come to this?
EDGAR: Who gives anything to poor Tom? whom the foul fiend hath led through fire and through flame, through ford and whirlpool, o'er bog and quagmire; that hath laid knives under his pillow and halters in his pew, set ratsbane by his porridge; made him proud of heart, to ride on a bay trotting-horse over four -inched bridges, to course his own shadow for a traitor. Bless thy five wits! Tom's a-cold. O, do de, do de, do de. Bless thee from whirlwinds, starblasting, and taking! Do poor Tom some charity, whom the foul fiend vexes. There could I have him now – and there – and there again – and there.

3.4.45–62

So, as Tom raves, the King descends into madness.

He learns something on the way. He learns that human beings exist in utter desolation. But pity is not enough. He feels a need to be identified with the naked, with Poor Tom, and so he tears at his clothes. Later, when he's reunited with his daughter Cordelia, she takes pains to dress him again in his proper condition. But then she dies, his greatest loss, and we see him again for the last time fumbling at his clothes before he dies:

　　　　No, no, no life!
Why should a dog, a horse, a rat have life,
And thou no breath at all? Thou'lt come no more,
Never, never, never, never, never.
Pray you undo this button. Thank you, sir.
Do you see this? Look on her. Look, her lips.
Look there, look there!

5.3.306–11

We are used to images of violence and horror. We have them on the television and in the newspapers. War and famine, senility, concentration camps – we have domesticated them. We look at them and wait for the next programme to begin. But perhaps one of the things that *King Lear* does is to de-familiarise these images of horror. Of course it doesn't explain them. We have to do that ourselves. And, of course, if we want to, we can simply resist them and turn them back into comfortable television images.

The history of this play could very well be written in terms of the way in which people have resisted its assault on their comfortable notions of natural and social justice. It presents a world wildly at odds with the world that they would prefer to live in. And, even in Shakespeare's own time, it seems that there may have been some resistance and that one or two of the scenes may have been thought too mad or too painful for performance. One such scene is in the hovel where Lear makes the Madman and the Fool act as judges in the trial of his two wicked daughters. The daughters have to be played by stools:

> LEAR: Thou robed man of justice, take thy place.
>   And thou, his yoke-fellow of equity,
>   Bench by his side. You are o' th' commission,
>   Sit you too.
> EDGAR: Let us deal justly.
> LEAR: Arraign her first; 'tis Goneril. I here take my oath before this honourable assembly she kick'd the poor King her father.
> FOOL: Come hither, mistress. Is your name Goneril?
> LEAR: She cannot deny it.
> FOOL: Cry you mercy, I took you for a joint-stool.
> LEAR: And here's another, whose warp'd looks proclaim
>   What store her heart is made on. Stop her there!
>   Arms, arms, sword, fire! Corruption in the place!
>   False justicer, why hast thou let her scape?

3.6.36–55

The great critic, Samuel Johnson, was another who resisted this play. In fact, he says he found it so painful that he could hardly bear even to read it. He thought that the death of Cordelia was contrary to the natural ideas of justice and I think he was even more shocked that, in all the other versions of the Lear story, Cordelia survives. Only in Shakespeare's version is she murdered. Another famous and very bitter resister was Tolstoy. He repeatedly attacked *King Lear*. George Orwell suggested that one reason for this obsession could have been that Tolstoy was half conscious of his own resemblance to the king. Anyway, Tolstoy

KING LEAR

preferred the early pre-Shakespearean version of the play in which everything comes out all right and divine and human justice prevail. So he thought that Shakespeare's play was wicked and worthless and believed too that anybody who thought otherwise was the victim of a vast cultural conspiracy.

But whatever we think of these matters, we know that we can't count on divine or human justice to intervene in the worst moments of life and what *King Lear* tries to do is to make us give our real assent to that knowledge. That's why it's the cruellest play. Its great climax and, to my mind the supreme stretch of Shakespeare's imagination, is the scene between the crazed king and the blind Gloucester at Dover:

GLOUCESTER: O ruin'd piece of nature! This great world
    Shall so wear out to nought. Dost thou know me?
LEAR: I remember thine eyes well enough. Dost thou squiny at
    me? No, do thy worst, blind Cupid; I'll not love. Read thou
    this challenge; mark but the penning of it.
GLOUCESTER: Were all thy letters suns, I could not see one.
EDGAR: I would not take this from report. It is,
    And my heart break at it.
LEAR: Read.
GLOUCESTER: What, with the case of eyes?
LEAR: O, ho, are you there with me? No eyes in your head nor no
    money in your purse? Your eyes are in a heavy case, your
    purse in a light; yet you see how this world goes.
GLOUCESTER: I see it feelingly.
LEAR: What, art mad? A man may see how this world goes with
    no eyes.
    Look with thine ears.

4.6.134–151

Gloucester is patient under this horrible teasing, but he wants to die. He tells Edgar that rather than continue his stumbling flight he'll sit down and rot, but Edgar won't have it:

    Men must endure
Their going hence, even as their coming hither:
Ripeness is all. Come on.

5.2.9–11

And on they go. The old man must pass through all the prescribed stages. There is no short cut to nothingness.

Certain words echo through this play: 'nothing' is one of them and 'eyes' another. And clothes is another repeated idea. Nowadays splendid clothes are not for everyday, but in Shakespeare's time they were both more ostentatious and more common. They are symbols of wealth, power and sex – all the things that Poor Tom lacks as he faces the storm. Lear develops quite a philosophy of clothes. Because he is obsessed with justice, he thinks most of the gowns of judges and of court officials. He addresses an imaginary beadle whipping a whore:

Thou rascal beadle, hold thy bloody hand.
Why dost thou lash that whore? Strip thy own back;
Thou hotly lusts to use her in that kind
For which thou whip'st her. The usurer hangs the cozener.
Through tatter'd clothes small vices do appear;
Robes and furr'd gowns hide all.

4.6.160–5

Shakespeare's England still entertained the old doctrine of the king's two bodies. One body is identified with his dignity, his inherited and God-given authority, and that body is immortal: 'the king is dead, long live the king'. But the other body is mortal. At his funeral, his mortal body lies naked in the coffin. His immortal body is represented by an effigy wearing his crown and robes. Lear never sorted out his two bodies. As one of his cruel daughters said 'he hath ever but slenderly known himself' and it's true. He thinks he can retain the dignity with his mortal body. We see that mortal body stripped of its 'additions' and its dignity.

When Lear was King, he thought that he could command love, measure it and reward it accordingly. Now he has handed over that power to his two wicked daughters. It is they who now ration out love. Which of them loves him better? Which will allow him fifty followers? But they reply that he only needs twenty-five:

REGAN: I entreat you
    To bring but five and twenty. To no more
    Will I give place or notice.
LEAR: I gave you all.
REGAN: And in good time you gave it.
LEAR: Made you my guardians, my depositaries;
    But kept a reservation to be followed
    With such a number. What, must I come to you
    With five and twenty, Regan? Said you so?
REGAN: And speak't again, my lord. No more with me.
LEAR: Those wicked creatures yet do look well-favour'd
    When others are more wicked; not being the worst

> Stands in some rank of praise. I'll go with thee.
> Thy fifty yet doth double five and twenty,
> And thou art twice her love.
> GONERIL: Hear me, my lord:
> What need you five and twenty, ten, or five,
> To follow in a house where twice so many
> Have a command to tend you?
> REGAN: What need one?

2.4.246–62

What are we to make of these villains? Edmund and the two sisters are wantonly cruel and self-seeking. That is obvious, but what about their servant, Oswald? He's simply there to fetch and carry. It is a trivial part, and it could have stayed trivial, but he becomes a very important representative of another sort of evil. It is the kind of evil that Hannah Arendt, thinking of Adolf Eichmann and other people of his kind, had in mind when she spoke of 'the banality of evil', the evil that is practised by those who simply carry out and augment the horrors that their masters have devised. It is of such people that Kent is thinking when he says

> Such smiling rogues as these,
> Like rats, oft bite the holy cords a-twain
> Which are too intrinse t' unloose; . . . .

2.2.68–70

Love and mutual respect are the holy cords and there is always an Oswald ready to gnaw at them. He lives, like his masters, in a state of nature where a man is a wolf to man. That is the way the wicked always do live in Shakespeare. Of course, in the end they are destroyed, but so are Lear, Gloucester and Cordelia – the sinned against as well as the sinning.

Such is the injustice we prefer not to look at. The remedy seems to be patience. Like Job, Lear is tried to the uttermost, but unlike Job's, his losses aren't made good. And the play often reminds us that this is the way the world ends, not in restored happiness but in dismay. It speaks of the horrors of the last days which according to the Bible, must precede the end of time: unnaturalness between the child and the parent, death, dearth and dissolutions of ancient amities. At the end, when Lear deludes himself into thinking that Cordelia is still alive, Kent asks 'is this the promis'd end?'. Edgar echoes him 'or image of that horror'. An image, then, of the end of the world and of ourselves which for each individual amounts to the same thing. It's not surprising that Dr Johnson found the play contrary to the natural ideas of justice. All through the play people are looking at the state of their world and trying to find evidence that it is just. When something that seems fair happens a character says 'this shows you are above/ You justicers', but to Lear the justices are rogues, thieves in fur gowns. And if it weren't for the fidelity of Kent and the charity of Cordelia, we might think that the play was dismissing the whole notion of justice as fraudulent, as if under the fine word as under the fine clothes there was nothing but greed and lust.

So *King Lear* is not just a play about a foolish king. It is about a king who loses his palace, his crown and his robes and finds himself an unsheltered mortal. It is also about a man without his dignity, lurking in hovels, without authority, without reason. We all live in societies that depend upon our belief in them and the belief of others. Without that belief they afford no shelter. I think Shakespeare, in his greatest years, was much preoccupied with that theme. He wanted here to express it unequivocally, if necessary cruelly. Sanity, dignity and love depend upon a structure of belief which might even be a structure of illusion. He shows us the rats gnawing at the holy cords and the collapse of the structure which is like the end of the world. In that situation we find ourselves naked, blind, deprived of reason. We babble the dialects of privation. Our life is as cheap as beasts. That is why *King Lear* is the cruellest play. 'Thou must be patient', says the mad Lear to the blind Gloucester,

> we came crying hither.
> Thou know'st the first time that we smell the air
> We wawl and cry.

4.6.179–81

But Gloucester has no eyes and cannot cry. The world has become an instrument of torture to the King himself. 'O let him pass!', says Kent

> He hates him
> That would upon the rack of this tough world
> Stretch him out longer.

5.3.313–5

Lear himself says that he is bound upon a wheel of fire. So we leave the theatre, switch off the television and return to our temporary certainties and devices by which we make the world familiar and acceptable, but it seems right that for a moment we should have had a glimpse of it as it appeared to the stripped king.

KING LEAR
Tony Church

Tony Church is associated with the Royal Shakespeare Company and the Northcott Theatre. Besides Gloucester and the title role in King Lear, *his other leading parts have included Henry IV. He played the Speaker in the BBC TV production of* Henry VIII *and the Banished Duke in the production of* As You Like it.

I think that *King Lear* is the most extraordinary and perhaps the greatest play in the English language, possibly even in world drama. Its central character, the King of Britain, has lived over eighty years before the play begins. In his remaining very short life span we find out almost everything that a play can tell us about a human being. There are other characters who are each explored in as great a depth as if they were leading roles in any other play. The story is complex and the motives of all the characters are as devious as they would be in real life.

In the very first scene you see in Lear the whole concluded man in his shell of absolute power, divine right and total self-regard. He comes in with his three daughters: the elder two, Goneril and Regan, with their husbands, Albany and Cornwall, and the third, Cordelia, who is being courted by both the King of France and the Duke of Burgundy. Lear says that, in view of his great age, he is going to divide up his kingdom between his three daughters so that 'future strife/May be prevented now'. Remember this wish to prevent 'future strife'. Now as we watch this scene we understand that the two married daughters have never actually had their dowries. We also realise that the Duke of Burgundy and the King of France have been kept waiting quite a long time to find out which of them is going to get Cordelia. Lear says that he is going to divide up the kingdom according to how much each of his three daughters says that she loves him. The elder two, Goneril and Regan, manage this pretty well. But the third daughter, Cordelia, is unable to stomach the situation and refuses to say how much she loves him until she is forced into a corner by her angry father:

LEAR: Now, our joy,
   Although our last and least; to whose young love
   The vines of France and milk of Burgundy
   Strive to be interess'd; what can you say to draw
   A third more opulent than your sisters? Speak.
CORDELIA: Nothing, my lord.
LEAR: Nothing!
CORDELIA: Nothing.
LEAR: Nothing will come of nothing. Speak again.
CORDELIA: Unhappy that I am, I cannot heave
   My heart into my mouth. I love you Majesty
   According to my bond; no more nor less.
LEAR: How, how, Cordelia! mend your speech a little,
   Lest you may mar your fortunes.
CORDELIA: Good my lord,
   You have begot me, bred me, lov'd me; I
   Return those duties back as are right fit,
   Obey you, love you, and most honour you.   1.1.81–97

If only she had stopped there: the play could have ended happily enough after four pages. I think that Lear would have accepted her speech. But Cordelia will not leave the matter alone: 'Why have my sisters husbands, if they say/They love you all?'. Cordelia is right, but why say so now? Why not please Daddy instead? The competitive situation between the two elder daughters has affected her as well. At this point the whole roof falls in as the King, in a mad rage, banishes her.

One of his ministers, the Earl of Kent, interferes by maintaining that people should not be expected to put their love into words. Lear banishes him as well and then turns round to Cordelia's two suitors. He asks the Duke of Burgundy whether he will take her without a dowry. Burgundy declines, but the King of France then suddenly throws the whole thing into question by saying that Cordelia is wonderful, Lear stupid, and a marriage must still take place. The worst possible political situation promptly develops, for France is now a bitter enemy of the kingdom. The 'future strife', which Lear had hoped to prevent, is more or less assured. The other two daughters are left at the end of the scene wondering what they are going to do with their impossible father, who has banished both his favourite daughter and his devoted minister. They seem to dread his proposed visits to them. The seeds of an appalling situation are thus sown.

The emotional blackmail of the 'how much do you love me?'

competition is central to our understanding of the play. Few performances in the theatre have convinced me of what is really going on here. If Lear had genuinely intended to reward the best and most convincing demonstrator of daughterly love, he would have waited until all three has spoken before apportioning the shares. Instead, he responds to Goneril and Regan immediately they have spoken by giving them a third of the kingdom. It is obvious that it is a negative game. It is only when Cordelia refuses to play that her pre-arranged best third is withdrawn. It is like showing a dog his favourite biscuit and then making him beg for it. Why does a father treat his children in this way? Why do the children react in the way that they do? It was customary until 1962 to dismiss Goneril's and Regan's declarations of love as being overwritten, over-fanciful and hypocritical. But Peter Brook's production in 1962 with Paul Scofield, together with Trevor Nunn's in 1976–7 with Donald Sinden, the two productions in which I have played Lear, and many others now, have set the record straight. We are now much more likely to accept that the balance of sympathy at the beginning of the play tends to be partly with the two elder daughters because of the position in which Lear has put them. We also realise that Shakespeare was writing something much, much deeper than just a simple Ugly Sisters and Cinderella situation. I am myself a father of three children and know enough to understand what has been going on for years in the Lear household prior to the beginning of the play. The absolute monarch wooed by flattery is only a reflection of the flattery and blackmail current and common in the familial scene. Later on, Lear knows what he appears not to know at the beginning of the play:

> They flatter'd me like a dog, and told me I had white hairs in my beard ere the black ones were there. To say 'ay' and 'no' to everything that I said! 'Ay' and 'no' too was no good divinity. When the rain came to wet me once, and the wind to make me chatter; when the thunder would not peace at my bidding; there I found 'em, there I smelt 'em out. Go to, they are not men o' their words. They told me I was everything; 'tis a lie – I am not ague-proof.

4.6.96–105

When we see him at the start of the play, Lear gives up the responsibility of power but makes it quite clear that he does not intend to give up any other part of it. He wants to keep his 100 knights, live alternately month by month with his two elder daughters and to end his days having a really splendid time doing what he wants. But when we see him in Goneril's house during his first monthly residence it is clear that a very nasty situation has already arisen. There is a clash of opinion about the behaviour of Lear and his knights. Goneril argues that these knights are unruly and riotous because Lear is no longer able to control them. She urges him:

> A little to disquantity your train;
> And the remainders that shall still depend
> To be such men as may besort your age,
> Which know themselves and you.   1.4.248–51

Whereupon he delivers a curse on her womb, which is horrific in its rage and detail:

> Hear, Nature, hear; dear goddess, hear.
> Suspend thy purpose, if thou didst intend
> To make this creature fruitful.
> Into her womb convey sterility;
> Dry up in her the organs of increase;
> And from her derogate body never spring
> A babe to honour her! If she must teem,
> Create her child of spleen, that it may live
> And be a thwart disnatur'd torment to her.
> Let it stamp wrinkles in her brow of youth,
> With cadent tears fret channels in her cheeks,
> Turn all her mother's pains and benefits
> To laughter and contempt, that she may feel
> How sharper than a serpent's tooth it is
> To have a thankless child.   1.4.275–89

It is unbelievable for a father to say that to his daughter. He storms out of the house to go to his second daughter, but we already know that Goneril has written to Regan and together they mean to control their father. Eventually there is a ruthless confrontation between Lear and his daughters, in which the number of knights that they will allow him falls from fifty to twenty-five and then to none at all. The scene is a terrible echo of the measurement of love at the beginning of the play.

Lear takes himself out into the night and the storm. Then follows the crucial moment when Cornwall, Goneril and Regan shut the doors against him to prevent his coming back – the crossing of the Rubicon in the play: war has now finally been declared between Lear and his elder daughters. During the storm

Lear's only companion is his Fool, one of the strangest creations in this strange play. He appears first in Goneril's house, his witty inversions of reality naming Lear as Fool, himself the sane man: Lear's folly is seen to include his blindness to the true worth of Cordelia, his ready response to the flattery of his other daughters, his failure to understand the selfish nature of man. The Fool also blames his master for his continual insistence on his own authority and rightness, and on the ingratitude of others: Lear in his own eyes is never to blame. Despite his piercing analysis of the truth through joke and song, the Fool is totally dependent on Lear, and suffers deprivation with him in the fury of the storm. The irony is that the thunder, lightning and the rain are never equal, in Lear's mind, to his own rage: he calls them 'servile ministers'. His injunctions to the 'great gods/That keep this dreadful pudder o'er our heads' are, however, most terribly obeyed: the rest of the play is the story of how what he calls forth actually occurs.

At this point the other elements of the plot start to impinge, so I must pick up the story of Gloucester, the King's chief minister. Things are no better in his family than they are in Lear's. Gloucester has two sons: Edgar, slightly the elder, was born in wedlock, but Edmund is a bastard. Edmund will not inherit anything from Gloucester on account of both his age and his illegitimacy. He therefore tricks his father by means of a phoney letter into thinking that Edgar has been plotting to usurp him. The extraordinary thing is that Gloucester instantly believes Edmund, thus revealing that his sympathies have always been with the illegitimate child (perhaps because of the fun surrounding his conception in the first place). It also reveals that Gloucester does not understand his elder son at all. We are asked to believe that Gloucester is blind in relation to his family. He orders Edgar's arrest, and almost certain execution, and leaves, blaming the King's behaviour to Cordelia and Edgar's to himself on the stars and destiny: 'these late eclipses in the sun and moon portend no good to us'. Edmund, left alone, rejects such an astrological viewpoint:

> This is the excellent foppery of the world, that, when we are sick in fortune, often the surfeits of our own behaviour, we make guilty of our disasters the sun, the moon, and stars; as if we were villains on necessity; fools by heavenly compulsion; knaves, thieves, and treachers, by spherical predominance; drunkards, liars, and adulterers, by an enforc'd obedience of planetary influence; and all that we are evil in, by a divine thrusting on –

an admirable evasion of whoremaster man, to lay his goatish
disposition on the charge of a star! 1.2.115–25

Edgar escapes and for most of the play we see him on the run and
disguised as Poor Tom, a mad wretch lurking in hovels and
ditches.

The catastrophic events called down by Lear now begin to roll
forward. Gloucester himself sides with Lear against his
daughters. Edmund betrays his father and, in a terrifying scene,
Cornwall and Regan pluck out his eyes. He is now literally blind as
well. Lear's own life is in peril, not least because it is feared that he
will join up with Cordelia, who has landed at Dover with a French
army. Naked ambition and jealousy appear to ride roughshod over
what should be the true relationship between a father and his
children, a master and his servants. Amazing discoveries are
nevertheless made in the midst of all the horrors. When Lear is at
the mercy of the elements, he reaches a climax of self-regard and
self-pity. He presents himself as 'a man more sinn'd against than
sinning', which is a very questionable notion at this point. As his
'wits begin to turn', he shows more interest in his companions. At
the point when madness enters into Lear, sympathy and understanding for other people replace the passionate self-obsession:

> Poor naked wretches, whereso'er you are,
> That bide the pelting of this pitiless storm,
> How shall your houseless heads and unfed sides,
> Your loop'd and window'd raggedness, defend you
> From seasons such as these? O, I have ta'en
> Too little care of this! Take physic, pomp;
> Expose thyself to feel what wretches feel,
> That thou mayst shake the superflux to them,
> And show the heavens more just.

3.4.28–36

Poor Tom and Lear then have an extraordinary encounter, which
culminates in these lines of Lear's:

> Why, thou wert better in a grave than to answer with thy
> uncover'd body this extremity of the skies. Is man no more than
> this? Consider him well. Thou ow'st the worm no silk, the beast
> no hide, the sheep no wool, the cat no perfume. Ha! here's
> three on's are sophisticated! Thou art the thing itself: un-
> accommodated man is no more than but such a poor, bare,
> forked animal as thou art.

3.4.100–9

Lear's response on seeing the naked Tom is then to start tearing his own clothes off. It is as if the person who comes on at the beginning of the play is a massive onion, the skins of which are gradually taken off by the events that happen to Lear and eventually by his own wish. It is part of the search for the core of his identity and for the nature of his responsibility to himself and others.

Gloucester, blinded, abandoned and wanting to die, also meets Poor Tom and asks to be led by him, unaware that he is speaking to his own rejected son. He claims it as 'the times' plague when mad men lead the blind'. He then goes on to experience the same vision of the injustice of the world, which was perceived by Lear in the previous scene. Gloucester's blindness enables him to see, in the same way that Lear's madness produces clarity of vision and a sympathy for other people:

> Let the superfluous and lust-dieted man
> That slaves your ordinance, that will not see
> Because he does not feel, feel your power quickly;
> So distribution should undo excess
> And each man have enough.   4.1.68–72

Lear's rage is finally spent after the weird scene in which he puts Goneril on trial in the form of a joint stool, and cuts Regan up in an imaginary anatomy lesson. He is then taken to Dover to meet Cordelia but escapes his attendants and in his peak of apparent madness, with flowers in his hair, meets Gloucester on Dover Cliff. I say apparent because in this scene Lear's penetrating eye exposes the whole structure of so-called justice and civilisation as the rotten edifice of our common experience. He knows now what only the fall from the throne, loss of absolute power, and suffering of the lowly can teach:

> Thou rascal beadle, hold thy bloody hand.
> Why dost thou lash that whore? Strip thy own back;
> Thou hotly lusts to use her in that kind
> For which thou whip'st her. The usurer hangs the cozener.
> Through tatter'd clothes small vices do appear;
> Robes and furr'd gowns hide all.   4.6.160–5

Then a second later, such is the wonder of the scene, Lear recognises Gloucester for the first time:

> I know thee well enough; thy name is Gloucester.
> Thou must be patient; we came crying hither.

Thou know'st the first time that we smell the air
We wawl and cry.   4.6.178.81

This is a play on so many levels. It is about relationships between
fathers and their children. Practically all the horrors that occur
within families occur here in enlarged or extreme form. There is
massive love, horror and jealousy, together with emotional
blackmail for all kinds. There is also a great deal of social criticism
about the way that things are ordered and the hypocrisy of power
as well as its injustice. It is also a study of the rise of Renaissance
man, embodied in the person of Edmund, who cuts his way
through the old world by climbing up on the shoulders of everybody else. Other themes include personal responsibility and the
encounter of men and madness. We know so much more about
schizophrenia than they did in Shakespeare's time, yet psycholo-
gists have told me that Shakespeare seems to be delineating a
casebook schizophrenic, particularly in the beginning of the
Dover scene. There is also a vast amount of animal imagery in the
play, which seems to say that the underlying nature of human
beings is that of the worst of jungle animals. Throughout, Shakespeare conducts a detailed investigation into, and a searching
assessment of, what man's relationship to man should be. Finally,
the play is concerned with man's confrontation with the end of his
life. Edgar says in his last line to Gloucester 'Men must endure
their going hence, even as their coming hither'.

Lear has to endure more, it seems, than Job. When Cordelia's
army is defeated by Goneril and Regan, Lear and Cordelia,
recently reunited after a painful and moving reconciliation, are
ordered to prison. Cordelia protests, but Lear answers with a
beautiful vision of separation from the stupid, hideous world we
see around us:

No, no, no, no! Come, let's away to prison.
We two alone will sing like birds i' the cage;
When thou dost ask me blessing, I'll kneel down
And ask of thee forgiveness; so we'll live,
And pray, and sing, and tell old tales, and laugh
At gilded butterflies, and hear poor rogues
Talk of court news; and we'll talk with them too –
Who loses and who wins; who's in, who's out –
And take upon's the mystery of things
As if we were God's spies; and we'll wear out
In a wall'd prison packs and sects of great ones
That ebb and flow by th' moon.   5.3.8–19

It is, however, the final hubris, and Shakespeare denies Lear the realisation of that dream. Man must endure this world: he cannot escape his personal responsibility, so he must face the end *alone*. The final scene has the most enigmatic ending in drama. But then what is *King Lear* but a massive series of questions to which we must find our own answers?

THE MERRY WIVES OF WINDSOR

Jilly Cooper

Jilly Cooper is a journalist who wrote a column for The Sunday Times *for a number of years, and now contributes to* The Mail on Sunday. *She has published several novels, such as* Harriet *and* Emily, *as well as books on contemporary social attitudes. She made this programme on location at Dorney Court, near Windsor.*

Queen Elizabeth, the Queen Mother, once told reporters that her favourite programme was *Mrs Dale's Diary*. 'I try never to miss it', she went on, 'because it's the only way of finding out what goes on in a middle-class family'. In just the same way, Queen Elizabeth the First must often have gazed down from her great castle, poised above the bustling little town of Windsor, and wondered what sort of lives her subjects led. Shakespeare told her in *The Merry Wives of Windsor*. Instead of writing about kings, princes, field marshals and heads of state as he usually did, he turned his attention to solid, rich burghers and their cheerful, dependable wives. He sets the play firmly in Windsor which was a town he knew well, instead of in some faraway place like Athens or Venice which he had only read about. Of all Shakespeare's plays this is thus the one most likely to tell us what middle class life in Elizabethan England was really like. It is a sort of Elizabethan *Mrs Dale's Diary* with Sir John Falstaff as guest star. Falstaff had already made an appearance in Shakespeare's *Henry IV* and the Queen is said to have been so enchanted by the character that she asked Shakespeare to write another play showing the fat knight in love. Shakespeare, being a true pro, responded with alacrity and produced *The Merry Wives*, all five acts of it, in a fortnight flat. The Queen, according to tradition, was delighted. And so she should have been, for the play is a marvellously funny, knockabout comedy which, because it was written so fast, crackles along at a rip-roaring pace with never a dull moment.

Today's merry wives go to the hypermarket, load up their trolleys with jumbo washing powder and frozen scampi. Mistress

Ford and Mistress Page must have gone shopping together, although they would have been able to order their manservants to carry home the spoils. With so many overseas markets opening up, Elizabethan England was for some people a land of opportunity and the newly rich middle classes in particular were ostentatiously hospitable. When you dined out, according to a contemporary report, there were so many dishes on the table that they had to be piled one on top of another. Goodness knows how the merry wives managed without a deep freeze when their equally hospitable husbands were always bringing troops of impromptu guests home for dinner or, even worse, breakfast. Sir John Falstaff was one of these impromptu guests. He is a knight and so regards the Fords and Pages as rather beneath him socially but despite his expansive, rather patronising manner he is on his beam ends. He and his gang of rascally retainers, Bardolph, Nym and Pistol, are all staying at the local pub, drinking their heads off and running up bills of ten pounds a week, an astronomical sum in those days. Falstaff hits on a plan to salvage his wrecked finances, after dining at the Pages and sampling, among other things, hot venison pasty, pippins and cheese. He is accustomed to drinking sack, a kind of sherry, in four pint mugs and has equally grandiose ideas when it comes to women. He will seduce not one, but two, of the merry wives and make them so dotingly in love with him that they will squander all their rich husbands' fortunes on him:

> FALSTAFF: I have writ me here a letter to her; and here another to Page's wife, who even now gave me good eyes too, examin'd my parts with most judicious oeillades; sometimes the beam of her view gilded my foot, sometimes my portly belly.
> PISTOL: Then did the sun on dunghill shine.
> NYM: I thank thee for that humour
> FALSTAFF: O, she did so course o'er my exteriors with such a greedy intention that the appetite of her eye did seem to scorch me up like a burning glass! She bears the purse too; she is a region in Guiana, all gold and bounty. I will be cheaters to them both, and they shall be exchequers to me; they shall be my East and West Indies, and I will trade to them both.

1.3.55–68

Falstaff is completely out of his depth with middle-class women, as he is only accustomed to tarts, barmaids and the sophisticated ladies of the Court. In one scene, for example, he accuses Mistress Ford of 'carving'. This was a gesture made by trollops in which they waggled their little finger at a man when they drank in order to encourage him. I wonder how many ladies at vicarage tea parties today realise the original meaning of that ever so refined and genteel gesture. Falstaff completely underestimates the iron-knickered respectability of the middle classes. The 'merry wives' may have enjoyed leading a man on, but a mistress is the last thing either Mistress Ford or Mistress Page want to be:

> MRS PAGE: (*reads*)
> Thine own true knight,
> By day or night,
> Or any kind of light,
> With all his might,
> For thee to fight,
> JOHN FALSTAFF.

What a Herod of Jewry is this! O wicked, wicked world! One that is well-nigh worn to pieces with age to show himself a young gallant! What an unweighed behaviour hath this Flemish drunkard pick'd – with the devil's name! – out of my conversation, that he dares in this manner assay me? Why, he hath not been thrice in my company! What should I say to him? I was then frugal of my mirth. Heaven forgive me! Why, I'll exhibit a bill in the parliament for the putting down of men. How shall I be reveng'd on him? for revenged I will be, as sure as his guts are made of puddings.

2.1.15–26

I am convinced that, if Falstaff had been wildly attractive, the merry 'waives' would not have been nearly so outraged. They are incensed that a drunken, scruffy, old lech with a seventy-two inch waist, that is five times bigger than Scarlett O'Hara's, and chilblained feet sticking through the holes in his shoes should actually think that they were giving him the come-on. No wonder they spend the rest of the play trying to get their own back. Falstaff is curiously naïve in that he writes identical love letters to both wives and expects them not to compare notes. He is also naïve in his attitude towards Nym and Pistol. He tells them that he intends to seduce the wives then, when they refuse to deliver his amorous missives, he sacks them but still expects them to remain loyal. I suppose that today Nym and Pistol would have gone straight to *The News of the World* and sold the story of 'Prince's Friend Sir John in Windsor Wife Swap Orgy' for thousands of pounds. In Shakespeare's day, they merely tipped off the husbands.

Tradition has it that *The Merry Wives* was first performed for the Garter celebrations of 1597. The motto of the Knights of the Garter is 'Honi Soit Qui Mal Y Pense' or 'Evil Unto Him Who Thinks Evil' and in a way this is one of the great themes of the play. Mistress Page's husband is a happy man because he trusts his wife implicitly and refuses to listen to any scandal-mongering from Nym and Pistol. Mr Ford, on the other hand, does not trust his wife an inch and suffers agonisingly as a result. According to Simon Forman, the fashionable doctor and astrologer, Elizabethan men were obsessed with the possibility that their wives might be unfaithful, and with some grounds too. Many of the wives who came to consult Forman wanted to know how to make their lovers more amorous. So the insanely jealous Mr Ford is a character that Elizabethan audiences would have laughed at but identified with. The Fords are in fact childless and poor Ford must have been subjected to endless sly digs about his lack of virility. When he gets one of his jealous brainstorms, he is like a small boy swinging a brick round on the end of a piece of rope and not caring whom he hits. He passionately resents Page for trusting his wife. He is also wildly suspicious of Mistress Page's friendship with Mistress Ford. Today I suppose that he would have bugged their telephone conversations. But most of all he detests a fat fortune-teller called the Old Woman of Brainford, whom he no doubt suspects of filling his wife's head with loads of rubbish about dark, or grossly overweight, strangers. Ford, jealousy aflame, comes roaring down the street with a rabble of friends, intent on catching his wife *in flagrante*. The merry wives have the brilliant idea, however, of dressing Falstaff up as the Old Woman of Brainford.

Half the fun for Mistress Ford is making an idiot of her frightful husband as well as of Falstaff. On an earlier occasion when Ford storms in in a jealous rage, Falstaff is smuggled out in a vast laundry basket full of dirty washing. It must have been jolly dirty because the Elizabethans were not great washers. Poor Falstaff is then emptied into the Thames – no fun in the middle of winter. One of the reasons we love Falstaff is his resilience. He may have an 'alacrity in sinking', but he soon perks up again at the prospect of a large drink. Like Dylan Thomas, another amorist fuelled by alcohol, Falstaff has the gift of the gab, and like all poets, capitalises on his disasters:

FALSTAFF: Go fetch me a quart of sack; put a toast in 't. Have I liv'd to be carried in a basket, like a barrow of butcher's offal, and to be thrown in the Thames? Well, if I be serv'd such another trick, I'll have my brains ta'en out and butter'd, and give them to a dog for a new-years gift. The rogues slighted me into the river with as little remorse as they would have drown'd a blind bitch's puppies, fifteen i' th' litter; and you may know by my size that I have a kind of alacrity in sinking; if the bottom were as deep as hell I should down. I had been drown'd but that the shore was shelvy and shallow – a death that I abhor; for the water swells a man; and what a thing should I have been when I had been swell'd! I should have been a mountain of mummy.

3.5.2–16

Apart from Falstaff's amorous scufflings, *The Merry Wives* never flags as a play because there is a host of marvellously drawn minor characters and a very strong sub-plot. Unlike the Fords, the Pages have two children. Master William is still at school and, with typical middle-class pushiness, the Pages are panicking about his education. I suppose that today Mistress Page would have been forking out for late-night coaching, charging along to maths workshops to help with the new maths homework and upstaging all the other mothers at the PTA with wildly exaggerated accounts of Master William's progress. Shakespeare must have drawn directly from his own experience at Stratford Grammar School for the hilarious scene in which Master William has a Latin test:

WILLIAM: Accusativo, hinc.

EVANS: I pray you, have your remembrance, child. Accusativo, hung, hang, hog.

MISTRESS QUICKLY: 'Hang-hog' is Latin for bacon, I warrant you.

EVANS: Leave your prabbles, oman. What is your genitive case plural, William?

WILLIAM: Genitive case?

EVENS: Ay.

WILLIAM: Genitive: horum, harum, horum.

MISTRESS QUICKLY: Vengeance of Jenny's case; fie on her! Never name her, child, if she be a whore.

EVANS: For shame, oman.

MISTRESS QUICKLY: You do ill to teach the child such words. He teaches him to hick and to hack, which they'll do fast enough of themselves; and to call 'horum'; fie upon you!

EVANS: Oman, art thou lunatics? Hast thou no understandings for thy cases, and the numbers of the genders? Thou art as foolish Christian creatures as I would desires.

MRS PAGE: I prithee hold thy peace.

EVANS: Go your ways and play; go.

MRS PAGE: He is a better scholar than I thought he was.

EVANS: His is a good sprag memory.

4.1.41–75

The Pages also have a daughter, Anne, who is a sensible, practical girl, much sought after both for her fortune and her beauty. Lucky thing, you might think, but unfortunately both her parents are determined that she shall make a brilliant match. Her mother favours a fashionable French doctor who is stinking rich, but has a foul temper. Anne Page does not fancy him at all. Rather than marry him, she would prefer to 'be set quick i' th' earth/ And bowl'd to death with turnips'.

Mistress Page should not have been surprised by Anne's rebellion, for her daughter is a chip off the old block. Elizabethan women were not shrinking violets like Victorian wives, but immensely powerful both in the home and in public affairs. Despite the bluster of men like Ford, women ran their husbands as efficiently as they ran their houses. But, like most mothers, Mistress Page did not expect her daughter to display a similar independence of spirit. Anne Page is even less enthusiastic about her father's candidate for her hand: a chinless wonder from the sticks with a vast estate but an IQ in single figures. He is unable to woo unless he has his book of sonnets to quote from and is reluctantly being pushed into marriage by his kinsman, the bumbling Justice Shallow. His proposal to Anne could not be more lukewarm:

SHALLOW: He will make you a hundred and fifty pounds jointure.

ANNE: Good Master Shallow, let him woo for himself.

SHALLOW: Marry, I thank you for it; I thank you for that good comfort. She calls you, coz; I'll leave you.

ANNE: Now, Master Slender –

SLENDER: Now, good Mistress Anne –

ANNE: What is your will?

SLENDER: My will! 'Od's heartlings, that's a pretty jest indeed! I ne'er made my will yet, I thank heaven; I am not such a sickly creature, I give heaven praise.

ANNE: I mean, Master Slender, what would you with me?

SLENDER: Truly, for mine own part I would little or nothing with you. Your father and my uncle hath made motions; if it be my luck, so; if not, happy man be his dole! They can tell you how things go better than I can. You may ask your father; here he comes.

3.4.49–65

Middle class girls, egged on by poets and ballad-mongers singing of romantic love, were beginning to kick over the traces and resist the marriages arranged by their parents. Anne loves Master Fenton and he truly loves her in return. Anne's parents, however, disapprove of him. They regard him as an up-market fortune hunter who has squandered his inheritance whooping it up with the 'fast set'. He is one of those young men who keeps cropping up in the gossip columns.

Finally, there is the hare-brained chatterbox, Mistress Quickly, to add to the fun. She is the original Mrs Malaprop, as well as being an inspired moonlighter. She not only housekeeps for the French doctor and acts as a go-between for Falstaff and the merry wives, but she also furthers the cause of each of Anne Page's three suitors and takes money from everybody:

FENTON: I thank thee; and I pray thee, once to-night
Give my sweet Nan this ring. There's for thy pains.
MISTRESS QUICKLY: Now heaven send thee good fortune! A kind heart he hath; a woman would run through fire and water for such a kind heart. But yet I would my master had Mistress Anne; or I would Master Slender had her; or in sooth, I would Master Fenton had her; I will do what I can for them all three, for so I have promis'd, and I'll be as good as my word; but speciously for Master Fenton. Well, I must of another errand to Sir John Falstaff from my two mistresses. What a beast am I to slack it!

3.4.97–108

Mistress Quickly must have had amazing powers of persuasion. Falstaff has been dumped in the Thames and thrashed whilst in drag, but she still manages to talk him in to an even more outlandish rendezvous with the elusive Mistress Ford.

This time he has to dress up as Herne the Hunter, the ghost of a gamekeeper believed to haunt Windsor Forest at midnight in the depths of winter. A grotesque figure wearing huge antlers, clanking his chain and quivering with lust therefore suddenly enters the Forest. The next moment he is measuring his length on the frosty grass, frightened out of his wits by a gang of nasty little children dressed as fairies. They proceed to pinch him black and blue and sing an extremely precocious song, attacking him for his

THE MERRY WIVES OF WINDSOR

lechery. One hopes they catch their death of cold by going out so late without their thermal underwear. I suppose that feminists today would see *The Merry Wives* as a triumph for the sisterhood of Mistress Page and Mistress Ford over a fat male chauvinist pig like Falstaff. But despite his bounderish behaviour, bragging and lying, we still want Sir John to win out, particularly when the Pages and Fords gang up against him. We cannot bear to see him so humiliated, nor thank goodness can Shakespeare. So Falstaff is saved and, while the Pages were making an idiot of him, their daughter was making idiots of them by slipping off and marrying Master Fenton. Fenton is only too happy to tear a strip off his new in-laws for trying to marry their daughter 'most shamefully/ Where there was no proportion held in love'. Shakespeare, who had been pushed into a miserably unhappy marriage himself, attacks through Fenton the dislocated values of the middle classes, who put such a high premium on fidelity and then make it almost impossible to achieve by forcing their children into loveless marriages for financial gain. Fortunately, the Pages are a good-natured couple who take their defeat in good part. They end, as they began, with lavish hospitality, inviting everyone including Falstaff home for a good laugh in front of a country fire. Soon, no doubt, he will be knocking back possets in four-pint mugs and regaling the company with more and more exaggerated accounts of his midnight stag party. Once he gets his chilblained feet under the table, I fear the Pages may have a house guest for many years to come.

THE MERRY WIVES OF WINDSOR

Prunella Scales

Prunella Scales played Mistress Page in the BBC TV production of The Merry Wives of Windsor. *Her previous Shakespearean parts include Olivia in* Twelfth Night *and Hermia in* A Midsummer Night's Dream. *She also played Sybil in the television series* Fawlty Towers.

A curious theory has grown up about *The Merry Wives of Windsor*. In his two history plays about the reign of Henry IV, Shakespeare had created one of the great comic characters of all time: Sir John Falstaff, the fat, bawdy, greedy, drunken knight who spent most of his time in the Boar's Head Tavern in Eastcheap with his gang of thieves. Falstaff was so popular with Elizabethan audiences, that it is said that Queen Elizabeth the First herself asked Shakespeare to write another play about Falstaff and his gang in which the fat knight would be seen 'in love'. It is also said that she gave him fourteen days, possibly only ten, to finish it. *The Merry Wives* has always been a great favourite with audiences, but this story of the royal commission, although it can't be proved, has led to a certain neglect of the play in academic criticism. It is often treated as little more than a poorly-made farcical potboiler, written to squeeze extra mileage out of the character of Falstaff.

For me, nothing could be further from the truth. *The Merry Wives* certainly has several elements of farce, but I find it splendidly constructed, with some of the best character writing and richest dialogue in all Shakespeare. It also gives a unique and beautifully observed picture of provincial middle class life in England as the year 1600 approached.

The plot *is* rather complicated. Sir John Falstaff turns up in Windsor, short of cash and with his band of villainous army renegades about him. In order to acquire money to support them all, he decides to make love to the wives of two of Windsor's richest citizens, Frank Ford and George Page. Now the idea of

Falstaff actually earning money from these escapades was probably funny in itself to those who knew him from the earlier plays.
But at the start of *The Merry Wives of Windsor* we have not seen the
two wives, so we don't know how they are going to respond.
Indeed we never find out whether Falstaff himself imagines they
are going to pay him for his services, as a sort of Elizabethan
'midnight cowboy', or whether he's planning a course of straightforward blackmail. He writes two identical letters, a kind of
amorous circular, and sends one to each wife on the somewhat
naive assumption that they won't show them to one another. But
Mrs Ford and Mrs Page are great friends and they immediately
show one another the letters, while two of the gang, Nym and
Pistol, go straight off and betray Falstaff to the two husbands.

George Page has perfect confidence in his wife and simply takes
the news as a good joke, but Ford, whose marriage is far less
secure, thinks his wife may well respond to Falstaff and is thrown
into paroxysms of jealousy. He decides to disguise himself under
the name of Brook so that he can give Falstaff money to encourage
him in his wooing of Mrs. Ford. Ford also urges Falstaff to pave
the way for 'Brook' to seduce her too, as a way of testing his own
wife. So the plot thickens. Both the wives are in fact incorruptibly
virtuous, but they decide to lead Falstaff on in order to turn the
tables on him and have some fun themselves at his expense. As
Mrs Page says,

> Let's be reveng'd on him; let's appoint him a meeting, give him
> a show of comfort in his suit, and lead him on with a fine-baited
> delay, till he hath pawn'd his horses to mine host of the Garter.
>
> 2.1.82–5

In other words they intend to flirt with him to the point where he is
broke.

The rest of the play consists of three great practical jokes played
by Mrs Ford and Mrs Page to humiliate Falstaff. First of all Mrs
Ford invites Falstaff to her house when her husband is out. Mrs
Page hides outside the room until Falstaff arrives and, as soon as
he begins his amorous declaration, she bursts in on them with the
announcement that Ford is on his way. Falstaff hides behind a
curtain, but eventually they persuade him to climb into a laundry
basket full of dirty linen. Then, to their considerable surprise,
Ford really does turn up. The buckbasket is carried out under
Ford's very eyes, Falstaff is tipped into the Thames like a bundle
of laundry, and Ford searches the house in vain. The wives don't
know why Ford had suspected that Falstaff would be there,

because they are not aware that Ford, disguised as Brook, has learnt of the assignation, but they enjoy hugely the humiliation of Falstaff and the bafflement of Ford. Falstaff is not so amused:

> Have I liv'd to be carried in a basket, like a barrow of butcher's offal, and to be thrown in the Thames? Well, if I be serv'd such another trick, I'll have my brains ta'en out and butter'd, and give them to a dog for a new-year's gift. The rogues slighted me into the river with as little remorse as they would have drown'd a blind bitch's puppies, fifteen i' th' litter; and you may know by my size that I have a kind of alacrity in sinking; if the bottom were as deep as hell I should down. I had been drown'd but that the shore was shelvy and shallow – a death that I abhor; for the water swells a man; and what a thing should I have been when I had been swell'd! I should have been a mountain of mummy.
> 3.5.3–16

Later on he tells his story to Ford himself, who is once again disguised as Brook:

> I suffered the pangs of three several deaths: first, an intolerable fright to be detected with a jealous rotten bell-wether; next, to be compass'd like a good bilbo in the circumference of a peck, hilt to point, heel to head; and then, to be stopp'd in, like a strong distillation, with stinking clothes that fretted in their own grease. Think of that – a man of my kidney. Think of that – that am as subject to heat as butter; a man of continual dissolution and thaw. It was a miracle to scape suffocation. And in the height of this bath, when I was more than half-stew'd in grease, like a Dutch dish, to be thrown into the Thames, and cool'd, glowing hot, in that surge, like a horse-shoe; think of that – hissing hot. Think of that, Master Brook.
> 3.5.93–108

The second humiliation of Falstaff is what we used to call in our rehearsals the 'wives strike again' scene. Falstaff is invited once again to the Ford Household while Ford is out, and again Mrs Page enters while Falstaff is flirting with Mrs Ford, this time with a genuine warning that Ford is on his way. Falstaff refuses to get into the buckbasket a second time, so they send him upstairs to disguise himself in some clothes they have planted there belonging to a local character, the Old Woman of Brainford (an old name for Brentford). Mrs Ford knows that her husband loathes the Old Woman. When Ford arrives to find the laundry basket empty, and when Falstaff comes downstairs in his disguise, Ford beats him up and throws him out of the house, again to the delight of the two wives.

At this point they finally tell their husbands what they have been up to. Ford and Mrs Ford are reconciled, and they all decide to trick Falstaff yet again. They make a third appointment, this time in Windsor Great Park. Falstaff is to arrive at midnight for this assignation, disguised as the legendary Herne the Hunter, with great horns on his head. He keeps the appointment, but so does the entire village, with all the children disguised as fairies. Falstaff is taunted, humiliated, pricked and burnt. Then all the company remove their masks, rebuke Falstaff for his lustful behaviour and go home with everyone, well nearly everyone having had a very good time. Mrs Page includes Falstaff in the final festivities:

> Good husband, let us every one go home,
> And laugh this sport o'er by a country fire;
> Sir John and all.

5.5.228–30

From everything I have said so far, you would be quite right in thinking that *The Merry Wives* is a romp, full of mistaken identities, hiding in laundry baskets and dressing up in women's clothes. It is indeed a sort of bedroom farce, with plenty of the kind of purely physical gags that we see in some present day situation comedies on television. But I think that there is more to it than that. It is also a very finely observed comedy of manners, gently mocking certain aspects of middle class provincial life in Shakespeare's time. There is an interesting sub-plot concerning the Pages' daughter, Anne. Page wants her to marry Abraham Slender, a country gentleman who has come up from Gloucestershire with his Uncle Shallow. Shallow is a Justice of the Peace whose country estate has been poached by Falstaff and the gang, and has chased them up to Windsor to get satisfaction. Mrs Page regards Slender, not without reason, as an idiot, in spite of all his property. She wants Anne to marry the local doctor, a Frenchman called Dr Caius, because he is rich and has friends at Windsor Castle – (we have to remember that Windsor was a royal residence: we may doubt the famous story that Queen Elizabeth the First actually commissioned the play, but it seems almost certain that she saw it performed, which could explain a good deal of the monarchical flattery in it). Anne Page herself wants to marry Fenton, a young aristocrat. The Pages dislike him because of his very aristocracy: despite their snobbery, they are not anxious for a connection with the London Court. They mistrust Fenton's riotous past and disapprove of his poverty.

There is a further sub-plot about a proposed duel between Dr Caius and Sir Hugh Evans, the Welsh schoolmaster, which is foiled by the local publican, the Host of the Garter Inn. And Mistress Quickly, housekeeper to Dr Caius, links all the plots together as a sort of combined matchmaker and postmistress. There are also some very charming minor characters: Slender's servant Peter Simple, Dr Caius's servant John Rugby, the schoolboy William Page and Falstaff's little servant Robin. The setting is Windsor village, a little more important than the average village because of the Castle, but still then a village, inhabited by a new Elizabethan bourgeois society, the emerging merchant class, stoutly defending their goods, their money, their position and their attitudes against all comers.

The Merry Wives is the only one of Shakespeare's Comedies to be set entirely in England – his other comedies all take place in exotic, sometimes imaginary places. But this English suburban society, which doesn't appear anywhere else in Shakespeare, is just as accurately observed as the feudal society of aristocrat and peasant in that other unique Shakespearean comedy, *Love's Labour's Lost*. The two worlds are differentiated with a faultless ear. *Love's Labour's Lost* is written almost entirely in verse – an unusually mannered academic text of 'taffeta phrases, silken terms precise', extremely difficult for present-day actors. But the thick, good-quality homespun prose of *The Merry Wives*, lavishly embroidered with sixteenth-century idioms and clichés, and perfectly suited to Elizabethan Windsor, is in its own way just as difficult to read and to act. It may sound extravagant to say so, but I think it's a more difficult text than *King Lear*. Some of the expressions have survived to the twentieth century – Mrs Page at one point says, 'I cannot tell what the dickens his name is . . . ', but other passages are quite obscure and hard to interpret, and need actors who are prepared to research their speeches, and when they have found exactly what the modern equivalent would be, have the skill and comic technique to deliver the lines so that they sound natural and clear to a modern audience. Given such actors, the lines can come out as fresh and funny as in any popular modern comedy.

Though how many popular comedies today have up to eighteen really good parts in them? Besides being a situation comedy and a comedy of manners, *The Merry Wives* is above all a comedy of character. I have heard the parts in *The Merry Wives* referred to as 'stock' characters: but although Shakespeare may have started with 'stock' characters – the Jealous Husband, the Comic Welshman and so on – here each one of them is individually fleshed out, with unique personal mannerisms and verbal eccentricities. The Host of the Garter tries to make peace between Dr Caius and Sir Hugh:

> Peace, I say, Gallia and Gaul, French and Welsh, soul-curer and body-curer. . . . Peace, I say. Hear mine host of the Garter. Am I politic? am I subtle? am I a Machiavel? Shall I lose my parson, my priest, my Sir Hugh? No, he gives me the proverbs and the noverbs. Give me thy hand, terrestrial; so. Give me thy hand, celestial; so. Boys of art, I have deceiv'd you both; I have directed you to wrong places; your hearts are mighty, your skins are whole, and let burnt sack be the issue. Come, lay their swords to pawn. Follow me, lads of peace; follow, follow, follow.   3.1.90–102

Justice Shallow can never use a phrase without repeating it again and again:

> He hath wrong'd me, Master Page. . . . He hath wrong'd me, indeed he hath; at a word he hath, believe me. Robert Shallow, esquire, saith he is wronged.   1.1.90–6

And I find Mistress Quickly a far richer and more rewarding part than the Mistress Quickly of *Henry IV*. There are passages in it to rival the Nurse in *Romeo and Juliet*. Here she is delivering Mistress Ford's first invitation to an impatient Falstaff, larded with invention and malapropisms. By 'canaries' we assume she means 'quandaries':

> Marry, this is the short and the long of it: you have brought her into such a canaries as 'tis wonderful. The best courtier of them all, when the court lay at Windsor, could never have brought her to such a canary. Yet there has been knights, and lords, and gentlemen, with their coaches; I warrant you, coach after coach, letter after letter, gift after gift; smelling so sweetly, all musk, and so rushling, I warrant you, in silk and gold; and in such alligant terms; and in such wine and sugar of the best and fairest, that would have won any woman's heart; and I warrant you, they could never get an eye-wink of her.   2.2.53–64

Even Fenton, the stock romantic juvenile, is given a special development. He confesses to Anne Page that he came to her first as a fortune-hunter, but has come to love her for herself – and since Page has threatened to cut off her dowry unless she marries Slender, I think we should believe that Fenton marries Anne for love alone. We can feel he has earned the right to rebuke Mr and Mrs Page for their commercial and hard-hearted attitude towards their daughter!

> You would have married her most shamefully,
> Where there was no proportion held in love.
> The truth is, she and I, long since contracted,
> And now so sure that nothing can dissolve us.
> Th' offence is holy that she hath committed;
> And this deceit loses the name of craft,
> Of disobedience, or unduteous title,
> Since therein she doth evitate and shun
> A thousand irreligious cursed hours,
> Which forced marriage would have brought upon her.

5.5.208–17

Fenton is the only character who always speaks in verse, which seems to oblige anyone addressing him to speak verse too. This could, I suppose, signify the virtuous and ennobling influence he has on the people of Windsor, but it also gives the rather charming effect of people using posh language to talk to the grand young man from London. Though even the prose of the play has wonderfully poetic passages and phrases: Mrs Ford of Falstaff, 'What tempest, I trow, threw this whale, with so many tuns of oil in his belly, ashore at Windsor?'. And Falstaff, complaining of his own stupidity, says, 'Have I laid my brain in the sun and dried it, that it wants matter to prevent so gross an o'er reaching as this?'. I love the image of someone taking his brain out and drying it in the sun.

We tried in the television production to find an accurate Berkshire accent for the Windsor characters, which is certainly nearer the speech of Shakespeare's own time than modern BBC English, and seemed to help the dialogue come alive. I loved playing Mrs Page. When I first started working on the part I thought, I know this lady, and lots of people like her – she's just like me in some ways. One of my favourite scenes is one that directors very often cut altogether, but in our production was set in the market place with the schoolboys playing football in the background:

MISTRESS QUICKLY: Mistress Ford desires you to come suddenly.

MRS PAGE: I'll be with her by and by; I'll but bring my young man here to school. Look where his master comes; 'tis a playing day, I see. How now, Sir Hugh, no school to-day?

EVANS: No; Master Slender is let the boys leave to play.
MISTRESS QUICKLY: Blessing of his heart!
MRS PAGE: Sir Hugh, my husband says my son profits nothing in
   the world at his book; I pray you ask him some questions . . . .

4.1.5–15

I've had that sort of conversation so often when my own sons were
at primary school: the details of everyday life in the play, that
haven't changed in nearly 400 years, I find even more delightful
than the big set pieces.

Mr and Mrs Page, though by no means the most important
parts in the play, could be seen as the heart of it, representing
Windsor, standing for good sense and good behaviour, a core for
the eccentrics like Falstaff and Ford to revolve around. Falstaff is,
of course, a famous part for actors, but I have never understood
why the part of Ford is so neglected. In a comic idiom, it offers just
as exciting and comprehensive a study of jealousy as *Othello*, and
the progress from suspicion to conviction to jealous mania and
then to realisation of Mrs Ford's innocence, Ford's apology and
whole-hearted participation in the final romp, his gentle defence
to Page of love in marriage, make a charming story which deserves
to be better known.

I don't want to claim too much for *The Merry Wives of Windsor*.
It doesn't pretend to be anything more than a situation comedy.
But it's a beautifully written one, and the themes that run through
it, of goodness, and of a certain loyalty to each other and to the
community are not negligible: Page is really deeply concerned to
stop the duel between Caius and Evans, not only to protect his
property and his bourgeois principles – he is anxious that people
shouldn't fight each other. When the townspeople mobilise to stop
the fight between schoolmaster and doctor, and to stop Falstaff
disrupting two marriages, they are not simply trying to preserve
the status quo: they are defending a certain standard of decent
behaviour which Shakespeare commends in the play, even though
he mocks it at the same time. For all their smugness and snobbery,
I think Shakespeare likes the citizens of Windsor, and wants us to
like them too, even while we are laughing at them.

CYMBELINE

Dennis Potter

Dennis Potter writes for television, cinema and stage. His highly acclaimed television work, which includes Pennies from Heaven, *was the subject of a tribute by the National Film Theatre in 1982. He made this programme on location in the Forest of Dean.*

One of the problems of introducing – no, commending – a play such as *Cymbeline* is how not to be caught in some ridiculous posture which still fails to give adequate measure to its sweetly ridiculous plot. In the circumstances, the producer was probably quite right to adduce that a background of book-lined walls and maybe me with a pipe stuck in my face would be marginally less satisfactory in evoking the mood and atmosphere of the play than these rocks and caves, woods and stonily mysterious landscapes of both my own childhood and all our fairytale-riddled memories. In any case, I quite like standing on the edge of my native Forest of Dean, though at bat-winged dusk would have been better if only to distance myself quite literally from the airless academicism which has too often disfigured those very things in Shakespeare which he knew his audiences wanted and would always want and, even while staring into the voracious maw of television, in my opinion still want.

It's difficult for any of us to be capable of a direct or unmediated response to anything by the Bard, but this is exactly the way in which *Cymbeline* needs to be enjoyed. Fortunately, it's not too often performed nowadays and not too many modern directors have taken the chance to express themselves, which can be to masturbate all over it. Nowadays, too, it's not often on the ordinary examination syllabus, which is another piece of good news. The chances are therefore that, like me, you will come upon *Cymbeline* anew without the squeak of blackboard chalk to set your teeth on edge and without the debilitating memory of pedagogic droning to bump about the inside of your head like a fat bluebottle laying its eggs here, there and everywhere on the genuine freshness and delight of this play. Cast your mind back, instead, to the dusky evenings of childhood. Your eyelids are drooping and the warm, cosy house is preparing itself to drift off, unanchored, into the night when from a soft and fading voice, outside yourself, that becomes a picture inside yourself and that is yours and yours alone – a soldier, home from the wars, comes marching down the high road – one, two – with his knapsack on his back and his sword at his side – one, two – and on his way he meets a witch. . . .

This is the world of *Cymbeline*. The extravagant, imperious improbable, tender, shocking, comical and entrancing realm of 'once upon a time', the kingdom where love has to be cruelly tested before emerging 'happy ever after', where the handsome but poor man wins the beautiful and true princess, where the rich and powerful are dissembling oafs and hypocrites, and foundlings come at long, long last upon their true inheritance. This is the kingdom where the heroine has to hide in lowly disguise like a Snow White among the Dwarfs and, not least, where the truly, yet comically wicked get a deserved come-uppance which not only tickles the ribs, but also severs with a satisfying crunch some more important bits of bone. And just as *Snow White* is called *Snow White* and *Cinderella* called *Cinderella*, so *Cymbeline* should more properly, if less euphoniously, be called *Imogen*. Sweet and true Imogen, the lovely and innocent princess whose very soul, not her borrowed shoes, is made of the clearest and purest crystal:

IMOGEN: But, good Pisanio,
  When shall we hear from him?
PISANIO: Be assur'd, madam,
  With his next vantage.
IMOGEN: I did not take my leave of him, but had
Most pretty things to say. Ere I could tell him
How I would think on him at certain hours
Such thoughts and such; or I could make him swear
The shes of Italy should not betray
Mine interest and his honour; or have charg'd him,
At the sixth hour of morn, at noon, at midnight,
T'encounter me with orisons, for then
I am in heaven for him; or ere I could
Give him that parting kiss which I had set
Betwixt two charming words, comes in my father,
And like the tyrannous breathing of the north
Shakes all our buds from growing.

1.3.22–37

Imogen's father, Cymbeline, who bears the title of the play as ill-fittingly as his own sense of judgement, is a gullible and, for most of the time, mean-minded old fart. He is the King of Britain who has by his second and more unwise marriage got himself a handsome but cunning Queen who can twist him every which way round her crooked little finger, a Queen – it's simplified – who is evil enough to poison cats and dogs in her chamber. She is the very stereotype of the wicked fairytale queen, who is even allowed a nod in that direction when she has the nerve to tell Imogen

No, be assur'd you shall not find me, daughter,
After the slander of most stepmothers,
Evil-ey'd unto you.

I.1.70–2

Is she kidding! She wants her stupendously stupid son, Cloten, to marry Imogen, the King's daughter by his first marriage.

Poor, beautiful, put-upon Imogen – brave, faithful, chaste, again the very model of the model fairytale stepdaughter, but only in the circumstances of the plot. Too fair, too bright, to want the proffered hand of the oaf, Cloten, a belligerent clod if ever there was, she has secretly and disobediently married the upright Posthumus, the man 'she'd break her eyestrings to see', but a man whose status in the sniggery and fawning Court is not high enough for such nuptials. In consequence, Posthumus has been sent packing. The young blade has been exiled on pain of death to Rome. This is supposed to be the Rome of the great Empire, but the playwright has taken his licence to pander to the prejudices of his audience and instead show Posthumus marooned in foppish, woppish, despicable, contemporary Italy. Question: can he possibly remain uncorrupted and as true in his heart and mind as he vows upon leaving her?

POSTHUMUS: What lady would you choose to assail?
IACHIMO: Yours, whom in constancy you think stands so safe. I will lay you ten thousand ducats to your ring that, commend me to the court where your lady is, with no more advantage than the opportunity of a second conference, and I will bring from thence that honour of hers which you imagine so reserv'd.
POSTHUMUS: I will wage against your gold gold to it. My ring I hold dear as my finger; 'tis part of it.

I.4.120–8

Dr Johnson was only one of many since who have been miffed by the improbabilities of a plot which has more twists and turns than a drunken morris dance, but I think it not only adds to the fun but also provides the opportunity for several startlingly unexpected epiphanies which come at one like a sudden view in the zigzag of the narrative. Take dumbhead, even sometimes smelly and always metaphorically malodorous Cloten. He's definitely set there for us to jeer at, demonstrably a swaggering coward as well as a loud-mouthed fool, but he's allowed by the exigencies of the tuppenny-coloured plot, to say nothing of his creator's theatrical fondness for banging words together in an up-yours, patriotic bluster, to become for a moment, in confrontation with the shuttling ambassador of mighty Rome, the latest spokesman for that bluff, down-to-the-bloody earth, well-there-it-bloody-well-is brand of mock-naïve patriotism that the English always affect at times of threat. It's the other wicked creature, the poisonous Queen, who's given one of those splendid, sea-girt-England bits of tub-thump which must have confused the hissing rabble somewhat, but Cloten has already made clear that Ancient Britain is a world in itself which will not pay tribute to Rome.

All this is being set up so that Posthumus can return and be valiant, thus allowing true love, happiness and Britain to triumph, with villainy cast down into death, defeat or disappointment. Who was it who said that drama shouldn't present new stories, only new relationships? Shakespeare had gone back, rich and comfortable, to Stratford where he could rake all over the ground he has already deep-furrowed. There are still gold and silver coins to be found where he has already taken treasure, but he always did know how to make any number of cast-off plots and tales, or whole troops of secondhand characters, jump back vividly in all their pristine glory. *Cymbeline* is like a hall full of echoes and yet the language is bubblingly alive and sinuous, handled with the easy competence of a genius who has got an armlock on a plot which, if it ever got away, would run and run until it collapsed in the puddle of its own sweat. Now that's not to scorn the three-fold interlacing of stories or story in *Cymbeline* as so many critics have done with the unnecessarily aloof sniff of those who so obviously think that drama is just words on a page. The old professional, back in Stratford with his paunch and his shekels intact, knew his audiences inside out. The London theatres had been shut down for close on eighteen months during and just before the time he was writing *Cymbeline*, so Shakespeare had plenty of time not only to play again with the characters and situations and passions he had already explored, but also to recall with apparent cynicism or lordly contempt – I think with sharp yearning – the particular, minute-by-minute atmosphere and expectation of the playhouse.

Out of what is, in any circumstances, an especially outrageous but undeniably tense and beautiful piece of theatre, the exiled Posthumus, grieving for home and Imogen, is tricked by a wily Italian into believing that Imogen has been unfaithful. Alone on stage, the bitter and misinformed Posthumus gives vent to a speech of such relentless misogyny that any modern male who dares to give even a nod in its direction, would soon be made to feel like the central character in a Bateman cartoon:

> This yellow Iachimo in an hour – was't not?
> Or less! – at first? Perchance he spoke not, but,
> Like a full-acorn'd boar, a German one,
> Cried 'O!' and mounted; found no opposition
> But what he look'd for should oppose and she
> Should from encounter guard. Could I find out
> The woman's part in me! For there's no motion
> That tends to vice in man but I affirm
> It is the woman's part. Be it lying, note it,
> The woman's; flattering, hers; deceiving, hers;
> Lust and rank thoughts, hers, hers; revenges, hers;
> Ambitions, covetings, change of prides, disdain,
> Nice longing, slanders, mutability,
> All faults that man may name, nay, that hell knows,
> Why, hers, in part or all; but rather all;
> For even to vice
> They are not constant, but are changing still
> One vice but of a minute old for one
> Not half so old as that.

2.5.14–32

Exit, pursued by a she-bear. This pain and hatred is his punishment for making a wager on Imogen's fidelity. She, of course, has been totally without blemish and the audience knows this for sure, but as a technique for showing passion or prejudice and at the same time undermining what appears to be the truth of it while still leaving the conviction of the speaker intact, this is drama working flat out in that unique combination of language, circumstances and character which ultimately justifies every serpentine twist of the plot. That old, old way of showing the workings, the accidents and the opportunities of what used to be called Destiny can still fit modern apprehensions, if not modern intellects.

Drama, of course, is older than the other surviving kinds of fiction and it retains very much less anxiety about the distinctions between form and content than are perhaps acceptable to current intellectual taste. It's the poor old novel, clapped out though it may be, which has to take the weight of contemporary critical ideologies, most of which seem to be in lumbering, flat-footed, tongue-tied motion towards the universal and the systematic where character is seen as a tedious illusion, a bourgeois invention and the plot – a plot for God's sake! – well that's just a place where you bury things which ought not to be allowed above ground in the clear air of vigorous and respectable discourse. Shakespeare, of course, could not have anticipated any part of the long, slow, sick dream which threatens to become the intellectual condition of present-day arts. But the greatest writers of the past are not totally landlocked in the plateau of yesterday. They can still provide escape hatches punched into the restricting carapace of our present habits and presumptions, and show how the universal and the archetypal can still yet reverberate with an individual nerve. *Cymbeline*, for example, is using old forms, old tales and almost shameless improprieties of narrative to get at something new. It's creating Romance which is still an embryonic form out of the setting gelatine of the folk tale. Imogen, a fairyland princess in all the details of her plight and her ultimate redemption, is still nevertheless genuinely human, unmistakably real.

Now I'm not *Reader's Digest* for all my bland exterior and occasional philistinism, so I can't possibly scale down for you here and now all the reasons why Cloten, the really quite likeable oaf, is found by drug-awakening Imogen in wild Wales with his head chopped off. She's dressed as a boy and he, in one hell of a huff, is dressed in her exiled husband's old clothes. Now understandably and I hesitate to use such a reasonable-sounding word – but understandably she thinks this headless body is Posthumus:

A headless man? The garments of Posthumus?
I know the shape of's leg; this is his hand,
His foot Mercurial, his Martial thigh,
The brawns of Hercules; but his Jovial face –
Murder in heaven! How! 'Tis gone, Pisanio,
All curses madded Hecuba gave the Greeks,
And mine to boot, be darted on thee! Thou,
Conspir'd with that irregulous devil, Cloten,
Hath here cut off my lord. To write and read
Be henceforth treacherous! Damn'd Pisanio
Hath with his forged letters – damn'd Pisanio –
From this most bravest vessel of the world
Struck the main-top. O Posthumus! alas,

Where is thy head? Where's that? Ay me! where's that?

4.2.309–22

I mean it's the sort of question you'd ask about anybody lying there without a head, whether strewn with flowers or no. And you don't have to be an exceptionally acute critic to get the idea that the cunning old Bard was deliberately writing about twelve miles off the ground with more than half an eye on tickling his own ribs as well as losing somebody else's cranium. *Cymbeline* is a wondrously crank-sided vessel, quite deliberately upturned just when our expectations are about to be becalmed.

In this part of the play, the other main strand is being unravelled. Cymbeline, the King, has much earlier lost and presumed dead his two sons, Arviragus and Guiderius, brothers to Imogen. In fact, they have been brought up in the purest rustic innocence, living in a Welsh cave without corruption and princely to the bone, though not knowing who or what they are. When they stumble across their disguised sister, blood and sensibility combine in the force of their attraction for the 'he' who is in fact a 'she'. Babes in the Wood? Hansel and Gretel? Fairytale land complete? Yes and no. For once again genuine emotion is released like a songbird let out of an impossibly ornate cage:

> GUIDERIUS: Fear no more the lightning flash,
> ARVIRAGUS: Nor th'all-dreaded thunder-stone;
> GUIDERIUS: Fear not slander, censure rash;
> ARVIRAGUS: Thou hast finish'd joy and moan.
> BOTH: All lovers young, all lovers must
>   Consign to thee and come to dust.
> GUIDERIUS: No exorciser harm thee!
> ARVIRAGUS: Nor no witchcraft charm thee!
> GUIDERIUS: Ghost unlaid forbear thee!
> ARVIRAGUS: Nothing ill come near thee!
> BOTH: Quiet consummation have,
>   And renowned be thy grave!

4.2.271–82

A throat-narrowing, skin-prickling, true prayer for the dead, which in the text is immediately followed by the old man of the cave bearing poor old Cloten's comically headless body. I tell you, it's difficult to know which of opposing expressions to hold for long on one's face. But playing with that which is serious, making serious the comic, breaking the crust of the old forms and yet also inhabiting them – that is *Cymbeline*, a fairy tale, romance, comedy and adventure.

CYMBELINE

Jeffery Dench

Jeffery Dench is a member of the Royal Shakespeare Company. Besides the title role in Cymbeline, *his parts have included the French King in* Henry V *and Sir Andrew Aguecheek in* Twelfth Night.

Cymbeline is probably a play that you don't know. It is unlikely that you were made to do it at school and you won't have had many opportunities to see it performed. You might, of course, have come to see it at Stratford in 1979. It was quite evident to me from playing Cymbeline in that production that the play performs much better than people believe. It is much more fun to do as an actor simply because audiences do not know it well. As they have no preconceived ideas about it, they are unable to sit there agonising over previous performances. I suppose that the play is rarely performed because it is not counted as one of Shakespeare's great plays. It has some good poetry in it. Although it has a convoluted story line, it is still a ripping yarn which carries you along with it all the time. The audience can't wait to get back after the interval to know what is going to happen next. Shakespeare keeps his secrets up his sleeve, revealing them a little at a time. He builds event on event so that by the end everything is on show and he has to tie it all up. Although *Cymbeline* may not be amongst Shakespeare's greatest plays, it is not an immature piece. It was written towards the end of Shakespeare's working life. We can tell that it was a late play by the shortened use of language, the fairly difficult use of verse and the way in which the prose itself almost scans. I would say that it is either the first or the second of Shakespeare's three Romances: *Cymbeline*, *The Winter's Tale* and *The Tempest*. He had really learnt how to write a romance by the time of *The Tempest*. We know that this was his last play, which was written in Stratford and, I think, possibly never meant to be performed. *Cymbeline* is probably the first of these Romances because Shakespeare is still experimenting with the form. He learnt enough from writing *Cymbeline* to take the experiment one stage further in *The Winter's Tale*. The original was called *The Tragedy of Cymbeline*, although *The Romance of Cymbeline* would be nearer the mark. Tragedy is, after all, a one-way ticket to self-destruction, whereas the Romances are concerned with a different kind of journey towards redemption and reconciliation.

I should also warn you that the fact that it is called *Cymbeline* at all is odd, because it is not really the play of Cymbeline. If anything it should be called *Imogen*, as she is really the core of the play. Shakespeare chose this shadowy King from the Dark Ages, Cymbeline probably being based on Cunnebelinus, and wrote a story about his family life. I say a story, but there are in fact three stories that we see developed in the play. First, there is the story of Imogen, daughter to Cymbeline, and her love affair with Posthumus Leonatus. This is the strongest theme and it really dominates the play, certainly in the first half. Secondly, there is the story of Cymbeline's two sons, Guiderius and Arviragus, who were stolen from their nursery as infants. As far as Cymbeline knows they are dead, or at least he believes that there is no hope of seeing them again after twenty years. Finally, as a kind of blackcloth, there is the story of the developing political confrontation between Cymbeline and the Romans, which eventually leads to war.

The play opens with a family confrontation caused by a forbidden marriage, which was one of Shakespeare's favourite themes. Imogen has secretly married Posthumus Leonatus, a poor but worthy underling who has been fostered since childhood under Cymbeline's protection. She is locked up and her husband is banished. Cymbeline, or more likely the Queen, had other plans for her. The Queen wanted her to marry her step-brother, Cloten, the Queen's son by a previous marriage. The imminent departure of Posthumus places Imogen directly at the mercy of the two people, the Queen and Cloten, whom she ought to fear the most. We get the measure of both of them very quickly. The first time we see the Queen she has arranged a secret meeting between Imogen and Posthumus so that they can say a last goodbye before he leaves the country:

> QUEEN: No, be assur'd you shall not find me, daughter,
> After the slander of most stepmothers,
> Evil-ey'd unto you. You're my prisoner, but
> Your gaoler shall deliver you the keys
> That lock up your restraint. For you, Posthumus,
> So soon as I can win th' offended King,
> I will be known your advocate. Marry, yet
> The fire of rage is in him, and 'twere good

You lean'd unto his sentence with what patience
Your wisdom may inform you.
POSTHUMUS: Please your Highness,
I will from hence to-day.
QUEEN: You know the peril.
I'll fetch a turn about the garden, pitying
The pangs of barr'd affections, though the King
Hath charg'd you should not speak together.   I.i.70–83

How sympathetic of her to walk around the garden while the two young things say goodbye! What she actually does is go and fetch the King who storms in and 'strikes fourteen'. She is a two-faced manipulator who in fact even leads you, the audience, up the garden path. Her real ambition is to get Cloten on the throne, preferably by marriage to Imogen, but failing that by the removal of Imogen. We see her later on very casually giving a box to Imogen's servant. It contains a drug which she claims has saved the King's life five times, which is not true. She believes that she is handing over a fatal poison which will destroy Imogen. We have to keep an eye on this box as Shakespeare has some tricks up his sleeve. The Queen is a delightful cameo part for the actor. She does not feature much after the early scenes but when she is on she is very strong, perhaps even caricatured. I am sure that Walt Disney used her later, only with apples rather than pills! When I played Cymbeline, I always fancied that the Queen controlled him with drugs, sending her ladies out to pick herbs so that she could cool him down or heat him up when she wanted to get something done.

Her son Cloten is quite the opposite: a brash fool and bumpkin. He is usually played for laughs, which oddly enough he gets, even through to the end by which time it is clear that he is paranoid, malevolent and dangerous. To begin with, though, he is shown as merely stupid and aggressive, as well as smelly and unwholesome even to his sycophantic followers:

Sir, I would advise you to shift a shirt; the violence of action hath made you reek as a sacrifice. Where air comes out, air comes in; there's none abroad so wholesome as that you vent.

I.2.1–4

We are clearly meant to see that Imogen will not so much as look at Cloten, despite the fact that he has a song called 'Hark, Hark the Lark' performed outside her door at daybreak. It is all too much for Imogen when he tries to get to her by insulting her husband:

IMOGEN: Profane fellow!
　Wert thou the son of Jupiter, and no more
　But what thou art besides, thou wert too base
　To be his groom. Thou wert dignified enough,
　Even to the point of envy, if 'twere made
　Comparative for your virtues to be styl'd
　The under-hangman of his kingdom, and hated
　For being preferr'd so well.
CLOTEN: The south fog rot him.
IMOGEN: He never can meet more mischance than come
　To be but nam'd of thee. His mean'st garment
　That ever hath but clipp'd his body is dearer
　In my respect than all the hairs above thee,
　Were they all made such men.

                                              2.3.124–36

The pestering Cloten is the least of Imogen's tribulations because
the play takes a new turn here. This is based on a story that
Shakespeare seems to have taken from Bocaccio's *Decameron*,
although it had been going around Europe in various forms for
200 years. We see Posthumus as a foreign visitor in Rome getting
on rather well with some new-found friends. They discuss
women, and more particularly the loyalty of their wives, over the
wine after a meal. Posthumus gets into an argument with one
Iachimo, who claims that no woman is ever totally loyal. They
settle their dispute with a wager: Iachimo will try to seduce
Imogen and if he succeeds he will win the diamond ring that
Imogen gave to Posthumus, but if he fails it will cost him 10,000
ducats. Iachimo is another gem of a role. Shakespeare was always
willing to exploit the prejudice of his audience about foreigners.
Sometimes he questions it very severely as he does with Shylock,
but not here. Iachimo is presented, plain and simple, as a slippery
Italian. You have to lock up your women and keep an eye on the
silver when he is around. He takes over the Roman dinner party,
even though it is not his party. He is a smooth talker if ever there
was one, who always seems to be one move ahead. Imogen trusts
him completely when he travels to England. She fully believes him
when he tells her that Posthumus is having a whale of a time in
Rome and seems to have turned his back on her. Iachimo puts a
direct proposition to her to 'be reveng'd':

IMOGEN: Reveng'd?
　How should I be reveng'd? If this be true –
　As I have such a heart that both mine ears

Must not in haste abuse – if it be true,
How should I be reveng'd?
IACHIMO: Should he make me
Live like Diana's priest betwixt cold sheets,
Whiles he is vaulting variable ramps,
In your despite, upon your purse? Revenge it.
I dedicate myself to your sweet pleasure,
More noble than that runagate to your bed,
And will continue fast to your affection,
Still close as sure.

1.6.127–37

This attempt to seduce Imogen fails, so you might think that
Iachimo is about to be kicked into the moat. Yet he means to win,
not so much her as the ring, which is worth a small fortune. So he
throws himself straightaway at her feet with profuse apologies and
extravagant praise for her fidelity and honour. He says it was all a
clumsy way of trying to strengthen rather than weaken the marriage of two lovely people. She of course forgives him and he tries
another tack by asking her to do him a favour:

IACHIMO: Some dozen Romans of us, and your lord –
The best feather of our wing – have mingled sums
To buy a present for the Emperor;
Which I, the factor for the rest, have done
In France. 'Tis plate of rare device, and jewels
Of rich and exquisite form, their values great;
And I am something curious, being strange,
To have them in safe stowage. May it please you
To take them in protection?
IMOGEN: Willingly;
And pawn mine honour for their safety. Since
My lord hath interest in them, I will keep them
In my bedchamber.

1.6.184–95

Yet when the trunk is wheeled in, it contains not the 'plate of rare
device' but Iachimo himself. He steals about Imogen's room
whilst she sleeps taking careful note of all its details. He also
studies her, finding a little mole beneath her breast. He takes her
bracelet, a wedding gift from Posthumus, and hurries back to
Rome with a wealth of circumstantial evidence which he unfolds
piece by piece.

Posthumus refuses to accept this evidence at first, but Iachimo
leads him step by step, just as Iago leads Othello, from scepticism

to suspicion and then from suspicion to conviction. Posthumus is thus finally convinced that Imogen has been seduced and so Iachimo wins the ring. This pushes Posthumus right over the edge and he delivers what must have been a highly provocative attack on women even in Shakespeare's time:

> Is there no way for men to be, but women
> Must be half-workers? We are all bastards,
> And that most venerable man which I
> Did call my father was I know not where
> When I was stamp'd. Some coiner with his tools
> Made me a counterfeit; yet my mother seem'd
> The Dian of that time. So doth my wife
> The nonpareil of this. O, vengeance, vengeance!
> Me of my lawful pleasure she restrain'd,
> And pray'd me oft forbearance; did it with
> A pudency so rosy, the sweet view on't
> Might well have warm'd old Saturn; that I thought her
> As chaste as unsunn'd snow. O, all the devils!
> This yellow Iachimo in an hour – was't not?
> Or less! – at first? Perchance he spoke not, but,
> Like a full-acorn'd boar, a German one,
> Cried 'O!' and mounted; found no opposition
> But what he look'd for should oppose and she
> Should from encounter guard. Could I find out
> The woman's part in me! For there's no motion
> That tends to vice in man but I affirm
> It is the woman's part. Be it lying, note it,
> The woman's; flattering, hers; deceiving, hers;
> Lust and rank thoughts, hers, hers; revenges, hers;
> Ambitions, covetings, change of prides, disdain,
> Nice longing, slanders, mutability,
> All faults that man may name, nay, that hell knows,
> Why, hers, in part or all; but rather all;
> . . . .

2.5.1–28

We leave him at this point and the next thing we hear about him is that he has actually planned his terrible vengeance. Back in Britain his servant Pisanio receives two letters from him. The first is for Imogen, asking her to meet him at Milford Haven. The second is for Pisanio himself, telling him to accompany Imogen to Milford Haven and then kill her:

Thy mistress, Pisanio, hath play'd the strumpet in my bed, the
testimonies whereof lie bleeding in me. I speak not out of weak
surmises, but from proof as strong as my grief and as certain as I
expect my revenge. That part thou, Pisanio, must act for me, if
thy faith be not tainted with the breach of hers. Let thine own
hands take away her life; . . . .

3.4.21–6

Pisanio does take her to Milford Haven, but with a few miles to go
he stops and tells her everything. Her reaction is a perfect
counterpoint to Posthumus's invective against women in general.
Even now she won't believe that it is all his doing, believing that
'some jay of Italy' must obviously have betrayed him. Pisanio is a
little more perceptive, suggesting that a villain 'singular in his art'
has plotted against them.

Pisanio is an interesting supporting character, who blocks the
downward path to tragedy. It is as though Shakespeare were
saying that tragedy is not inevitable because people can step in and
stop it. The courageous, loyal and conscientious can often stop it
by refusing to do what they are told. Antigonus saves the infant
Perdita in *The Winter's Tale* by not quite following his orders.
Pisanio does the same thing here, as well as planning the next
move. He has brought along a bag of boys' clothing, into which he
tells Imogen to change. He then instructs her to seek out Posthumus on board a Roman ship at Milford Haven and to sort things
out with him. Pisanio himself will confirm to Posthumus that
Imogen is dead and send him some bloody sign of it. Imogen's
apparent disappearance will also reinforce this evidence. Before
she goes, he gives her the Queen's box:

What's in't is precious. If you are sick at sea
Or stomach-qualm'd at land, a dram of this
Will drive away distemper.

3.4.188–90

That is what he thinks anyway. As a matter of fact a reliable map
would have served Imogen much better for she never gets to the
dockside at Milford Haven.

We see her wandering and lost until she comes across the cave
where an old man is living with his two sons. This great coinci-
dence introduces the play's second story. We have already met
these rustic hunters because Shakespeare dovetails the three
stories together in his construction of the plot. He pushes each
one forward a little at a time towards the point where they collide.

It is all done very artfully, so we don't meet these new characters until halfway through Act Three. A less experienced writer might have been tempted to lay all his cards on the table in Act One and crowd it out with a confusion of detail. But Shakespeare keeps us waiting and then suddenly gives the play this great surge of energy at this mid-point. Who is this old man? He is Belarius, who some twenty years before was Cymbeline's trusted henchman. He was, however, falsely accused of treason. All is not well in this strange one-parent family. The two young men, whom we presume are Belarius's sons, are feeling restless. They know that there is a whole world beyond their wild and woolly mountainside, as their father has told them about it. He has tried to convince them of its corruption, but they are unwilling to take his word for it. When these boys finally depart up the mountain to go hunting, Belarius turns to us and spills the beans:

How hard it is to hide the sparks of nature!
These boys know little they are sons to th' King,
Nor Cymbeline dreams that they are alive.
They think they are mine; and though train'd up thus meanly
I' th' cave wherein they bow, their thoughts do hit
The roofs of palaces, and nature prompts them
In simple and low things to prince it much
Beyond the trick of others.

3.3.79–86

He goes on to explain how he stole the Princes from Cymbeline just after he had been banished. Shakespeare always had a strong fascination for the relationship of parent to child. He was interested in the bonds that can't be broken and the state of bondage that is created by them. Belarius perceives that twenty years of upbringing away from their real father does not truly break the bonds of inheritance. There is always something, a 'spark of Nature', which can't be removed. As mentioned, Imogen arrives at this cave dressed as a boy. She is dejected and bedraggled after sleeping rough for two nights. She is taken in as one of the family, which of course is just what she is. Shakespeare creates in a few scenes a golden, arcadian atmosphere which provides glimpses of another life. As Imogen says,

These are kind creatures. Gods, what lies I have heard!
Our courtiers say all's savage but at court.
Experience, O, thou disprov'st report!

4.2.32–4

But Imogen is not safe even here. Her disappearance has been reported to Cymbeline and Cloten forces Pisanio to tell him where she is. Cloten, the buffoon, flies into a mad rage and we now realise just how dark and dangerous he is. He sets out after Imogen, but not before rehearsing to himself a psychotic and cruel fantasy about what he is going to do:

> She said upon a time – the bitterness of it I now belch from my heart – that she held the very garment of Posthumus in more respect than my noble and natural person, together with the adornment of my qualities. With that suit upon my back will I ravish her; first kill him, and in her eyes. There shall she see my valour, which will then be a torment to her contempt. He on the ground, my speech of insultment ended on his dead body, and when my lust hath dined – which, as I say, to vex her I will execute in the clothes that she so prais'd – to the court I'll knock her back, foot her home again. She hath despis'd me rejoicingly, and I'll be merry in my revenge.

3.5.134–46

But this is a play in which such villainy does not win through, so Cloten, swaggering to the last, is despatched in a fight with the two brothers. They return to the cave, however, only to find Imogen's lifeless body on the ground. They bear her out, cover her with flowers, and speak a lament over her body.

I'll let you discover the rest. Imogen is not in fact dead, but only in a death-like trance induced by the drug from the Queen's box. The climax of the story shows everybody finally caught up in a swift and bloody battle with the invading Romans, from which Belarius and his two sons, together with Posthumus himself, emerge as heroes. Even Jupiter contributes to the extravagant climax by descending from heaven and casting a thunderbolt. If this seems a little too much, I ought to say that it takes place within a dream. The final scene of the play is a technical tour-de-force. Everyone is assembled together. Some of them do not recognise each other yet, so we watch them finding out everything that we already know. Nobody on stage has any idea what has been going on, apart from what has happened to them. This is particularly true of Cymbeline himself. He still thinks, for instance, that the Queen is a true, adoring wife. Everyone supposes that Imogen is dead. Nobody knows who Belarius is. Only Belarius knows the true identity of the boys. Iachimo has not been fully exposed as a cheat and nobody seems to know what has happened to both Cloten and the unknown warrior who fought so heroically in the battle. I think that you are meant to laugh at this last scene. The actors would certainly have their work cut out trying to stop you. Repetition is usually funny and here we have people falling over with surprise time after time. There are still some things that the audience does not know and will have to wait for breathlessly. Will Iachimo confess? Can Belarius escape death for treason, kidnapping and *prima facie* murder? Can Posthumus actually get away with the attempted murder of his wife? How will Cymbeline judge these issues?

Finally, let me suggest that *Cymbeline* is a quite different dramatic experience from, say, *King Lear*. It is not a play that stops for long to ponder or analyse, for all its moments of very raw emotion. It provokes intriguing questions but does not itself give any answers. Imogen is at the core of the play. She is a pure girl on a hazardous journey who upholds the steadfast virtues of love and loyalty, even when beset and surrounded by rainbow-coloured people who seem to be the symbols of human fallibility and the human power of destruction. I think that it is a tale that appeals to that part of us that can still see as a child. It asks to be accepted for what it is and not misunderstood for what it is not.

MACBETH

Julian Symons

Julian Symons is a crime writer, whose numerous publications include The Blackheath Poisonings *and* The Man Who Killed Himself. *He has also written historical and biographical studies. He made this programme on location at Cawdor Castle.*

I always find the witches in *Macbeth* a problem. It's difficult not to see them as comic when one says 'where hast thou been, sister?' and the answer comes 'killing swine'. Yet the predictions of the witches are the pivot on which the play moves, and what may seem comic to us was deadly earnest for Shakespeare and his audience. Witches were burnt by the thousand in Europe during the sixteenth and seventeenth centuries. We usually hanged them in Britain. Even the King, James I, not only believed in witches, but actually wrote a book on demonology. One way to test for a witch was to truss her up and throw her into a pond. The guilty floated and the innocent sank. If she drowned before she could be fished out, that was just bad luck. I say 'she' because most people accused of witchcraft were, in fact, harmless old women. The witches meet Macbeth at the beginning of the play, as he comes hotfoot from putting down a rebellion against his King, Duncan. He seems to be a bluff, honest soldier and the epitome of a loyal captain. The witches greet him and his fellow soldier, Banquo, with startling prophecies:

1 WITCH: All hail, Macbeth! Hail to thee, Thane of Glamis!
2 WITCH: All hail, Macbeth! Hail to thee, Thane of Cawdor!
3 WITCH: All hail, Macbeth, that shalt be King hereafter!

1.3.48–50

Macbeth is already Thane of Glamis. A few minutes later messengers from the King tell him that he has been created Thane of Cawdor. So the first of the witches' prophecies is fulfilled.

Macbeth is a straightforward man, who is used to seeing the shortest way between two points. It occurs to him almost immediately that he may become king by murdering Duncan, but no sooner has the idea occurred to him than he rejects it. Yet very soon Macbeth will be murdering Duncan. It is his wife who makes him change his mind. When we first meet Lady Macbeth she is reading a letter from her husband telling her of the witches' predictions. She sees immediately that the way to the crown is through murder. She also recognises that Macbeth, although a vigorous man of action on the battlefield, may be indecisive off it:

> Hie thee hither,
> That I may pour my spirits in thine ear,
> And chastise with the valour of my tongue
> All that impedes thee from the golden round
> Which fate and metaphysical aid doth seem
> To have thee crown'd withal.

I.5.22–7

The relationship between Macbeth and Lady Macbeth is subtle, complicated, and at the very heart of the play. Although Lady Macbeth at first urges her husband on, she can't bring herself actually to kill Duncan because, as he sleeps, he reminds her of her father. Macbeth is reluctant at first to do anything at all to fulfil the witches' prophecy, but is prepared later on to move from one murder to the next.

The textbook term for the psychological condition which moved Macbeth and his wife jointly to murder is *folie à deux*. The textbook definition is 'a delusion or delusional system affecting two people, usually husband and wife or two sisters'. It means, in plainer language, that two people can incite each other to acts of violence that they would not commit alone. Good, bluff, honest Macbeth would never have embarked on his career of murder but for the urging of his wife. Lady Macbeth could imagine the deed, but not perform it. He's all action, whereas she's all scheming. Together they make a lethal combination at first to other people, finally to themselves.

Myra Hindley was one of the partners in the most horrifying *folie à deux* killings of modern times. Together with Ian Brady, she was found guilty of committing monstrous crimes. Although the word monstrous is often misused, no other one would be adequate here. For what Brady and Hindley did was to kidnap a young girl and then torture, sexually mistreat and finally kill her. They recorded much of what was done on tape for their own pleasure. The case of the American, Martha Beck, provides another example of *folie à deux*. She and Raymond Fernandez, who met through a lonely hearts club, sought out gullible women through such clubs in the late 1940s. Fernandez made love to these women, whilst Beck posed as his sister, then they were robbed and killed. Brady and Hindley are still in prison. Fernandez and Beck went to the electric chair. Martha Beck's last meal was Southern fried chicken.

There's one extraordinary feature common to both these cases. Myra Hindley was a moral, religious, hard-working girl, whose piety impressed all those who knew her, before she met Brady. Martha Beck was the head of a school for crippled children and a sympathetic, intelligent, trained nurse when she met Fernandez. Neither woman had ever been in trouble with the law, and although Brady and Fernandez weren't exactly good members of society, neither of them had engaged in any violent act before they met their partners. Some terrible emotional and physical chemistry worked when Brady met Hindley and when Fernandez met Beck.

I mentioned a career of murder, and Macbeth finds that he can't stop with a single death. Duncan is dead, Macbeth has become king. The prediction is fulfilled. But what about Banquo? He heard what the witches said, and then there were the curious words spoken to him by them, saying he would 'get kings, though thou be none'. Banquo must be disposed of, and his young son Fleance with him. In what might be called an early version of a modern contract killing, Macbeth calls on two murderers to get rid of them. They kill Banquo, but Fleance escapes. None of this is directly known to Lady Macbeth, yet there can be no doubt that she is responsible for his actions, it is she who put the machine of murder in motion.

Shakespeare dealt with this material as a man of the theatre, an actor and playwright, who was concerned with getting the words that he wrote onto the stage and seeing them played effectively as drama. He often wrote rather hurriedly, sometimes in collaboration with other dramatists. Some of his plays might be called 'school of Shakespeare', as we call paintings 'school of Leonardo'. He certainly was not interested in what later generations might have thought of the form, language or psychology of his plays. Nor did he worry much about historical accuracy. There was a real Macbeth who ruled in Scotland during the eleventh century. He took power after killing King Duncan and was killed by Duncan's son, Malcolm. These Scottish kings were rather like the Chicago gangsters of the 1920s. Shakespeare cut the seventeen years of Macbeth's reign down to a few weeks because he wanted speedy action rather than a long-drawn-out chronicle. Banquo was a partner in the murder of Duncan in the version of the Elizabethan chronicler, Holinshed, but as James I was descended from Banquo this would never do for Shakespeare. Instead, he inserted a delicate compliment to the King in the Witches' reference to the fact that Banquo 'shalt get kings, though thou be none'. Shakespeare changed the facts to suit himself.

I've mentioned the Chicago gang wars. Like medieval Scotland, twentieth century Chicago shows us a society essentially outside the rule of law. The law was for a time replaced by strict taboos. You might kill a fellow gangster, but not in his own home or in yours. You also had to make sure that you gave him the most lavish funeral money and bad taste could provide. And in Scotland one of the things that most disturbs Macbeth is that Duncan is his guest, somebody who should be kept safe from harm. The deed is made much worse by the fact that it is committed in Macbeth's own home. Like Al Capone, Jack Diamond and a number of other gangsters, Macbeth is very superstitious. Hitler placed great reliance on his astrologer and Macbeth comes to depend upon the witches' promises. He is undone when they turn out to be tricks. They tell him that he is safe until Birnam Wood comes to Dunsinane, and that no man born of woman can harm him. That makes him sound pretty safe, but Birnam Wood does in fact come to Dunsinane. His enemy, Macduff, was also 'from his mother's womb/ Untimely ripp'd' and so, strictly speaking, not born of woman. I've always thought that was a bit of outrageous dramatic licence.

But the play goes far beyond such ingenious devices to the hearts of the two central characters. They are tortured by guilt before, during and after Duncan's murder. When Macbeth kills Duncan he passes by the chamber where the King's sons, Malcolm and Donalbain, are sleeping:

MACBETH: One cried 'God bless us', and 'Amen' the other,
As they had seen me with these hangman's hands.
List'ning their fear, I could not say 'Amen'
When they did say 'God bless us!'

LADY MACBETH: Consider it not so deeply.

MACBETH: But wherefore could not I pronounce 'Amen'?
I had most need of blessing, and 'Amen'
Stuck in my throat.

LADY MACBETH: These deeds must not be thought
After these ways: so, it will make us mad.

2.2.26–34

Lady Macbeth is still seen as the strong one of the pair at this point. She believes that 'a little water clears us of this deed', but of course it doesn't. The image of blood and the impossibility of removing the bloodstain, which is also the taint of guilt, recurs again and again. As Macbeth says in one agonised soliloquy 'blood will have blood'. His wife washes her hands continually in vain attempts to wipe away the stain. After Duncan's death, terrible dreams oppress them both and the ghost of the murdered Banquo appears to Macbeth at a banquet in the palace hall. Although Shakespeare never visited Scotland, there is a guilt-haunted, covenanting feeling about the play that seems particularly Scottish. There's even something peculiarly Scottish about Macbeth as we see him at first: the brave, rugged chieftain putting down the rebellion against Duncan. He never quite loses this quality, though it soon turns to villainy. As soon as he has been given those apparently foolproof assurances by the three witches, he immediately contemplates the death of Macduff, Thane of Fife, and everybody connected with him:

> Time, thou anticipat'st my dread exploits.
> The flighty purpose never is o'ertook
> Unless the deed go with it. From this moment
> The very firstlings of my heart shall be
> The firstlings of my hand. And even now,
> To crown my thoughts with acts, be it thought and done:
> The castle of Macduff I will surprise,
> Seize upon Fife, give to the edge o' th' sword
> His wife, his babes, and all unfortunate souls
> That trace him in his line. No boasting like a fool:
> This deed I'll do, before this purpose cool.

4.1.144–54

As the play develops, the roles of husband and wife are reversed. Macbeth is only briefly distressed by the appearance of Banquo's ghost and, as this soliloquy illustrates, becomes more determined than ever to hold on to the power that he has gained through murder.

Repentance for crimes committed is not something that is ever considered in this play. So Lady Macbeth does not repent urging her husband to kill Duncan, but she does start walking in her sleep. Her sleep-walking should be construed as an expression of conscience by which the evil repressed in the daytime emerges at night. Conscience drives her to madness in the end. The blood will never go away:

Out, damned spot! out, I say! One, two; why then 'tis time to
do't. Hell is murky. Fie, my lord, fie! a soldier, and afeard?
What need we fear who knows it, when none can call our pow'r
to account? Yet who would have thought the old man to have
had so much blood in him?

5.1.33–8

Her doctor is baffled, as doctors often are. He is referred to in the
stage directions as a doctor of physic, but claims that Lady Macbeth really needs a doctor of divinity rather than a doctor of physic.
The distinction would have been important to Shakespeare's
contemporaries, for they had a faith in the divine that is almost lost
to-day. The distinction we would make instead is that between the
doctor of medicine and the doctor of the mind, or psychiatrist. We
would say that Lady Macbeth has become a psychiatric case. It is a
mark of her husband's rougher, coarser nature that he can't, or
won't, acknowledge this. He suggests to the doctor that there must
be some 'sweet oblivious antidote' to cure her. When he's told that
there is no such antidote, he responds that physic might as well be
thrown to the dogs. We are not told the physical cause of Lady
Macbeth's death, nor does Macbeth bother to ask it:

SEYTON: The Queen, my lord, is dead.
MACBETH: She should have died hereafter;
    There would have been a time for such a word.
    To-morrow, and to-morrow, and to-morrow,
    Creeps in this petty pace from day to day
    To the last syllable of recorded time,
    And all our yesterdays have lighted fools
    The way to dusty death. Out, out, brief candle!
    Life's but a walking shadow, a poor player,
    That struts and frets his hour upon the stage,
    And then is heard no more; it is a tale
    Told by an idiot, full of sound and fury,
    Signifying nothing.

5.5.16–28

Macbeth is one of the very greatest of Shakespeare's plays, but
where does the greatness lie? Not in the plot, which is simply
about power taken and then lost. Nor in the minor characters, who
are less important here than they are in a number of the other
tragedies. The play's greatness lies partly in the poetry, which is
perhaps the finest in any of the plays. It is not just that almost every
scene contains familiar quotations and memorable speeches.

Here these speeches, because of their intensity and because of the gloomy view of human nature they convey, do seem to reflect something in Shakespeare's own life at this time. We don't know what it may have been, but *Macbeth* does seem a much more personal play than any of the other great tragedies. It is significant that most of the great speeches come from Macbeth himself, or from his 'dearest chuck', the wife who draws him on to murder.

Perhaps Shakespeare only meant to show a pair of murderers, but his genius achieved much more. This is a play about ambition and greed, yet it transcends those plain motives to investigate the darkest recesses of the human personality in a way that reminds me of the self-torturing characters of Dostoievsky more than of any other writer. It is a measure of the play's greatness that by the end of it we feel some deep sympathy for Macbeth and Lady Macbeth. They have done terrible things, but they remain symbols of our human condition. They are weak enough to believe in the false prophecies of the witches, yet universal enough to engage our sympathy and imagination. There are moments when all of us might have committed murder, for love or gain or ambition, if the circumstances had made it easy. Macbeth is a villain, but by the end of the play we feel that he's not fully responsible for his own actions as he is being driven by forces outside himself towards an inevitable doom. And Lady Macbeth has changed for us too, from the murderous harpy of the early scenes into a guilt-racked figure full of pathos and pity. Through her and through Macbeth, Shakespeare is exploring the idea that love can be totally destructive, even when it is completely sincere.

MACBETH

Sara Kestelman

Sara Kestelman has played Lady Macbeth for both the Birmingham Repertory Company and The Royal Shakespeare Company. Her other Shakespearean parts have included Titania and Hippolyta in Peter Brook's production of A Midsummer Night's Dream *and Rosalind in* As You Like It. *Her non-Shakespearean parts have included the Countess in* The Marquis of Keith.

FIRST WITCH: When shall we three meet again?
  In thunder, lightning, or in rain?
SECOND WITCH: When the hurlyburly's done,
  When the battle's lost and won.
THIRD WITCH: That will be ere the set of sun.
FIRST WITCH: Where the place?
SECOND WITCH: Upon the heath.
THIRD WITCH: There to meet with Macbeth.

I.I.I–7

Macbeth is a popular play, popular with audiences and performers – a thrilling, swiftly-moving, damned good yarn! Its very popularity of course makes it well-known. Most of us have either studied the play at school or seen it performed in theatres or on television. It has been variously treated in the cinema by Orson Welles, Roman Polanski and by the Japanese director Kurosawa in *The Throne of Blood*. It lends itself brilliantly to the screen because of the intensely dramatic presentation and rhythm of the play, particularly in the opening scenes, which fling us into an extraordinary time structure where scenes are happening, as it were, simultaneously and with astonishing rapidity and introduce us to the principal protagonists. So in Scene One (which is just thirteen lines long and contains some of the best known and most quoted lines of Shakespeare!) we meet the three witches, weird sisters, call them what you will, and as they vanish we immediately cut to Scene Two: Duncan; King; War; Victory. We're told that the Thane of Cawdor is a traitor and that Macbeth is a hero. We see King Duncan sending Ross to find Macbeth and to honour him with the title of Cawdor. Suddenly we are in Scene Three, back on the blasted heath with the three weird sisters, and now we meet Macbeth and Banquo and see these creatures confront the two men with extraordinary prophecies. And already we as an audience are on the edge of our seats because we know that Ross is about to tell Macbeth that he has been made the Thane of Cawdor, yet here are these strange creatures privy to this knowledge and predicting the future! Who are they? They tell Banquo that, though he is not destined to be king himself, he will beget kings and then again they simply vanish into the air. No sooner have they gone but Ross arrives with the news that Macbeth is Thane of Cawdor. It all happens so fast!

We are now allowed to hear how Macbeth receives all this astonishing information. We discover, in his first soliloquy, a man volatile in personality with a mind teeming with emotional and rational reactions:

> This supernatural soliciting
> Cannot be ill; cannot be good. If ill,
> Why hath it given me earnest of success,
> Commencing in a truth? I am Thane of Cawdor.
> If good, why do I yield to that suggestion
> Whose horrid image doth unfix my hair
> And make my seated heart knock at my ribs
> Against the use of nature? Present fears
> Are less than horrible imaginings.

1.3.130–8

He is shocked and confused, as if a hidden nerve or desire has somehow been exposed by these prophecies. We don't know yet how or why. We watch him recover and rejoin his friends. Then we are whisked away into Scene Four: Macbeth meeting Duncan and arranging for him to spend that night at Macbeth's castle. Then wham! – we are at Macbeth's castle and we see a woman in the midst of reading a letter describing the meeting with the witches. So we know that it's from Macbeth and from her response to the letter we discover the woman to be Lady Macbeth. Her reaction to the prophecies is very different from her husband's. She takes a swift, positive line, translating the contents of the letter into action, though precisely what action we don't yet know. So both partners have teased us with something deep within them yet still withheld from us. She is clever, witty, passionate, ambitious for her husband and for herself and with an intimate knowledge of her man. She affectionately and acerbically describes for us his strengths and weaknesses, as she sees them, and anticipates how he will react to the idea forming in her mind:

> Glamis thou art, and Cawdor; and shalt be
> What thou art promis'd. Yet do I fear thy nature;
> It is too full o' th' milk of human kindness
> To catch the nearest way. Thou wouldst be great;
> Art not without ambition, but without
> The illness should attend it.

1.5.12–17

In the space of five scenes we are privy to an intense relationship.

A servant brings the news that the King and Macbeth are on their way to the castle. We then witness a truly terrifying phenomenon: a woman defies nature, invokes spirits to dispossess her of all weakness and feminine frailty, or rather to possess her of sufficient cruelty to commit an act. We still don't know what. Brilliant, witty and remarkable as she may be, we're looking at a monster. No sooner has she committed words to air but her husband arrives and with disarming simplicity she tells him her plan – to kill the King! We see his doubt countered immediately by her resolve and suddenly we are into Scene Six with the arrival of Duncan. He is welcomed, wined, dined and after everyone has gone to bed we hear the first of the great Macbeth soliloquies (and we're still only twenty minutes or so into the play!):

> If it were done when 'tis done, then 'twere well
> It were done quickly. If th' assassination
> Could trammel up the consequence, and catch,
> With his surcease, success; that but this blow
> Might be the be-all and end-all here –
> But here upon this bank and shoal of time –
> We'd jump the life to come. But in these cases
> We still have judgment here, that we but teach
> Bloody instructions, which being taught return
> To plague th' inventor. This even-handed justice
> Commends th' ingredience of our poison'd chalice
> To our own lips. He's here in double trust:
> First, as I am his kinsman and his subject –
> Strong both against the deed; then, as his host,
> Who should against his murderer shut the door,
> Not bear the knife myself. Besides, this Duncan
> Hath borne his faculties so meek, hath been
> So clear in his great office, that his virtues
> Will plead like angels, trumpet-tongu'd, against

The deep damnation of his taking-off;
And pity, like a naked new-born babe,
Striding the blast, or heaven's cherubin hors'd
Upon the sightless couriers of the air,
Shall blow the horrid deed in every eye,
That tears shall drown the wind. I have no spur
To prick the sides of my intent, but only
Vaulting ambition, which o'er-leaps itself,
And falls on th'other.

1.7.1–28

Shakespeare is serving the actor here with breathtaking perception and painful self-analysis. We begin to share the torment of this man and mysteriously ally ourselves with him so that his dilemma becomes our dilemma, his conscience our conscience, unaware that we have shifted our moral standpoint. Astonishing!

Just as Macbeth has convinced himself that he can't, won't go through with this murder, in pops madam and with brilliant, unswerving and often cruel wit she works him, woos him, wins him and finally seduces him. She charts the lot with chilling clarity: she'll get the King's bodyguards drunk; she'll leave the daggers for Macbeth; she'll give him a signal by ringing a bell when everything is ready; Macbeth will go to Duncan's chamber, kill the King, daub the bodyguards with blood so that it will appear that they are the murderers – and there you are! Breathtakingly simple – the perfect crime! Will he do it or won't he? He resolves to, he prepares to, and then his imagination begins to play the first of some frightful tricks:

Is this a dagger which I see before me,
The handle toward my hand? Come, let me clutch thee.
I have thee not, and yet I see thee still.
Art thou not, fatal vision, sensible
To feeling as to sight? or art thou but
A dagger of the mind, a false creation,
Proceeding from the heat-oppressed brain?
I see thee yet, in form as palpable
As this which now I draw.
Thou marshall'st me the way that I was going;
And such an instrument I was to use.
Mine eyes are made the fools o' th' other senses,
Or else worth all the rest. I see thee still;
And on thy blade and dudgeon gouts of blood,
Which was not so before. There's no such thing:

It is the bloody business which informs
Thus to mine eyes.

2.1.33–49

Then the signal bell is rung! Will he do it or won't he?

He kills the King, but forgets to leave the daggers by the bodyguards. What's more, he thinks that he's heard a voice crying 'Macbeth shall sleep no more' and is so frightened that he refuses to return the daggers to the chamber. He seems to be at the very edge. With ferocious determination his wife takes the daggers from him and goes to Duncan's chamber. Suddenly there's a knocking at the castle gate and there they are with their hands covered in blood. Macbeth, paralysed, is unable to let go of his fears, wandering, wavering. How can they possibly get away with it? We now see Lady Macbeth at her most practical and her most prosaic:

> retire we to our chamber.
> A little water clears us of this deed.
> How easy is it then! Your constancy
> Hath left you unattended. Hark! more knocking.
> Get on your nightgown, lest occasion call us
> And show us to be watchers. Be not lost
> So poorly in your thoughts.

2.2.66–72

Within moments Macduff arrives to waken the King, goes to the chamber, finds the King murdered and then all hell is let loose. If we had feared for Macbeth's stability before, we're now amazed by his performance. He seems to act the part of horrified host superbly, but then he delivers a body-blow. He confesses to killing the bodyguards – not part of the plan at all and executed without consultation with Lady Macbeth. This, though neither she nor we know it, is the first of many solo decisions to come. It's debatable whether the decision to kill the bodyguards is well thought out or an emotional reaction on the spur of the moment, but it prompts the inevitable question 'why?' from Macduff. Macbeth finds himself having to defend himself in a dangerously embroidered display of self-justification. A mixture of genuine shock and alarm that he may be about to betray his complicity forces Lady Macbeth to shift the focus quickly by collapsing in a faint.

With the sudden departure of the King's two sons, Malcolm and Donalbain, suspicion from many falls on them and almost immediately Macbeth and his wife are crowned King and Queen. They seem to have got away with it! And we're still only a third of the way through the play – it all happens so incredibly fast! From this point on we are in the agony of watching how these two people cope with the 'fruits of their success' and the tremendous cost involved. We watch this stunningly matched couple become estranged and finally collapse. We see this once popular, dependable, honourable warrior and man at the mercy of his imagination, ambition and conscience deny himself the glory and joy of leadership and turn murderer accepting, even embracing, the consequences of his actions. Helpless voyeurs, we witness his terrifying breakdown at the banquet, the severing himself from his wife as he catapults into paranoia committing atrocity after atrocity: the desperate murder of Banquo, the botched attempt to kill Banquo's son Fleance and the ghastly, gratuitous killings of Lady Macduff and her children. Each scene tumbling upon the other, careering towards isolation, madness and inevitably death.

The supernatural in the play has been argued and discussed endlessly by scholars, actors, directors and students and, though the supernatural forces may have had a particular impact on Shakespeare's audience, they are as resonant today with our contemporary experience of mediums, tarot cards and seances. We know, for instance, that the desire for some people to communicate with the 'other world' can be as addictive as a drug. Macbeth sacrifices himself to the occult and, as his personality undergoes a sea-change as dramatic as Jekyll and Hyde, he is compelled to return to the witches. So confident is he now that when told by them that 'none of woman born shall harm Macbeth' he laughs, and dismisses as an impossibility their prophecy that Birnam Wood will move. Much later, his wife by this time dead, and finding himself isolated in his castle preparing for battle threatened by the approaching armies of Malcolm and Old Siward with Macduff, a servant rushes in to tell Macbeth that he has seen Birnam Wood begin to move! And when Macduff declares that he was 'from his mother's womb untimely ripped' our Faustus is face to face with the Devil and the bloody circle is complete.

I've played Lady Macbeth twice. She's a lonely character to live with and a disturbing creature to know. There are of course an infinite variety of interpretations, as with all great Shakespearean roles, but her inability to grasp the implications of how Duncan's murder will affect them and her refusal to see beyond the act itself, reveals to me a serious character deficiency that finally can barely be described as normal. Many famous and distinguished actors have played Macbeth and Lady Macbeth and in reading about past performances, or in conversation with actors and audiences, I've formed the impression that somehow people expect to see something which can be easily identified as evil. But what is 'Evil' and how does it manifest itself? If the expectation is that Lady Macbeth should be portrayed as a ferocious demon then the complex personality created by Shakespeare is diminished. Moreover, the delicate balance between her undoubted strength and Macbeth's swerving commitment is absolutely crucial if we are to be allowed to identify his own personal ambition at odds with his conscience. So, in my view, it is essential that neither the character of Macbeth nor the actor playing him should be seen to be emasculated by a tyrant. Let me try to elaborate what I mean. I read a fascinating account of various people's responses after meeting a woman imprisoned for a particularly unpleasant murder. Without exception each person had expected to confront 'Evil' and to their astonishment they found themselves in the presence of someone who appeared quiet, mild, highly intelligent, well-read, charming, gracious, utterly feminine and disarmingly articulate. So amazed were they that they found themselves seduced into perhaps reversing or anyway significantly altering their view of this person. Without doubt she had charisma, but she never ever demonstrated 'Evil'. Both this woman and Lady Macbeth are possessed of remarkable power. She's charming and her reward from Duncan is a great fat diamond! She's gracious, clever; seen from a certain viewpoint, she's brave and undoubtedly fiercely loyal, but her imagination is limited and naive, her vision tunnelled and she's insensitive to the fears that consume her husband. She appears to have no moral foundation upon which to base any judgement. She has no machinery to separate right from wrong and, possessed as she is with a relentless and all-consuming energy, she becomes a frighteningly powerful and dangerous weapon.

It has been suggested that some of Lady Macbeth's scenes are missing. There are, for instance, references to past conversations with Macbeth which we don't actually witness in the play. The absence of Lady Macbeth between the banquet and sleepwalking scene has also been used to support this view. Yet I have no doubt that the play is complete and intact. Its flow, rhythm and filmic technique are as spare as the situation requires, as rich as the moment needs. It is white, naked and raw with its own energy and momentum. All this is not accidental but quite deliberately and brilliantly conceived by Shakespeare.

By the banquet Macbeth and his wife could not have been

driven further apart. All her energy has always been channelled through and for him: without him she's nothing and before our very eyes she becomes nothing. Redundant, useless, broken, rejected and, in an astonishing psychological study, we witness the breakdown of a human being as we're presented with a warped flashback of the action, desperately revealed in her nightmare sleepwalking. George Bernard Shaw once advised an actress to concentrate all her creative energy on the scenes with Macbeth, begging her to leave the sleepwalking scene alone. 'It is brilliantly constructed and will play itself' I believe he said. And he was right. It required no embroidery, no pyrotechnics, it is what it is – deeply, deeply shocking. And how pathetic this Lady Macbeth is, how tender, how very very sad. Small wonder that not long afterwards she takes her own life – what little there is left of it:

MACBETH: Wherefore was that cry?
SEYTON: The Queen, my lord, is dead.
MACBETH: She should have died hereafter;
    There would have been a time for such a word.
    To-morrow, and to-morrow, and to-morrow,
    Creeps in this petty pace from day to day
    To the last syllable of recorded time,
    And all our yesterdays have lighted fools
    The way to dusty death.

                                        5.5.15–23

He's lost all power to feel, he's doomed. There is no excuse, no vindication for this woman or her husband, yet we feel inextricably involved. We've shared with a man intimate thoughts expressed with such poetic self-awareness, such vulnerability and such frankness that to witness his bloody, awful self-destruction is to witness a tragedy.

THE TWO GENTLEMEN OF VERONA

Russell Davies

Russell Davies is the television critic of The Sunday
Times *and a well-known presenter of radio and
television programmes. He made this programme on
location at St John's College, Cambridge.*

Verona must have been a beautiful place with its Renaissance
turrets, conspiratorial stairways, ancient squares and shadowy
arcades. But I have never been there and I think that it is highly
unlikely that William Shakespeare ever saw the place either. Far
from being familiar with Italy, he wasn't even very sure of the map.
If he had been, he would hardly have sent the central characters of
The Two Gentlemen of Verona from that city to Milan by sea. In
fact, it is a straight overland hop across the top of Italy which today
you can accomplish very speedily by means of the autostrada. So I
am not abroad, but in Cambridge, England. The time of year is
known hereabouts as May Week which, this being very English
England, is held in June. It is a season when this town, at least in
the environs of the University, tries to give the impression that
time is suspended. When the weather is right, there are parties all
afternoon in Elysian fields and gardens and in the evenings some
of the colleges, though not as many nor as lavishly as once upon a
time, hold a May Ball. Here the ladies come in their long dresses
and the gentlemen are dressed up like me, give or take the odd
monocle or opera cloak or pair of spats. You can walk around the
streets like this and nobody will stare at you because they know
exactly what you are up to. You are involved in a pleasurable ritual.
It is a convention. I don't know whether the ladies are inviting the
men these days. At sixty guineas a ticket, they would be well
advised to stick to the old-fashioned policy. But inviting someone
to these ostentatiously formal occasions is still a good way of
cementing a friendship or pursuing a friendship. It is also a good
place for the ageing outsider to watch these activities in progress.

Most young adults, like the undergraduates here at St John's
College, live their emotional lives on that rather exhausting

borderline between friendship and love. One factor or the other is always there to preoccupy you. The moral and social assumptions of our lives have changed a great deal since Shakespeare's time, but it is still true that friendship and love can make rival claims on the individual's conscience. To favour one is to neglect and possibly destroy the other. This was one of the obsessions of the Elizabethan age. A vast amount of writing was devoted to defining and proclaiming love, diagnosing it, indeed, as the disease it is so often said to be. Shakespeare wrote *The Two Gentlemen of Verona* in his own comparative youth. The play itself leaves you in no doubt that its subject is to be love and its distorting effect upon duty and loyalty. It also distorts language. In the first fifty lines of the play the word love itself, let alone its various derivatives, occurs fifteen times:

> PROTEUS: Wilt thou be gone? Sweet Valentine, adieu!
>   Think on thy Proteus, when thou haply seest
>   Some rare noteworthy object in thy travel.
>   Wish me partaker in thy happiness
>   When thou dost meet good hap; and in thy danger,
>   If ever danger do environ thee,
>   Commend thy grievance to my holy prayers,
>   For I will be thy beadsman, Valentine.
> VALENTINE: And on a love-book pray for my success?
> PROTEUS: Upon some book I love I'll pray for thee.
> VALENTINE: That's on some shallow story of deep love:
>   How young Leander cross'd the Hellespont.
> PROTEUS: That's a deep story of a deeper love;
>   For he was more than over shoes in love.
> VALENTINE: 'Tis true; for you are over boots in love,
>   And yet you never swum the Hellespont.
> PROTEUS: Over the boots! Nay, give me not the boots.
> VALENTINE: No, I will not, for it boots thee not.
> PROTEUS: What?
> VALENTINE: To be in love – I.I.II–29

Here, then, are the Two Gentlemen of Verona, so-called. I hear a slight ironic tinge in that title, but then I have probably lived too long in Cambridge where people have traditionally tut-tutted over the riotous tendencies of what they call the 'young gentlemen of the university'. Our two young men are called Valentine and Proteus, the names already implying what we should expect from them. Valentine, like the February saint, is a true and constant lover. Proteus, like his forebear in Greek mythology, tends to change his shape, or at least the shape of his mind.

Valentine is off to see the world at the Court of the Duke of
Milan. In Italy where Castiglione's *The Book of the Courtier* was the
modern manual of character-building, courtly life was seen as the
best education of all. Universities seem to have taken over that
position now and, indeed, university was an option even then. But
Proteus was denied all these possibilities, a disadvantage that his
family and servants were aware of:

> ANTONIO: Tell me, Panthino, what sad talk was that
>   Wherewith my brother held you in the cloister?
> PANTHINO: 'Twas of his nephew Proteus, your son.
> ANTONIO: Why, what of him?
> PANTHINO: He wond'red that your lordship
>   Would suffer him to spend his youth at home,
>   While other men, of slender reputation,
>   Put forth their sons to seek preferment out:
>   Some to the wars, to try their fortune there;
>   Some to discover islands far away;
>   Some to the studious universities.
>   For any, or for all these exercises,
>   He said that Proteus, your son, was meet;
>   And did request me to importune you
>   To let him spend his time no more at home,
>   Which would be great impeachment to his age,
>   In having known no travel in his youth.

1.3.1–16

But though Proteus has so far been denied experience at the
university of life, he is fortunate in one respect. He is in love. He is
unfortunate as well, of course, because love is a plague of sighings
and longings and general frustration. He shows all the conventional signs of the affliction. He sends, for example, the conven-
tionally passionate love letter, though he employs Valentine's
servant to deliver it. It is one of the pleasant, complicating features
of this play that people are always presenting their emotions by
proxy, in letters and songs and token rings.

The recipient of Proteus's letter is Julia. This is the young
woman who will be grievously wronged by Proteus and, although
one always has that romantic-story feeling that they will end up
together, one can't be all that pleased about it. She is the earliest of
the Shakespeare heroines who are what's known as a 'sparky' girl
and one simply feels that she deserves better than Proteus. If there
is one indication in the play that they are ultimately suited to each

other, it is in Julia's first scene when Proteus's letter arrives. Just as he is destined to change his mind about her, so she is unable to make her mind up about his love letter. At first she refuses to receive it, then she snatches it from her maid, Lucetta, then finally she tears it up before even reading it, a gesture she immediately regrets:

> But twice or thrice was 'Proteus' written down.
> Be calm, good wind, blow not a word away
> Till I have found each letter in the letter –
> Except mine own name; that some whirlwind bear
> Unto a ragged, fearful, hanging rock,
> And throw it thence into the raging sea.
> Lo, here in one line is his name twice writ:
> 'Poor forlorn Proteus, passionate Proteus,
> To the sweet Julia'. That I'll tear away;
> And yet I will not, sith so prettily
> He couples it to his complaining names.
> Thus will I fold them one upon another;
> Now kiss, embrace, contend, do what you will.

> 1.2.117–29

Julia's vacillating remorse is very prettily done by Shakespeare and it shows why the women in the play, or this woman at least, is a more successfully complex character than the men. She does not have to embody traditional virtues, or the lack of them, as they do, so her psychology can be more naturally presented. Mind you, there is the odd sign within the play that Shakespeare was acquainted with the traditional male's dim view of female psychology. He has the maid, Lucetta, say 'I have no other but a woman's reason:/ I think him so, because I think him so'. But then, as always with Shakespeare, his humanity overflows the vessel of convention.

Nor does he let the conventional heart-searching about love go maundering on unchallenged by cynics and peasant unbelievers. *The Two Gentlemen* has its full complement of clownish servants: Launce who is the servant of Proteus and Speed who attends, not always very closely, upon Valentine. Launce and Speed are the allies of that considerable part of Shakespeare's audience who will have felt that, although this love-and-duty stuff is all very fine and sometimes very beautiful, it is really the preserve of the privileged class who can afford to indulge it. Launce and Speed have what you might call an unexalted view of womankind. In fact, to call it down-to-earth would be putting it a bit high. Launce carries with him a written list of the vices and virtues of his intended and the two clowns go through this catalogue together, Speed doing the reading. It is a version of the 'first the good news, then the bad news' game:

> SPEED: 'Here follow her vices'.
>
> LAUNCE: Close at the heels of her virtues.
>
> SPEED: 'Item: she is not to be kiss'd fasting, in respect of her breath'.
>
> LAUNCE: Well, that fault may be mended with a breakfast. Read on.
>
> SPEED: 'Item: she hath a sweet mouth'.
>
> LAUNCE: That makes amends for her sour breath.
>
> SPEED: 'Item: she doth talk in her sleep'.
>
> LAUNCE: It's no matter for that, so she sleep not in her talk.
>
> SPEED: 'Item: she is slow in words'.
>
> LAUNCE: O villain, that set down among her vices! To be slow in words is a woman's only virtue. I pray thee, out with't; and place it for her chief virtue.
>
> SPEED: 'Item: She is proud'.
>
> LAUNCE: Out with that too; it was Eve's legacy, and cannot be ta'en from her.
>
> SPEED: 'Item: she hath no teeth'.
>
> LAUNCE: I care not for that neither, because I love crusts.
>
> SPEED: 'Item: she is curst'.
>
> LAUNCE: Well, the best is, she hath no teeth to bite.
>
> SPEED: 'Item: she will often praise her liquor'.
>
> LAUNCE: If her liquor be good, she shall; if she will not, I will; for good things should be praised.
>
> SPEED: 'Item: she is too liberal'.
>
> LAUNCE: Of her tongue she cannot, for that's writ down she is slow of; of her purse she shall not, for that I'll keep shut. Now of another thing she may, and that cannot I help. Well, proceed.

3.1.313–43

Much of what the servants do is a below-stairs travesty of the other action, but it does have its own lugubrious dignity as well. Take Launce's memorable, if theatrically risky, appearance with his dog, Crab. This is one of those grimly hilarious relationships that has not changed much in popular literature since the Middle Ages. Whenever I imagine Launce and Crab, the picture I see is of Dennis the Menace and his equally appalling hound, Gnasher. Launce spends his working days on the receiving end of a master-

and-servant relationship so, when he is alone with Crab, he naturally makes a meal of his unaccustomed position as the master. When the dog disgraces itself – and dogs in Shakespeare often stand for disgrace – it gives Launce a chance to feel doubly superior. Yet something within him is stirred to pity for the awful animal. Both he and it, after all, are in line for a whipping if they misbehave. Underdog doesn't eat dog, you might say. So, in the end, Launce takes the punishment on the dog's behalf. It is another of those instances in the play where a stand-in carries the can:

> You shall judge. He thrusts me himself into the company of three or four gentleman-like dogs under the Duke's table; he had not been there, bless the mark, a pissing while but all the chamber smelt him. 'Out with the dog' says one; 'What cur is that?' says another; 'Whip him out' says the third; 'Hang him up' says the Duke. I, having been acquainted with the smell before, knew it was Crab, and goes me to the fellow that whips the dogs. 'Friend', quoth I 'you mean to whip the dog'. 'Ay, marry do I' quoth he. 'You do him the more wrong;' quoth I ''twas I did the thing you wot of'. He makes me no more ado, but whips me out of the chamber. How many masters would do this for his servant? Nay, I'll be sworn, I have sat in the stocks for puddings he hath stol'n, otherwise he had been executed; I have stood on the pillory for geese he hath kill'd, otherwise he had suffer'd for't. Thou think'st not of this now. Nay, I remember the trick you serv'd me when I took my leave of Madam Silvia. Did not I bid thee still mark me and do as I do? When didst thou see me heave up my leg and make water against a gentlewoman's farthingale? Didst thou ever see me do such a trick?
>
> 4.4.14–36

There is something about Launce's comical self-sacrifice, high-principled yet sordid at the same time, that implies a whole structure of nature: not just the nitrogen cycle to which Crab has contributed, but a moral order in which man participates passionately, or cruelly, according to his temperament. Naturally nothing comes of these thoughts in a play which is in every way a comedy of immaturity, but in later years Shakespeare was to build them into the great theme of a tragedy as noble as *King Lear*.

It has rather been the fate of *The Two Gentlemen of Verona* to be seen as a forerunner of other achievements. There are more reminders of *Romeo and Juliet* than anything else. *Romeo and Juliet* is itself set in Verona, though it is only after the scene of *The Two*

Gentlemen shifts to Milan, confusingly enough, that the resemblances show. The same conspiratorial world of balconies, rope ladders and friars' cells is common to both plays. So what happend here? Valentine, as you would expect, falls in love with Silvia, the daughter of the Duke, when he arrives in Milan. She falls in love with him too and signals it by commissioning him to compose a love letter on her behalf, which she immediately hands back to him but he doesn't get it. It is one of those instances that has to be played rather carefully in case it dawns on the audience too soon that these young men are too obtuse to be taken seriously:

> VALENTINE: What means your ladyship? Do you not like it?
> SILVIA: Yes, yes; the lines are very quaintly writ;
>   But, since unwillingly, take them again.
>   Nay, take them.
> VALENTINE: Madam, they are for you.
> SILVIA: Ay, ay, you writ them, sir, at my request;
>   But I will none of them; they are for you:
>   I would have had them writ more movingly.
> VALENTINE: Please you, I'll write your ladyship another.
> SILVIA: And when it's writ, for my sake read it over;
>   And if it please you, so; if not, why, so.
> VALENTINE: If it please me, madam, what then?
> SILVIA: Why, if it please you, take it for your labour.
>   And so good morrow, servant.

2.1.110–23

Now Proteus arrives in Milan and, of course, he likewise falls in love with Silvia. His only way of advancing his own cause is to do down his old friend and this is where the duties of friendship take a clobbering from the demands of love. Proteus tells the Duke that Valentine plans to elope with Silvia, so Valentine is apprehended and banished to the surrounding woodland where he falls in with a band of comic opera brigands who appoint him their leader on the grounds that he can speak foreign languages. By now, though, one further convention has been piled on those we have already seen, which is that Julia has come from Verona – by road too which is curiously authentic of her – to Milan. She appears disguised as a page-boy, Sebastian, and is just in time to see her beloved Proteus pressing his suit, in that wonderful English phrase, with the beautiful Silvia. Proteus allows himself to be employed as a serenading minstrel on behalf of another suitor, an obvious no-hoper called Thurio, yet another example of the third party representative doing the emotional donkey work. But the justly famous aspect of the scene is the song itself, 'Who is Silvia?', ancestor of a thousand pop songs based on girls' names and a composition that has been set to music by more than fifty copyrighted composers. The most famous was, of course, Schubert, but every musical generation has taken its own delight in these, the purest verses in the play:

Who is Silvia? What is she,
    That all our swains commend her?
Holy, fair, and wise is she;
    The heaven such grace did lend her,
That she might admired be.

Is she kind as she is fair?
    For beauty lives with kindness.
Love doth to her eyes repair,
    To help him of his blindness;
And, being help'd, inhabits there.

Then to Silvia let us sing
    That Silvia is excelling;
She excels each mortal thing
    Upon the dull earth dwelling.
To her let us garlands bring.

4.2.38–53

This song is probably the one undisputedly successful feature of the play. It must seem like a consolation prize to the actress who plays Silvia because otherwise hers is a part that fizzles out rather strangely. In a way, she is too much like Proteus's mistaken view of her. Silvia is very much a love object to him. It is the beauty he perceives with the eye that he is smitten by, not any beauty of mind or soul within. If he can't have Silvia herself – and he can't – then he insists on having her picture which, one senses, he is nearly as much in love with as he is with the woman herself. The trouble is that Silvia who is rather underdone by Shakespeare does turn out like this: a bit cold and distant, a beautiful image-like apparition. In present-day terms, she would be a sort of sex symbol whose photograph is much passed around, but who is seldom to be seen in person.

The Two Gentlemen of Verona is a highly imperfect play and the critics have always treated it harshly, but with regretful harshness in some cases. Take Samuel Johnson. Dr Johnson said 'in this play there is a strange mixture of knowledge and ignorance, care and negligence'. Johnson points out, what is certainly true, that Proteus, having met Silvia and conversed with her, says that he has only seen her picture. It is a remark that it is difficult for an actor to bend into a metaphor. Then William Hazlitt says of the play 'this is little more than the first outlines of a comedy, loosely sketched in'. He finds plenty to praise in the poetry, though, and he does approve of the dog. But there are many more judgements in the archive far more savage than these and the real reason for them is the last scene in the play. I think that if some way could be found of removing or sidestepping this problem in production, then the whole reputation of this play would be instantly revived. As it is, *The Two Gentlemen of Verona* is rather rarely performed, which just puts you more in suspense about how this final scene is going to be treated. It is so condensed, possibly because there are bits missing, that it just seems to give the audience one slap in the face after another. Granted a grand reconciliation scene is inevitable once Silvia has fled from home and joined Valentine in his outlaw retreat and Proteus clearly has to be there, too, so that he can acknowledge the great wrong that he has done. But it is the way Valentine accepts his apology that causes the difficulty. It is not just amazingly abrupt, but is is followed by a self-sacrificing gesture so absurdly, destructively extravagant that it is as much as an audience can do to stop themselves leaping up and shouting 'no, no, you've got it wrong!'.

The revels here at the May Ball are ended for this year. Some of the participants will remember this as the place where they realised they were in love. Some may even have made their first commitment to a life's partner. We tend to think of it in terms of conscious commitment nowadays. We accept the mating urge as a permanent physical condition and treat the social contract – engagement and marriage – as a separate rational decision. It was different for the Elizabethans. They saw love as a syndrome, a concerted attack upon all the senses at once including the sense of self and the sense of citizenship. It was partly through their studies of love that they began the separation of moral philosophy from religion. It was, and is, a mountainous subject and it would be wrong to claim that Shakespeare had done much more than tackle a few friendly foothills in *The Two Gentlemen of Verona*. But when you know a man is capable of greatness, it is fascinating just to watch him in training even if he does run through some of the obstacles – obstacles which in later life he will vault with the most glorious authority and grace.

THE TWO GENTLEMEN OF VERONA

Geoffrey Hutchings

Geoffrey Hutchings is a member of the Royal Shake-speare Company. Apart from Launce in The Two Gentlemen of Verona, *his parts have included Bottom in* A Midsummer Night's Dream *and Autoclycus in* A Winter's Tale. *His non-Shakespearean roles have included Lady Dodo in* Poppy.

Do you remember the first time you were in love? Maybe it was a very long time ago, maybe it has yet to happen, maybe it is happening to you now for the very first time. It is an impossible state to describe. Our whole personality changes. We do silly things. There seems to be no reason for the way in which we behave. Reason in fact goes out of the window. For most of us this is a teenage experience. At a time when we are striving to cope with the enormous physiological changes that are happening to us, we are thrown headlong into a mental state of mind that renders all normal behaviour impossible.

The Two Gentlemen of Verona is an exploration of this unique and universal experience. I expect most of you think that you know nothing about this play which is, after all, one of Shakespeare's least known comedies. But do you remember singing 'Who is Sylvia?' in the school choir? You are probably still asking who Sylvia is. Well, that may become clear if I briefly outline the plot. Valentine and Proteus are the two gentlemen of the title who grew up together in Verona as firm friends. Valentine goes to Milan at the beginning of the play, leaving Proteus to moon over Julia, his love. Proteus is then ordered to follow Valentine. He reluctantly bids farewell to Julia and swears an oath of constancy to her. Meanwhile, in Milan, Valentine has fallen in love with the Duke's daughter, Sylvia. She has been promised to Thurio, but in fact loves Valentine. When Proteus arrives, Valentine confides to him about his love for Sylvia and how it has had to be concealed from the Duke. Despairing of ever getting the Duke's approval, the two lovers are planning to escape that night to Mantua. Proteus, infatuated by Sylvia at first sight, proves a faithless lover and a false friend by revealing the planned elopement to the Duke, who banishes Valentine. Meanwhile, Julia arrives, disguised as a boy, and secures a post for herself as Proteus's page. She soon discovers his love for Sylvia. Her only consolation is that Sylvia does not return his love. Valentine, on leaving Milan, is set upon by robbers who make him an offer he can't refuse: either he lives with them and becomes their leader or they will kill him! Sylvia decides to follow Valentine and is captured by the same robbers. Proteus, accompanied by Julia as his page, arrives in time to rescue her. He then tries to win her love by force, watched by the concealed Valentine who intervenes in time. Rejected by his friend, Proteus begs forgiveness. Valentine recognises the sincerity of his repentance and so reaffirms their friendship. Julia then reveals her identity and finally the lovers are reunited: Julia with Proteus, Sylvia with Valentine. That's the plot.

One of the problems a modern-day audience is faced with is the sudden change that takes place from one mood to another. So it has to be remembered that the play is about adolescent love and irrational behaviour. We should also remember that the Elizabethans had the mercurial ability to change from mood to mood far more quickly than we do today. They were far more 'Latin' in their temperament than we post-Victorians. The play runs the gamut of love from Proteus's naive and immature love for Julia to the ultimate example of unconditional love when at the end of the play Valentine forgives Proteus. Here are some examples of the different kinds of love that we find in the play. This is how Proteus describes his love for Julia:

Thou, Julia, thou hast metamorphis'd me,
Made me neglect my studies, lose my time,
War with good counsel, set the world at nought;
Made wit with musing weak, heart sick with thought.

1.1.66–9

Then there is Julia's love for Proteus:

Lo, here in one line is his name twice writ:
'Poor forlorn Proteus, passionate Proteus,
To the sweet Julia'. That I'll tear away;
And yet I will not, sith so prettily
He couples it to his complaining names.
Thus will I fold them one upon another;
Now kiss, embrace, contend, do what you will.   1.2.123–9

Proteus himself comments on the unpredictability of love:

> Thus have I shunn'd the fire for fear of burning,
> And drench'd me in the sea, where I am drown'd.
> I fear'd to show my father Julia's letter,
> Lest he should take exceptions to my love;
> And with the vantage of mine own excuse
> Hath he expected most against my love.
> O, how this spring of love resembleth
> The uncertain glory of an April day,
> Which now shows all the beauty of the sun,
> And by and by a cloud takes all away!
>
> 1.3.78–87

Speed, Valentine's servant, comments on the transparency of love when asked by his master 'how know you that I am in love?':

> Marry, by these special marks: first, you have learn'd, like Sir Proteus, to wreath your arms like a malcontent; to relish a love-song, like a robin redbreast; to walk alone, like one that had the pestilence; to sigh, like a school-boy that had lost his ABC; to weep, like a young wench that had buried her grandam; to fast, like one that takes diet; to watch, like one that fears robbing; to speak puling, like a beggar at Hallowmas. You were wont, when you laughed, to crow like a cock; when you walk'd, to walk like one of the lions; when you fasted, it was presently after dinner; when you look'd sadly, it was for want of money. And now you are metamorphis'd with a mistress, that, when I look on you, I can hardly think you my master.
>
> 2.1.16–28

Love is also shown as being fickle. On leaving Julia, Proteus swears his oath:

> Here is my hand for my true constancy;
> And when that hour o'erslips me in the day
> Wherein I sigh not, Julia, for thy sake,
> The next ensuing hour some foul mischance
> Torment me for my love's forgetfulness!
>
> 2.2.8–12

Yet two scenes later he meets Sylvia and it is love at first sight:

> Even as one heat another heat expels
> Or as one nail by strength drives out another,
> So the remembrance of my former love
> Is by a newer object quite forgotten.   2.4.188–91

He struggles to make sense of his behaviour, both as a lover and a friend:

> Methinks my zeal to Valentine is cold,
> And that I love him not as I was wont.
> O! but I love his lady too too much,
> And that's the reason I love him so little.

2.4.199–202

Then there is the single-minded strength of Julia's love:

> The more thou dam'st it up, the more it burns.
> The current that with gentle murmur glides,
> Thou know'st, being stopp'd, impatiently doth rage;
> But when his fair course is not hindered,
> He makes sweet music with th' enamell'd stones,
> Giving a gentle kiss to every sedge
> He overtaketh in his pilgrimage;
> And so by many winding nooks he strays,
> With willing sport, to the wild ocean.
> Then let me go, and hinder not my course.
> I'll be as patient as a gentle stream,
> And make a pastime of each weary step,
> Till the last step have brought me to my love;
> And there I'll rest as, after much turmoil,
> A blessed soul doth in Elysium.

2.7.24–38

We are also given an example of what an Elizabethan lover might do if he wanted to woo by the book. Valentine instructs the Duke:

> VALENTINE: Win her with gifts, if she respect not words:
>   Dumb jewels often in their silent kind
>   More than quick words do move a woman's mind.
> DUKE: But she did scorn a present that I sent her.
> VALENTINE: A woman sometime scorns what best contents her.
>   Send her another; never give her o'er,
>   For scorn at first makes after-love the more.
>   If she do frown, 'tis not in hate of you,
>   But rather to beget more love in you;
>   If she do chide, 'tis not to have you gone,
>   For why the fools are mad if left alone.

3.1.89–99

But for me the outstanding love relationship in the play, which is a microcosm of all the others, is the love between Launce and his dog. Maybe Launce didn't appreciate what he was letting himself in for when he saved Crab from drowning when he was a puppy, but since then their relationship has followed almost to the letter the marriage ceremony: 'for better or for worse, for richer for poorer, in sickness and in health, till death do us part . . .'. Their relationship demonstrates the ultimate in self-sacrifice:

> When a man's servant shall play the cur with him, look you, it goes hard – one that I brought up of a puppy; one that I sav'd from drowning, when three or four of his blind brothers and sisters went to it. I have taught him, even as one would say precisely 'Thus I would teach a dog'. I was sent to deliver him as a present to Mistress Silvia from my master; and I came no sooner into the dining-chamber, but he steps me to her tren-cher and steals her capon's leg. O, 'tis a foul thing when a cur cannot keep himself in all companies! I would have, as one should say, one that takes upon him to be a dog indeed, to be, as it were, a dog at all things. If I had not had more wit than he, to take a fault upon me that he did, I think verily he had been hang'd for't; sure as I live, he had suffer'd for't. You shall judge. He thrusts me himself into the company of three or four gentlemen-like dogs under the Duke's table; he had not been there, bless the mark, a pissing while but all the chamber smelt him. 'Out with the dog' says one; 'What cur is that?' says another; 'Whip him out' says the third; 'Hang him up', says the Duke. I, having been acquainted with the smell before, knew it was Crab, and goes me to the fellow that whips the dogs. 'Friend', quoth I "you mean to whip the dog'. 'Ay, marry do I' quoth he. 'You do him the more wrong;' quoth I 'twas I did the thing you wot of'. He makes me no more ado, but whips me out of the chamber. How many masters would do this for his servant? Nay, I'll be sworn, I have sat in the stocks for puddings he hath stol'n, otherwise he had been executed; I have stood on the pillory for geese he hath kill'd, otherwise he had suffer'd for't. Thou think'st not of this now. Nay, I remember the trick you serv'd me when I took my leave of Madam Silvia. Did not I bid thee still mark me and do a I do? When didst thou see me heave up my leg and make water against a gentlewoman's farthingale? Didst thou ever see me do such a trick?

4.4.1–36

I have played Launce twice now and I know from bitter experience how vital it is to cast the right dog for the part. It must be a dog, not a bitch, and a mangy looking dog to boot. It has to be a real pub dog. My first dog was like that and we built up a good working relationship. The second dog was a huge old English sheepdog bitch, neurotic and very bad casting. Apart from anything else it was difficult to know which way it was facing.

For me, the play has an inspiring message that there is no such thing as unrequited love. Shakespeare's concept of love is greater than the notion of romantic love. Many of us have felt that by loving someone, we were losing a piece of ourselves by exposing ourselves to hurt. Yet Shakespeare is saying that there is no such thing as a vacuum in love. We never lose out, but can only gain if we love and trust each other. Love enduring all, suffering all, giving all, forgiving all:

Who by repentance is not satisfied
Is nor of heaven, nor earth. . . .

5.4.79–80

PERICLES

P. J. Kavanagh

P. J. Kavanagh is a poet whose Selected Poems *was published in 1982. He has also written novels, such as the highly acclaimed* A Song and Dance. *He made this programme on location at the Minach Theatre, Porthcurno, Cornwall.*

Shakespeare was moving on to something new when he wrote Pericles. He had written his comedies, his histories, and his tragedies about flawed heroes. He had written, in short, about the things of this world with this world's limitations. We sense that he now wants to turn his imagination free from bonds of time and place, and now we find that after a hard, ambitious and successful life he has not become jaded and cynical or embittered. On the contrary, he seems to have become more hopeful and, in a sense, more of a poet than he had ever been. This is the period that culminates, we believe, in *The Tempest*, that play of music and magic, of reunion and the final resolution of difficulties, of young love and middle-aged forgiveness. There is nothing sentimental or easy about this escape from realism, no self-delusion or funking of reality but, rather, a transcendence: a seeing so clearly and deeply into human life that we are taken above and beyond it to a glimpse of some guessed-at final harmony, to the sound of the music of the spheres. That is what I mean when I say, rather absurdly, that Shakespeare became even more of a poet than before. Because at the heart of poetry, its essence perhaps, is this search for harmony and shape: exasperation and despair, certainly, at its absence, nevertheless a belief that somehow it exists. *Pericles* is Shakespeare's first attempt to turn his imagination loose and to free it along these lines.

As he usually did, Shakespeare went back to an old story for his plot – if *Pericles* can be said to have a plot at all. Shakespeare is moving away even from that. What he chose for his framework was one of the most popular stories of the Middle Ages, *The Romance of Apollonius of Tyre*. He puts it into the mouth of the old poet, John Gower (who had told it himself a couple of hundred years before) to distance himself and his audience from this story. He, as it were, 'alienates' us from it by warning that what is going to unroll before us is more in the nature of a pageant, to be done in dance, music and mime:

> To sing a song that old was sung,
> From ashes ancient Gower is come,
> Assuming man's infirmities,
> To glad your ear and please your eyes.
> It hath been sung at festivals,
> On ember-eves and holy-ales;
> And lords and ladies in their lives
> Have read it for restoratives.
> The purchase is to make men glorious;
> Et bonum quo antiquius, eo melius.

1–10

'The older a good thing is, the better it is', says Gower in Latin, telling the audience in an old language that they are going to hear an old story they probably know already and alerting them, surely, to pay less attention to the story than to what the dramatist is going to make of it.

The play begins with Pericles, Prince of Tyre, away from home, attempting to win a bride. To do so, he must first solve a riddle, on pain of death if he fails. On such an unpromisingly archaic note does the play begin. He does solve the riddle. The answer to it is fairly obvious, but unfortunately makes it impossible for him to marry the girl because it reveals that she has been committing incest with her father:

> PERICLES: Fair glass of light, I lov'd you, and could still,
> Were not this glorious casket stor'd with ill.
> But I must tell you now my thoughts revolt;
> For he's no man on whom perfections wait
> That, knowing sin within, will touch the gate.
> You are a fair viol, and your sense the strings;
> Who, finger'd to make man his lawful music,
> Would draw heaven down, and all the gods, to hearken;
> But, being play'd upon before your time,
> Hell only danceth at so harsh a chime.

1.1.76–85

This is the first reference to music in a play bursting with such references, and with music and harmony themselves. Here sin has put the music out of tune. Pericles flees the anger of the King, who is angry because his shameful secret has been discovered and, for the first time in the play but certainly not for the last, Pericles takes to the sea.

The sea is almost a central character in the play from now on. We can feel its presence all the time, and are meant to. There is a sense of warm salt, white ribbed sands and sea-girt statues with that strange archaic smile, but that is not because these things are Greek but because they are timeless. This is the sea of life, with its storms and calms, its shipwrecks and disasters, its slow, steady pulse and magical restitutions! the sea as a repository of power and mystery. Pericles moves from place to place about this sea and this world as though it is a unity, and speaks the same language; which to some extent the ancient world was, and did. He is subject to the moods of the sea, which are those of life. He comes upon famine, for this world is not a good or easy place, and relieves it with stores from his ships. In other words, he is being presented to us as a personification of the good man worked on by the apparent hostility of the world; or by what in this play amounts to the same thing, the caprices of the sea.

But he is a passive sufferer, unlike most other Shakespearean heroes. His sufferings are not his own fault and in this way he can stand for man in general rather than as a particular man with particular faults. Pericles in fact appears to have no faults. Gower comes on again at the beginning of the next act to suggest how man should deal with these undeserved sufferings:

> Be quiet, then, as men should be,
> Till he hath pass'd necessity.
> I'll show you those in troubles reign,
> Losing a mite, a mountain gain.

5–8

In other words, do not complain, as most Shakespearean heroes do. Then Gower, or rather the playwright, will show us 'those in troubles reign,/ Losing a mite, a mountain gain'. This is the announcement of a key theme of the play, the value of patience: when all seems lost it may only be a little thing or 'mite' and the sufferer may have gained a 'mountain'. In the last act Shakespeare, as only he could do, sets about showing us how this may be so.

But, to go back to the beginning, when Pericles receives the news that he is being pursued by the incestuous King he is told this in mime. This is astonishing because here is Shakespeare at the height of his powers going back to the rather clumsy convention of the medieval morality play. It is true, of course, that in courtly masques and revels they used dumb show and mime, but I think that it is clear that he is pointing backwards to an earlier time. I think this is another suggestion – and there are many such in *Pericles* – that he is concerned with timelessness, and not with ordinary events at all; with experiences which are somehow beyond words in the way that music moves beyond words.

Straightaway Pericles suffers one of his many storms at sea and at once the note of patience, already struck by Gower, is brought in:

> Yet cease your ire, you angry stars of heaven!
> Wind, rain, and thunder, remember earthly man
> Is but a substance that must yield to you;
> And I, as fits my nature, do obey you.

2.1.1–4

He does not defy or rebuke the tempest like King Lear. He submits to it. Perhaps because of this patience the sea does not only destroy, it also yields up. Some fisherman finds the much-treasured armour of Pericles's father, so that not all organic continuity with the past is lost: for although he is destitute he has his father's armour, in which he is able to woo and win the daughter of the local king. If Pericles has a foible, it is that he seems to fall in love very easily. Yet we have already been warned against naturalistic quibbles in such a play, and the stylised competition for the princess's hand, which also takes place in dumb show, makes this warning even more obvious. Although there is a continuity inside time because her father reminds Pericles of his own father, the wooing itself takes place as though outside time, and beyond words, with dancing and music.

But all is not happiness and harmony, or not yet. We now come to Act Three. We need to say, that from this point in the play, the language and subtlety suddenly take a great leap upwards. The contrast with what has gone before is very marked and it is possible that Shakespeare did not write the first two acts. Scholars have argued about it for years, but we need not make too much of this because we can at least allow that Shakespeare knew what he was doing. If he did not write the first two acts, he was obviously happy to use them. They suited him as a launching pad for the last great scenes, so he let them stand. Act Three finds Pericles at sea, with his pregnant wife, journeying home. They are caught in a storm and his wife dies in childbirth. Her body is put in a bitumined cask, to preserve it, and entrusted to the waves, while the widowed Pericles and his infant daughter take refuge further along the coast. Unknown to him, this cask containing his wife is washed ashore. She is then revived by a ceremonious old man appropriately called Cerimon. She is revived by knowledge for, as he says, he has 'turned over' many books, and also, of course, by music and harmony:

> CERIMON: The music there! I pray you give her air.
>   Gentlemen,
>   This queen will live; nature awakes; a warmth
>   Breathes out of her. She hath not been entranc'd
>   About five hours. See how she gins to blow
>   Into life's flower again!
> IST GENTLEMAN: The heavens,
>   Through you, increase our wonder, and set up
>   Your fame for ever.
> CERIMON: She is alive. Behold,
>   Her eyelids, cases to those heavenly jewels
>   Which Pericles hath lost, begin to part
>   Their fringes of bright gold; the diamonds
>   Of a most praised water do appear,
>   To make the world twice rich. Live, and make
>   Us weep to hear your fate, fair creature,
>   Rare as you seem to be.
> THAISA: O dear Diana, where am I?
>   Where's my lord? What world is this?

> 3.2.96–III

So the first words of his wife, Thaisa, when she comes round, are 'O dear Diana', addressed to the Goddess. Shakespeare is not concerned with any specifically Christian allegory of suffering and renewal, nor would he have been allowed to be so on the secular stage, although that is the tradition of mystical insight in which he lived. However, from now on the references to the gods are frequent and insistent.

Now, with the help of Gower, we jump fourteen years. Marina, the sea-born daughter of Pericles, is brought up in Tarsus, where she becomes adept (of course) at music. Pericles, separated from her, reigns in Tyre. Marina is so entrancing a girl that her guardian becomes jealous of her and decides to have her murdered, but before this can happen she is captured by pirates and sold into a brothel in Mytilene.

The contrast is shocking, from a storm-tossed idyll to the sweaty stews, and Shakespeare, returning to realism, enjoys himself. It would have been easy for him to highlight the virtue of

Marina against the obvious vice of her captors, but he doesn't because he rather enjoys them. He allows the pimps and bawds to condemn themselves out of their own mouths and to show the audience their tragi-comic benightedness and moral narrowness. Interestingly, it is not virtue that is seen as constricting or constricted, but vice. Marina's virtue is so eloquent in the brothel that we believe in it and in her. How good Shakespeare is at intelligent, virtuous young girls! You feel he must have had some happy experiences, and, notice how often he returns to the relationship of father and daughter. This play, for example, begins with a father and daughter whose nearness has corrupted them and it ends with a daughter being the means of her own father's resurrection.

We learn from the trusty Gower that Pericles now believes Marina dead. We see him, again in dumb show, putting on sackcloth and we learn that he has vowed never to wash or cut his hair again. He has withdrawn from the world. He is, apparently, finished. A ship bearing this dishevelled, dumb Pericles puts in to Mytilene for stores. The governor of the town comes on board and, seeing a princely personage in such a condition, it occurs to him that the one person who might be able to charm him out of it would be Marina, who has charmed him and the rest of the town with her music, conversation and sweet harmony of spirit. She is sent for and comes on board. The scene is set for the last great operatic act – the point, one feels, of the play. Marina sings to Pericles. The text of the song, alas, has not come down to us. But it seems not to work. Pericles pushes her away and this offends her because she replies rather proudly with hints of her own lineage and suffering. He is not the only grand person who has suffered, she seems to be telling him. So, at last, Pericles looks at her and something stirs in him. He says,

> Pray you turn your eyes upon me.
> You are like something that – What countrywoman?
> Here of these shores? 5.1.100–2

The dawn of Pericles's belief that this is indeed his daughter is slow and full of the kind of emotional suspense beloved of audiences, for after all we are in the secret as Marina and Pericles are not. It is so psychologically and dramatically paced that it is one of the great Shakespearean scenes. We share Pericles's disbelief because, after all, the reunion is very unlikely. We rejoice as his incredulity slowly diminishes, as step by step he tests the ground in front of him, as it were, and finds that it holds:

MARINA: Is it no more to be your daughter than
    To say my mother's name was Thaisa?
    Thaisa was my mother, who did end
    The minute I began.
PERICLES: Now blessing on thee! Rise; thou art my child.
    Give me fresh garments. Mine own, Helicanus –
    She is not dead at Tharsus, as she should have been
    By savage Cleon. She shall tell thee all;
    When thou shalt kneel, and justify in knowledge
    She is thy very princess. Who is this?
HELICANUS: Sir, 'tis the Governor of Mytilene,
    Who, hearing of your melancholy state,
    Did come to see you.
PERICLES: I embrace you.
    Give me my robes. I am wild in my beholding.
    O heavens bless my girl! But hark, what music?
    Tell Helicanus, my Marina, tell him
    O'er, point by point, for yet he seems to doubt
    How sure you are my daughter. But, what music?
HELICANUS: My lord, I hear none.
PERICLES: None?
    The music of the spheres! List, my Marina.
LYSIMACHUS: It is not good to cross him; give him way.
PERICLES: Rarest sounds! Do ye not hear?
LYSIMACHUS: My lord, I hear.
PERICLES: Most heavenly music!
    It nips me unto list'ning, and thick slumber
    Hangs upon mine eyes: let me rest.

5.1.208–33

At last, there it is – the music of the spheres. Only Pericles can hear, and possibly Marina. Only they are pure enough to have access to an eternal, underlying harmony which, like patience, smiles on suffering and transcends it.

But this is not all. Pericles is summoned in a dream to the Temple of Diana where he is reunited with his supposedly dead wife. This reunion, taking place in a temple, is explicitly religious. When Pericles sees his wife, his first words are addressed not to her but to the Goddess. It is much more than a conventional happy ending: suffering has, literally, changed them all beyond recognition. They are all sea-changed. Marina was sea-born, Thaisa was cast up by the sea and the sea and its effects have so battered Pericles that he is now like a man cleansed, purged and salted until his ears are keen enough to hear the divine harmoniousness to which others are deaf.

More than 200 years later, Matthew Arnold described the sea thus:

> Listen! you hear the grating roar
> Of pebbles which the waves draw back and fling,
> At their return, up the high strand,
> Begin, and cease, and then begin again,
> With tremendous cadence slow, and bring
> The eternal note of sadness in.

That is not Shakespeare's note in *Pericles*. There is incest, attempted murder, disease, famine and lust. There is bereavement and unendurable grief. There is also patience, music, harmony and redemption. There is no sadness. As Gower told us at the beginning, 'the purchase is to make men glorious'.

PERICLES

Amanda Redman

Amanda Redman played Marina in the BBC TV production of Pericles. *She has also played leading roles in* Richard's Things *and* Oxbridge Blues.

Ben Jonson apparently thought that *Pericles* was a 'mouldy tale'. It didn't strike me that way, even though the first time I ever came across it was on the read through for the BBC Television production. I was surprised how much it made me laugh even though we were just stumbling through it. It was also easy to follow. It is a crowded story but not a complex one. It pulls you along with it because you can't predict what is coming next. *Pericles* isn't fundamentally comic or tragic. It's a Romance, a story about love, loss and restoration with something to suggest about the rise and fall of fortune. It follows that rhythm all the way through with Pericles falling in love with someone and then losing her, falling in love with somebody else and losing her and then losing his daughter and being totally heartbroken because of it. At the end he gets restored, not only to his daughter and his wife, but to his former self. He becomes a whole man again. Although he is impulsive and perhaps lacks wisdom, he is essentially a good man. What befalls him isn't due to any fault of his own. We see him grow up the hard way. He starts off as this boy about town, this have-a-go Jack the lad, and finishes with a daunting realisation of what life can do to you.

This play, like all good stories, gets down to business right away with an extravagant fairy tale beginning. Pericles, Prince of Tyre, sails into Antioch. He has heard of the sumptuous beauty of the daughter of King Antiochus and he goes there knowing that all her previous suitors have been given a riddle to work out. If they get it wrong, and it seems that they all have, their heads are chopped off and displayed round the city. It is as if the King didn't want his daughter to marry and when Pericles sees the riddle the truth dawns on him:

I am no viper, yet I feed
On mother's flesh which did me breed.
I sought a husband, in which labour
I found that kindness in a father.
He's father, son, and husband mild;
I mother, wife, and yet his child.
How they may be, and yet in two,
As you will live, resolve it you.

1.1.64–71

As riddles go, it is not too difficult to infer the incestuous relationship between the King and his daughter. Pericles tries to hide
the fact that he's tumbled to the answer. You might wonder why
the King takes the risk of having his dark secret written up in a
word game, but it takes Pericles about two seconds to realise that it
is a game that can't be won. Nobody is meant to get out alive.
Antiochus confirms this later in the scene:

He hath found the meaning,
For which we mean to have his head.
He must not live to trumpet forth my infamy,
Nor tell the world Antiochus doth sin
In such a loathed manner;
And therefore instantly this prince must die;
For by his fall my honour must keep high.

1.1.143–9

Our young adventurer makes a quick escape back home to Tyre,
but he's followed by an assassin, the long arm of Antiochus.
Realising that Antiochus might even send an army and destroy his
city, Pericles decides to go into exile for the time being and takes to
the sea. It is a curious and isolated episode. We don't hear
anymore about it, except to learn much later that Antiochus has
died. But this first adventure sets the pace and is the first link in a
chain of events that wouldn't otherwise happen.

The story of Pericles, originally a Greek tale, had been in
existence since Classical times. It was revived in the fourteenth
century by the English poet John Gower in his *Confessio Amantis*.
It reappeared in 1576 as *The Pattern of Painful Adventures* by
Lawrence Twine and as a novel by George Wilkins in 1608.
Shakespeare's version, or alleged version, was published the very
next year so it is a late play. I say alleged version because the play's
authenticity is surrounded by mystery. It is generally agreed that in
the first two acts there is not a lot that is recognisable as Shakespeare's own work. One theory suggests that the play was pirated

by two different people, one of whom did an incompetent job. Others have wondered if it is the work of two writers badly patched together. If it was pirated, Shakespeare's company (The King's Men) never replaced it with an authentic version, which they had done on previous occasions. It does not appear in the 1623 Folio. The result is what one critic has called 'a submerged play', like a rich landscape that's been silted up. You don't have to be a scholar to read the play through and see what this critic meant: a lot of the language, certainly in the first two acts, is plain, pedestrian and sometimes downright clumsy. It does its job, but doesn't have any of that Shakespearean flair about it, the surefooted way with words that you start to discover from Act Three onwards. But I wonder how much it matters? Obviously one feels cheated knowing that Shakespeare may have written a better and richer piece than what we have now. But the experience of reading the play from a printed page, when you've got time to pause and ponder, is quite different from the experience of seeing and hearing it. However much it worries the scholar, the actor has got to pull it together and make it work. It's the way you tell it, as they say, and, whatever is missing from the poetry, the story is still intact. It is a racy yarn full of vigour and intense emotion.

Another unusual feature about *Pericles* is the way it uses a story teller. Shakespeare often resorts to choruses, prologues and epilogues, but here the whole structure is dependent on a narrator. He is Old Gower, or John Gower the poet whose version of the story is being used. He would have been sitting front-stage, I imagine, like a master of ceremonies, being rather chummy with his audience and waving actors on and off. At three points the stage directions give detailed instructions for a dumb show, which is a mime to illustrate the story teller's words. In fact some quite major events are covered in this way, rather than being dramatised. It's like being taken through a photograph album, dwelling on some things and skipping through others. This gives a cinematic pace to what could otherwise be something of a marathon. Incidentally, the use of narration and mime seems to have been a deliberate harking back to a more primitive style of presentation. Gower says right at the beginning 'if you, born in those latter times,/ When wit's more ripe, accept my rhymes', which is perhaps a dig in the ribs for the fashionable Ben Jonson fans.

Pericles is at sea. A great storm blows up and he is shipwrecked. He is washed up on a strange coast where he meets three fishermen:

1ST FISHERMAN: . . . this is call'd Pentapolis, and our king the good Simonides.

PERICLES: The good Simonides, do you call him?

1ST FISHERMAN: Ay, sir; and he deserves so to be call'd for his peaceable reign and good government.

PERICLES: He is a happy king, since he gains from his subjects the name of good by his government. How far is his court distant from this shore?

1ST FISHERMAN: Marry, sir, half a day's journey; and I'll tell you, he hath a fair daughter, and to-morrow is her birthday, and there are princes and knights come from all parts of the world to joust and tourney for her love.

PERICLES: Were my fortunes equal to my desires, I could wish to make one there.

1ST FISHERMAN: O sir, things must be as they may; and what a man cannot get he may lawfully deal for – his wife's soul.

2ND FISHERMAN: Help, master, help! Here's a fish hangs in the net like a poor man's right in the law; 'twill hardly come out. Ha! Bots on't! 'Tis come at last, and 'tis turn'd to a rusty armour.

2.1.98–117

Well, it is rusty armour – Pericles's own armour left to him by his father. The fishermen agree to hand it over, if he comes back and repays them when he can. So he makes his way to the court at Pentapolis to join the tournament and to get him a princess. There follow two very gentle and rather whimsical scenes with Pericles tattered and covered in rust, causing a lot of polite amusement, but of course winning the tournament and the hand of Princess Thaisa. More than that, he wins her heart as well. They fall head-over-heels in best Cartland tradition.

But it doesn't last. The story teller whips us away from golden romance to black catastrophe. Thaisa is pregnant and goes into labour on the homeward journey by sea to Tyre at the height of another great storm. The nurse comes to Pericles:

LYCHORIDA: Here is a thing too young for such a place,
　　Who, if it had conceit, would die, as I
　　Am like to do. Take in your arms this piece
　　Of your dead queen.

PERICLES:　　　　　　　How, how, Lychorida?

LYCHORIDA: Patience, good sir; do not assist the storm.
　　Here's all that is left living of your queen –
　　A little daughter. For the sake of it,

Be manly, and take comfort.
PERICLES: O you gods!
Why do you make us love your goodly gifts,
And snatch them straight away? We here below
Recall not what we give, and therein may
Use honour with you.   3.1.15–26

The sailors insist that Thaisa must be buried at sea because of a superstition: 'the wind is loud, and will not lie till the ship be clear'd of the dead'. The grief-stricken Pericles throws the coffin overboard and makes for Tarsus where he put the newborn Marina into the care of Cleon the Governor. I shall leave you to discover how the coffin of Thaisa drifts ashore into caring and friendly hands. At this point Pericles's world has been blown apart and he disappears into a kind of limbo.

In the second half of the play, from Act Four onwards, the focus shifts very much onto Pericles's daughter, Marina. A long time has passed and she is now fourteen (though in our production we have discreetly made it seventeen). Old Gower tells us that she is a clever girl, obviously well brought up in Cleon's house. She is accomplished in the arts – weaving, embroidery and singing to the lute – and devout on her spiritual allegiance to Diana, Goddess of chastity. But straight away black villainy is abroad in the shape of a jealous foster mother, who provides another of the play's fairy tale elements. Cleon's wife, Dionyza, is obsessively jealous of Marina because she outshines their own daughter in all her accomplishments. So Dionyza arranges to have Marina taken out and killed by a servant, even though she knows that Pericles is expected any day now to take his daughter back. Marina's murder would therefore be pointless in any practical sense. It is an act of pure evil and insane revenge. It seems to suggest that evil doesn't have to be purposeful or deserved, it just is and it comes like a bolt from the blue.

There is nothing weak or wilting about Marina. Certain things are of course expected of a romantic heroine: to be virtuous, courageous, steadfast and resourceful in defending her honour and integrity. Shakespeare manages to make her achieve these qualities without seeming priggish or untouchable. I found her a strong and self-sufficient girl, despite her youth and vulnerability to physical violence. She is intelligent and articulate, as she needs to be when confronted on the sea shore by her would be murderer. She saves herself more than once by appealing to the moral sense of her tormentors, the sense of decency or of pity that she trusts is in there somewhere. On this occasion such an appeal does at least buy her time. As her killer hesitates, there comes another bolt from the blue. Three pirates jump out from the bushes and carry her off to their ship.

Then there is comic relief with a rapid shift of scene 100 miles along the coast to a bawdy house at Mytilene. It is one of the points in the play where you think 'yes, this has got to be Shakespeare'. It has the raw knockabout wit, which conceals a dramatic fist waiting to hit you between the eyes. Business is terrible in this particular bawdy house:

> PANDER: Search the market narrowly. Mytilene is full of gal-lants. We lost too much money this mart by being too wenchless.
>
> BAWD: We were never so much out of creatures. We have but poor three, and they can do no more than they can do; and they with continual action are even as good as rotten.
>
> PANDER: Therefore let's have fresh ones, whate'er we pay for them. If there be not a conscience to be us'd in every trade, we shall never prosper.
>
> BAWD: Thou say'st true; 'tis not our bringing up of poor bas-tards – as, I think, I have brought up some eleven –
>
> BOULT: Ay, to eleven; and brought them down again. But shall I search the market?
>
> BAWD: What else, man? The stuff we have, a strong wind will blow it to pieces, they are so pitifully sodden.

4.2.3–20

But the comic relief soon turns sour, underneath the raucous humour the scene is horrific. Shakespeare had no illusions about the brothels of his day. Just as the fishermen on the shore symbo-lised honesty and wholesomeness, so the bawdy house is the symbol of urban corruption. It is a place of filth and degradation, a staging post for every disease going and there were quite a few on offer. It is a place for lost souls who are contemptuously exploited as social outcasts. This is where Marina is brought and sold by the pirates. She is then kept prisoner by the Bawd and her two pimps, Pander and Boult.

Marina's ordeal is portrayed with great realism in two unusually long scenes, which give it a nightmarish relentless quality and a feeling of no escape. At first this wide-eyed innocent can hardly understand what is going on or what these people expect of her. There are heavy lesbian overtones when the Bawd and her pimps touch Marina and size her up like a piece of meat. Of course her very fearfulness and naivety, and not least her chastity, add up to a good sales pitch: 'cry "He that will give most shall have her first". Such a maidenhead were no cheap thing, if men were as they have been'. The Bawd tells Marina:

> You have fortunes coming upon you. Mark me: you must seem to that fearfully which you commit willingly; to despise profit where you have most gain. To weep that you live as ye do makes pity in your lovers; seldom but that pity begets you a good opinion, and that opinion a mere profit.

> 4.2.117–22

Marina slowly realises the truth and horror of what she is being dragged in to. She prays to Diana to keep her intact. 'What have we to do with Diana,' retorts the Bawd. This scene is broken by an elaborate mime which portrays Pericles arriving at Tarsus, only to be told that Marina is dead. Cleon and his wife have hypocritically erected a great monument to her memory. Marina is, in reality, actually fighting off the hundreds of customers who come along and successfully too because they all leave after being lectured to. Some are converted to religion, vow to give up whoring and make straight for the temple.

One day Lysimachus, the Governor of Mytilene, turns up. I think we have to believe that he is an upright and decent chap really, a bit of a lad who slinks in once a week with his collar turned up for a bit of sin on the side. We have to believe this for the simple reason that he is Marina's future husband. She captivates him at first by resorting to her well-practised approach of appealing to his sense of shame:

> Do you know this house to be a place of such resort, and will come into't? I hear say you're of honourable parts, and are the governor of the place. . . . If you were born to honour, show it now; . . . .

> 4.6.77–91

I should say here that one of the problems with the play is that Lysimachus caves in so easily when Marina hasn't really said very much:

MARINA: For me,
    That am a maid, though most ungentle fortune
    Have plac'd me in this sty, where, since I came,
    Diseases have been sold dearer than physic –
    That the gods

Would set me free from this unhallowed place,
Though they did change me to the meanest bird
That flies i' th' purer air!
LYSIMACHUS: I did not think
Thou couldst have spoke so well; ne'er dreamt thou couldst.
Had I brought hither a corrupted mind,
Thy speech had altered it.

4.6.94–104

As Lysimachus is swayed without protest or argument on his part, it is generally assumed that there must have been a more eloquent and persuasive speech here which has been lost. This is, after all, a highly charged confrontation. This chance meeting eventually turns the whole tide of misfortune and brings the play back into sunlight. Surely no dramatist would pass lightly through a moment like this one. Our solution in the television version is to bridge the void by using a passage from the George Wilkins novel:

What reason is there in your justice
Which hath power over all, to undo any?
If you take from me mine honour,
You are like him that makes a gap in forbidden ground,
After whom too many enter.
My life is yet unspotted, my chastity unstained in thought.
If your violence deface this building,
This workmanship of heaven,
You do kill your own honour
Abuse your own justice and impoverish me.

Lysimachus is morally outraged and strides away. The management is mortified that Marina has had the gall to spurn the Governor and decide to punish her:

BAWD: Boult, take her away; use her at thy pleasure. Crack the glass of her virginity, and make the rest malleable.
BOULT: An if she were a thornier piece of ground than she is, she shall be ploughed.
MARINA: Hark, hark, you gods!
BAWD: She conjures. Away with her.

4.6.140–7

The intended violation of Marina is not just to make her change her mind. It is gratuitous revenge designed to bring her down to their level, an expression of hatred for being something they are not. Yet she saves herself for the last time by her own eloquence, which somehow wins through to Boult's better nature. With his help, she persuades the others to let her go and enter some respectable house where she can teach the arts and crafts that she is so good at as a sort of adult education tutor.

The play begins to resolve itself. Three months later, Gower tells us, a strange ship came into the harbour blown off course by an unfavourable wind. Pericles – who else? But the bold adventurer is now a despairing and broken man, sunk into middle age, withdrawn and brooding over the loss and failure of his life. He's dirty and dishevelled, dressed in sackcloth with long hair that he's vowed never to cut. What we see next is the joyful climax of the play. Marina is brought on board by Lysimachus as somebody who might get through to Pericles by singing and talking to him. At first he strikes her and pushes her away, but she doesn't give in. Even though you who are watching know everything and can't be taken by surprise, the real magic of the scene is the way Shakespeare plays it to and fro, keeping us waiting hankies at the ready, slowly winding it up until the spring is finally released. Pericles, having seen Marina's tomb in Tarsus with his own eyes, can't believe it isn't a cruel mockery:

PERICLES: But are you flesh and blood?
    Have you a working pulse, and are no fairy?
    Motion! Well; speak on. Where were you born?
    And wherefore call'd Marina?
MARINA: Call'd Marina
    For I was born at sea.
PERICLES: At sea! what mother?
MARINA: My mother was the daughter of a king;
    Who died the minute I was born,
    As my good nurse Lychorida hath oft
    Delivered weeping.
PERICLES: O, stop there a little!
    This is the rarest dream that e'er dull sleep
    Did mock sad fools withal.

                                    5.1.151–61

The tide of fortune has finally turned and, just as chance has brought about the reconciliation of father and daughter, it's another supernatural intervention that brings back Thaisa.

I have given you the merest glimpse of what this eventful story is about. Like most romances it's extravagant, a trifle absurd and doesn't stand up to a lot of analysis. But what seems to be larger than life may still be a reflection of the smaller lives that most of us know about. You can be tempted to scoff at the improbabilities and chance happenings, but that would be missing the point. The constant image of the sea and the wind is behind the play. The sea is unpredictable: you don't know whether you'll be taken where you want to go or be driven somewhere else or lose everything you have on the way. You don't know whom you'll meet or what will confront you. Pericles makes ten voyages from place to place. He meets his wife because of a storm and loses her in another. His life is saved by wind and current, whereas his daughter's is saved by pirates who come from the sea. Finally it is a chance wind on Neptune's feast day that reunites father and daughter. If the sea is the underlying metaphor, what does it suggest? That life doesn't go to plan and we can't live in a cocoon shut away from the things we don't want to know about. It suggests that good and evil confront us out of the blue and that life is down to chance with an occasional hint of supernatural interventions. But when Marina comes into the play an element of hope begins to take shape. It becomes more moral in its implications that ultimately our lives are not ruled by random events but by our responses to them. The events may determine the options, but there are still choices to be made. We've seen Pericles at the beginning: courageous, competitive and ready to throw the dice and seize his chances. We've seen him at the other end in full retreat from life when the dice have gone against him. One senses that Marina has a kind of inner strength that her father doesn't possess. She has what it takes to save herself and, in doing that she also leads her father back to life. I wonder if that is the final thought the play leaves behind: nobody makes it alone.

THE COMEDY OF ERRORS
Roy Hudd

Roy Hudd is a comedian who has worked in summer shows, pantomimes, television, radio and theatre, including Shakespeare. He also writes and broadcasts on the history of comedy. He made this programme on location at the City Varieties Music Hall in Leeds.

I'm sure that you are asking yourself why old Huddy is here to tell you all about William Shakespeare's *The Comedy of Errors*. Well, many of the old music hall gags, routines and songs that fascinate me date back to Will Shakespeare's time and beyond. There's nothing wrong with old gags. Shakespeare himself used many of them in his plays. What I am going to try to do is to show you how the gags and the situations that Shakespeare used in *The Comedy of Errors* were subsequently used in music hall, pantomime and variety. Some of them are still used today, particularly if you come and see my act!

I have been told that I have to start by giving you an idea of the plot of *The Comedy of Errors*. There was a very popular variety comedian just after the war called Leon Cortez, who used to specialise in potted Shakespeare:

> There was this 'ere geezer called 'amlet, see? And he was a snotty so-and-so. Nuffink made 'im happy, but he did enjoy Ophelia, a feel yah see. Now, don't be higgorant, don't be higgorant – Ophelia, Ophelia, see? That was the name of 'is bit o' crumpet.

Leon Cortez used to be able to get the plot of *Hamlet* across in about three minutes, but I think that even he would have had trouble trying to tell you the story of *The Comedy of Errors*. It is such a marvellously complicated plot. Time and time again you think that the whole thing is going to disappear up its own back-side. But no, Shakespeare manages to keep all the balls in the air and pulls off one of the greatest theatrical juggling acts of all time. The play is about identical twins. So is this gag by Ken Dodd:

By Jove, missus, I was walking along the front this morning and a woman is coming towards me. She's got two kids in a pram. I have never seen two kids look so alike in all my life. I said to her, 'By Jove, missus, they look just like two peas in a pod'. She said, 'So they should. He was a bachelor and I was canned'.

The Comedy of Errors is about identical twins both called Antipholus, one from Syracuse and the other from Ephesus. Yet Shakespeare does not just have one set of identical twins, he has two. The Antipholus twins, who were separated from each other in a shipwreck, had identical twins called Dromio as their servants. All this is explained in the first scene by Ægeon, the father of the Antipholus twins:

> There had she not been long but she became
> A joyful mother of two goodly sons;
> And, which was strange, the one so like the other
> As could not be distinguish'd but by names.
> That very hour, and in the self-same inn,
> A mean woman was delivered
> Of such a burden, male twins, both alike.
> Those, for their parents were exceeding poor,
> I bought, and brought up to attend my sons.   I.I.50–8

You get the picture? Identical twins called Antipholus with identical twins called Dromio as their servants. The shipwreck means that these two sets of twins are split up when kids. One Antipholus and one Dromio are brought up in Ephesus, their other halves in Syracuse. The shipwreck also separates the Antipholus twins from their parents.

The story really starts when the two from Syracuse arrive in Ephesus, the very place where their brothers live. From that moment on until the end of the play, the right servant is talking to the wrong master or the wrong servant to the right master:

> ANTIPHOLUS OF SYRACUSE: Now, as I am a Christian, answer me
>> In what safe place you have bestow'd my money,
>> Or I shall break that merry sconce of yours
>> That stands on tricks when I am undispos'd;
>> Where is the thousand marks thou hadst of me?
> DROMIO OF EPHESUS: I have some marks of yours upon my pate,
>> Some of my mistress' marks upon my shoulders,
>> But not a thousand marks between you both.
>> If I should pay your worship those again,

Perchance you will not bear them patiently.

ANTIPHOLUS OF SYRACUSE: Thy mistress' marks! What mistress, slave, hast thou?

DROMIO OF EPHESUS: Your worship's wife, my mistress at the Phoenix;

She that doth fast till you come home to dinner,

And prays that you will hie you home to dinner.

ANTIPHOLUS OF SYRACUSE: What, wilt thou flout me thus unto my face

Being forbid? There, take you that, sir knave.

1.2.76–92

Antipholus of Syracuse does not have a wife and things really start to warm up when the wife of his twin Antipholus of Ephesus mistakes him for her husband. Talking of warming up, here's Max Miller on the subject of twins:

I've fallen in love with twin sisters,
Two girls who I'd like you to meet.
One is called Annie, the other's called Fanny,
They've both come to live down my street.
I think I'd better describe them,
So that you'll be in no doubt.
Annie's the one with the teeth in
And Fanny's the one with them –
Dya da dedededeedle – a da da de!
Annie, she wears a blue costume,
It brings out her eyes, you can tell.
Fanny wears slacks that bring out all the facts
And most of the police force as well.
Now one of these girls I should marry.
To separate twins isn't fair.
So when I tie the knot,
With what little I've got,
I'll see they both get their fair share.

If you think that this Max Miller song, called 'The Twins', is rude and not at all the sort of thing that ought to be in a programme about one of the Bard's immortal masterpieces, then I am here to tell you that there are far naughtier gags than that in *The Comedy of Errors*. You have to listen for them, but they are there alright. You will listen for them, won't you? Yes I thought you would! Try this one. Dromio of Syracuse is telling his real master about a serving wench, who thinks that he is his twin brother. It becomes obvious, incidentally, that the twin brother and the serving wench are much more than just good friends:

> DROMIO OF SYRACUSE: . . . she is spherical, like a globe; I could find out countries in her.
>
> ANTIPHOLUS OF SYRACUSE: In what part of her body stands Ireland?
>
> DROMIO OF SYRACUSE: Marry, sir, in her buttocks. I found it out by the bogs.
>
> ANTIPHOLUS OF SYRACUSE: Where Scotland?
>
> DROMIO OF SYRACUSE: I found it by the barrenness, hard in the palm of her hand.
>
> ANTIPHOLUS OF SYRACUSE: Where France?
>
> DROMIO OF SYRACUSE: In her forehead, arm'd and reverted, making war against her heir.
>
> ANTIPHOLUS OF SYRACUSE: Where England?
>
> DROMIO OF SYRACUSE: I looked for the chalky cliffs, but I could find no whiteness in them. But I guess it stood in her chin, by the salt rheum that ran between France and it.
>
> ANTIPHOLUS OF SYRACUSE: Where Spain?
>
> DROMIO OF SYRACUSE: Faith, I saw it not, but I felt it hot in her breath.
>
> ANTIPHOLUS OF SYRACUSE: Where stood Belgia, the Netherlands?
>
> DROMIO OF SYRACUSE: O, sir, I did not look so low.

3.2.113–37

That is early Bill Shakespeare. The same gag was being used in Billy Bennett's monologue, 'The Road to Mandalay', in 1920:

> There's no maps for the soldiers
> In this land of Gunga Din.
> So they picked the toughest warrior out
> And tattooed all over him.
> On his back, he'd got Calcutta.
> Lower down, he's got Bombay
> And you'll find him sitting peacefully
> On the road to Mandalay!

The gag was also being used at the Croydon Empire in 1950:

> 'Ere, there's three of us sat round the table the other night in the digs. The landlady brought us in a beautiful chicken, but she didn't 'arf serve it in a funny way. She said to the first fella, 'what football team do you support?' 'E said, 'Liverpool' and she gave him the left leg. She said to the next fella, 'what team do you

support?' 'E said, 'Newcastle', and she gave 'im the right leg. She said to me, 'who do you support?' I said 'Arsenal, but I'm not hungry'.

These are the same kind of gags that Shakespeare used in *The Comedy of Errors* 400 years ago.

Many of the gags in the play are associated with double acts rather than stand-up routines: Antipholus and Dromio, master and servant, straight man and comedian. These double acts are really just like Eric and Ernie, Cannon and Ball, Flanagan and Allen. I would have loved to have seen Bud and Ches as Antipholus and Dromio:

BUD: What race am I in, sir?

CHES: The two-thirty

BUD: What time?

CHES: You're in the two-thirty race. You'll start about ten to one.

BUD: I start at ten to one?

CHES: Yes

BUD: In the two-thirty race.

CHES: Yes.

BUD: Well, I've got tons of time, haven't I? I can take liberties. What about the other horses?

CHES: Oh, they'll start about five to four.

BUD: Same day?

CHES: Same day, same race.

BUD: Five to four, and I start at ten to one. I can go 'ome for me dinner, can't I? You watch me at about 'arf past three. I won't 'arf be shifting.

CHES: Now, be very careful. I'm putting a monkey on this horse.

BUD: Oh?

CHES: And the trainer's putting a pony on it.

BUD: Well, where the 'ell am I going to sit?

CHES: You will sit on top of the horse.

BUD: What, with the monkey and the pony? I resign!

Variety comedians such as Frankie Howerd, Ken Dodd and Bill Maynard have appeared in Shakespeare and marvellous they were, too, because they brought their own comic personalities to the plays. Even this is an idea that we have knocked off from the sixteenth century. Shakespeare's most famous clown, Will Kemp, was renowned for making the plays a vehicle for his own comic personality. He was in fact always being told off for sticking in his own gags and routines. I would defend him, even though it is now harder to alter Shakespeare's own dialogue because it has become so famous. You can still add your own visual gags and tricks.

I myself played Shakespeare, and lost three nil! But I was lucky enough to be directed by Alexander Doré in a couple of plays and then by Frank Dunlop in *Much Ado About Nothing*. Once Frank was sure I knew the lines and what they meant, he really left the rest to me. Although my Dogberry owed more to the sergeant-major in the teabag advert than to a close study of the First Folio, it did get some good laughs. Shakespeare is great stuff for a comic to play because the situations are set up so well. One of the first parts that I had was Andrew Aguecheek in *Twelfth Night*. The script says something like 'comedy sword fight here', which by itself is not a great deal of help. It is a bit like a pantomime script where they have lots of blank pages that just say things like 'haunted house scene here' or 'kitchen scene here'. The comics usually manage to come up with something. Shakespeare gives a comic a lot to work on, as he always sets up these comedy routines so beautifully. Before you get to the 'comedy sword fight here' in *Twelfth Night*, Shakespeare has already clearly established the main protagonists in it. They are Andrew Aguecheek himself, a cowardly simpleton – no acting required! – and a girl disguised as a man who has never even held a sword, let alone fought a duel. This gives great scope for the introduction of comic business.

Shakespeare takes great pains to set up the individual gag as well as these essentially visual comic scenes. For instance, here is Adriana, the wife of Antipholus of Ephesus, leading off at the man that she thinks is her husband:

> ADRIANA: I am possess'd with an adulterate blot;
>   My blood is mingled with the crime of lust;
>   For if we two be one, and thou play false,
>   I do digest the poison of thy flesh,
>   Being strumpeted by thy contagion.
>   Keep then fair league and truce with thy true bed;
>   I live dis-stain'd, thou undishonoured.
> ANTIPHOLUS OF SYRACUSE: Plead you to me, fair dame?

2.2.139–46

It is a long set-up for that one-liner, 'plead you to me, fair dame'. It is rather like some of Spike Milligan's gags in *The Goon Show* or one of Basil Fawlty's replies to a long tirade from Sybil.

The Comedy of Errors has marvellous gags, routines and double acts, but it also has a terrific plot. The play starts with Ægeon, the father of the Antipholus twins, being arrested and sentenced to die, unless he is ransomed by the end of the day. We know that all of his family are in fact in town but, as the mix-ups between the two sets of twins get wilder and wilder and the time of the old man's execution gets nearer and nearer, you really do start to think 'for Gawd's sake, sort it all out or else the old boy is going to get the chop'. You laugh at the characters, but you care about them as well. This is a special brand of comedy. We all cared about Frank Spencer in *Some Mothers Do Have 'Em* or the old buffers in *Dad's Army*. We cared about the great comedians like Tony Hancock and Charlie Chaplin.

Chaplin used standard characters in his films such as the avaricious shopkeeper, the virginal girl and the bullying wife. Shakespeare also uses these kind of characters in *The Comedy of Errors*, but he did not invent them. They go back to at least Roman times to a playwright called Plautus. He was a great inventor of comic characters and situations. The successful Broadway musical, *A Funny Thing Happened on the Way to the Forum*, was in fact based around some of his comic inventions. Shakespeare also nicked the plot of one of Plautus's plays for *The Comedy of Errors*, but he adapted it for his own purposes. The original play only had one set of twins, but Shakespeare decided to add another set in order to create four possible double-acts instead of just the one. He added another double-act by building up the characters of Adriana and her sister Luciana. Here they are in a scene reminiscent of modern situation comedy trying to sort out just why Adriana's husband – the wrong one of course – has made love to her sister:

LUCIANA: Then pleaded I for you.
ADRIANA: And what said he?
LUCIANA: That love I begg'd for you he begg'd of me.
ADRIANA: With what persuasion did he tempt thy love?
LUCIANA: With words that in an honest suit might move
   First he did praise my beauty, then my speech.
ADRIANA: Didst speak him fair?
LUCIANA: Have patience, I beseech.
ADRIANA: I cannot nor I will not hold me still;
   My tongue, though not my heart, shall have his will.
   He is deformed, crooked, old and sere;
   Ill-faced, worse-bodied, shapeless everywhere;
   Vicious, ungentle, foolish, blunt, unkind,
   Stigmatical in making, worse in mind.
LUCIANA: Who would be jealous, then, of such a one?

No evil lost is wail'd when it is gone.
ADRIANA: Ah, but I think him better than I say.

4.2.11–25

Once again, Shakespeare provides a long build up for the important line, 'Ah, but I think him better than I say'.

Slapstick is one of the few comic elements of *The Comedy of Errors* that, sadly, you hardly see at all today. Yet all the kids I know, and their parents too if only they would admit it, love slapstick. Incidentally, it is called slapstick because a slap stick was actually used for walloping people. It doesn't hurt, but it makes a terrific sound and that is what gets an audience at it. Nowadays we call almost any form of physical comedy slapstick, but in *The Comedy of Errors* there are lots of genuine good hidings dished out. Shakespeare's clowns must have loved all this. Most of them were jugglers and tumblers and the chance of some real acrobatics and 'pratt falls' would have been meat and drink to them. Circus and traditional pantomime are the only places where you are likely to see this form of comedy today. Yet in Shakespeare's time, thanks to the influence of the Comedia Dell' Arte which was full of slapstick, it was another story. Still, lots of young performers today are learning juggling and tumbling, so perhaps we might see these sadly neglected arts coming back into comedy. We need it, as you never hear an audience laugh as loudly at words as they do at the antics of Laurel and Hardy, Buster Keaton and Charlie Chaplin.

Like Charlie Chaplin, I love coming back to the City Varieties in Leeds. This 'cave of conviviality' reeks of the great days of music hall and variety. But, best of all, the place is still a living, working theatre and happily not the only one in Leeds. I myself am appearing at the Grand Theatre, which is just around the corner. I am playing Fagin at the moment and, believe it or not, it is really quite a small part. Yet he is such a fascinating character that there are lots of different ways of playing him. He is really quite evil: exploiting children, teaching them to pick pockets and then living off the proceeds of what they nick. He is also such an eccentric old loony that you can't help laughing at him, even though you may be terrified of him. Shakespeare uses a similar mixture of comedy and terror in *The Comedy of Errors*. He introduces a character called Dr Pinch towards the end of the play. It is a great name. Adriana has become so mixed up by the proceedings that she decides that her husband must be possessed by demons, so she wheels in Dr Pinch, the exorcist, to drive them out. This scene is absolutely on the brink of comedy and terror. Like Fagin, Pinch is only a small part but it provides every actor with a great chance to do it his own way:

ADRIANA: Good Doctor Pinch, you are a conjuror:
  Establish him in his true sense again,
  And I will please you what you will demand.
LUCIANA: Alas, how fiery and how sharp he looks!
COURTESAN: Mark how he trembles in his ecstacy.
PINCH: Give me your hand, and let me feel your pulse.
ANTIPHOLUS OF EPHESUS: There is my hand, and let it feel your ear.
PINCH: I charge thee, Satan, hous'd within this man,
  To yield possession to my holy prayers,
  And to thy state of darkness hie thee straight.
  I conjure thee by all the saints in heaven.

4.4.44–54

This is where I should sum up *The Comedy of Errors* for you, but I can't. It does have a happy ending, but I expect that you have guessed that already. I am not going to spoil your fun by telling you exactly what happens at the end, but it is fascinating to see a play that has so many different plot lines going at once resolve itself so beautifully. It is also fascinating for me to see a play with all the characters, gags and routines that today's comics know so well. It warms the old cockles to know that they still work just as well today as when Bill Shakespeare, the Immortal Card, first wrote them or borrowed them. At least, I hope that they do work just as well today or else I shall be out of a job. I love comedy. It is a living tradition, not to be dissected, but to be acted and enjoyed on the small screen as well as in the theatre.

THE COMEDY OF ERRORS
Roger Rees

Roger Rees is a member of the Royal Shakespeare Company. He played Antipholus of Syracuse in the 1976 production of The Comedy of Errors. *He is playing Berowne in* Love's Labour's Lost *and the title role in* Hamlet *in the 1984–5 season. His other leading roles have included the title role in* Nicholas Nickleby.

This is a really funny play. But as with all really funny jokes, let us say, someone's approach to a banana-skin and our childlike joy in their undignified fall, we are ready to feel a little bit ashamed of ourselves afterwards. It is about the separation of twins and so very reminiscent in some respects of *Twelfth Night*. There are, however, two sets of twins in *The Comedy of Errors*. They are distinguished only by the name of the town from which they come. We have Antipholus of Syracuse and Antipholus of Ephesus. Then there are the twins who act as their servants, Dromio of Syracuse and Dromio of Ephesus.

Antipholus of Syracuse, together with Dromio of Syracuse, arrives in Ephesus. Although they have never been here before, all the inhabitants seem to recognise them. The merchants and their wives greet them as though they were old friends who had lived there all their lives. Ephesus is in fact a very lame footed place. It is full of jealous wives, anxious husbands and avaricious merchants. The Duke of Ephesus has in his power an old man who has been travelling around Greece and Asia for many years in search of one of his sons:

> Five summers have I spent in farthest Greece,
> Roaming clean through the bounds of Asia,
> And, coasting homeward, came to Ephesus;
> Hopeless to find, yet loath to leave unsought
> Or that or any place that harbours men.   I.I.133–7

This old man is given one day, which conveniently enough is the timespan of the play, to raise enough money to pay a fine, which has been imposed because inhabitants of Syracuse were forbidden to set foot in Ephesus. He will be executed at sunset if he does not pay. His life hangs in the balance throughout the play, and his fate frames the whole farcical conundrum of the play, giving it a profound ring. Another serious aspect of the play is linked with his name, which is Ægeon. Syracuse and Ephesus are separated by the Aegean Sea. The two words ring with similarity, and the sea holds the play together, in the same way that the name Ægeon holds the two sets of twins together. The sea symbolism thus provides an interesting parenthesis around the farcical action. The play finishes with hands being held out across this symbolic ocean:

> We came into the world like brother and brother,
> And now let's go hand in hand, not one before another.

5.1.423–4

This clasping together and celebration of being 'hand in hand' is all part of a seriousness that envelopes the farcical action.

Antipholus of Syracuse is rather like George Formby in one of those early 1930s films. He is the white-faced innocent abroad. He is a very loveable creature, who associates himself with the play's sea symbolism:

> I to the world am like a drop of water
> That in the ocean seeks another drop,
> Who, falling there to find his fellow forth,
> Unseen, inquisitive, confounds himself.

1.2.35–8

It's wonderful, but it's also dopey. He's the 'fall-guy', as he's too sympathetic, polite and sad to be anything else. The first of many mix-ups takes place when he sends his servant, Dromio of Syracuse, to go and put some money in the hotel. It is, of course, the other servant, Dromio of Ephesus, who has to explain about the money:

ANTIPHOLUS OF SYRACUSE: Where have you left the money that
  I gave you?
DROMIO OF EPHESUS: O – sixpence that I had a Wednesday last
  To pay the saddler for my mistress' crupper?
  The saddler had it, sir; I kept it not.
ANTIPHOLUS OF SYRACUSE: I am not in a sportive humour now;
  Tell me, and dally not, where is the money?
  We being strangers here, how dar'st thou trust
  So great a charge from thine own custody?
DROMIO OF EPHESUS: I pray you jest, sir, as you sit at dinner.
  I from my mistress come to you in post;

> If I return, I shall be post indeed,
> For she will score your fault upon my pate.
> Methinks your maw, like mine, should be your clock,
> And strike you home without a messenger.
> ANTIPHOLUS OF SYRACUSE: Come, Dromio, come, these jests
> are out of season;
> Reserve them till a merrier hour than this.
> Where is the gold I gave in charge of thee?
> DROMIO OF EPHESUS: To me, sir? Why, you gave no gold to me.
>
> 1.2.54–71

When Dromio of Syracuse finally appears on the scene, he is given a thrashing and told to stop messing about. Master and servant then sit down, perhaps at a café or maybe they are just taking their ease in the market square. They are almost immediately confronted by a woman, who greets Antipholus with a fierce, menacing 'where have you been darling?'. This is Adriana, wife of Antipholus of Ephesus, and she believes she is talking to her husband:

> ADRIANA: How dearly would it touch thee to the quick,
> Shouldst thou but hear I were licentious,
> And that this body, consecrate to thee,
> By ruffian lust should be contaminate!
> Wouldst thou not spit at me and spurn at me,
> And hurl the name of husband in my face,
> And tear the stain'd skin off my harlot-brow,
> And from my false hand cut the wedding-ring,
> And break it with a deep-divorcing vow?
> I know thou canst, and therefore see thou do it.
> I am possess'd with an adulterate blot;
> My blood is mingled with the crime of lust;
> For if we two be one, and thou play false,
> I do digest the poison of thy flesh,
> Being strumpeted by thy contagion.
> Keep then fair league and truce with thy true bed;
> I live dis-stain'd, thou dishonoured.
> ANTIPHOLUS OF SYRACUSE: Plead you to me, fair dame? I know
> you not:
> . . . .
>
> 2.2.129–46

This is a wonderful moment in the theatre. After Adriana has gone on for such a long time, Antipholus just says 'who are you?'. When I played the part I was lucky enough to have Judi Dench serving it up for me, like Chrissie Evert. Adriana goes crazy when she isn't recognised and keeps on at poor Antipholus so much that he agrees to have dinner with her. She says 'we will dine above', which I believe means more than coffee and sandwiches. Then along comes Adriana's real husband, Antipholus of Ephesus, and he is unable to get into his own house. The fact that it is Dromio of Syracuse who tells him to go away adds insult to injury. It is getting very convoluted and we've hardly started. Antipholus of Syracuse is given an expensive gold chain a little later on. It is one which his twin, Antipholus of Ephesus, was having made up for Adriana. As soon as the wrong Antipholus is given the chain, further complications are set in motion. The play is rather like one of those little toys that flip on two little strings: flipping right down and then starting back up again. It is a game of 'Consequences'.

People often say to actors 'I wish you'd done it as Shakespeare had written it'. They are really referring to Victorian productions, such as the extraordinary ones of *Henry VIII* with thousands of slaves, millions of courtiers and a budget to match. Today we don't have that sort of money, so our theatre is moving towards presenting Shakespeare in small arenas with few frills. We, not the Victorians, stage more exact reproductions of what actually happened in Shakespeare's day. Plays were performed then in the open air with no artificial lighting. The actors had to shout their heads off even to be heard above the noise of the bear-baiting and of the ferries on the river. It is highly likely that *The Comedy of Errors* was first produced with a considerable emphasis on music, interludes and farcical slapstick areas. The writing itself supports this, as Shakespeare sometimes leaves out rhythmic beats in the pentameter. You know that in a play like *The Comedy of Errors* this is when you have to hit someone round the face to complete the line with a thump: di dum, di dum, di dum, di dum, di smash. Modern productions also add comic routines to complete the action. I remember at one time I had to slide right across the length of the stage, from up in the wings at the top of the house, on a wire dressed to look like a laundry line. I swung right across the stage hanging onto a pair of underpants.

It is good to remember that Antipholus of Syracuse was frightened of Ephesus before he even got there. The place was notorious for being the home of witches, conjurers and mountebanks. St Paul mentions it as being a town of witchcraft and naughtiness. This is probably why Shakespeare changed the Epademnum of the original story into Ephesus. When the little 'Buster Keaton' figure of Antipholus of Syracuse comes into Ephesus, the seeds of fear have already been sown:

They say this town is full of cozenage;
As, nimble jugglers that deceive the eye,
Dark-working sorcerers that change the mind,
Soul-killing witches that deform the body,
Disguised cheaters, prating mountebanks,
And many such-like liberties of sin;
. . . .

I.2.97–102

He is genuinely frightened by the time the second act is well underway. Everybody appears to be possessed. They really need that joy and celebration at the end of the play. One of the characters, Dr Pinch, is described as a conjurer. I imagine him to be rather like Malvolio; bitter, crazy and mad. Pinch is employed by Adriana to exorcise the Devil from Antipholus of Ephesus and his Dromio. He calls the Devil forth from them; and it is very frightening. The thing about farce is that, if it is played with real feeling and truth, it can prove far more revealing than the darkest tragedy.

The Comedy of Errors is very like *The Merry Wives of Windsor* in that it deals with a domestic situation in true time. It is not like *Twelfth Night*, which has a double time sequence, or *Cymbeline*, where great liberties are taken with the chronology so that many years will pass in two or three minutes. *The Comedy of Errors* gives us the more realistic timescale of one day in the life of Ephesus. We know too that it is an early play because at this stage of his career Shakespeare, rather like me, tends to use a great many lines to express one thought. The language is sprawling and beyond the thought, placing the play very early, just coming up to *Romeo and Juliet*. When you come to later plays like *Cymbeline* and *The Winter's Tale*, you can find maybe five characters with two rhythmic beats each in a line sharing a lot of thoughts within that one line.

It is the strength of the comedy which spurs on the play. There is a very famous exchange between Antopholus of Syracuse and his Dromio which is reminscent of Max Miller, perhaps even more like Dean Martin and Jerry Lewis. Dromio has been chased by a kitchen wench who is a very fat girl. He says that she is so round that she is like a globe and claims to be able to find out countries in her:

ANTIPHOLUS OF SYRACUSE: In what part of her body stands Ireland?

DROMIO OF SYRACUSE: Marry, sir, in her buttocks. I found it out by the bogs.

ANTIPHOLUS OF SYRACUSE: Where Scotland?

DROMIO OF SYRACUSE: I found it by the barrenness, hard in the palm of her hand.

ANTIPHOLUS OF SYRACUSE: Where France?

DROMIO OF SYRACUSE: In her forehead, arm'd and reverted, making war against her heir.

ANTIPHOLUS OF SYRACUSE: Where England?

DROMIO OF SYRACUSE: I look'd for the chalky cliffs, but I could find no whiteness in them; but I guess it stood in her chin, by the salt rheum that ran between France and it.

ANTIPHOLUS OF SYRACUSE: Where Spain?

DROMIO OF SYRACUSE: Faith, I saw it not, but I felt it hot in her breath.

ANTIPHOLUS OF SYRACUSE: Where stood Belgia, the Netherlands?

DROMIO OF SYRACUSE: O, sir, I did not look so low.

3.2.115–37

The strength of the play lies in its verse as well as its comedy. There are some sensational pieces of verse, if you look for them and are brave enough not to cut them out. There are some wonderful descriptions. One of these which really fulfills the whole play for me is when Ægeon finally sees the first of his two sons. You'll remember that he has been looking for him for years and years and years, then he suddenly sees him protesting his innocence before the Duke in the market place. Ægeon is handcuffed and ready to be excuted. He sees his son, but he is unable to believe it. The boy ignores him because he has never seen his father before. Ægeon is at the end of his tether, his speech about growth and continuity is one of the sad grace-notes of the play:

> Not know my voice! O time's extremity,
> Hast thou so crack'd and splitted my poor tongue
> In seven short years that here my only son
> Knows not my feeble key of untun'd cares?
> Though now this grained face of mine be hid
> In sap-consuming winter's drizzled snow,
> And all the conduits of my blood froze up,
> Yet hath my night of life some memory,
> My wasting lamps some fading glimmer left,
> My dull deaf ears a little use to hear;
> All these old witnesses – I cannot err –
> Tell me thou art my son Antipholus.

5.1.306–17

This wonderful speech is there in the middle of a farce. Ægeon brought up Antipholus of Syracuse, although he has not seen him for seven years. He thinks that he is delivering the speech to him, but is in fact addressing Antipholus of Ephesus, whom he has not seen since he was a little baby. I find it very moving.

Adriana too is to be pitied, despite being the bossy, almost stereotyped, matriarchal figure in a farce. Her husband goes off with other women because she nags too much. Aemilia, who turns out to be the mother of the Antipholus twins, tells her as much in another of the play's wonderful speeches:

> The venom clamours of a jealous woman
> Poisons more deadly than a mad dog's tooth.
> It seems his sleeps were hind'red by thy railing,
> And thereof comes it that his head is light.
> Thou say'st his meat was sauc'd with thy upbraidings:
> Unquiet meals make ill digestions;
> Thereof the raging fire of fever bred;
> And what's a fever but a fit of madness?
> Thou say'st his sports were hind'red by thy brawls.
> Sweet recreation barr'd, what doth ensue
> But moody and dull melancholy,
> Kinsman to grim and comfortless despair,
> And at her heels a huge infectious troop
> Of pale distemperatures and foes to life?
> In food, in sport, and life-preserving rest,
> To be disturb'd would mad or man or beast.
> The consequence is, then, thy jealous fits
> Hath scar'd thy husband from the use of wits.

> 5.1.69–86

Kate has a wonderful speech of subservience to her mate Petruchio in the very last scene of *The Taming of the Shrew*. She puts her hand underneath his foot to show how subservient she is, but you don't know whether she is going to trip him up, pull his boot off or what. I think that even in Shakespeare's time that kind of subservience was very tongue-in-cheek. Adriana has a sister called Luciana, who falls in love with Antipholus of Syracuse thinking, of course, that he is her sister's husband. Although she says that men are very intelligent and wise and that women ought to be subservient to them, she really protests too much:

> LUCIANA: A man is master of his liberty;
>   Time is their master, and when they see time,

> They'll go or come. If so, be patient, sister.
> ADRIANA: Why should their liberty than ours be more?
> LUCIANA: Because their business still lies out o' door.
> ADRIANA: Look when I serve him so, he takes it ill.
> LUCIANA: O, know he is the bridle of your will.
> ADRIANA: There's none but asses will be bridled so.
> LUCIANA: Why, headstrong liberty is lash'd with woe.
> There's nothing situate under heaven's eye
> But hath his bound, in earth, in sea, in sky.
> The beasts, the fishes, and the winged fowls.
> Are their males' subjects, and at their controls.
> Man, more divine, the master of all these,
> Lord of the wide world and wild wat'ry seas,
> Indue'd with intellectual sense and souls,
> Of more pre-eminence than fish and fowls,
> Are masters to their females, and their lords;
> Then let you will attend on their accords.

2.1.7–24

When she finds true love with Antipholus of Syracuse, we suspect that she will not be quite so subservient.

The play could not be funny without the danger that old Ægeon *really* will be beheaded, and not be funny without the audience's supposition that, off-stage, Adriana might well have gone to bed with Antipholus of Syracuse. What is more patently serious about the play is the way in which the characters cope in this town of mistaken identity. A kind of rococo theme associated with Antipholus of Syracuse is 'who am I without my other half?', which is similar to the themes of *Twelfth Night*. Antipholus thinks that he has finally found himself when he meets Luciana:

> Call thyself sister, sweet, for I am thee;
> Thee will I love, and with thee lead my life;
> . . . .

3.2.66–7

When he says 'I am thee' he says that he is incomplete without her. The play is about people finding each other, and therefore, themselves.

When Adriana thinks that she is speaking to her husband, she declares that it would be easier for her to separate a drop of water from the ocean than it would be to separate out their love. Everybody in the play is looking for the other half of their jigsaw, just like us.

CORIOLANUS

General Sir John Hackett

General Sir John Hackett had a distinguished military career. He is the author of The Third World War *and* The Profession of Arms *and a frequent contributor to television programmes dealing with military questions. He made this programme at his home in Cheltenham.*

Shakespeare, like so many of his late Renaissance contemporaries, was enormously attracted by Ancient Rome. The story of *Coriolanus* is that of a warrior-aristocrat in the Rome of the fifth century BC, when this young city-state was struggling to maintain its sovereign independence against warlike neighbours. In such times, an outstanding fighting man was of first rate importance, however difficult he might be to accommodate within the structure of the Republic. In *Coriolanus*, even more than in most of his plays, Shakespeare was clearly influenced by the social and political climate of England at the beginning of the seventeenth century. The lively minds of Elizabethan and Jacobean England saw in Ancient Rome a beehive similarly buzzing. Old values had been challenged in a society under change. Was valour the whole of virtue? Was tradition the only regulator, or the chief regulator at least, of conduct? Could the aspirations of the citizenry be scorned without grave risk to the strength and even the safety of the state? Shakespeare and his contemporaries saw in Ancient Rome these problems being faced by people in whom they recognised mirror images of themselves. It was almost as though they were watching a preview of a drama now being enacted in real life. Coriolanus himself seemed like haughty Renaissance figures, such as the 'damnably proud' Sir Walter Raleigh. Jacobean society, like Ancient Rome, was plagued by social discontent. Shakespeare probably wrote *Coriolanus* in 1608, soon after peasant uprisings, caused in great part by shortage of corn in counties which included his own Warwickshire, which had been forcibly suppressed by the local gentry.

Coriolanus, or Caius Martius to give him his own name to which Coriolanus was to be added later as a mark of military distinction, had been brought up by his widowed mother, Volumnia, to regard valour as the chief part of virtue. Valour on the battlefield to the Ancient Romans, as in our time to the Nazis, was not only the chief part of virtue, it was probably the whole of it. Caius Martius was first in action at the age of sixteen when the Tarquins were expelled from Rome and, after that, more than twenty times as the struggling young Republic sought to defend itself against its warlike neighbours. His standing as a fighting man was high and so was his patrician contempt for the common people. The play opens with unrest among the citizens, brought on by the supposed hoarding of grain by the nobles in a time of great shortage. In the very first scene, Menenius, an older and politically wiser man than Coriolanus, seeks to soothe the mob by an ingenious allegory about the belly, which represents the nobles, and the rest of the body, which represents the plebeians. Although this does much to calm them down, Caius Martius soon has their backs up again with words of withering scorn:

> He that will give good words to thee will flatter
> Beneath abhorring. What would you have, you curs,
> That like nor peace nor war? The one affrights you,
> The other makes you proud. He that trusts to you,
> Where he should find you lions, finds you hares;
> Where foxes, geese; you are no surer, no,
> Than is the coal of fire upon the ice
> Or hailstone in the sun. Your virtue is
> To make him worthy whose offence subdues him,
> And curse that justice did it. Who deserves greatness
> Deserves your hate; Hang ye! Trust ye!   1.1.165–79

News now comes that the Volscians, warlike and hostile neighbours, are advancing to attack Rome under a leader who is the hated enemy of Caius Martius. The Romans move out to give battle under their General, Cominius, with Caius Martius as his subordinate, Shakespeare then introduces us to Volumnia, the mother of Caius Martius, in a very revealing little scene. Volumnia is no ordinary mother. A Danish critic has described her as 'the sublime mother force'. She is the matronly embodiment of the disciplines of Rome and Sparta and has taught her son that valour is the chief virtue, while instilling into him *pietas*, or family loyalty, and that crippling pride which will lead to his destruction. Caius Martius remains to the end his mother's son and never grows up. A citizen says of his battle service that he 'did it to please his mother and partly to be proud'. I recall a tough commando soldier in the war, who was told by his officer, a friend of mine, that he had been awarded the Military Medal for gallantry in the field. 'Oh', the rugged fellow burst out, 'mother will be pleased'! Caius Martius's mother longs for her son's glory, whereas his wife, Virgilia, is only interested in his safe return:

> VOLUMNIA: If my son were my husband, I should freelier rejoice in that absence wherein he won honour than in the embracements of his bed where he would show most love. When yet he was but tender-bodied, and the only son of my womb; when youth with comeliness pluck'd all gaze his way; when, for a day of kings' entreaties, a mother should not sell him an hour from her beholding; I, considering how honour would become such a person – that it was no better than picture-like to hang by th' wall, if renown made it not stir – was pleas'd to let him seek danger where he was like to find fame. To a cruel war I sent him, from whence he return'd his brows bound with oak. I tell thee, daughter, I sprang not more in joy at first hearing he was a man-child than now in first seeing he had proved himself a man.
>
> VIRGILIA: But had he died in the business, madam, how then?
> VOLUMNIA: Then his good report should have been my son; I therein would have found issue. Hear me profess sincerely: had I a dozen sons, each in my love alike, and none less dear than thine and my good Marcius, I had rather had eleven die nobly for their country than one voluptuously surfeit out of action.

1.3.2–25

The Roman attack on the Volscian city fails owing to the cowardice of the common soldiers, who are less concerned with the outcome of the battle than with the spoils. Caius Martius upbraids them bitterly:

> All the contagion of the south light on you,
> You shames of Rome! you herd of – Boils and plagues
> Plaster you o'er, that you may be abhorr'd
> Farther than seen, and one infect another
> Against the wind a mile! You souls of geese
> That bear the shapes of men, how have you run
> From slaves that apes would beat! Pluto and hell!
> All hurt behind! Backs red, and faces pale
> With flight and agued fear! Mend and charge home,
> Or, by the fires of heaven, I'll leave the foe
> And make my wars on you. Look to't.

1.4.30–40

He then shows his own foolhardiness by going off into the city by himself. The common soldiers will not follow him.

Did Shakespeare, who wrote so richly and freely about fighting men and war, ever see service under arms himself? It is not impossible. After the christening of his twins in 1585, Shakespeare disappears from the Stratford scene and we next find him as an established playwright seven years later in London. What happened in between? He was perhaps already, as we might say today, helping the authorities in their enquiries into a matter of deer poaching. It was a widely spread belief that the Earl of Leicester had protected him and indeed it would need nothing less than a grandee to save him from the law of the land. Queen Elizabeth sent a strong expeditionary force to fight the Spanish in the Netherlands in 1585, three years before the Spanish Armada. Its commander was the Earl of Leicester. It does not tax the imagination far to picture young Will Shakespeare, twenty one years old, making his way up over the thirteen miles to Kenilworth Castle, already possibly in some trouble, to enlist there as a soldier. Soldiers were just then in high demand. It is easier to think of his doing that than facing the hazardous ninety mile walk to seek an uncertain future in London. The Earl of Leicester lived only for three years more. His famous nephew, Sir Philip Sidney, who died in the Netherlands campaign, has left behind a letter in which he refers to one 'Will, a jesting player' in Leicester's entourage. Duff Cooper examines the evidence in a charming little book called *Sergeant Shakespeare*. I incline to accept Duff Cooper's case, as there is much in the plays to suggest that their author knew what service in the ranks was really like. Shakespeare deals accurately with the grudges that can be left behind by promotions, as with Cassio and Iago in *Othello*. His references to the looting habits of the rank-and-file also ring true – though in the last war we used to refer to it as 'liberating'. When I hear advice that runs 'in conflict . . . get the sun of them' and I recall how, in the Western Desert, the German tanks used to attack us of an evening out of the West with the setting sun behind them, I reckon that I am listening to somebody who has at least been under musketry instruction.

We must return to the battle for the city of Corioli. Shut in the city by himself, Caius Martius forces the enemy to capitulate at the edge of his own single sword and then comes out to go on after Aufidius, the leader of the Volscians and his hated enemy. What is it possible to make of Caius Martius Coriolanus as a military person in action, a general on the battlefield? I find him frankly unconvincing as a general. The praise he gets is for what he has done with his own weapons. He is not so much a commander as a killer. There is no evidence of skill in the disposal of forces. His command over his troops, as far as we are shown it here, seems to rest pretty well entirely on example and invective. Yet, as everyone who has commanded troops in battle knows, there is a clear limit to how far men can be got to go by example alone, while invective is a particularly ineffective tool. Caius Martius charges alone into Corioli and the gates are shut on him. But what happens here? He captures the city by himself: 'alone I did it'! If war-fighting were only a matter of individual personal assaults upon hated personal enemies this might be possible, but war-fighting is not like that. Coriolanus is much less of a general than a champion. The notion of the champion in ancient times, of a leader seeking out the leader of the other side to fight him and slay or be slain, was widely spread. A vestige of it persists in military command today. I recollect the portrait of Rommel in Monty's caravan in the desert in World War Two and Churchill's crisp injunction not so much to destroy the Afrika Korps as to defeat Rommel. But in the personalisation of military adversaries, and I say nothing about politicians here, there is no personal hatred. There is none of the personal animosity which is found in the relationship between Coriolanus and Aufidius.

It is now only right and proper that the victorious Coriolanus should stand for election to the consulship of Rome, though he would have made a catastrophic consul. Cominius, his commander in the battle, commends him to the Senate. He is enthusiastically accepted by the nobles, but then he must plead for election by the common people. In spite of Volumnia's sensible advice, this is something that so proud and stubborn a man cannot easily stomach. His mother has taught him his pitiless contempt for the common people, but she is astute enough to recognise the need for compromise. He can see nothing in compromise but cowardice. Carefully watched by Sicinius and Brutus, the two Tribunes of the people, he destroys his chances by his disdainful treatment of the common people. He is elected by them in the first instance on account of his great service, but then, for his insufferable insolence and arrogance, furiously rejected:

CORIOLANUS: Thou wretch, despite o'erwhelm thee!
What should the people do with these bald tribunes,
On whom depending, their obedience fails
To the greater bench? In a rebellion,
When what's not meet, but what must be, was law,

Then were they chosen; in a better hour
Let what is meet be said it must be meet,
And throw their power i' th' dust.
BRUTUS: Manifest treason!
SICINIUS: This a consul? No.   3.1.163–71

Popular feeling, manipulated and inflamed by the Tribunes, is now for the instant death of Coriolanus, hurled down from the Tarpeian rock according to the custom. But, on account of his earlier service to the city, this is mitigated to banishment.

Cast out from his beloved Rome, he thinks now only of revenge upon the city that has so dishonoured him. What does this extraordinary man do next? He makes his way to the Volscians and offers himself to none other than Aufidius. The Volsci welcome him warmly and make much of him. He is now to lead them into the field to storm, sack and burn Rome. Menenius, the old diplomat, comes up to try to talk him out of this, but the Volscian army under his leadership is already sweeping all before it and Coriolanius will not be moved. Then his revered mother, Volumnia, and his beloved wife, Virgilia, make their way to him in a last desperate attempt to save from his vengeance the city that he has loved and served so well. He is a plain dealer, so he won't hear them except in the presence of Aufidius and other Volscians, but the plea of his mother is something that he is unable to disregard:

VOLUMNIA: He turns away.
Down, ladies; let us shame him with our knees.
To his surname Coriolanus 'longs more pride
Than pity to our prayers. Down. An end;
This is the last. So we will home to Rome,
And die among our neighbours. Nay, behold's!
This boy, that cannot tell what he would have
But kneels and holds up hands for fellowship,
Does reason our petition with more strength
Than thou hast to deny't. Come, let us go.
This fellow had a Volscian to his mother;
His wife is in Corioli, and his child
Like him by chance. Yet give us our dispatch.
I am hush'd until our city be afire,
And then I'll speak a little.
                         (*He holds her by the hand, silent*)
CORIOLANUS: O mother, mother!
What have you done? Behold, the heavens do ope,
The gods look down, and this unnatural scene

>They laugh at. O my mother, mother! O!
>You have won a happy victory to Rome;
>But for your son – believe it, O, believe it! –
>Most dangerously you have with him prevail'd,
>If not most mortal to him. But let it come.

5.3.168–89

Aufidius is watching and biding his time. He will destroy Coriolanus when his chance comes. That is clear.

We now come to the highest point in the play. Coriolanus, unauthorised, strikes a peace treaty between Rome and the Volscians and brings it back with him. Aufidius will have none of it. When the document is presented to the elders, he confronts Coriolanus in full and open hostility. Aufidius knows, as the Roman Tribunes knew, that this man's vaunting pride, skilfully manipulated, can be relied upon to trigger off an uncontrollable and self-destructive fit of rage. Aufidius calls him 'boy', even 'boy of tears'. This evokes from Coriolanus a stinging reply. Its towering contempt seals his own doom:

>'Boy'! O slave!
>Pardon me, lords, 'tis the first time that ever
>I was forc'd to scold. Your judgements, my grave lords,
>Must give this cur the lie; and his own notion –
>Who wears my stripes impress'd upon him, that
>Must bear my beating to his grave – shall join
>To thrust the lie unto him.
>Cut me to pieces, Volsces; men and lads,
>Stain all your edges on me. 'Boy'! False hound!
>If you have writ your annals true, 'tis there
>That, like an eagle in a dove-cote, I
>Flutter'd your Volscians in Corioli.
>Alone I did it. 'Boy'!

5.6.104–17

'The offering of self is sealed', as Wagner wrote of Beethoven's *Coriolan Overture*, 'and the colossus crashes down'. But Coriolanus has not so much killed himself as surrendered to death and what was meant to be his total humiliation is to turn, in the end, into his triumph.

The play presents clear-cut extremes in black and white. To Coriolanus, those who lack valour deserve absolutely nothing from a state whose very existence depends upon it. They have no right to eat, let alone govern. He has no sympathy at all with the common people, no less a part of Rome than he is. He treats his own people with an uncompromising inhumanity reflected in his behaviour towards his (and their) enemies on the battlefield where, as Menenius says in a searing phrase, 'there is no more mercy in him than there is milk in a male tiger'. What bothers me a good deal is Coriolanus's ugly preoccupation with killing. I say again what I have said before, that it is the unlimited liability under which the man-at-arms serves which does more than anything else to lend his profession its especial dignity. I think it was John Ruskin who said that it is less important that a soldier should have to slay than that he must offer himself to be slain. In a good deal of wartime active service, I must myself have been responsible for the deaths of men, whilst always making that offer, like countless other men, myself. It was an offer of which the enemies of the sovereign I was serving tried freely to make use, twice with only partial success and on a third occasion with success which was very nearly total and I am lucky to be here. But I bore those who did this to me, and I bear them now, no grudge. For Coriolanus, however, all this is a personal affair. He glories in killing. He is, in fact, as a soldier little more than a killing machine and, knowing as I do that soldiers are mostly compassionate people, I find him not only repellent as a man but hardly credible as a general. Shakespeare never invites our affection or sympathy for Coriolanus. He is always shown in a harsh and blinding light, the central figure upon whom our attention is sharply focussed. It is this centralisation of interest together with the swift momentum of the action which gives this play what many people consider to be a unity unique in Shakespeare. When Coriolanus dies at the end – curiously enough it is the only on-stage death in the whole of the play's violent and tumultuous course – politics are shed, animosity dies, envy and rivalry disappear and something like redemption emerges. The hero's body is borne off and a dead march sounds. Am I alone here in finding an echo of Götterdämmerung?

CORIOLANUS

Ian Hogg

Ian Hogg played the title role in Coriolanus *in 1972 in the Royal Shakespeare Company's season of Roman plays. His other leading Shakespearean roles have included Edmund in* King Lear *and the title roles in* Macbeth *and* Henry V. *His non-Shakespearean work has included television serials such as* David Copperfield *and* Bleak House. *He played Banquo in the BBC TV production of* Macbeth.

I have come to look upon Shakespearean roles like Lear, Hamlet, Macbeth and Othello as theatrical initiations on the grandest scale. A unique master of the art of tragedy takes the actor by the hand and leads him into the circle of a test which, whether it is acknowledged to be a great success or a dismal flop, will bring him face to face with the physical, mental and spiritual centres of his being. Coriolanus I believe to be one of these initiations, even though academics and critics have questioned whether the play is indeed a tragedy. George Bernard Shaw called it Shakespeare's finest comedy. A critic called O. J. Campbell described it as a satire and another critic saw it as a form of debate. Samuel Johnson regarded it as

> one of the most amusing of our author's performances. The old man's merriment in Menenius; the lofty lady's dignity in Volumnia; the bridal modesty in Virgilia; the patrician and military haughtiness in Coriolanus; the plebeian malignity and tribunitian insolence in Brutus and Sicinius make a very pleasing and interesting variety. There is, perhaps, too much bustle in the first act and too little in the last.

In talking about the play I intend to re-examine the route of my own experience ten years ago. I am not going to submit myself to an academic discipline, but rather to an act of recall. My commission is to remember as faithfully as I can how the story, and eventually the presence of the character, began to become a physical and emotional conviction in me. When I played the part of Coriolanus at Stratford the play was to be acted as one of a cycle of plays covering the development and decline of Rome, as seen by Shakespeare. The plays were *Coriolanus, Julius Caesar, Antony and Cleopatra* and *Titus Andronicus*. The order of presentation was historical. So *Coriolanus*, which was written last, was performed first in this cycle. It deals with that savage and tribal Rome before it attained the subtlety and civilisation of the great city and then the empire.

Before I begin to read a play about a legendary or historical character who has an existence outside the playwright's mind, I always go to the source material. It is almost certainly what the playwright did and perhaps provides the only clue that I shall get about what excited him to tell this man's story. And so in the cases of Coriolanus I reached for North's Plutarch, as Shakespeare must have done, and read this:

> Caius Marcius, whose life we intend now to write, being left an orphan by his father, was brought up under his mother, a widow, who taught us by experience, that orphanage bringeth many discommodities to a child, but doth not hinder him to become an honest man, and to excel in virtue above the common sort. . . . This man also is a good proof to confirm some men's opinions: that a rare and excellent wit untaught, doth bring forth many good and evil things together, as a fat soil that lieth unmanured bringeth forth both herbs and weeds. For this Marcius' natural wit and great heart did marvellously stir up his courage to do and attempt notable acts. But on the other side for lack of education, he was so cholerick and impatient, that he would yield to no living creature: which made him churlish, uncivil, and altogether unfit for any man's conversation. Yet men marvelling much at his constancy, that he was never overcome with pleasure, or money, and how he would endure easily all manner of pains and travails: thereupon they well liked and commended his stoutness and temperancy. But for all that, they could not be acquainted with him, as one citizen useth to be with another in the city. . . . Now in those days, valiantness was honoured in Rome above all other virtues: which they call '*Virtus*'. . . .

The first image then of Coriolanus, as Caius Martius was later to become known, is of a figure of early Rome, which was emerging from the epoch of kings and chiefs and ceasing to be just a tribe. Here was a supreme and heroic soldier, who was a matchless example of the Roman virtues of courage, honour and endurance. But we are also alerted to the presence of arrogance, churlishness, political naïvety and aloofness, which are destined to separate him from other men.

The image, inspired by the source material, one established leads me to the next stage which is to read the play through, easily and openly, as if it were a story book and not an obstacle in an otherwise peaceful life. Before I try to work out the details and progression of Shakespeare's plot, I sit back and listen out for the 'voices', those fragments of the play that appeal to the subconscious. I allow my subconscious to decide the order of recall which, being dream-like, is not necessarily the order in which the lines are spoken in the text. And, in seeking out these voices of the play's dream, I felt in this case not unlike Coriolanus himself standing in the market place, cowled in wolfskin, and begging for votes or voices:

> Your voices. For your voices I have fought;
> Watch'd for your voices; for your voices bear
> Of wounds two dozen odd; battles thrice six
> I have seen and heard of; for your voices have
> Done many things, some less, some more. Your voices?
> Indeed, I would be consul.

2.3.123–8

Here are the 'voices' from my 'dream play' of *Coriolanus*:

> SICINIUS: Such a nature,
>   Tickled with good success, disdains the shadow
>   Which he treads on at noon.

1.2.257–9

> CORIOLANUS: Who deserves greatness
>   Deserves your hate; and your affections are
>   A sick man's appetite, who desires most that
>   Which would increase his evil. He that depends
>   Upon your favours swims with fins of lead,
>   And hews down oaks with rushes. Hang ye! Trust ye?
>   With every minute you do change a mind
>   And call him noble that was now your hate,
>   Him vile that was your garland.

1.1.174–82

> MENENIUS: Pray you, who does the wolf love?
> SICINIUS: The lamb.
> MENENIUS: Ay, to devour him, as the hungry plebeians would
>   the noble Marcius.
> BRUTUS: He's a lamb indeed, that baes like a bear.

MENENIUS: He's a bear indeed, that lives like a lamb.

2.1.6–10

Menenius's voice again:

His nature is too noble for the world:
He would not flatter Neptune for his trident,
Or Jove for's power to thunder. His heart's his mouth;
What his breast forges, that his tongue must vent;
And, being angry, does forget that ever
He heard the name of death.

3.1.255–60

Consider this: he has been bred i' th' wars
Since 'a could draw a sword, and is ill school'd
In bolted language; meal and bran together
He throws without distinction.

3.1.320–3

Volumnia's voice:

The breasts of Hecuba,
When she did suckle Hector, look'd not lovelier
Than Hector's forehead when it did spit forth blood
At Grecian sword, contemning.

1.3.40–3

I prithee now, my son,
Go to them with this bonnet in thy hand;
And thus far having stretch'd it – here be with them –
Thy knee bussing the stones – for in such business
Action is eloquence, and the eyes of th' ignorant
More learned than the ears – waving thy head,
Which often thus correcting thy stout heart,
Now humble as the ripest mulberry
That will not hold the handling.

3.2.72–80

Voices of the play's dream, fragments:

Most sweet voices!
Better it is to die, better to starve,
Then crave the hire which first we do deserve.
Why in this wolvish toge should I stand here
To beg of Hob and Dick that do appear
Their needless vouches? Custom calls me to't.
What custom wills, in all things should we do't,

243

The dust on antique time would lie unswept,
And mountainous error be too highly heap'd
For truth to o'erpeer. Rather than fool it so,
Let the high office and the honour go
To one that would do thus.

2.3.109–20

Aufidius's voice, as if heard in a temple, like a ritual curse:

Five times, Marcius,
I have fought with thee; so often hast thou beat me;
And wouldst do so, I think, should we encounter
As often as we eat. By th' elements,
If e'er again I meet him beard to beard,
He's mine or I am his.

1.10.7–12

Nor sleep nor sanctuary,
Being naked, sick, nor fane nor Capitol,
The prayers of priests nor times of sacrifice,
Embarquements all of fury, shall lift up
Their rotten privilege and custom 'gainst
My hate to Marcius. Where I find him, were it
At home, upon my brother's guard, even there,
Against the hospitable canon, would I
Wash my fierce hand in's heart.

1.10.19–27

Aufidius in a new space, but always like a voice whispering in the mind:

Let me twine
Mine arms about that body, where against
My grained ash an hundred times hath broke
And scarr'd the moon with splinters; here I clip
The anvil of my sword, and do contest
As hotly and as nobly with thy love
As ever in ambitious strength I did
Contend against thy valour. Know thou first,
I lov'd the maid I married; never man
Sigh'd truer breath; but that I see thee here,
Thou noble thing, more dances my rapt heart
Than when I first my wedded mistress saw
Bestride my threshold.

4.5.106–18

Voices moving in to destroy:

> CORIOLANUS: Hear'st thou, Mars?
> AUFIDIUS: Name not the god, thou of boy of tears-
> CORIOLANUS: Ha!
> AUFIDIUS: – no more
> CORIOLANUS: Measureless liar, thou hast made my heart
> Too great for what contains it. 'Boy'! O slave!
> Pardon me, lords, 'tis the first time that ever
> I was forced to scold. Your judgements, my grave lords,
> Must give this cur the lie; and his own notion –
> Who wears my stripes impress'd upon him, that
> Must bear my beating to his grave – shall join
> To thrust the lie unto him.
> Cut me to pieces, Volsces; men and lads,
> Stain all your edges on me. 'Boy'! False hound!
> If you have writ your annals true, 'tis there
> That, like an eagle in a dove-cote, I
> Flutter'd your Volscians in Corioli.
> Alone I did it. 'Boy'!   5.6.101–17

Very soon, incredibly but inevitably, a personal inner-play emerges. It is my 'play' and the academic would cry out in horror, but at this stage I am reaching for this subjective viewpoint. It is in this crucible that my personal dream within the play is born.

The next stage is to read the text again, but this time to discover the basic storyline. Having dreamt the play, I now see if I can report as clearly as possible the plot and its development. Invariably I am surprised at the gaps my dream has left in the full story. In this case the political struggle and the conflict with the people take a second place for me to the striking themes of war, excellence and immaturity. The pace of the play is austere and relentless. From the first scene we are plunged into the midst of a crowd of plebeians in tumult and on their way to break open the granaries for the grain which is being held from them by the patricians. Caius Martius's name is immediately used as the chief enemy, a figure of arrogance and hate. The citizenry are held in a state of oppression and usury. Menenius, the avuncular elder statesman, halts them by virtue of his class and presence. The plebeians listen attentively to his tale of the belly and the spell of the patrician class works yet again. Martius walks into this situation with arrogant invulnerability for this society instinctively obeys the patricians. The news arrives of restored hostilities with

Rome's arch enemies, the Volscians. Martius, now a creature in his element, leads the poor out to battle as if they were vermin. The new representatives of the people, the Tribunes Sicinius and Brutus, observe all this. They are men of cunning and political acumen, who are well able to out-manoeuvre this spoilt child Martius.

In the next third of the play we see Martius at the height of his powers in battle, questing for Aufidius and caring less and less for his cackling farmyard of an army that betrays him and gets in his way. He takes Corioli single-handed and charges from one conflict to another until at last he meets Aufidius. The major fight of the play happens. Martius progressively flays Aufidius and is at the moment of the kill when the Antiates, Aufidius's personal guard, rush in and save him. This leaves Martius, at the peak of his battle fury, alone on stage and robbed of his completed victory. The Roman army finally catches up with him. He recoils from any praise like an awkward adolescent, which would be an endearing characteristic were it not for his brutal contempt which shadows him all the time. Even when he specifically requests mercy for a poor man of Corioli, he spoils this moment of compassionate generosity because he is unable to remember the man's name. The only name he is unable to forget is Tullus Aufidius. Martius is a supreme athlete and an unbearable whelp. He is a sort of martial John McEnroe, except that he is thirty or more years old and so no longer an uncertain adolescent. He returns in honour and glory to a waiting and parental Rome that will demand that he grow up; a resentful and perceptive Rome that is going to play the unforgiving adult game of politics and power. The title of Coriolanus is presented to him and Shakespeare gives a fleeting glimpse of his family life and with his wife, son and mother. This reveals perhaps a domestic life of boyish and awkward affection, but no more than a glimpse is allowed. Menenius steers him towards the Consulship and for the first time in his life he goes through the charade of standing in robes of humility in the market place to woo the plebeians for election. He survives the experience without destroying his chances, but only just.

Coriolanus again seems to be at the height of his power: a Consul of Rome and, to make his joy complete, news of more action against the Volsces arrives. This is soon interrupted, however, by news from those scheming Tribunes, Sicinius and Brutus, who announce that the people's vote has been reversed. Coriolanus turns on them with blistering contempt and lightning wit. Sicinius, poor soul, makes the mistake of using a seemingly innocent little word in his response, whereupon Coriolanus reveals a command of words that sears patricians and plebeians alike:

> SICINIUS: It is a mind
> That shall remain a poison where it is,
> Not poison any further,
> CORIOLANUS: Shall remain!
> Hear you this Triton of the minnows? Mark you
> His absolute 'shall'?
> COMINIUS: 'Twas from the canon.
> CORIOLANUS: 'Shall'!
> O good but most unwise patricians! Why,
> You grave but reckless senators, have you thus
> Given Hydra here to choose an officer
> That with his peremptory 'shall', being but
> The horn and noise o' th' monster's, wants not spirit
> To say he'll turn your current in a ditch,
> And make your channel his? If he have power,
> Then vail your ignorance; if none, awake
> Your dangerous lenity. If you are learn'd,
> Be not as common fools; if you are not,
> Let them have cushions by you. You are plebeians,
> If they be senators; and they are no less,
> When, both your voices blended, the great'st taste
> Most palates theirs. They choose their magistrate;
> And such a one as he, who puts his 'shall',
> His popular 'shall', against a graver bench
> Than ever frown'd in Greece.

3.1.86–107

His rage reaches boiling point and he manhandles Sicinius for calling him a traitor. His fellow patricians have to save him from the crowd who are baying for his death. The patricians are stunned by the blind passion that has put them all at risk. It is Menenius once again who manages to speak up for Coriolanus and is left with the task of persuading him to face a trial before the plebeians. The next scene in which his mother, Volumnia, who has schooled him to be an ideal hero of Roman 'Virtus', now joins Menenius to tutor him in the arts of duplicity and politics is both painful and comic. Coriolanus becomes a spoilt child but finally, albeit petulantly, obeys. He walks like a lamb to slaughter. Sicinius goads him into defiant rage with contemptuous ease and the sentence of banishment becomes inevitable. But out of the silence which prologues his reply, Coriolanus delivers one of the most chilling and calculated speeches of contempt and threat ever written:

> You common cry of curs, whose breath I hate
> As reek o' th' rotten fens, whose loves I prize
> As the dead carcasses of unburied men
> That do corrupt my air – I banish you.
> And here remain with your uncertainty!
> Let every feeble rumour shake your hearts;
> Your enemies, with nodding of their plumes,
> Fan you into despair! Have the power still
> To banish your defenders, till at length
> Your ignorance – which finds not till it feels,
> Making but reservation of yourselves
> Still your own foes – deliver you
> As most abated captives to some nation
> That won you without blows! Despising
> For you the city, thus I turn my back;
> There is a world elsewhere.

3.3.122–37

The dynamic of his character changes. He seems somehow to have matured and takes leave of his wife, family and friends with charm and wit. He then runs out through the gate alone, dismissing everything Roman.

The second half of the play records his entry into the world of the Volsces. Theirs is an atavistic society which has not, like Rome, been caught up in the rising aspirations of the people. Coriolanus chooses to enter Aufidius's city, Antium, like a beggar. I imagine him having spent weeks wandering over the desert lands until he is dishevelled, almost like an ascetic fakir. His first exile has been into himself alone. It is his test. He is now indistinguishable from the Roman plebeians he despises. His meeting and joining with Tullus Aufidius is like a love scene. He thrives and grows in the tribal society which adores him and worships his way. Aufidius grows more and more bitter as Coriolanus outshines him. At last Coriolanus is in his element, a romantic loner like T. E. Lawrence who donned the dress and the ways of the Bedhouin. He becomes a warlord bent on Rome's destruction. The city shudders in paralysed fear at the inevitable return of Coriolanus in vengeance. Menenius, with his pathetic belief in his ability to persuade, is rejected as brutally as Falstaff is by Hal when he became King. Finally Volumnia and his wife and son come to him. His inner armour melts and he is a child again before his mother, but now he sees the emotional blackmail. His passion has always been honest and true to his belief in the natural order. His heart overwhelms him and he sinks to his knees in obedience to it. But he also sees that his death at the hands of the Volsces, who despise such sentiment, is now inevitable:

> O mother, mother!
> What have you done? Behold, the heavens do ope,
> The gods look down, and this unnatural scene
> They laugh at. O my mother, mother! O!
> You have won a happy victory to Rome;
> But for your son – believe it, O, believe it! –
> Most dangerously you have with him prevail'd,
> If not most mortal to him. But let it come.

> 5.3.182–9

After making peace with Rome, he returns deliberately to Corioli with the peace terms to face the consequence of what he recognises has been a betrayal. Aufidius knows exactly which taunts to use: he breaks Coriolanus's control by calling him Martius and then a 'boy of tears'. Coriolanus is hemmed in and destroyed by a crowd of assassins, who deny him the space he has always needed, even in death. The space and isolation return as they all stand back in awe at what they have destroyed and the ease with which they have done it:

> AUFIDIUS: My rage is gone,
> And I am struck with sorrow. Take him up.
> Help, three o' th' chiefest soldiers; I'll be one.
> Beat thou the drum, that it speak mournfully;
> Trail your steel pikes. Though in this city he
> Hath widowed and unchilded many a one,
> Which to this hour bewail the injury,
> Yet he shall have a noble memory.

> 5.6.147–54

My final act is to leave you with some impression of the contest with which an actor playing Coriolanus is faced. Reading the play and dreaming the dream casts down these questions as part of the challenge. How do I, as Coriolanus, master the alchemy of a man with the chemical elements of Mohammed Ali at his peak, John McEnroe at his most unbearable and Lawrence of Arabia at his most beguiling? How do I digest the fact that he has a mother like Volumnia who is both Queen Victoria and Edith Evans in her most commanding and living mood? How do I become a man who devours an uncle and mentor like Menenius, who is Dennis Healey and Robert Morley in one man? How do I become a man who both hates and loves Tullus Aufidius, who is a mix of Tarzan of the Apes and Richard Nixon? I have to be all this and be true to my own persona. I have to move in a society that is the USA of 1968 during the Chicago riots, or Poland faced by the shadowy eminence of the USSR. The challenge excites the whole body, mind and spirit, yet, at the same time, once the dream beast is unleashed, it terrifies the actor about the strength of his techniques and control. If you add to the formula the aqua vita of Shakespeare's genius for a turn of phrase, you can anticipate a major theatrical event. I remember that Shakespeare, like a poker player, placed a card down on the table in front of me and whispered 'There you are; make a man out of that, if you can'.

KING JOHN
Sir Peter Parker

Sir Peter Parker had a distinguished acting career at Oxford, playing the titles roles in both Hamlet *and* King Lear. *He had a successful career in business and was Chairman of the British Rail Board from 1976 to 1983. The programme was made at his home in Minster Lovell.*

For me, Shakespeare's *King John* has a triple fascination. The story itself has the speed of a good, blood-curdling thriller. Then there is the Shakespearean verve and vision that transfigures the medieval underworld of crooked kings and their baronial Mafia. But I also find in it an anatomy of the relationships of power and personality. It's a revelation of the nature of leadership and in terms not only of the unacceptable face of feudalism in England 800 years ago, but any time – including now.

The effigy of King John at Worcester Cathedral is said to be the earliest royal effigy in England. Already, it strikes me, it is well into the hushed, polite tradition of not speaking too unkindly of the kingly dead. It wants to tell us, it seems, that here lies a king who had everything it takes to wear a crown: the wide, high brow to mark his intelligence, the stern, judging poise and the slim nobility. So far, so good – and it does square with some of the historical facts. In some ways, John was one of our most competent royals. He did have a magnificent library and he had the demonic energy of his parents. Queen Eleanor, his mother, was one of the richest and most remarkable women in Europe in her prime. Henry II, his father, was famous for 'being impatient of repose and did not hesitate to disrupt half Christendom'. Certainly, in that rampaging family tradition, John was a true son, but the truth seemed to be not in him otherwise. From a different angle, there are hints even in this effigy that tell us more of what he really was: a brilliant thug and, finally, a failure. The intelligent face and tilting poise suggest to me equally subtly a fatal tension between hesitancy and cruelty, the creepy and the sudden, wilful ferocity that ruined his reign. From this angle, the stone mask slips and the judgement of history stands. Even Churchill, that most generous of historians who, after all, could make history for himself, concluded 'no

SIR PETER PARKER

animal is more full of contradictions than John'. In history his reign from 1199 to 1216 reads as an exhausting saga of cunning skill, weakness, war and collapse.

In theatre, however, it's a different story. Shakespeare's hand of glory transforms all this sad stuff, above all, into an entertainment for his times – some might say for all time. But I've a shrewd idea that Shakespeare, the playwright and businessman, was aiming to fill his theatre. After all, eventually he had shares in it. In a sense he was always aiming at the Globe, not the world. The last speech in this play has been popular for centuries in our patriotic repertoire, but there were special good reasons why it was superb box office in its own Elizabethan times:

> BASTARD: This England never did, nor never shall,
> Lie at the proud foot of a conqueror,
> But when it first did help to wound itself.
> Now these her princes are come home again,
> Come the three corners of the world in arms,
> And we shall shock them. Nought shall make us rue,
> If England to itself do rest but true.   5.7.112–8

In a play often criticised for its lack of focus on a hero the Bastard, the lovechild of Richard the Lionheart, turns out to be the only real man around. In historical fact, he was the most fictional character. Most of the other names have some historical basis but he, self-aware, funny, tough, rough and piratical, is the one we can learn to feel with and for. He ends by speaking for us in an astonishingly vivid, modern tone. More, he ends by speaking for England. Love of country turns out to be the passion that survives and subsumes the undergrowth of intrigue and selfishness. This political thriller, more your hot war than your cold war, is about England at bay, England at stake, and England truly was embattled in the 1590s when the best guesses reckon this play was written. The Spanish Armada of 1588 had been smashed, but the island was still under threat, fighting for its life, fighting for its new Protestantism and fighting for its adamant Queen. This play must have been aimed at the Armada factor. The box-office appeal of 'Come the three corners of the world in arms/And we shall shock them' must have been as rousing as three cheers. By the way, it's not four corners but three. John was fighting Spain, the Pope and France, and nearly four hundred years later Shakespeare's England was fighting Spain, the Pope and, from time to time, France. There's something in this play we seem to need in times of crisis – unity.

As John's star shoots down, the Bastard's rises steadily up and that star-crossed pattern gives a shape and balance to the play. John starts in a blaze of over-confidence. He defies the challenge of France who claim his throne on behalf of Prince Arthur, the son of John's dead elder brother, Geoffrey, and his wife, Constance. How those Elizabethan audiences seemed to enjoy the procession of royal detail. They seemed to enjoy clambering over royal family trees like kids over climbing frames in a playground. The French ambassador talks of John's 'borrowed majesty' and Shakespeare ruthlessly confirms John as a usurper. I say ruthlessly because the rules of primogeniture were anything but clear in those days. Shakespeare, however, gives John no benefit of the doubt. Queen Eleanor, listening, is unmoved by the high-flown argy-bargy of John and the French ambassador. She brings her son down to brass tacks. She tells him off for going over the top into war and then, realistically, chillingly, reminds him that he has no right to what he's got, so now he had better fight for it. Mother knows best. Possession is all ten points of the law:

> ELINOR: What now, my son! Have I not ever said
> How that ambitious Constance would not cease
> Till she had kindled France and all the world
> Upon the right and party of her son?
> This might have been prevented and made whole
> With very easy arguments of love,
> Which now the manage of two kingdoms must
> With fearful bloody issue arbitrate.
> JOHN: Our strong possession and our right for us!
> ELINOR: Your strong possession much more than your right,
> Or else it must go wrong with you and me;
> So much my conscience whispers in your ear,
> Which none but heaven and you and I shall hear.

I.I.31–43

The First Act concentrates on the ambiguities of power and legitimacy. The Bastard prefers to rely on his illegitimacy. He prefers to rely on his illegitimate noble blood to prove himself. 'I will take my chance', he says. John lacks that cool assurance. The usurper hotly argues his rights. At the start, they are the two faces of the debased coin of power, but at once we are made to feel that one is a man, the other a royal mouse – well, more than a mouse, King Rat.

The plot thickens and quickens, pell mell, after this. John

invades France, a dazzling model of military decision and despatch. The two colliding armies of England and France meet at Angiers and each claim that city, which has sensibly shut its gates. They tangle in an elaborate, bloody farce of ritual bombast, of vaunting and taunting, of wheeling and dealing. The spokesman for Angiers says that they want to be loyal, but they have a problem. Loyal to whom? 'He that proves the King,/To him will we prove loyal', he says. At the end of this hot, malicious day Hubert saves his city and everybody's face by suggesting a marriage between King John's niece, Blanche, and the French King's son, the Dauphin Louis. This is a Machiavellian marriage of total expediency. Both sides have betrayed their original purposes and alliances in the sell-out. This crude, patched-up peace between the Kings lasts no time. The Papal delegate appears and isolates John in his defiance of Rome. Once again, for a flashing moment, John must have seemed to the Elizabethan audiences a star, the unsteady morning star of Protestantism 300 years before the Reformation. But with more war, more alarums and excursions, the star fades deathly pale.

The plot darkens. John loses his way and his nerve. His capture of Arthur tempts him to murder. His plot fails but, anyway, Arthur dies trying to escape. His mysterious death infects the land. The air is filled with omens:

> HUBERT: Old men and beldams in the streets
>   Do prophesy upon it dangerously;
>   Young Arthur's death is common in their mouths;
>   And when they talk of him, they shake their heads,
>   And whisper one another in the ear;
>   And he that speaks doth gripe the hearer's wrist,
>   Whilst he that hears makes fearful action
>   With wrinkled brows, with nods, with rolling eyes.
>   I saw a smith stand with his hammer, thus,
>   The whilst his iron did on the anvil cool,
>   With open mouth swallowing a tailor's news;
>   Who, with his shears and measure in his hand,
>   Standing on slippers, which his nimble haste
>   Had falsely thrust upon contrary feet,
>   Told of a many thousand warlike French
>   That were embattailed and rank'd in Kent.
>   Another lean unwashed artificer
>   Cuts off his tale, and talks of Arthur's death.

4.2.185–202

The play works up to a climax of double-crossing at the top. John is burning out by now. The two armies of England and France slog themselves to a standstill. French reinforcements founder on the Goodwin sands and the English forces are lost in the Wash. John, sickening, is poisoned by a priest and peace breaks out the only way it ever could, over his dead body. The Bastard's famous call for unity is the requiem.

But there's more to this complex thriller than its final flourish of a Tudor political broadcast. Somehow, through the war and chaos of Shakespeare's play, we're drawn above it all into the peace of his world. In an exaltation of language and spirit, we are freed to see our life and that of others in a larger reality, in larger detail, yet in larger mystery. I take it to be a young man's play. Shakespeare was probably about thirty when he wrote it. The language is full of fire, literally. It goes for the speed and for the body. It's full of personalised, sensual imagery: eyes, lips, hands (amazing how many mentions of hands), uproarious bawdy, sex and rape. All the spills and thrills of the Plantagenets are here and there is room still for the great themes that seem to matter to Shakespeare throughout his working life. There are three in particular and all variations on the main theme of power: power and innocence; power failing; and power and personality. First, the fate of Prince Arthur is at the heart of the violation of innocence theme. Inexorably, there comes the brutal encounter between innocence and power, innocence armed only with its own helplessness against the force of evil. In Shakespeare, innocence is never enough. Over and over again his characters, men, women and children, protest their innocence, loyalties and worthiness, but their unilateral declaration of disarmament is ignored. Most pathetic, of course, are the children: the two Princes in the Tower in *Richard III*, Macduff's son in *Macbeth* and here little Arthur. The build-up to the horror is masterly. After the tumult and the shouting of battle, John goes deadly quiet and slips into his lowest gear. He seduces his agent, Hubert, into a mood of murder. Craftily, he fumbles through dark, velvety folds of hints, half sentences and suppressed desires. Words, carefully, almost fail him. Hubert falls for it and John pounces. The crunch comes in one line of blank verse:

JOHN: Then, in despite of brooded watchful day,
    I would into thy bosom pour my thoughts.
    But, ah, I will not! Yet I love thee well;
    And, by my troth, I think thou lov'st me well.
HUBERT: So well that what you bid me undertake,

Though that my death were adjunct to my act,
By heaven, I would do it.
JOHN: Do not I know thou wouldst?
Good Hubert, Hubert, Hubert, throw thine eye
On yon young boy. I'll tell thee what, my friend,
He is a very serpent in my way;
And wheresoe'er this foot of mine doth tread,
He lies before me. Dost thou understand me?
Thou art his keeper.
HUBERT: And I'll keep him so
That he shall not offend your Majesty.
JOHN: Death.
HUBERT: My lord?
JOHN: A grave.
HUBERT: He shall not live.
JOHN: Enough!
I could be merry now. Hubert, I love thee.

3.3.52–67

Arthur's mother, Constance, is the manifestation of another recurring theme in Shakespeare: power failing but proud. Constance has operatic arias, too many for my liking, of vengeful grief, but she has one exquisite moment of truth. It echoes the moment in *Richard II* when despair bears the King down through hierarchical layers of pomp and circumstance and he bumps to earth: 'let us sit upon the ground/And tell sad stories of the death of kings'. Constance, after her rantings, is wonderfully moving when she too earths the lightning:

SALISBURY: Pardon me, madam,
I may not go without you to the kings.
CONSTANCE: Thou mayst, thou shalt; I will not go with thee;
I will instruct my sorrows to be proud,
For grief is proud, and makes his owner stoop.
To me, and to the state of my great grief,
Let kings assemble; for my grief's so great
That no supporter but the huge firm earth
Can hold it up. Here I and sorrows sit;
Here is my throne, bid kings come bow to it.

3.1.65–74

The rise and fall of kings and queens. This is the rhythm of each of Shakespeare's nine Plantagenet plays. Praise be, Shakespeare converts these dynastic quarrels, these medieval star wars, into men and women we can all understand.

To make a play work in theatre ideas have to be personalised. Not even Shakespeare could cast a constitutional issue. For him politics, the management of power, is never left to party lines or lineage. For him, at least it seems so to my managerial eye, the legitimacy of power shows finally through the character of leadership:

> BASTARD: Mad world! mad kings! mad composition!
> John, to stop Arthur's title in the whole,
> Hath willingly departed with a part;
> And France, whose armour conscience buckled on,
> Whom zeal and charity brought to the field
> As God's own soldier, rounded in the ear
> With that same purpose-changer, that sly devil,
> That broker that still breaks the pate of faith,
> That daily break-vow, he that wins all,
> Of kings, of beggars, old men, young men, maids,
> Who having no external thing to lose
> But the word 'maid', cheats the poor maid of that;
> That smooth-fac'd gentleman, tickling commodity,
> Commodity, the bias of the world –
> The world, who of itself is peised well,
> Made to run even upon even ground,
> Till this advantage, this vile-drawing bias,
> This sway of motion, this commodity,
> Makes it take head from all indifferency,
> From all direction, purpose, course, intent –
> And this same bias, this commodity,
> This bawd, this broker, this all-changing word,
> Clapp'd on the outward eye of fickle France,
> Hath drawn him from his own determin'd aid,
> From a resolv'd and honourable war,
> To a most base and vile-concluded peace.

2.1.561–86

The play's anatomy of power interests me enormously. I know it's a book not often set for schools. I can understand that. Wasn't it Auden who said that history is too criminal a subject for the young? But it could well be set for management schools. Any of us who have to manage anything, who hold accountable authority, must have some concept or even philosophy of power. To get anything done in an organisation of any size – a company, a union, national government, local government, any institution – there must be an answer to the sovereign question: why should an order be obeyed? Any organisation needs orders. What is the sanction of the orders? Where is the source of sovereignty? Politics is the human, fallible process of trying to fix that point of sovereignty in a society, so there is law and order. And in any organisation that has to get things to happen, there is the same problem. Order-giving and order-taking must make sense to the individual ultimately at each end of the communication, Democracy, the worst sort of government except for every other sort of government as the saying goes, seeks to establish the legitimacy of authority through the individual vote. Too often with romantic over-precision, we trace back the rights of the individual to that misty ceremony at Runnymede where John was forced to sign the Magna Carta. For most people the Magna Carta is the one thing to be remembered about the bad King John's reign, certainly the only good thing. But Shakespeare, writing as far in time from John as we are from Shakespeare today, ignored it completely. What interested him and his audiences was not constitutional development but the personalities of power. Were they up to it? He who wears the crown can stand only if he can deliver. A weak king is the worst of kings. He breaks the power that is given to him in trust by society. He breaks his social contract.

John loses power because he has not the character to use it properly. The Bastard is unable to change him:

> Be great in act, as you have been in thought;
> Let not the world see fear and sad distrust
> Govern the motion of a kingly eye.
> Be stirring as the time; be fire with fire;
> Threaten the threat'ner, and outface the brow
> Of bragging horror; so shall inferior eyes,
> That borrow their behaviours from the great,
> Grow great by your example and put on
> The dauntless spirit of resolution.

5.1.45–53

All the royal picture cards land face up in this power play. The Jack, the Dauphin, calls it a game, an easy match played for a crown and thinks that he's the winning card. The Queen knows that the game is fixed and tries to mark her son's card, the King. John thinks that he is trumps, but all the King's horses and all the King's men cannot save him. The Ace, the Bastard, is high. For me he is the only character with real character. 'I am I', he says, 'Howe'er I was begot'. That's his Magna Carta. He grows to greatness. The leader emerges. We almost wish he would pick up the crown and wear it to end the tug and the scramble, but Shakespeare has no intention of leaving us with the Fuehrer principle, the cult of personality, centre stage. After all, the triumph of individual character and leadership is to serve. So the Bastard, as the curtain falls, falls to his knees to accept the young Prince Henry as his King who, in historical fact, went on to reign fifty-six years, one of our longest reigns. The Bastard cannot be the hero. England is.

KING JOHN
Emrys James

Emrys James is a member of the Royal Shakespeare Company. Besides the title role in King John, *his leading roles have included Iago, Shylock and Henry IV. He played Enobarbus in the BBC TV production of* Antony and Cleopatra *and the Player King in the production of* Hamlet.

King John has never had a good press. A. A. Milne said:

> King John was not a good man
> He had his little ways
> And sometimes no-one spoke to him
> For days and days and days.

And the play that Shakespeare wrote about him has not had a particularly good press either. Let me quote James Agate, a leading theatre critic, who said in 1941:

> What a bad play this is, all about a war in which it is not possible to take the slightest interest. No critic has ever had much to say for King John.

Theatre critics often get it wrong! But no less an editor than John Dover Wilson said, in his edition of the play:

> Shakespeare's life and death of King John is not from the literary standpoint one of his best or most interesting plays and though, as I am told by actors who have played it, by no means ineffective in the theatre, it is rarely seen upon the modern stage.

At least he allows that the actors might know something about its quality. When you come to look at the actors who've played King John the list contains some formidable talents: Garrick, Kean, Macready, Kemble and Beerbohm Tree. When Beerbohm Tree played it he incorporated a scene in dumb show where the barons were seen advancing on John and forcing him to sign Magna Carta, whereupon John was seen throwing himself on the floor and biting the rushes in his rage. Oddly enough so dramatic a scene as the signing of the Magna Carta has no place at all in Shakespeare's play. It's not even mentioned. That episode of history didn't gain its hallowed place in English thought until some fifty or sixty years after Shakespeare's death, in the struggle between the Stuart kings and parliament. But let me turn to another and greater critic, Dr Johnson, who said this:

> The tragedy is varied with a very pleasing interchange of incidents and characters. The lady's grief is very affecting, and the character of the Bastard contains that mixture of greatness and levity which this author delighted to exhibit.

Good old Dr Johnson. He invariably gets it right and he unerringly pinpoints two of the great characters of the play: the first Constance, or 'Crying Constance' as the part was called, a bravura role for actresses since the day of Mrs Siddons, and the second, the illegitimate son of one of England's great heroes, Richard the Lionheart, the Bastard Falconbridge who has I suppose the lines in the play most people would recognise:

> This England never did, nor never shall,
> Lie at the proud foot of a conqueror,
> But when it first did help to wound itself.
> Now these her princes are come home again,
> Come the three corners of the world in arms,
> And we shall shock them. Naught shall make us rue,
> If England to itself do rest but true.   5.7.112–8

It's odd though that Johnson calls it a tragedy. No epic fall of a great man occurs and though sad things happen there are no elevated themes with tragic endings. Given the swiftness of the story and of events the play is more of a chronicle history.

What does actually happen? Richard the First, The Lionheart or Coeur-de-Lion as he's called in the play, is dead. He had no legitimate heir so the crown should have passed to his next brother Geoffrey – but he's dead too, killed in a tournament. So the younger brother John, backed by his mother, a strong character, Eleanor of Aquitaine has grabbed the throne. I say grabbed because Geoffrey has a young son Arthur whose strong claim to be King is backed by his mother Constance and by the King of France. The first three acts depict the challenges and battles that arise from the two claims to the throne. John takes the war to France. When it looks as if the struggle will be settled by a marriage between the son of the King of France, the Dauphin, and Blanche, John's niece, thus dropping Arthur's claim, the church tries to grab a piece of the action. Cardinal Pandulph, the Legate of Rome, enters and in a whirlwind of zeal excommunicates John and spurs the French into re-opening hostilities. A battle takes place in which John captures young Arthur to the huge despair of Arthur's mother, Constance. The rest of the play takes place in England. Arthur dies accidentally but unhappily for John it looks like 'accident done-a-purpose.' The English barons, then as now an unpredictable and eccentric group, outraged at Arthur's presumed murder, decide to join the French who at their second attempt invade England – their first attempt fell foul of that mixed blessing the English weather. In the ensuing battle the barons learn that the French have a cunning plot to execute them once they have gained power. So they decide to return to King John's side and the French are held off. John however is dying, worn out by bad luck, sickened by a fever and finally poisoned by a monk. The play ends with the retreat of the French. All England's princes do come home again and unite under John's son, Prince Henry, who becomes Henry III. The mainspring of the plot is the claim and fate of Arthur. The action is a see-saw struggle for power, a chronicle of greed, ambition, religious interference and expedience. It is in fact a very modern story, the very essence of a successful television series about power and what its pursuit does to people.

I've been in *King John* twice. The first time was in 1960 at the Old Vic when I played Chatillon, the French Ambassador, and the second time with the Royal Shakespeare Company when I played the King himself. That was eleven years ago in 1974. When I started thinking about this programme I went back to the text and read it through and despite what some critics have said I was immediately struck by what an extraordinarily good play it is. So good in fact that my actor's instinct made me want to do it again and soon. *King John* is written throughout in verse, that bold iambic pentameter, the striding ten beats to the line that Shakespeare used so brilliantly. The poetry has a lean and sinewy quality about it. There is no padding and everything is said directly and forcefully. This gives the play one of its most striking characteristics – the speed at which events occur.

Take the very beginning. King John addresses the French ambassador:

KING JOHN: Now, say, Chatillon, what would France with us?
CHATILLON: Thus, after greeting, speaks the King of France
In my behaviour to the majesty,
The borrowed majesty, of England here

ELINOR: A strange beginning – 'borrowed majesty'!
KING JOHN: Silence, good mother; hear the embassy.

1.1.1–6

There it is, straightaway, the confrontation between England and France, and we learn too that John's mother, Queen Eleanor, likes to interfere. There follows shortly a declaration of war and an admission that John's claim to the throne is doubtful. As Eleanor says to him 'Your strong possession much more than you right'. Then we meet one of Shakespeare's most attractive characters, the Bastard Falconbridge, and we're only fifty lines into the play.

Or take the middle. Where in other writers the action often sags, here we have several breathtakingly swift scenes: John proposes the murder of the imprisoned Arthur to one of his followers, Hubert:

KING JOHN: I'll tell thee what, my friend,
   He is a very serpent in my way;
   And whereso'er this foot of mine doth tread,
   He lies before me. Dost thou understand me?
   Thou art his keeper.
HUBERT: And I'll keep him so,
   That he shall not offend your Majesty.
KING JOHN: Death.

3.3.60–5

In the next scene comes Constance's lament for Arthur:

Grief fills the room up of my absent child,
Lies in his bed, walks up and down with me,
Puts on his pretty looks, repeats his words,
Remembers me of all his gracious parts,
Stuffs out his vacant garments with his form;
Then, have I reason to be fond of grief.

3.4.93–8

After that lament with what chilling effect on the audience follows the torture scene. 'Must you with hot irons burn out both mine eyes?', Arthur cries. 'Young boy, I must' says Hubert, although at the end he relents and leaves Arthur unharmed. In the next scene John is brought news of the French invasion and is told of his mother's death, the mother on whom he was so dependent:

KING JOHN: O, where hath our intelligence been drunk?
   Where hath it slept? Where is my mother's care?
   That such an army could be drawn in France,

263

And she not hear of it?
MESSENGER: My liege, her ear
  Is stopp'd with dust: the first of April died
  Your noble mother; and as I hear, my Lord,
  The Lady Constance in a frenzy died
  Three days before; . . . .
KING JOHN: Withold thy speed, dreadful occasion!

4.2.116–25

Then Arthur kills himself when attempting to escape and there is a squabble over who's to blame. No wonder Shakespeare wrote in another play of the two hour traffic of the stage.

The speed of the action does not prevent fine and skilful character drawing, from the smallest to the largest parts. Take the smallest. James Gurney has four words. There's a name for a good four square man of the soil. Does it perhaps remind you of one of the characters who went to Widdecombe Fair with Old Uncle Tom Cobleigh and all? James Gurney escorts the Bastard's mother, Lady Falconbridge. The Bastard asks him to leave them while they discuss private matters:

BASTARD: James Gurney, wilt thou give us leave awhile?
GURNEY: Good leave, good Philip.

1.1.230–1

And the Bastard, who a moment before has been knighted, bridles,

Philip – Sparrow! James,
There's toys abroad – anon I'll tell thee more.

1.1.231–2

Exit Gurney. With what skill is drawn there the relationship between the two men: men who are clearly affectionate with each other, who have met, say, in the stables or out hunting and who are used to each other and easy with each other. And of course that says something about the down-to-earth qualities of the Bastard too.

Then take a major character, John himself. John seems to me to be a quite remarkable portrayal of a weak man in a position of power. We saw something of that in that key first scene. He is dependent on his mother, but shows a lot of spirit in rebuffing the French Ambassador:

Be thou as lightning in the eyes of France;
For ere thou canst report I will be there,

The thunder of my cannon shall be heard.
So hence! Be thou the trumpet of our wrath
And sullen presage of your own decay.

1.1.24–8

But he is also an adept player of the power game: wicked, devious, unscrupulous and murderous. Consider the way that he prepares Hubert, his henchman, for murder. Hubert is I suppose the medieval equivalent of the rising middle class. He wants to get on and the King begins by saying to him 'I owe you an awful lot, you're a good fellow. I wish I could unburden myself to you, but there's something in my way.' He continues:

> KING JOHN: Or if that thou couldst see me without eyes,
> Hear me without thine ears, and make reply
> Without a tongue, using conceit alone,
> Without eyes, ears, and harmful sound of words –
> Then, in despite of brooded watchful day,
> I would into thy bosom pour my thoughts.
> But, ah, I will not! Yet I love thee well;
> And, by my troth, I think thou lov'st me well.
> HUBERT: So well that what you bid me undertake,
> Though that my death were adjunct to my act,
> By heaven, I would do it.
> KING JOHN: Do not I know thou wouldst?
> Good Hubert, Hubert, Hubert, throw thine eye
> On yon young boy. I'll tell thee what, my friend,
> He is a very serpent in my way;
> And wheresoe'r this foot of mine doth tread,
> He lies before me. Dost thou understand me?
> Thou art his keeper.
> HUBERT: And I'll keep him so
> That he shall not offend your Majesty.
> KING JOHN: Death.
> HUBERT: My lord?
> KING JOHN: A grave.
> HUBERT: He shall not live.
> KING JOHN: Enough!

3.3.48–65

Notice the way he uses the man's name: 'Good Hubert, Hubert, Hubert' and the brilliance of that last exchange. This in fact lasts just over the ten beat line and the extra beat reinforces the jaggedness. Another thing about this scene, and indeed about much of the character portrayal, is Shakespeare's unerring eye for psychological truth. The moment that Hubert has agreed to murder Arthur, John, a man who knows that he is doing wrong, immediately feels a great relief:

> I could be merry now. Hubert, I love thee.
> Well, I'll not say what I intend for thee.
> Remember.

3.3.66–9

Though John is weak, he has resilience. In the same scene where he is beaten down by the invasion of the French, the desertion of the nobles and the news of his mother's death, he bounces back with

> I was amaz'd
> Under the tide; but now I breathe again
> Aloft the flood, and can give audience
> To any tongue, speak it of what it will.

4.2.137–40

In fact for all John's many bad qualities there remains a good deal in his character we are forced to admire. He is an undaunted fighter who has the capacity to make good men like Hubert and the Bastard love him.

What a character the Bastard is. One of Shakespeare's great characters, of the line of Mercutio and Hotspur in his energy, wit and bravery. He is also the one character of the play who is not mentioned in Shakespeare's historical sources – in other words he is an invention of the playwright. He is set up at the beginning as a sturdy, down-to-earth, good thinking chap, almost the essence of Englishness, or as the English like to see themselves. But he is also like a Western hero, not perhaps John Wayne maybe Paul Newman. For instance, his first confrontation with the braggart Archduke of Austria, who wears on his shoulders the lion skin he took from Coeur-de-lion, seems to me the kind of wisecrack that appears in any Western:

> CONSTANCE: Thou wear a lion's hide! Doff it for shame,
>   And hang a calf's skin on those recreant limbs.
> AUSTRIA: O that a man should speak those words to me!
> BASTARD: And hang a calf's skin on those recreant limbs.
> AUSTRIA: Thou dar'st not say so, villain, for thy life.
> BASTARD: And hang a calf's-skin on those recreant limbs.

3.1.127–33

He begins as a ribald careless soldier but, as the play unfolds, he loses something of his gaiety and rises in personal consequence. Here he is encouraging John:

> BASTARD: But wherefore do you droop? Why look you sad?
>   Be great in act, as you have been in thought;
>   Let not the world see fear and sad distrust
>   Govern the motion of a kingly eye.
>   Be stirring as the time; be fire with fire;
>   Threaten the threat'ner, and out-face the brow
>   Of bragging horror; so shall inferior eyes,
>   That borrow their behaviours from the great,
>   Grow great by your example and put on
>   The dauntless spirit of resolution.
>   Away, and glister like the god of war
>   When he intendeth to become the field;
>   Show boldness and aspiring confidence.

5.1.44–56

The date generally given to the play is 1596, which is interesting when we think what happened to Shakespeare in that year. It's just eight years after the great Spanish Armada attempted to invade England and in the play Shakespeare makes King Philip of France, England's enemy, say:

> So by a roaring tempest on the flood
> A whole Armado of convicted sail
> Is scattered and disjoin'd from fellowship.

3.4.1–3

And that is an exact description of what happened to the Spanish Armada, which set sail for these shores and was finally routed by a spell of British weather.

On the 11th August 1596 the parish register of Stratford upon Avon records the burial of Hamnet Shakespeare, son of William Shakespeare. That day was buried Hamnet, son of William, twin of Judith, both of them named after Hamnet and Judith Sadler, neighbours and friends, who in their turn, when they had a son in 1598 called him after their great friend William. I find it difficult to believe that the loss of that twelve-and-a-half year old boy in 1596 is not echoed in the lament of Constance for her son. It is worth quoting again:

> Grief fills the room up of my absent child,
> Lies in his bed, walks up and down with me,
> Puts on his pretty looks, repeats his words,

Remembers me of all his gracious parts,
Stuffs out his vacant garments with his form;
Then have I reason to be fond of grief.
Fare you well; had you such a loss as I,
I could give better comfort than you do.
I will not keep this form upon my head,
When there is such disorder in my wit.
O Lord! my boy, my Arthur, my fair son!
My life, my joy, my food, my all the world!
My widow-comfort, and my sorrows' cure!

3.4.93–105

If we accept the date of 1596 for the composition of the play it's just three years after Henry IV of France, a Protestant King, dismayed his English allies (Elizabeth was after all the daughter of England's first Protestant King Henry VIII) by a breathtaking piece of political expediency. He renounced Protestantism, accepted Catholicism and with it the rule of Paris with the famous words, 'Paris is worth a mass.' With this in mind we can appreciate more fully the speech of the Bastard when he has seen this sort of politics in action. John and Philip of France have just negotiated an agreement and gone off to celebrate:

Mad world! mad kings! mad composition!
John, to stop Arthur's title in the whole,
Hath willingly departed with a part;
And France, whose armour conscience buckled on,
Whom zeal and charity brought to the field
As God's own soldier, rounded in the ear
With that same purpose-changer, that sly devil,
That broker that still breaks the pate of faith,
That daily break-vow, he that wins of all,
Of kings, of beggars, old men, young men, maids,
Who having no external things to lose
But the word 'maid', cheats the poor maid of that;
That smooth-fac'd gentleman, tickling commodity,
Commodity, the bias of the world –
The world, who of itself is peised well,
Made to run even upon even ground,
Till this advantage, this vile-drawing bias,
This sway of motion, this commodity,
Makes it take head from all indifferency,
From all directions, purpose, course, intent –
And this same bias, this commodity,

This bawd, this broker, this all-changing word,
Clapp'd on the outward eye of fickle France,
Hath drawn him from his own determin'd aid,
From a resolv'd and honourable war,
To a most base and vile-concluded peace.

2.1.561–86

What he calls 'commodity' we would nowadays call 'expedience'.
As many of the characters of the play act on the basis of expedience we are, in a sense, watching what is almost a gangster story
because, let's face it, John, Philip of France, Lewis the Dauphin
and the barons are all out for what they can get. This sense of
gangsters at work, of irresponsible power, often surfaces in the
play. How topical for instance is the plight of the citizens caught in
the crossfire between two warring powers. It reminds one uncomfortably of the innocent people in Iran and Iraq scuttling about in
the brief hours between curfews wishing it would all go away. And
how eloquently poor Blanche, niece of King John, but shortly
betrothed to Lewis the Dauphin in an attempt to reconcile the
warring powers, sums up the plight of these innocent people
caught in crossfire:

The sun's o'ercast with blood. Fair day, adieu!
Which is the side that I must go withal?
I am with both: each army hath a hand;
And in their rage, I having hold of both,
They whirl asunder and dismember me.

3.1.326–30

In the same way, and again how uncomfortably one is reminded of
our present time, Shakespeare makes a very stirring indictment of
cruelty when Arthur, talking about his imminent torture by
Hubert, notices that the irons which have been heated to burn out
his eyes have become cold:

ARTHUR: the fire is dead with grief,
    Being create for comfort, to be us'd
    In undeserved extremes. See else yourself:
    There is no malice in this burning coal;
    The breath of heaven hath blown his spirit out,
    And strew'd repentant ashes on his head.
HUBERT: But with my breath I can revive it, boy.
ARTHUR: An if you do, you will make it blush
    And glow with shame of your proceedings, Hubert.
    Nay, it perchance will sparkle in your eyes,

> And, like a dog that is compell'd to fight,
> Snatch at his master that doth tarre him on.
> All things that you should use to do me wrong
> Deny their office; . . . .
>
> 4.1.106–19

And that basically is one of the statements of the play: that it is misuse that leads us to do wrong. The misuse of John's power leads to his undoing and his misuse of friendship leads him to embroil a good man, Hubert, in attempted murder. The barons misuse their position and their oath of loyalty, whilst Pandulph misuses the power of the church. Promises are broken, loyalties thrown aside and nothing and nobody holds true.

There is of course one exception. The Bastard shows his contempt in the great speech about commodity or 'expedience' for the way these leaders of the world break their faith. For it is one of the strengths of his character that the Bastard does keep faith. Virtually the only promise that is kept in the play is the Bastard's promise to strip Austria of his misgotten lion skin. Despite the lack of kingly qualities he must see in John, he does remain true to him, probably because he recognises that to replace John with a weaker man, or worse, a foreigner would be detrimental to England. His only moment of doubt comes when he sees the death of innocence and beauty as represented by Arthur:

> I am amaz'd, methinks, and lose my way
> Among the thorns and dangers of this world.
> How easy dost thou take all England up!
> From forth this morsel of dead royalty
> The life, the right, and truth of all this realm
> Is fled to heaven; and England now is left
> To tug and scramble, and to part by th'teeth
> The unowed interest of proud-swelling state.
>
> 4.3.140–7

But his fighting spirit reasserts itself and it is the Bastard who is left at the end of the play to sum up the course of action which will unite the country and its people:

> This England never did, nor never shall,
> Lie at the proud foot of a conqueror,
> But when it first did help to wound itself.
> Now these her princes are come home again,
> Come the three corners of the world in arms,
> And we shall shock them. Nought shall make us rue,
> If England to itself do rest but true.
>
> 5.7.112–8

MUCH ADO ABOUT NOTHING

Eleanor Bron

Eleanor Bron starred in a number of satirical programmes such as Not So Much A Programme More A Way of Life. *Her other television roles include the part of Natasha in* A Month In The Country. *She has also played a wide range of leading roles in the theatre, including Shakespearean ones. She made this programme at Broughton Park.*

Watching *Much Ado About Nothing* the audience is in a rather ironic position. They are eavesdropping. Perhaps any audience is eavesdropping, but here they are eavesdropping on a play about eavesdropping. *Much Ado About Nothing* is a play about what it can be like to exist in an enclosed society – the Civil Service or the BBC, or any great household, or a court not unlike the Court of the first Elizabeth – where the inmates live in constant hope of advancement but also with the constant possibility that at any moment they may be stabbed in the back, literally or metaphorically. The courtiers of Elizabeth were perpetually jockeying for position and for favour and – who knows – perhaps the company of actors at the Globe theatre were not without their internal politics. We could certainly find parallels in any repertory company today and indeed in any small hierarchical community, since human nature doesn't seem to have changed very much. In such a community it's impossible to have any sort of private life. It's rather like living in a goldfish bowl: not only is everything public, but there's very little room for manoeuvre. In the world of the play there is ceaseless manoeuvring; plotting, intrigue and gossip, and no privacy. The walls have eyes as well as ears, the gardens are bugged – that's the system. Some of the characters use the system and some of them abuse it. It's faster and more certain than the telephone. A word dropped here, a word dropped there, and rumours become facts, facts become rumours, lies become truth, and reputations are made or marred in a moment. The wonder is that the courtiers who spend their lives in this atmosphere remain so gullible and fall headlong into the traps that are laid for them. Though I admit I have noticed that whenever I read a newspaper interview with a total stranger I believe every word of it, whereas if it happens to be with someone that I know I almost always find it full of lies and inaccuracies.

The play has a heroine called Hero and a hero called Claudio and the action is set in motion by Claudio's decision to marry Hero. There's another couple on the scene, their friends and companions Beatrice and Benedick, who at the outset of the play have no intention in the world of ever marrying, either each other or anybody else. They offer a vivid counterpoint to the first two and though their story seems to be a sub-plot incidental to the main action, it is they who will command our attention as real human beings. Hero and Claudio are merely creatures of the Court without any minds or substance of their own. Although we learn that Claudio, who has just returned from battle, is a brave soldier and hero, in civilian life he behaves more like a weather-vane. He changes direction with every gust that blows. He falls in love with Hero, but in an extraordinary circumspect fashion. For example, before he's too far gone he makes sure that the match will have the approval of his royal patron, Don Pedro, and checks at the same time on what Hero's chances of inheritance are:

CLAUDIO: My liege, your Highness now may do me good.
DON PEDRO: My love is thine to teach; teach it but how,
   And thou shalt see how apt it is to learn
   Any hard lesson that may do thee good.
CLAUDIO: Hath Leonato any son, my lord?
DON PEDRO: No child but Hero; she's his only heir.
   Dost thou affect her, Claudio?
CLAUDIO: O, my lord,
   When you went onward on this ended action,
   I look'd upon her with a soldier's eye,
   That lik'd, but had a rougher task in hand
   Than to drive liking to the name of love;
   But now I am return'd, and that war-thoughts
   Have left their places vacant, in their rooms
   Come thronging soft and delicate desires,
   All prompting me how fair young Hero is,
   Saying I lik'd her ere I went to wars.
DON PEDRO: Thou wilt be like a lover presently,
   And tire the hearer with a book of words.

If thou dost love fair Hero, cherish it;
And I will break with her, and with her father,
And thou shalt have her. Was't not to this end
That thou began'st to twist so fine a story?   1.1.252–73

The Duke, Don Pedro, sets the tone for the behaviour of his followers and everyone who comes within the influence of his Court. Half their time seems to be spent eavesdropping so that the other half can be spent in devising plots and schemes. In the hands of the Duke these are lighthearted enough. He uses his power to play games and even to play Cupid. 'His glory shall be ours', he says, 'for we are the only love-gods'. One of his acts as Cupid is, in accordance with a common practice of the time, to offer to woo Hero on Claudio's behalf at a masked ball.

Wickedness can also flourish in such an atmosphere of intrigue and courtly machinations. Don Pedro has a bastard brother, Don John, who is eaten up with jealousy and melancholia. He has no power except what he can muster by plotting for his own quite gratuitously evil ends. It is through Don John that Hero and Claudio fall victim to some of the pernicious effects of Court life, when he maligns Hero to Claudio at this same masked ball. Claudio, who throws himself with a will into some of the other plotting that goes on in the play, shows himself nonetheless totally gullible in the face of Don John's insinuations. He believes the worst of Hero immediately; he puts up no fight at all and not only gives her no opportunity to clear her name, but actually resolves to humiliate her; he jilts her like the worst cad. He turns up at the church all right, but once there he hurls abuse at her as well as some extremely vague accusations, before the very altar itself:

CLAUDIO: Stand thee by, friar. Father, by your leave:
  Will you with free and unconstrained soul
  Give me this maid, your daughter?
LEONATO: As freely, son, as God did give her me.
CLAUDIO: And what have I to give you back whose worth
  May counterpoise this rich and precious gift?
DON PEDRO: Nothing, unless you render her again.
CLAUDIO: Sweet Prince, you learn me noble thankfulness.
  There, Leonato, take her back again;
  Give not this rotten orange to your friend;
  She's but the sign and semblance of her honour.
  Behold how like a maid she blushes here.
  O, what authority and show of truth
  Can cunning sin cover itself withal!

Comes not that blood as modest evidence
To witness simple virtue? Would you not swear,
All you that see her, that she were a maid
By these exterior shows? But she is none:
She knows the heat of a luxurious bed;
Her blush is guiltiness, not modesty.

4.1.22–41

That the two of them should find it so easy to believe a young daughter of good house to be already debauched says as much, or as little, about their own morals as it does about the morals of young daughters.

Claudio, for me, is a bit of a problem – he does seem such a rotter. It's hard to believe that he's anything but a very vain, very shallow creature of society. He lacks loyalty and integrity, he's moody and doesn't seem to learn from his mistakes. He goes step by step, according to society's book. He comes back from the wars elated and ambitious. He decides that it's time to marry. He rushes into marriage. He could easily take time to get to know Hero, but he's thoughtless and impatient. Hero, on the other hand, doesn't get the opportunity to know Claudio any better, even if she wanted it. Far from being debauched, she is the very model of good daughterdom and apparently prepared to accept any husband her father, Leonato, proposes, in spite of Beatrice urging her to reject any suitor she doesn't like:

Yes, faith; it is my cousin's duty to make curtsy, and say 'Father, as it please you'. But yet for all that, cousin, let him be a handsome fellow, or else make another curtsy and say 'Father, as it please me'.

2.1.43–7

Beatrice, Hero's cousin and confidante, is a woman from another stable altogether. She's shrewder, wiser, a woman who thinks for herself and who does do exactly 'as it pleases her', as far as that was possible for a woman of that time. In terms of spirit as well as wit and intellect, she's well matched with Benedick. He is another of Don Pedro's courtiers and, although a friend of Claudio's, as different from him as Beatrice is from Hero. At first glance, they may both seem to suffer from all the infirmities bred by Court life, but in reality there is no comparison in scale or scope of these two with Claudio and Hero. Sub-plot they may be, but they provide the weight, richness and depth of the play. Although they are shining and accomplished ornaments of a Court which revels in the spoken word, fine language, wit and verbal fireworks, they are the only two in the Court who have any integrity. For this reason they stand out from the rest and, when they meet, sparks do fly:

BEATRICE: I wonder that you will still be talking, Signior Benedick; nobody marks you.

BENEDICK: What, my dear Lady Disdain! Are you yet living?

BEATRICE: Is it possible disdain should die while she hath such meet food to feed it as Signior Benedick? Courtesy itself must convert to disdain if you come in her presence.

BENEDICK: Then is courtesy a turncoat. But it is certain I am loved of all ladies, only you excepted; and I would I could find in my heart that I had not a hard heart, for, truly, I love none.

BEATRICE: A dear happiness to women! They would else have been troubled with a pernicious suitor. I thank God, and my cold blood, I am of your humour for that: I had rather hear my dog bark at a crow than a man swear he loves me.

BENEDICK: God keep your ladyship still in that mind! So some gentleman or other shall scape a predestinate scratch'd face.

BEATRICE: Scratching could not make it worse, an 'twere such a face as yours were.

BENEDICK: Well, you are a rare parrot-teacher.

BEATRICE: A bird of my tongue is better than a beast of yours.

BENEDICK: I would my horse had the speed of your tongue, and so good a continuer. But keep your way a God's name, I have done.

BEATRICE: You always end with a jade's trick; I know you of old.

I.I.99–124

The public nature of life at Court would force any creatures of intelligence and sensibility to protect themselves, and underneath the verbal display and dazzle of the 'merry war' we sense two sensitive and vulnerable people. Theirs is one of the least sentimental and most romantic relationships in English literature. Jane Austen's Emma and Mr Knightley and Noel Coward's Amanda and Elyot in *Private Lives* are happy descendants of this noble breed.

In fact, Beatrice is just a little too successful in protecting herself. Her resistance to marriage is not perhaps all that surprising in a woman of her intelligence and especially in those days, when marriage really was a market. For the woman especially it meant losing-giving up-everything. She simply became part of her husband's goods and chattels, and Beatrice is too proud and too sensible to be prepared to sell herself to the first or to the highest bidder. She wants something better. It's not that she's without feeling – she is a very passionate being – but she does have impossibly high standards. She puts any man to the most severe tests. Benedick refers several times to her disdainfulness in the fiercest terms, likening her to a fury:

> She speaks poniards, and every word stabs; if her breath were as terrible as her terminations, there were no living near her; she would infect to the north star. I would not marry her though she were endowed with all that Adam had left him before he transgress'd; she would have made Hercules have turn'd spit, yea, and have cleft his club to make the fire too. Come, talk not of her; you shall find her the infernal Ate in good apparel. I would to God some scholar would conjure her; for certainly, while she is here, a man may live as quiet in hell as in a sanctuary; and people sin upon purpose, because they would go thither; so, indeed, all disquiet, horror, and perturbation, follows her.

2.1.218–32

It seems very likely that Beatrice, in her despairing self-defence, has gone a little too far and proved just too much for Benedick.

But I think that the gracious Lord Benedick also protests just a little too much. Beatrice appears to best him in almost every exchange, but there seems to me to be an element of almost old-fashioned chivalry in Benedick, which makes him gentler with her than she is with him; although of course – perish the thought – she may simply be cleverer than he is. He has a great reputation as a womaniser, which may be another reason for Beatrice's fierceness in a society which has one standard for men and another standard for women. There's a strong suggestion, too, that in this respect Benedick merely goes along with Court practice and that his superficiality is only on the surface. He practically admits to Claudio that he has two faces: one for the Court and another one, his real one. He pronounces himself very strongly against marriage, which is strange as he is a man and has very little to lose by it. Perhaps, like Beatrice, he is also an idealist. Or there is another possibility. Beatrice makes one reference to something in the past between them, a dalliance, the beginnings of an amour that went awry in the way that true love is proverbially supposed to do:

DON PEDRO: Come, lady, come; you have lost the heart of Signior Benedick.
BEATRICE: Indeed, my lord, he lent it me awhile; and I gave him use for it, a double heart for his single one; marry, once

> before he won it of me with false dice, therefore your Grace
> may well say I have lost it.

DON PEDRO: You have put him down, lady, you have put him
down.

BEATRICE: So I would not he should do me, my lord, lest I
should prove the mother of fools.

2.1.247–55

The device by which they are tricked back into love is a benign
version of other devices employed throughout the play. Beatrice
and Benedick are led to acknowledge their affection for each other
through a plot of Don Pedro's. He arranges for them each in turn
to eavesdrop on two scenes played out for their benefit in the
garden. The courtiers gossip first about Beatrice's passion for
Benedick and then about Benedick's passion for Beatrice. Each of
them overhears, disbelieves at first, but then falls hook, line and
sinker for the bait. You could say that there is an element of vanity
in their willingness to believe, against all appearances, that they
are the object of a grand passion; but it's also possible that they are
able to accept this unlikely thought just because they can project
onto it their own carefully disguised feelings. So the Duke's
decision to turn matchmaker is not as arbitrary or perverse as it
may seem and it does provide us with one of the great delights of
the play. One of the pleasures of *Much Ado* is that so much of what
happens is spelt out before it happens. The trap that is laid for
Claudio and the traps laid for Beatrice and for Benedick, followed
by the meeting that they have afterwards: in all of these things our
delight is to see how they will behave.

The structure of the plot brings out yet more contrasts between
the two couples. Claudio's rejection of Hero finally prompts the
declaration of love between Beatrice and Benedick, but there is no
romantic swooning into each other's arms because it is precisely at
this tender moment that Beatrice chooses to put their new relationship to the fiercest test:

BENEDICK: By my sword, Beatrice, thou lovest me.

BEATRICE: Do not swear, and eat it.

BENEDICK: I will swear by it that you love me; and I will make
him eat it that says I love not you.

BEATRICE: Will you not eat your word?

BENEDICK: With no sauce that can be devised to it; I protest I
love thee.

BEATRICE: Why, then, God forgive me!

BENEDICK: What offence, sweet Beatrice?

BEATRICE: You have stayed me in a happy hour; I was about to protest I loved you.

BENEDICK: And do it with all thy heart?

BEATRICE: I love you with so much of my heart that none is left to protest.

BENEDICK: Come, bid me do anything for thee.

BEATRICE: Kill Claudio.

BENEDICK: Ha! not for the wide world.

BEATRICE: You kill me to deny it. Farewell.

4.1.272–89

Beatrice's cheek at this moment is as incredible as the proof of love she demands, and so is her courage. The risk she takes of losing Benedick is breathtaking because by now we really believe in their feeling for each other. Up till now, the public world of the Court has treated serious things lightly and made rather too light of serious things, such as Hero's honour and reputation. The glittering goldfish bowl of the Court has brought us to a point where its own intrigues have brutally separated two of its company, and the one couple we feel are really meant for each other, in preparing to challenge the values of the Court, are poised to lose everything. Any denunciation of Claudio by Benedick is bound to include the Duke, their patron, and it's a measure of Benedick's integrity and of his love that he does not balk at this test:

Fare you well, boy; you know my mind. I will leave you now to your gossip-like humour; you break jests as braggarts do their blades, which, God be thanked, hurt not. My lord, for your many courtesies I thank you. I must discontinue your company. Your brother the bastard is fled from Messina. You have among you kill'd a sweet and innocent lady.

5.1.178–83

His indictment includes the whole Court and their way of life.

It's a wonderful moment, but Benedick's indignation is not enough. The tangled webs that have been woven by the Court sophisticates have to be untangled somehow if *Much Ado* is to fulfil its promise and remain a comedy. The characters who are enlisted for this difficult task only appear towards the end of the play. They are drawn from the society's humbler citizens and led by Dogberry, Constable of the Watch. They are ignorant, pompous and foolish. They give themselves airs and ape their social superiors, whom they resemble in only one thing, which is in their sense of their own importance. Dogberry wears the mantle of his authority very heavily, much more heavily than the Duke does his.

He is officious, inefficient, stupid, cowardly, vain, contorting the English language which has been tripping so elegantly off more courtly tongues and trying the patience of his auditors. But it is his doggedness, suggested in his name, which finally uncovers the villains and leads to the discovery of their plot. The opposition of the stupidity of Dogberry and his team to the impatient intelligences of the Court creates a wonderful stumbling-block to delay the progress towards justice and build up tension. But stupidity finally triumphs over sophistication, so that evil is undone and the play can come to a happy conclusion.

For me the play, with its contrivance to bring about a happy ending, works almost on the level of a fairy-tale. It has the same strong moral tone as a fairy tale. Without the final ironing-out of troubles, like the *deus ex machina* in a Greek drama, it could easily have been a tragedy. People could have got killed. The best plays, whether comedy or tragedy, the best art, make us aware of the thin line between life and death and heighten our sense of the value of life. Characters like Beatrice and Benedick allow us to see how well, how richly, life can be lived even in a society whose morality is not all that it should be. They do it entertainingly, with humility, great wit and charm and what could be better than that?

MUCH ADO ABOUT NOTHING

Kenneth Haigh

Kenneth Haigh played Benedick in the 69 Theatre Company's production of Much Ado About Nothing *at Manchester Cathedral in 1976. He also played a number of leading parts during the American Shakespeare Festival of 1979. He created the part of Jimmy Porter in* Look Back in Anger, *and played Achilles in the BBC TV production of* Troilus and Cressida.

I love acting in comedies, but rehearsing them is another matter. Day after day, week after week you go into a hall at ten in the morning and try to be witty. It is as if you are wearing lead boots and ploughing through treacle. What is so funny about *Much Ado About Nothing*? There is nothing funny about it until the audience is sitting there and you are performing it for real. Then the laughter rolls in and you feel like a god. When this happens you think 'aren't I clever?', but you're not. The laughter has always been there because the play is well-written. So, after those dull plodding days of rehearsal, the actors are saying two weeks into the run 'aren't we lucky? we're in one of the funniest comedies ever written'.

Much Ado About Nothing is set in Messina in Sicily, but that isn't important. It is important, however, that it begins at the end of a war. The men who were in the trenches together, fought together, saved each other and drank together are now home. The dangers are over and they are ready to enjoy themselves. It is a tremendous release. It's usually after such homecomings that all the girls in the village get pregnant. Two of these returning soldiers, Benedick and Claudio, are good friends. They are also members of the Court and friends of the Prince, who is called Don Pedro. But they are very different people: Benedick is the older and a confirmed bachelor. In the first scene he is set upon by Beatrice, a confirmed spinster:

BEATRICE: I wonder that you will still be talking, Signior Benedick; nobody marks you.

BENEDICK: What, my dear Lady Disdain! Are you yet living?

BEATRICE: Is it possible disdain should die while she hath such
meet food to feed it as Signior Benedick? Courtesy itself
must convert to disdain if you come in her presence.

BENEDICK: Then is courtesy a turncoat. But it is certain I am
loved of all ladies, only you excepted; and I would I could find
in my heart that I had not a hard heart, for truly, I love none.

BEATRICE: A dear happiness to women! They would else have
been troubled with a pernicious suitor. I thank God, and my
cold blood, I am of your humour for that: I had rather hear
my dog bark at a crow than a man swear he loves me.

BENEDICK: God keep your ladyship still in that mind! So some
gentleman or other shall scape a predestinate scratch'd face.

BEATRICE: Scratching could not make it worse, an 'twere such a
face as yours were.

1.1.99–116

Claudio, on the other hand, is captivated by the beauty of a young
girl called Hero, who is Beatrice's cousin. As he says to Don
Pedro,

> O, my lord,
> When you went onward on this ended action,
> I look'd upon her with a soldier's eye,
> That lik'd, but had a rougher task in hand
> Than to drive liking to the name of love;
> But now I am return'd, and that war-thoughts
> Have left their places vacant, in their rooms
> Come thronging soft and delicate desires,
> All prompting me how fair young Hero is,
> Saying I lik'd her ere I went to wars.

1.1.258–67

Don Pedro agrees to sound out Hero's father, Leonato, on the
subject and arrange a marriage if he can. This he does
successfully.

Claudio of course wants to get married immediately, but Leonato tells him that he will have to wait while all the preparations are
made. In the meantime, says Don Pedro, they will amuse themselves by bringing 'Signior Benedick and the Lady Beatrice into a
mountain of affection, th'one with th' other'. The deception of
both Beatrice and Benedick is carried out by the same simple
expedient in two funny scenes. First of all, Benedick is made to

overhear his friends Don Pedro, Claudio and Leonato in conversation:

> DON PEDRO: Come hither, Leonato. What was it you told me of to-day – that your niece Beatrice was in love with Signior Benedick?
> CLAUDIO: O ay; stalk on, stalk on; the fowl sits. I did never think that lady would have loved any man.
> LEONATO: No, nor I neither; but most wonderful that she should so dote on Signior Benedick, whom she hath in all outward behaviours seem'd ever to abhor.
> BENEDICK: Is't possible? Sits the wind in that corner?
> LEONATO: By my troth, my lord, I cannot tell what to think of it; but that she loves him with an enraged affection – it is past the infinite of thought.
> DON PEDRO: May be she doth but counterfeit.
> CLAUDIO: Faith, like enough.
> LEONATO: O God, counterfeit! There was never counterfeit of passion came so near the life of passion as she discovers it.

> 2.3.82–98

Then, in just the same way, Beatrice is made to overhear Hero telling her maid that Benedick is languishing for her. Each of them, who have so far been mocking each other and the very idea of love, is now a pushover. As Benedick says,

> This can be no trick: the conference was sadly borne; they have the truth of this from Hero; they seem to pity the lady; it seems her affections have their full bent. Love me! Why, it must be requited. I hear how I am censur'd: they say I will bear myself proudly if I perceive the love come from her; they say, too, that she will rather die than give any sign of affection. I did never think to marry. I must not seem proud; happy are they that hear their detractions and can put them to mending. They say the lady is fair; 'tis a truth, I can bear them witness; and virtuous; 'tis so, I cannot reprove it; and wise, but for loving me. By my troth, it is no addition to her wit; nor no great argument of her folly, for I will be horribly in love with her. I may chance have some odd quirks and remnants of wit broken on me because I have railed so long against marriage; but doth not the appetite alter? A man loves the meat in his youth that he cannot endure in his age. Shall quips, and sentences, and these paper bullets of the brain, awe a man from the career of his humour? No; the world

must be peopled. When I said I would die a bachelor, I did not think I should live till I were married.

2.3.201–20

But now Don John, the bastard brother of Don Pedro, comes on to stir up trouble for the young lovers. He claims that Hero is unfaithful and that he can prove it if Claudio and Don Pedro will watch with him that night outside her window. Don John has planned with his henchmen in an earlier scene to make it appear that Hero is seen talking to a ruffian at her window, when in fact it will only be someone dressed like her. Don John is only lightly sketched as to give him more weight would unbalance the comedy. But it was his rebellion that caused the war which has just ended and he still resents his brother. His resentment is also aimed at Claudio who gained a lot of glory in that war.

We then meet Dogberry, the Constable in charge of the watch but not in command of the English language. He is accompanied by Verges and the other members of the watch:

DOGBERRY: You are thought here to be the most senseless and fit man for the constable of the watch; therefore bear you the lantern. This is your charge: you shall comprehend all vagrom men; you are to bid any man stand, in the Prince's name.

SECOND WATCH: How if 'a will not stand?

DOGBERRY: Why, then, take no note of him, but let him go; and presently call the rest of the watch together, and thank God you are rid of a knave.

VERGES: If he will not stand when he is bidden, he is none of the Prince's subjects.

DOGBERRY: True, and they are to meddle with none but the Prince's subjects. You shall also make no noise in the streets; for for the watch to babble and to talk is most tolerable and not to be endured.

SECOND WATCH: We will rather sleep than talk; we know what belongs to a watch.

DOGBERRY: Why, you speak like an ancient and most quiet watchman, for I cannot see how sleeping should offend; only, have a care that your bills be not stol'n. Well, you are to call at all the ale-houses, and bid those that are drunk get them to bed.

SECOND WATCH: How if they will not?

DOGBERRY: Why, then, let them alone till they are sober; . . . .

3.3.19–42

Dogberry is one of Shakespeare's dumbest characters. He reminds me in a way of Inspector Clouseau, the mad detective played by Peter Sellers who is so thick and yet manages to stumble onto the truth. The men of the Watch do their best to sit quietly, but onto the stage come two of Don John's henchmen who have just helped him deceive Claudio. These two discuss their crime and are overheard by the Watch, who arrest them. But incompetence will out. When Dogberry reports the case in the morning to Leonato, he is so slow about it that Leonato, who is about to go to his daughter's wedding, loses patience.

The next scene, the church wedding of Hero and Claudio, is the most dramatic of the play. Claudio rejects Hero before the priest and this gathering of friends and relations because he is convinced that she has betrayed him. This could be a painful moment, but for the audience it does not overcome the comedy because Shakespeare has taken care that some of the conspirators have already been arrested. The audience knows that it is only a matter of time before the plot against the young people is revealed. Hero faints and is carried from the stage. Beatrice and Benedick are left alone, each believing that the other's love is a secret known only to them. Benedick is faced with a crisis of loyalty: he is torn between, on the one hand, his friends Claudio and Don Pedro and, on the other, Beatrice who is now weeping for her cousin's dishonour and distress:

BENEDICK: By my sword, Beatrice, thou lovest me.

BEATRICE: Do not swear, and eat it.

BENEDICK: I will swear by it that you love me; and I will make him eat it that says I love not you.

BEATRICE: Will you not eat your word?

BENEDICK: With no sauce that can be devised to it; I protest I love thee.

BEATRICE: Why, then, God forgive me!

BENEDICK: What offence, sweet Beatrice?

BEATRICE: You have stayed me in a happy hour; I was about to protest I loved you.

BENEDICK: And do it with all thy heart?

BEATRICE: I love you with so much of my heart that none is left to protest.

BENEDICK: Come, bid me do anything for thee.

BEATRICE: Kill Claudio.

BENEDICK: Ha! not for the wide world.   4.1.272–88

This scene can be very difficult to put over. But here I should say that when I played it we did the production in Manchester Cathedral, which was a great help. It is as if divine intervention gave us this immense set, plus organ, large window and candles. In such a setting the ringing silence built up such a dense emotional feeling that the audience were wrapt in attention and followed every word and every gesture. Although, believe me, it isn't easy getting laughs in a cold cathedral in winter.

Benedick does in fact resolve to challenge his friend Claudio to a duel. But, just in case the audience starts thinking that the play is going to become a tragicomedy, the next scene has Dogberry and Verges back. They have been told to examine the prisoners themselves and, amazingly, the mischief is brought to light. But before the plot is reported to Leonato, who, remember is Hero's father, we see him attempting to challenge Claudio to a duel. Then Benedick does the same in fulfilment of his promise to Beatrice. Now, when Hero fainted, the Friar who was about to marry her to Claudio suggested to Leonato that he announce that she is dead, to make Claudio suffer remorse for his callousness. When it is at last revealed that he has been deceived by Don John, Claudio says to Leonato

> I know not how to pray your patience,
> Yet I must speak. Choose your revenge yourself;
> Impose me to what penance your invention
> Can lay upon my sin; . . . .

5.1.257–60

Leonato says that he will forgive him if he will marry another niece of his in place of the 'dead' Hero. Claudio makes a mournful visit to Hero's tomb and then presents himself to Leonato's house to wed his bride, whose features are veiled. It is, of course, Hero so the couple are reunited and married. Beatrice and Benedick affirm their love and the play ends with a dance.

When I saw *Much Ado* for the first time as a young actor I was captivated by that marvellous pair, Benedick and Beatrice, perhaps the greatest sub-plot ever written. Yet I was also puzzled as to what was going on in the play with Hero and Claudio. It isn't easy for us to understand the dilemma of these two young people. So when I came to do the play myself I was particularly concerned to watch as much as I could of the rehearsals with Claudio and Hero. The actress playing Hero was completely flabbergasted as to how to deal with her situation because it just wouldn't have occurred to her. She found it difficult to say her lines with conviction. Instead of fainting, she would have replied to Claudio something like 'if you won't take my word for my innocence, then as far as I'm concerned the marriage is off anyway'. It is true that in the age of Elizabeth I, as in the age of Victoria, a woman's virtue was highly prized, but there is more to it than that. Hero's situation is also a modern one: she wants to be regarded and loved for herself not by what other people have said about her. She is shocked that Claudio does not believe her and that he has decided that she is guilty before facing her. When she says 'and seemed I ever otherwise to you?', she appeals directly to his own knowledge of her. When she adds a few lines later 'is my lord well, that he doth speak so wide?', we see her commitment to Claudio in that she can still call him 'my lord'. And what makes it worse for her is that Leonato, her own father, is at first inclined to believe her accusers. Here, by the way, it is worth noting that the men in the play are not all that impressive: they seem weak and a little superficial, but the women, especially Beatrice, seem stronger as they are in closer touch with their feelings.

As for Claudio, I think that we have to see him as young and insecure. He lacks belief in himself. His readiness to doubt others, to doubt Hero, reveals his own doubt in himself. Is he capable of being loved? It was, after all, his Prince, Don Pedro, who did his wooing for him. He does not address a word to Hero until the marriage has been agreed. What happens to him in the play is that at the beginning he is not ready for love and must endure this crucible of doubt, love and loss in order to find himself. Happiness can't be given as simply as that, it is there at the end if he can find it.

The youth and inexperience of Claudio and Hero provide a contrast to the more sceptical, maturer attitudes of Benedick and Beatrice. They are more interested in intelligence than looks. The darker area touched on by Claudio and Hero's experiences gives more point to their wit. It comes as a release. The audience is glad to see Benedick and Beatrice come back to amuse them and they know too that this couple will not be hurt in the same way. Beatrice is perhaps the most vivid, three-dimensional woman in Shakespeare's work. The eminent critic John Dover Wilson said of her: 'the first woman in our literature, perhaps in the literature of Europe, who not only has a brain but delights in the employment of it'. Here she is talking to Leonato and Hero:

LEONATO: Well, niece, I hope to see you one day fitted with a husband.

BEATRICE: Not till God make men of some other metal than

earth. Would it not grieve a woman to be over-master'd with a piece of valiant dust, to make an account of her life to a clod of wayward marl? No, uncle, I'll none: Adam's sons are my brethren; and, truly, I hold it a sin to match in my kindred.

LEONATO: Daughter, remember what I told you: if the Prince do solicit you in that kind, you know your answer.

BEATRICE: The fault will be in the music, cousin, if you be not wooed in good time. If the Prince be too important, tell him there is measure in everything, and so dance out the answer. For, hear me, Hero: wooing, wedding, and repenting, is as a Scotch jig, a measure, and a cinquepace; the first suit is hot and hasty, like a Scotch jig, and full as fantastical; the wedding, mannerly modest, as a measure, full of state and ancientry; and then comes repentance, and, with his bad legs, falls into the cinquepace faster and faster, till he sink into his grave.

LEONATO: Cousin, you apprehend passing shrewdly.

BEATRICE: I have a good eye, uncle; I can see a church by daylight.

2.1.48–70

Though she can see a church by daylight, she has not realised that her mocking of Benedick is really a way of flirting with him. When she is fooled into thinking that he is in love with her she does not, like him, go into self-justification. Her surrender is direct and simple:

> Can this be true?
> Stand I condemn'd for pride and scorn so much?
> Contempt, farewell! and maiden pride, adieu!
> No glory lives behind the back of such.
> And, Benedick, love on; I will requite thee,
> Taming my wild heart to thy loving hand;
> If thou dost love, my kindness shall incite thee
> To bind our loves up in a holy band;
> . . . .

3.1.107–14

I remember the first time I went round the Uffizi Gallery in Florence. a Leonardo had been placed in a room of religious paintings, which were very beautiful and sacred but done in a two-dimensional style. It stood out like cobalt. You could see immediately how he sent art and our awareness rocketing forward. Beatrice comes out of Shakespeare's work with just such an amazing jolt. Rosalind has not attained womanhood and Cleopatra is making her last grab for it, but Beatrice is there, the thing itself.

Benedick is the part I've played. It has great visual moments, like the business of the beard. Benedick has a beard, which Beatrice does not like. So, when Benedick hears that Beatrice has fallen in love with him, he returns for the next scene without his beard. A couple of minutes later the audience stops laughing. Benedick is a character who seems at the start to be supremely confident to deal with any social situation he encounters. He is happy to help his friend Claudio, keep Don Pedro amused and be as polite as he can to Beatrice. He is a man who wants everything to be just okay and who will not permit himself a moment of self-analysis or self-criticism. The crucial scene for him, as well as for Hero and Claudio, is that remarkable one in the church. When he comes to the church he is no longer the soldier, cynic and extrovert, but halfway to turning into a lover. An obvious way of showing his transition is by way of a change of costume. We didn't have the money for two costumes in this production, so there I was in my soldier's uniform with the problem of showing this change in Benedick. At the dress-rehearsal I spotted some lilies in a vase beside our stage in Manchester Cathedral. I picked them up and carried them on the stage. The incongruity of these flowers with the uniform did the trick and it got a laugh throughout the run. When he is left alone on stage with Beatrice, he turns to her and sees that she has been weeping: 'Lady Beatrice, have you wept all this while?'. This open display of her feelings allows him for the first time to stop masking his own: 'I do love nothing in the world so well as you. Is not that strange?'.

Beatrice and Benedick have a final exchange in the last act. He does not say that he loves her, but asks if she loves him. He is still reluctant to remove the mask over his feelings before his friends. Anyone can say 'I love you' privately, but it is a far greater confession in public. So Beatrice has to tease it out of him:

> BENEDICK: Come, I will have thee; but, by this light, I take thee for pity.
> BEATRICE: I would not deny you; but by this good day, I yield upon great persuasion; and partly to save your life for I was told you were in a consumption.
> BENEDICK: Peace; I will stop your mouth.

5.4.92–7

He kisses her which is, of course, a public confession before the

Court. The stage direction for the kiss comes, according to the scholars, from Shakespeare's own hand. When I played it the director wanted me to kiss Beatrice earlier, but I said 'no, you mustn't, not until Shakespeare says so'. When the kiss happens, all the problems of the play are resolved and the audience tingle because they have wanted it so much.

So here we have two couples: a young pair of lovers who are in the grip of something they don't understand though they know it means committing themselves for the rest of their lives, and a funnier, maturer pair who are working out the same problem. It is a very adult play. There are comparisons with the golden comedies, *Twelfth Night* and *As You Like it*, but this isn't all 'boy meets girl' stuff. Beatrice and Benedick are grown up people who are not ready for love and each other. That they do finally succeed shows Shakespeare's immense optimism about human relationships. He was to lose this optimism a few years later when he came to write *Troilus and Cressida, Measure for Measure, Hamlet* and the other tragedies. But here in *Much Ado About Nothing* it remains: a tremendous adult warmth as Beatrice and Benedick pass from witty dissonance, and Hero and Claudio pass from discord, to the blissful resolution. As Benedick says

> Come, come. We are friends. Let's have a dance ere we are married, that we may lighten our own hearts and our wives' heels.

5.4.113–5

The perfect metaphor.

LOVE'S LABOUR'S LOST
Emma Tennant

Emma Tennant is a novelist whose publications include Alice Fell, Queen of Stones *and* Woman Beware Woman. *She made this programme on location in the gardens at Althelhampton.*

Here is a riddle. What is planned but always changing? Green and white and read all over, but seldom seen? You could say the answer is a garden and it's in a garden that I see *Love's Labour's Lost* as set, a garden that's planned and formal and changes its colours with the seasons of the year, from daisies pied to icicles. And you could say the answer is the play itself, which is planned as a stately dance with the partners forever masking and unmasking and changing places. As for being read but seldom seen, *Love's Labour's Lost* is seldom performed and is seen more as a play on words than a play that comes to life on the stage. Why is this? Is it boring? Hard to understand? Hopelessly out of date? I'd say none of these things. For me, coming to it for the first time, it's the fact that there is less enshrining of, pontificating over, this play than, say, *Hamlet* or *A Midsummer Night's Dream*, that makes it possible to look at things with a fresh eye. And the first thing a fresh eye does see is that *Love's Labour's Lost* is a glorious send-up of precisely those qualities – over-reverence for the intellect, pomposity and pontification – which have always been with us and always are, and always will be, in need of sending up. We aren't taken off, either, to a distant land where we are not going to be able to recognise the characters. Shakespeare gives us curates, schoolmasters, lofty toffs with an 'e' at the end of their name and pretentious foreigners with new-fangled theories. They are all the targets of ridicule and satire just as much today as they were then. So there is no reason for someone in the last quarter of the twentieth century not to identify immediately with the fools, pundits and lovers made into fools by love that walked the boards in the last quarter of the sixteenth century.

Love's Labour's Lost was first performed in 1593, probably before a private audience of Queen Bess and her courtiers. They laughed at the idea, and who wouldn't, of four arrogant young men pledging to give up the company of women for three years in order to further their education. They laughed in the way that, say, an Alan Ayckbourn audience would laugh when, before the ink is even dry on the agreement, four lovely young ladies turn up and present themselves on urgent business. They agreed, as we do, with Berowne – he of the cynical manner and the 'e' at the end of his name – that these famous studies are likely to be very short-lived indeed:

> BEROWNE: 'Item. If any man be seen to talk with a woman within the term of three years, he shall endure such public shame as the rest of the court can possibly devise.'
> This article, my liege, yourself must break;
> For well you know here comes in embassy
> The French king's daughter, with yourself to speak –
> A maid of grace and complete majesty –
> About surrender up of Aquitaine
> To her decrepit, sick, and bedrid father;
> Therefore this article is made in vain,
> Or vainly comes th' admired princess hither.
> KING: What say you, lords? Why, this was quite forgot.
> BEROWNE: So study evermore is over-shot.
> While it doth study to have what it would,
> It doth forget to do the thing it should;
> And when it hath the thing it hunteth most,
> 'Tis won as towns with fire – so won, so lost.
> KING: We must of force dispense with this decree;
> She must lie here on mere necessity.
> BEROWNE: Necessity will make us all forsworn
> Three thousand times within this three years' space;
> For every man with his affects is born,
> Not by might mast'red, but by special grace.

> I.I.128–50

It is a play in which almost every comic device is put to full use. There is the 'fantastic Spaniard' Armado, who is so ashamed of falling in love with a humble dairymaid that he shoots out sonnets that would curdle the milk. There are mistaken identities, disguises and slips of the tongue. There is even a page called Moth, a clown called Costard and a schoolmaster, Holofernes, who says of Armado 'I abhor these fanatical phantasimes'. Yet, in a play where even a village pageant falls flat and a flat-footed bobby tries to get in on the act, in a pavane of punnery, an

ever-shifting charade, Berowne's deeply felt warning is heard
under the froth of the superficial:

> For every man with his affects is born
> Not by might mast'red, but by special grace.

It is love, Berowne pleads, that brings true wisdom, not superficial
learning. Until a man can learn to say 'I am a fool, and full of
poverty', he has learnt nothing at all. In *Love's Labour's Lost* we're
invited to partake in a Feast of Fools and to stay until the lovers get
their deserts.

As in all true love stories, there is resistance at first. The
treatment of the female visitors by the budding scholars is hardly
chivalrous. It seems the stars in women's eyes will not prove more
alluring than the stars of the new science of Copernican
astronomy, or the shining new words that are racing into the
language. The French Princess is a pretty girl and she quickly
obtains a good property deal for her father, but she still isn't
allowed in the house. Instead, she and her ladies must camp in the
garden at a safe distance from the seat of learning. She's a pretty
girl but she's a spirited girl too, and the King soon sees what he's
up against:

> KING: Fair Princess, welcome to the court of Navarre.
> PRINCESS: 'Fair' I give you back again; and 'welcome' I have not
>   yet. The roof of this court is too high to be yours, and
>   welcome to the wide fields to base to be mine.

> 2.1.90–3

The scholar King soon falls for what he's up against, so to speak,
but he still doesn't offer sheltered accomodation. The Princess,
who is falling fast too, is pleased to hear from her courtier, Boyet,
that the King's love is plainly visible:

> BOYET: If my observation, which very seldom lies,
>   By the heart's still rhetoric disclosed with eyes,
>   Deceive me not now, Navarre is infected.
> PRINCESS: With what?
> BOYET: With that which we lovers entitle 'affected'.
> PRINCESS: Your reason?
> BOYET: Why, all his behaviours did make their retire
>   To the court of his eye, peeping thorough desire.

> 2.1.227–34

And Berowne falls for the Princess's dark lady, Rosaline. What's
so seductive about the courtship dances in *Love's Labour's Lost* is

the extraordinary range of word-music that accompanies them. The stately, formal language of courtly love with its roots in the wooing of beautiful, remote ladies in their Provencal towers, is an affectation Shakespeare loves to poke fun at, like setting a mouse under the feet of self-satisfied dancers and watching them trip up. As the music changes, so does the dance. It's 'Here We Go Round The Mulberry Bush' or a children's chant like 'Pat-a-cake, Pat-a-cake, Baker's Man' with the words hit back at their owners like clapping hands:

> BEROWNE: What's her name in the cap?
> BOYET: Rosaline, by good hap.
> BEROWNE: Is she wedded or no?
> BOYET: To her will, sir, or so.
> BEROWNE: You are welcome, sir; adieu!
> BOYET: Farewell to me, sir, and welcome to you.

2.1.208–13

It almost goes without saying that our other two swots, Longaville and Dumain, have fallen head over heels with the remaining two in the ladies doubles. The dance is paired. The mis-steps, mistakes and misunderstandings of love are set in train.

The chief battle behind this decorous dance was the battle between the School of Life and the School of Night, which was a coterie run by Sir Walter Raleigh to back the new scientific theories of the age. Raleigh was the rival of the Essex-Southampton gang and, as it's thought that Shakespeare was very much on the Essex-Southampton side, it wouldn't be surprising to find him ridiculing Raleigh and his friends. Everything they stood for – atheism, the new mathematics, astronomy, the intellectual's way of looking at life – was the opposite of Shakespeare's instinctive feeling for things. The poet Chapman, translator of Homer, seems to have been the chief rhymester of the Raleigh group. In a poem called 'Shadow of Night' he wrote the lines:

> No pen can anything eternal write
> That is not steeped in humour of the Night.

Night seems to mean to him contemplation of the deeper matters where a black sky with an unknown star can bring a sense of chaos. Study and vigorous intellectual work are what the poet needs or the sky may open up and he might vanish into infinity. But Shakespeare wants nothing of the sky. He can pull it down to him when it suits. There's plenty going on in the full daylight of the School of Life without going to the stars. Shakespeare may have seen and feared a new age of materialism:

> These earthly godfathers of heaven's lights
> That give a name to every fixed star
> Have no more profit of their shining nights
> Than those that walk and wot not what they are.

1.1.88–91

Night plays a strong part in this aristocratic entertainment where the strongest contrast you're likely to find will be of the dappled-shade variety like, say, Fragonard's 'Girl on a Swing' going back and forth. Night in *Love's Labour's Lost* – 'Black is the badge of hell, the hue of dungeons and the School of Night' – stands for more than Shakespeare's possible hatred of the Raleigh faction. It stands, amusingly for us at least, for a 'Gentlemen Prefer Blondes' attitude in a country that worshipped Good Queen Bess. Rosaline, the dark lady of Berowne's heart, needs much defending for being a brunette. At one stage she's even compared to an old boot. In the reign of Astraea the 'henna' if you can't join 'em – dye it.

Love's Labour's Lost isn't just a battle of wits, even if it seems so at first glance. In the real-life Court of Navarre, King Henry IV had founded an academy where neo-platonism held sway. Words, music and the new mathematics were studied with the aim of finding a unity, or language of the Gods. Shakespeare must have drawn on accounts of the scholarly French Court in the play. Academies of this kind were also springing up in the England of his day. Shakespeare is scoffing at the pretensions of the nutty professors who ran them throughout *Love's Labour's Lost*. Yet his admiration for the bringing together of many disciplines in the service of one 'higher' voice is also evident. As a poet, he could bring together the beautiful and the ugly, the absurd and the sad. He could show the sky in a puddle. And he wanted life and learning reflected in that sky, clear and not choppy with clouds.

When we laugh at the schoolmaster Holofernes and the 'fantastic Spaniard' Armado, we see one side of the Channel mocking the other. For what are these ludicrous figures but equivalents of the present-day French semioticians, the disciples of Barthes, Derrida and Lacan? These foreign intellectuals with their concepts so alien to the pragmatic English way of thinking would amuse Shakespeare just as much if he were here today. Not all intellectuals in Shakespeare's time were in search of harmony and unity. A contemporary portrait of a scholar in an age of High Latin for the few and illiteracy for the rest stated that 'his mind is made up of divers shreds like a cushion'. Holofernes is just the same:

ARMADO: Arts-man, preambulate; we will be singuled from the barbarous. Do you not educate youth at the charge-house on the top of the mountain?

HOLOFERNES: Or mons, the hill.

ARMADO: At your sweet pleasure, for the mountain.

HOLOFERNES: I do, sans question.

ARMADO: Sir, it is the King's most sweet pleasure and affection to congratulate the Princess at her pavilion, in the posteriors of this day; which the rude multitude call the afternoon.

HOLOFERNES: The posterior of the day, most generous sir, is liable, congruent, and measurable, for the afternoon. The word is well cull'd, chose, sweet, and apt, I do assure you, sir, I do assure.

5.1.67–81

What does become clear to us as we take in the absurd plot and the frequent meaninglessness of the words is that words are meant to be meaningless. They exist on their own, in their sound or in their own 'write'. They fly off, as it were, and anyone who tries to pin them down will brush the gold dust from their wings. In this Platonic academy where the meaning of life is study no one would have been able to tell you, in simple English, the time of day. If we laugh at these affected people and their present-day counterparts, it is because we sense in them a contempt for ordinary people. Holofernes and the curate, Nathaniel, express contempt for the poor local copper, Dull, but Dull manages to stump them with a riddle:

DULL: I said the deer was not a haud credo; 'twas a pricket.

HOLOFERNES: Twice-sod simplicity, bis coctus! O thou monster Ignorance, how deformed dost thou look!

NATHANIEL: Sir, he hath never fed of the dainties that are bred in a book; He hath not eat paper, as it were; he hath not drunk ink; his intellect is not replenished; he is only an animal, only sensible in the duller parts;
And such barren plants are set before us that we thankful should be –
Which we of taste and feeling are – for those parts that do fructify in us more than he.
For as it would ill become me to be vain, indiscreet, or a fool,
So, were there a patch set on learning, to see him in a school.
But, omne bene, say I, being of an old father's mind:
Many can brook the weather that love not the wind.

DULL: You two are book-men: can you tell me by your wit
  What was a month old at Cain's birth that's not five weeks old
    as yet?
HOLOFERNES: Dictynna, goodman Dull; Dictynna, goodman
    Dull.
DULL: What is Dictynna?
NATHANIEL: A title to Phoebe, to Luna, to the moon.
HOLOFERNES: The moon was a month old when Adam was no
    more,
  And raught not to five weeks when he came to five-score.
  Th' allusion holds in the exchange.
DULL: 'Tis true, indeed; the collusion holds in the exchange.
HOLOFERNES: God comfort thy capacity! I say th' allusion holds
    in the exchange.
DULL: And I say the polusion holds in the exchange; for the
    moon is never but a month old; and I say, beside, that 'twas a
    pricket that the Princess kill'd.   4.2.18–46

As well as sending up the vanity and pomposity of these know-alls,
Shakespeare no doubt enjoyed parodying such writers as John
Lyly who was the begetter of the euphuism. This was a language
of alliteration, antithesis and simile. Yet throughout this play
Shakespeare enjoys being better at doing what he sends up. Two
can play at that game. The courtly pairs are well versed in the rules
of rhetoric, the finer points of debate, the turning of an argument
and the 'odiferous flowers of Fancy'. The appetite of Shakespeare's audience is as keen on the meringue-wit of the courtiers
as it is on the lardy-cake talk of their hangers-on. For this was a
time when the English language was in a state of great mix,
Latinate words and newly coined ones all coming in together.
Love's Labour's Lost is like a glorious summer pudding, stirred in
with puns and metaphors. It's sweetened by Arcadian rhetoric and
made sickly by sheer excess.

If the words are young, sounding often as if they had been made
up by children, this suits a play where everything is a game. The
shining hour can pass without being too much improved upon.
There is hide-and-seek and that old standby, the dressing-up
box. This provides strange and wonderful disguises as when the
Nine Worthies put in an appearance – among them Hector of
Troy, Pompey the Great and Alexander. At another point the four
ladies find themselves playing host to four mysterious suitors in
Russian dress. The Muscovite look was all the rage at the time. As
for hide-and-seek, we see Berowne hide and eavesdrop on the

outpourings of the lovesick Lords: '"All hid, all hid" – an old infant play.'

Love's Labour's Lost is supposed to date from roughly the period when Shakespeare was writing the Sonnets. As a poet, he was exploring to the limit ideas and feelings about love – love fleshly, godly, unending, passing and unrecompensed. Flirts and swains are set to the dance in his early public comedies like *Love's Labour's Lost* and *The Two Gentlemen of Verona*, but the private poet was attacking the idea of the lover-versemaker and the sonnet form itself. Even the most romantic of his Sonnets

> Shall I compare thee to a summer's day
> Thou art more lovely and temperate

is an attack on the 'darling buds of May' that nod through the poetry of his time. It is also, of course, a marvellous love poem. In his plays, love in all its manifestations and in all its tribulations is treated as a serious theme, however much fun Shakespeare has with the silly behaviour of its victims, inexperienced and doomed in *Romeo and Juliet* or mature and worldy-wise in *Much Ado About Nothing*. It's a dramatic theme which Lyly, again, pioneered in light, delicious court comedies like *Campaspe*. But here the workings of love are seen without the power, ambition and grief of the other plays. Because love has so many faces, it can be dismissed in a world ruled by power. By making Berowne plead for that 'special grace', without which our lives would have no meaning, Shakespeare shows his deep belief in the power of love.

There is not much hint, when Berowne and his friends catch each other displaying their first-draft love-draughts, that love has taken serious hold. Berowne himself is soon caught out when his own letter to Rosaline – 'I sent a letter to my love and on the way I dropped it' – is brought accidentally to the scene. It shows him to be as much of a fool as the rest of them. Berowne swears that he will never more trust to speeches penned, nor to woo in rhyme. Love is too serious a matter for that:

> For valour, is not Love a Hercules,
> Still climbing trees in the Hesperides?
> Subtle as Sphinx; as sweet and musical
> As bright Apollo's lute, strung with his hair.

4.3.336–9

When all is said and done, love is all, but in the end, if love isn't exactly lost it's put aside. News comes of the death of the Princess's father. The harshness of the outside world comes in and, as the year begins to die, so does the rash, impulsive side of love. The seasons turn, the dancing in the garden has to stop, and a year must go by to test the faithfulness of the sonneteering suitors. The King must go to an isolated hermitage and Berowne, too witty for his own good, is sent off to a hospital – not one hopes with a repertoire of sick jokes – and the year in this garden that is always planned and always changing will be marked by seasonal songs:

> When icicles hang by the wall,
> And Dick the shepherd blows his nail,
> And Tom bears logs into the hall,
> And milk comes frozen home in pail,
> When blood is nipp'd, and ways be foul,
> Then nightly sings the staring owl:
> 'Tu-who;
> Tu-whit, Tu-who' – a merry note,
> While greasy Joan doth keel the pot.

5.2.899–907

LOVE'S LABOUR'S LOST
Kenneth Branagh

Kenneth Branagh is a member of the Royal Shake-speare Company. His parts in the 1984–5 season include the King of Navarre in Love's Labour's Lost *and the title role in* Henry V. *His non-Shakespearean roles have included Judd in* Another Country.

*L*ove's Labour's Lost concerns the King of Navarre and his three courtiers, Berowne, Dumaine and Longaville. They decide to form an 'academe', or university, which they will support themselves in for three years, forswearing the company of women and devoting themselves to 'living art'. The King is convinced, in company with Longaville and Dumaine, that the idea is feasible. But Berowne starts to puncture their dream from the word go. He reminds everybody that a woman, the Princess of France indeed, is due to arrive imminently:

> KING: We must of force dispense with this decree;
>   She must lie here on mere necessity.
> BEROWNE: Necessity will make all forsworn
>   Three thousand times within this three years' space;
>   For every man with his affects is born,
>   Not by might mast'red, but by special grace.
>   If I break faith, this word shall speak for me:
>   I am forsworn on mere necessity.

1.1.145–52

They are forced to meet the Princess and her three ladies, so the idea of avoiding the company of woman is knocked on the head immediately. As one can imagine, the four men take a shine to the four ladies and vice versa. The story of the play, then, concerns the trials of having to cope with forswearing the very serious oaths that they have taken because they all fall head-over-heels in love.

There is also a gallery of comic characters at the Court of Navarre. Don Armado, referred to as 'a refined traveller of Spain', is a familiar of the King's. He will be used to amuse the courtiers:

KING: One who the music of his own vain tongue
　　Doth ravish like enchanting harmony;
　　A man of complements, whom right and wrong
　　Have chose as umpire of their mutiny.
　　This child of fancy, that Armado hight,
　　For interim to our studies shall relate,
　　In high-born words, the worth of many a knight
　　From tawny Spain lost in the world's debate.
　　How you delight, my lords, I know not, I;
　　But I protest I love to hear him lie,
　　And I will use him for my ministrelsy.

　　　　　　　　　　　　　　　　　　1.1.164–74

Like all the other characters in this play, Armado has a great delight in words but, unfortunately, he can't use them very well. His wonderful vocabulary is all askew, which is why the King finds him so amusing. He travels with a young boy called Moth. They form a kind of double act with Moth, who is a very bright youngster, pricking the bubble of Armado's vanity. Armado chooses to stay with the King and to follow the three year vow. He becomes a grotesque mirror of the courtiers' own behaviour; one of the targets that Shakespeare attacks in this play, which is a satire on all manner of people who abuse language. As well as Don Armado, there is a schoolmaster called Holofernes, who is obsessed with Latin and, again, unable to use it correctly or succinctly. His malapropisms are a constant source of amusement.

After the four men have become entangled with the four women, each of them has to hide the fact that they are enamoured of the woman in question. The King has fallen for the Princess of France. Berowne, the renegade figure, has fallen for Rosaline, who amongst the ladies is the most sharp-witted of them all. The four women are all in fact quite strong and spirited. Indeed, when they meet the men for the first time, the Princess is more than a match for the King:

KING: Fair Princess, welcome to the court of Navarre.
PRINCESS: 'Fair' I give you back again; and 'welcome' I have not yet. The roof of this court is too high to be yours, and welcome to the wide fields too base to be mine.
KING: You shall be welcome, madam, to my court.
PRINCESS: I will be welcome then; conduct me thither.
KING: Hear me, dear lady: I have sworn an oath –
PRINCESS: Our Lady help my lord! He'll be forsworn.

KING: Not for the world, fair madam, by my will.
PRINCESS: Why, will shall break it; will, and nothing else.

2.1.90–9

It is a point-scoring exercise between the men and the women, which continues right through the play. It is, I think, one of the fascinations of the men for the women. Berowne and Rosaline are the two most barbed adversaries. They are very much models for Beatrice and Benedick in *Much Ado About Nothing*, who are more refined and disciplined versions of the same kind of creature. The attraction is both physical and one of two fascinated and intrigued intellects. As the play goes on, it's quite clear that the women, although more reserved than the men, are fascinated by them.

The four men are discovered to be hopelessly in love in one hilarious scene. This happens very swiftly, after only one meeting with the women. First of all we see Berowne writing a sonnet to his love, Rosaline. He's then interrupted by the King and so hides. The King reveals that he is head-over-heels in love with the Princess by reading a poem that he has written. He is in turn interrupted by Longaville and so hides. Longaville reveals that he is head-over-heels in love with Maria. He reads his sonnet and is then interrupted by Dumaine, who is in love with Katherine. Dumaine finishes his poem, only to be surprised and verbally set upon by Longaville, who takes great delight in self-righteously denouncing the fact that he has gone back on the oath. Then the King, outraged that Longaville should be doing this, comes in with another dose of self-righteousness:

Come, sir, you blush; as his, your case is such.
You chide at him, offending twice as much:
You do not love Maria! Longaville
Did never sonnet for her sake compile;
Nor never lay his wreathed arms athwart
His loving bosom, to keep down his heart.

4.3.127–32

He goes on to ask:

What will Berowne say when that he shall hear
Faith infringed which such zeal did swear?
How will he scorn, how will he spend his wit!
How will he triumph, leap, and laugh at it!
For all the wealth that ever I did see,
I would not have him know so much by me.

4.3.141–6

At which point out steps Berowne and says:

> Now step I forth to whip hypocrisy.
> Ah, good my liege, I pray thee pardon me.

4.3.147–8

And then proceeds to denounce the King. He, of course, tops the lot with the moral indignation of his reprimand:

> O, what a scene of fool'ry have I seen,
> Of sighs, of groans, of sorrow, and of teen!
> O me, with what strict patience have I sat,
> To see a king transformed to a gnat!

4.3.159–62

They are all, of course, thunder-struck with grief and guilt and he just doesn't let them off the hook:

> KING: Too bitter is thy jest.
> Are we betrayed thus to thy over-view?
> BEROWNE: Not you by me, but I betrayed to you.
> I that am honest, I that hold it sin
> To break the vow I am engaged in;
> I am betrayed by keeping company
> With men like you, men of inconstancy.

4.3.170–6

All this is from the worst offender, as he is by far the most in love!

At which point, Costard, a swain, and Jaquenetta, a maid romantically involved with Don Armado, arrive to deliver to the King a letter which has been 'mistook'. Costard, having been charged by Berowne to deliver it to Rosaline, confuses it with a letter that Don Armado has asked him to take to Jaquenetta. Holofernes, the schoolmaster, discovers this discrepancy and asks Jaquenetta to redeliver the letter. So at this point Berowne's sonnet, sent to Rosaline, is placed in the hands of the King. The whole business of Berowne's infatuation with Rosaline is now blown open. The whole scene is a miracle of comedic simplicity.

Costard and Jaquenetta leave and so the four men, in what becomes the pivotal scene of the play, indulge in relief that everything is out in the open. They do so through the verbal duels which are so characteristic of this play. Their poetry has brightness, vitality and density. They then begin an argument, like undergraduates, about whose love is the fairest. Dumaine starts by claiming that Berowne's love, Rosaline, is too dark:

> DUMAINE: To look like her are chimney-sweepers black.
> LONGAVILLE: And since her time are colliers counted bright.

KING: And Ethiopes of their sweet complexion crack.
DUMAINE: Dark needs no candles now, for dark is light.

4.3.262–5

The images complement and bounce off each other. The play is full of rhymed line endings. Verbally, or musically, it is a 'great feast of language'. This presents some difficulties for actors and producers. They have to decide whether to play the language to the hilt knowing that, because it is so dense, the audience isn't necessarily going to pick up everything, or whether to slow it down a bit in order to try to give away as much of the meaning as possible. This may be a reason why the play has been neglected since Shakespeare's day really until this century. People have felt that it was too rooted in its own time. The fantastical characters, such as Holofernes and Don Armado, with their extravagant, eccentric use of language full of Elizabethan puns and wordplay, were thought to have no appeal for latter-day audiences. The play does not have a massive leading role, so it didn't have much appeal for the actor-managers from Shakespeare's day onwards. It is very much an ensemble piece. There have, however, been several famous productions this century. The play has been rediscovered because it works magnificently in the theatre. There are wonderful set pieces, such as the 'discovery' scene which I have already mentioned.

The four men decide to pursue their love affairs. The King suggests that they put on an entertainment for the women, so they decide to dress up and stage a masque. I think it is the King who comes up with the idea that they should dress themselves up as Muscovites, or Russians, to appear before the women. Unfortunately this plan is discovered by Boyet. He is a kind of Oscar Wilde or Pandarus figure, a diplomat and father figure who has probably been through all the shenannigans of young love with which the play is concerned with. He warns the ladies so that, when the men arrive disguised as Muscovites, they tease them mercilessly. The women change the favours, or presents, that the men have sent in advance of the meeting. So, although the men think that they are wooing the woman they fancy, they are in fact wooing someone else. The masque is a disaster as the women also make fun of the accents and manners of the Muscovites. The King, Berowne, Dumaine and Longaville leave not having achieved what they wanted to at all. I think it is important when playing this scene for the men to believe that they are absolutely convincing as Muscovites. This says something about their rather wild and high spirited mood. They come back to be found out by the women and they are, of course, mortified by this. It means cards-on-the-table-time. They have to admit that they have broken their oaths to forswear the company of women. Berowne is the one who finally decides to come clean. He decides to make clear why they have done it in a speech to Rosaline, but which is aimed at all the women:

> Here stand I, lady – dart thy skill at me,
> Bruise me with scorn, confound me with a flout,
> Thrust thy sharp wit quite through my ignorance,
> Cut me to pieces with thy keen conceit;
> And I will wish thee never more to dance,
> Nor never more in Russian habit wait.
> O, never will I trust to speeches penn'd,
> Nor to the motion of a school-boy's tongue,
> Nor never come in vizard to my friend,
> Nor woo in rhyme, like a blind harper's song.
> Taffeta phrases, silken terms precise,
> Three-pil'd hyperboles, spruce affectation,
> Figures pedantical – these summer-flies
> Have blown me full of maggot ostentation.
> I do forswear them; and I here protest,
> By this white glove – how white the hand, God knows! –
> Henceforth my wooing mind shall be express'd
> In russet yeas, and honest kersey noes.

5.2.396–413

The men decide, for the first time, to be honest. They put aside the artifice with which the play is riddled. It has, until now, been full of the kind of affectation and games playing that people can indulge in when they are in love.

Then Costard and the rest of the low life characters appear to put on a show, which is rather like the play within the play at the end of *A Midsummer Night's Dream*. It is the Pageant of the Nine Worthies and presents mythical figures like Hercules and Pompey the Great. The actors who present the show are Costard himself, Holofernes and his sidekick Sir Nathaniel, a curate who complements the schoolmaster's ego. Moth and Don Armado are also in this show, which comes at just the right point to prevent any further disagreements between the men and the women. So, especially after the Muscovite disaster, the men look on it as a chance to impress the women. It is then revealed during the performance, to sensational effect, that Armado has made

Jaquenetta pregnant. This is the culmination of a whole series of comic disasters that happen throughout the show. A fight breaks out between Armado and Costard. You can imagine how embarrassing this is to the King and to the Princess. Everything has suddenly become much more serious. Costard and Armado, egged on by Berowne, Dumaine, Longaville and the assembled villagers, almost come to blows. Then Marcade arrives, dressed in black, in the middle of this absurd quarrel, to tell the Princess in a few brief words that the King, her father, is dead. At which point the play turns on a sixpence. The atmosphere changes, just as it would if you were with any group of people and someone walks into the room and says that there has been a bereavement for one of them.

The Princess's father is described earlier on as being 'decrepit, sick, and bedrid'. His death is therefore not a surprise, but it is still a shock. The things that are still to be resolved are the relationships that have begun. What is to be the end of all this 'midsummer madness'? The men react in a remarkably insensitive way to this news. The Princess says to the King of Navarre

> Farewell, worthy lord.
> A heavy heart bears not a nimble tongue.
> Excuse me so, coming too short of thanks
> For my great suit so easily obtain'd.

5.2.724–7

The King replies:

> The extreme parts of time extremely forms
> All causes to the purpose of his speed:
> And often at his very loose decides
> That which long process could not arbitrate.
> And though the mourning brow of progeny
> Forbid the smiling courtesy of love
> The holy suit which fain it would convince,
> Yet, since love's argument was first on foot,
> Let not the cloud of sorrow justle it
> From what it purpos'd; since to wail friends lost
> Is not by much so wholesome-profitable
> As to rejoice at friends but newly found.

5.2.728–39

To which she answers 'I understand you not; my griefs are double'. The men are unable to cope with the idea that the women will leave. Yet the Princess has to cope both with the death of her

305

father and this insensitivity. The sense that the women have been instructing the men throughout the play because they are wiser and more mature starts to come through very strongly here. *Love's Labour's Lost* is the work of a young playwright. There are lots of things which do not seem cohesive: the Armado and Holofernes scenes and the scenes between the lovers sometimes seem to belong to different, almost irreconcilable, worlds. Yet you begin to see the playwright that will emerge through the remarkable way he portrays the women in this scene. It is full of wisdom and spirit. The King of Navarre wants the Princess to stay:

> Now, at the latest minute of the hour,
> Grant us your loves.

> 5.2.775–6

But she replies:

> A time, methinks, too short
> To make a world-without-end bargain in.
> No, no, my lord, your Grace is perjur'd much
> Full of dear guiltiness; . . . .

> 5.2.776–9

She suggests that their love, to date, has been a merriment: a round of jests and play-acting. She thus proposes to the King that, if he really loves her, then he should go away for a year as a kind of test and become a hermit. If this doesn't nip the 'gaudy blossoms' of his love, then she will be his. The King says

> If this, or more than this, I would deny,
> To flatter up these powers of mine with rest,
> The sudden hand of death close up mine eye!
> Hence hermit then, my heart is in thy breast.

> 5.2.801–4

And in turn the other three couples, with Berowne and Rosaline last of all, make the same commitment. Then they are forced to leave.

There should be question marks left over all these relationships at the end of the play. All through this last section of the play there is this terrible sense, caught beautifully in every line, of people being helplessly torn apart. The men come to understand that they have the opportunity to discover whether what they have been doing up to now has been love or merely infatuation. Their commitment not to see the women for a year is not so dissimilar from their decision at the beginning of the play to spend three years in an academe. It's still a rude awakening and a bit of a jolt for everyone. Nevertheless, the possibility of real love runs through this last section as well. If the play is served properly, one should see the potential for this seriousness of the playwright's purpose all the way through.

Just as we are coming to terms with this seriousness, Shakespeare brings on all the comic characters again. They have written a song to come at the end of their show and want to perform it. 'The Owl and the Cuckoo' concerns the renewal of the seasons. The cycle of life, and of love as well, goes on. This song also brings together some of Shakespeare's thoughts on nature in this play. It is very much a country piece, lyrical and pastoral. Armado finishes the whole thing off with a beautifully simple parting shot: 'The words of Mercury are harsh after the songs of Apollo. You that way: we this way'. The final act turns the play on its head and leaves one with knowledge of a much darker and more melancholic element to this play than one suspects on first reading it. And indeed the parting of the lovers at the end of the play brings us back, perhaps, to its title, *Love's Labour's Lost*.

TITUS ANDRONICUS
Anthony Clare

Anthony Clare is the Professor of Psychological Medicine at St Bartholomew's Hospital in London. He is a well-known radio and television presenter, whose programmes include In The Psychiatrist's Chair *and* Motives. *He made this programme on location in Highgate Cemetery.*

If there is one Shakespearean play which would appear to merit one of those pre-transmission warnings about the sensibilities of viewers being offended by some of the scenes which are such a feature of many of today's X-rated movies, it must be *Titus Andronicus*. One critic wrote that, if the play had six acts instead of five, Shakespeare would get at the spectators sitting in the first row of the stalls and let them die in agony because on the stage no-one, except Lucius, remains alive. Indeed, before the curtain even rises, twenty-five of Titus's sons have already died in battle. Thirty-five people die during the play itself. The usual defence of Shakespeare, mounted by those who would be horrified at any suggestion that *Titus Andronicus* is the sixteenth century equivalent of today's video nasties, is that he does not attack our sensibilities. They claim that the murders are symbolic, or take place dutifully out of sight, and are thus purified and sanitised of their arousing or disturbing effects. But this is not so with *Titus*. Ten major murders are committed in full view of the audience. Titus has his hand chopped off. The two sons of the Queen of the Goths have their throats cut. A nurse is strangled. Off-stage mercifully, Titus's daughter, Lavinia, has her arms cut off, her tongue cut out and is twice raped. Add to all this the play's torture and cannibalism and you can see why the need for the pre-transmission warning becomes irresistible.

Nor can the play be dismissed, as some have tried to dismiss it, as not by Shakespeare or as an immature work by a man who was later to use much of the character of Titus in Lear and of the black Moor, Aaron, in the white devil, Iago. *Titus Andronicus* was not an aberration written for money and best forgotten. It was one of the most successful plays in Shakespeare's time. Elizabethan and

Jacobean audiences voted it into their Top Ten. Ben Jonson commented sourly on its success and the dates of its earliest performances – 1594, 1600 and 1611– suggested to one critic an almost continuous run, which was by no means always the case as far as Shakespeare's plays were concerned. There is even a drawing, known as the Longleat or Peachum drawing, which depicts a particular scene from the play. Not everybody, however, liked it. For plays like *Titus*, and it does belong to the Theatre of Revenge which includes Marlowe's *The Jew of Malta* and Thomas Kyd's *The Spanish Tragedy*, provoked observations from the Puritan critics of the time concerning the debasement of the soul which results from playgoing. Such observations bear more than a passing resemblance to the protestations concerning *The Romans in Britain* which were advanced by Mary Whitehouse and the Festival of Light. One critic, Philip Stubbes, would have none of the argument that watching plays might ultimately have a morally uplifting and cleansing impact. After its popularity in the sixteenth and seventeenth centuries *Titus* languished and, indeed, my Victorian collection of Shakespeare's plays does not even include it. I am not greatly surprised. The blood-letting, violation of taboos and the unqualified portrayal of untrammelled lust, greed, deceit and power would have been too much for Victorian sensibilities. Besides which, *Titus Andronicus* gives a picture of family life which the Victorians, those founders of today's much revered institution, could hardly be expected to stomach. Yet in these post-Freudian days, it is the picture of beastly family and intra-family relationships which modern audiences, familiar with the notion of the family as the bosom of all manner of reptilian desires, even madness itself, will find quite acceptable.

Titus Andronicus, whatever else it is about, is about family relationships. It deals with family loyalty on whose behalf anything, even murder itself, is justified. It shows family honour which, when disfigured, permits the grossest acts whereby its virtue is restated. The opening speech of the play has Saturninus staking his claim to the Roman throne as the first-born son of the late Emperor. Filial rivalry sees Bassianus, his brother, contesting the claim. The Tribunes are anxious to award the crown outside the family to the victorious general, Titus Andronicus, back from the long and bloody war against the Goths. As mentioned, this war has already claimed twenty-five of Titus's sons. The play is barely minutes old before Titus and his living sons declare their intention of spilling more blood, this time that of Alarbus, the first son of Tamora, the prisoner Queen of the Goths. The purpose of this bloodshedding is to appease the groaning shadows of the sons already dead. Tamora, no pure and undefiled saint herself, pleads not as a queen but as a mother for the life of her first-born, but to no avail. Remorselessly the blood sacrifice is enacted and, remorselessly, the tragedy unfolds – Titus and his family are engulfed and Rome becomes a jungle of tigers devouring their prey:

LUCIUS: See, lord and father, how we have perform'd
    Our Roman rites: Alarbus' limbs are lopp'd,
    And entrails feed the sacrificing fire,
    Whose smoke like incense doth perfume the sky.
    Remaineth nought but to inter our brethen,
    And with loud 'larums welcome them to Rome.
TITUS:Let it be so, and let Andronicus
    Make this his latest farewell to their souls.
    In peace and honour rest you here, my sons;
    Rome's readiest champions, repose you here in rest,
    Secure from worldly chances and mishaps!
    Here lurks no treason, here no envy swells,
    Here grow no damned drugs, here are no storms,
    No noise, but silence and eternal sleep.
    In peace and honour rest you here, my sons!

                            1.1.142–56

There is much reverence shown to one's own dead in *Titus*. The death of others is of little moment. Poor benighted Titus was not the first, nor indeed the last, to believe that one could satisfy honour, defend one's family and bring about a lasting peace through blood.

Worse still, he is utterly naive and backs away from the offer of the Imperial crown in favour of the unscrupulous Saturninus. Emperor now, Saturninus promptly lays claim to the hand of the daughter of Titus, the fair Lavinia. This provokes sibling jealousy once again for Lavinia belongs to brother Bassianus, who promptly seizes her and with the help of the sons of Titus makes off with her. Saturninus is not greatly shaken by this turn of events and promptly switches his affections to Tamora, the Queen of the Goths. But Titus, ever the man of principle, is outraged at this affront to the Emperor's honour and kills his own son, Mutius. It is the one intra-familial murder in the play, the one of blood by blood. The Emperor makes off with his new bride, leaving Titus to engage in one of those empty, pointless family wrangles about the funeral, about whether the dishonoured dead son should be buried along with the rest of his family in the family vault:

MARCUS: O Titus, see, O see what thou hast done!
    In a bad quarrel slain a virtuous son.
TITUS: No, foolish Tribune, no; no son of mine –
    Nor thou, nor these, confederates in the deed
    That hath dishonoured all our family;
    Unworthy brother and unworthy sons!
LUCIUS: But let us give him burial, as becomes;
    Give Mutius burial with our bretheren.
TITUS: Traitors, away! he rests not in this tomb.
    This monument five hundred years hath stood,
    Which I have sumptuously re-edified;
    Here none but soldiers and Rome's servitors
    Repose in fame; none basely slain in brawls.
    Bury him where you can, he comes not here.

                                        1.1.341–54

It is the sort of row that tears apart families in two-up, two-down suburbia and casts a chilly shadow over Yuletide family gatherings.

What follows is not so much a river of blood as a tidal wave. Within a scene's breath, we see Tamora's evil sons, Chiron and Demetrius, vying with each other in their lust for Lavinia. Influenced by the reprehensible Aaron, they make common cause to murder Bassianus and rape Lavinia. As this is a play where the thought but occurs and action quickly follows, the opportunity rapidly presents itself. But Shakespeare does not waste such an opportunity to portray family life in one of its less attractive aspects. Not content with his novel portrayal of brothers-in-arms, he provides an interesting twist to the notion of the powerful mother behind every man of action. After Bassianus has been stabbed on stage, Lavinia pleads for her virtue by appealing to Tamora as one woman to another. But there are stronger bonds than mere sex:

LAVINIA: O, do not learn her wrath – she taught it thee;
    The milk thou suck'dst from her did turn to marble,
    Even at thy teat thou hadst thy tyranny.
    Yet every mother breeds not sons alike:
    Do thou entreat her show a woman's pity.
CHIRON: What, wouldst thou have me prove myself a bastard?
LAVINIA: 'Tis true, the raven doth not hatch a lark.
    Yet have I heard – O, could I find it now! –
    The lion, mov'd with pity, did endure
    To have his princely paws par'd all away.

Some say that ravens foster forlorn children,
The whilst their own birds famish in their nests;
O, be to me, though thy hard heart say no,
Nothing so kind, but something pitiful!

TAMORA: I know not what it means; away with her!

LAVINIA: O, let me teach thee! For my father's sake,
That gave thee life when well he might have slain thee,
Be not obdurate, open thy deaf ears.

TAMORA: Had'st thou in person ne'er offended me,
Even for his sake am I pitiless.
Remember, boys, I pour'd forth tears in vain
To save your brother from the sacrifice;
But fierce Andronicus would not relent.
Therefore away with her, and use her as you will:
The worse to her the better lov'd of me.

LAVINIA: O Tamora, be call'd a gentle queen,
And with thine own hands kill me in this place!
For 'tis not life that I have begg'd so long;
Poor I was slain when Bassianus died.

TAMORA: What beg'st thou, then? Fond woman, let me go.

LAVINIA: 'Tis present death I beg; and one thing more,
That womanhood denies my tongue to tell:
O, keep me from their worse than killing lust,
And tumble me into some loathsome pit,
Where never man's eye may behold my body;
Do this, and be a charitable murderer.

TAMORA: So should I rob my sweet sons of their fee;
No, let them satisfy their lust on thee.

2.3.143–80

''tis true, the raven doth not hatch a lark', says Lavinia. This theme, that vice cannot beget virtue, becomes a refrain on the limitations and influences of family transmission and genetic effects. How do we explain depraved behaviour, sickening violence and perverted destruction? Is it, we ask ourselves, the fault of our parents? Is it the society in which we live? Is it the result of watching degrading television serials, plays and films? Lavinia appeals to Chiron to ask his mother to intercede. Chiron replies that, were his mother to show pity, this would declare him a bastard and no true son of hers. It is a chilling vision of the genetic penetrance of evil.

Worse is to follow. In Act Three we return to the city from the hunting wood where Bassanius was murdered and Lavinia raped.

We see Titus, who so religiously sacrificed Tamora's son, earnestly pleading for the lives of two of his own, falsely accused of the murder of Bassianus. He is told that, if he severs his own hand and sends it to the Emperor Saturninus, his sons will be spared. He persuades Aaron without too much difficulty to assist him in this deed, but his hand and the heads of his sons are returned. This provokes Titus to an anguished plea to be released from the nightmare and then, as he surveys the butchered, mangled remains of what was once his family, the inevitable cry of revenge:

> Why, I have not another tear to shed;
> Besides, this sorrow is an enemy,
> And would usurp upon my wat'ry eyes
> And make them blind with tributary tears.
> Then which way shall I find Revenge's cave?
> For these two heads do seem to speak to me,
> And threat me I shall never come to bliss
> Till all these mischiefs be return'd again
> Even in their throats that have committed them.
> Come, let me see what task I have to do.
> You heavy people, circle me about,
> That I may turn me to each one of you
> And swear unto my soul to right your wrongs.
> The vow is made.

3.1.267–80

And so it was war between the family of Titus and the Emperor and his Queen of the Goths. Titus teeters on madness, that affliction from which many families suffer and which, if a certain school of psychiatry is to be believed, some families cause. There has been much discussion about the madness of Titus, some of it surrounding a celebrated scene in which his brother Marcus kills a fly and provokes Titus into an intemperate rage:

> MARCUS: Alas, my lord, I have but kill'd a fly.
> TITUS: 'But'! How if that fly had a father and mother?
> How would he hang his slender gilded wings
> And buzz lamenting doings in the air',
> Poor harmless fly,
> That with his pretty buzzing melody
> Came here to make us merry! And thou hast kill'd him.
> MARCUS: Pardon me, sir; it was a black ill-favour'd fly,
>   Like to the Empress' Moor; therefore I kill'd him.
> TITUS: O,O,O!

Then pardon me for reprehending thee,
For thou hast done a charitable deed.
Give me they knife, I will insult on him,
Flattering myself as if it were the Moor
Come hither purposely to poison me.
There's for thyself, and that's for Tamora.
Ah, sirrah!
Yet, I think, we are not brought so low
But that between us we can kill a fly
That comes in likeness of a coal-black Moor.
MARCUS: Alas, poor man! grief has so wrought on him,
He takes false shadows for true substances.

3.2.59–80

Within this exchange is packed a small sermon on the difficulty which even men of war encounter when asked to kill those with whom they can share their common humanity. Once you imagine a grieving father and desolate mother, it is hard to recapture the ease, nay, the satisfaction with which men kill when they have successfully depersonalised and dehumanised their target. 'How if that fly had a father and mother?', asks Titus, even though he spurned Tamora's pleadings for her first-born and killed his own son, Mutius. This is the same Titus who, in the short space of three acts, has seen his daughter mutilated and two sons beheaded. But the ambiguity about family relationships is not only Shakespeare's. Today we recoil from family murder, yet cope thoughtlessly with the statistic that, if we are to be murdered, it is most likely to be by someone to whom we are related or by whom we are known. This is not the bountiful, respectable Victorian stereotype of the family. This is the nest of vipers, the source of all our strengths and the genesis of both our noblest hopes and foullest desires. Titus Andronicus is the archetype of the flawed paternal figure, the victorious general and the incompetent father at whose hands, directly and indirectly, his children perish.

The succession of violent spectacles abates in Act Four, but the theme of family murderousness persists. Indeed, Shakespeare now shows us a cameo of the transmission of violence through a vision of the grandson of Titus, the young Lucius, being initiated into the whole sorry catalogue of violence and revenge. The speechless Lavinia writes the names of her assailants and the result is yet another declaration of family purpose and intent which today still strikes a disturbingly apposite note:

BOY: I say, my lord, that if I were a man

Their mother's bedchamber should not be safe
For these base bondmen to the yoke of Rome.
MARCUS: Ay, that's my boy! Thy father hath full oft
For his ungrateful country done the like.
BOY: And, uncle, so will I, an if I live.
TITUS: Come, go with me into mine armoury.
Lucius, I'll fit thee; and withal my boy
Shall carry from me to the Empress' sons
Presents that I intend to send them both.
Come, come; thou'lt do my message, wilt thou not?
BOY: Ay, with my dagger in their bosoms, grandsire.
TITUS: No, boy, not so; I'll teach thee another course.

4.1.108–20

The play moves to its culmination, a succession of stabbings
which act as both a climax and a catharsis. Titus captures Tamora's vicious sons, Chiron and Demetrius, and cuts their throats.
This particular mayhem is carried out on stage with the assistance
of the mutilated Lavinia, who catches their blood in a basin which
she carries helpfully between her mangled stumps! Titus then
prepares the banquet to which he has invited Saturninus and
Tamora. Dressed as a cook, Titus serves what must be the most
infamous meat pie in theatrical history. It is indeed significant that
Tamora eats her sons at a meal. As any mother knows the meal,
that great symbol of family unity and devotion over which she has
sweated long and hard, can be wrecked in acrimony and become a
source of disharmony and dissent. So dominant is this mother that
literally, albeit mistakenly, she eats that which she has created.
This is no raven that has hatched a lark. This is a sow that eats her
farrow.

But this being Shakespeare, there is a puzzle. Aaron is so
implacable in his perversity that Shakespeare made him black,
which he had more than a tendency to do in those days. Although
Aaron is given lines which can only remind modern audiences of
pantomime's Demon King, he is also allowed one moment of
human sensibility about his son. His adulterous relationship with
Tamora has produced a black infant whom everyone wishes to
kill. Aaron fights for the life of his son, although his own is about to
end:

Stay, murderous villains, will you kill your brother!
Now, by the burning tapers of the sky
That shone so brightly when this boy was got,
He dies upon my scimitar's sharp point

That touches this my first-born son and heir.
I tell you, younglings, not Enceladus,
With all his threat'ning band of Typhon's brood,
Nor great Alcides, nor the god of war,
Shall seize this prey out of his father's hands.
What, what, ye sanguine, shallow-hearted boys!
Ye white-lim'd walls! ye alehouse painted signs!
Coal-black is better than another hue
In that it scorns to bear another hue;
For all the water in the ocean
Can never turn the swan's black legs to white,
Although she lave them hourly in the flood.
Tell the Empress from me I am of age
To keep mine own – excuse it how she can.

4.2.88–105

'For all the water in the ocean/Can never turn the swan's black legs to white'. *Titus Andronicus* is a play which appears to endorse a particularly blunt view of the transmission of personal characteristics, values and patterns of behaviour. That which we breed ourselves, small things but our own, carry intractably our vices and our virtues. The ultimate mark of the civilised man is his devotion to his own blood. Yet Aaron is far from civilised and the goodly Titus kills his own son. There is nothing more revered than a mother's love, yet Tamora goads her two sons to ravish an innocent girl and, by way of comment on her dominance over them, ends up eating them in a pie. It is a bleak, pitilessly bleak, vision of the corruption of power and of the manner in which political life is conditioned by lust, greed, ambition, cruelty and revenge. But it is more than an exercise in political and imperial depravity. It is an exploration of what, in the name of family ties, brotherly love, fatherly responsibility and maternal possessiveness, we have done to each other and are still doing today.

TITUS ANDRONICUS
Patrick Stewart

*Patrick Stewart is a member of the Royal Shake-
speare Company. Apart from playing both Aaron and
the title role in* Titus Andronicus, *his rôles have
included Cassius in* Julius Caesar, *Oberon in* A
Midsummer Night's Dream *and Shylock in* The
Merchant of Venice. *He also played Claudius in
the BBC TV production of* Hamlet.

My lovely Aaron, wherefore look'st thou sad
When everything doth make a gleeful boast?
The birds chant melody on every bush;
The snakes lie rolled in the cheerful sun;
The green leaves quiver with the cooling wind
And make a chequer'd shadow on the ground;
Under their sweet shade, Aaron, let us sit,
And whilst the babbling echo mocks the hounds,
Replying shrilly to the well-tun'd horns,
As if a double hunt were heard at once,
Let us sit down and mark their yellowing noise;
And – after conflict such as was suppos'd
The wand'ring prince and Dido once enjoyed,
When with a happy storm they were surpris'd,
And curtain'd with a counsel-keeping cave –
We may, each wreathed in the other's arms,
Our pastimes done, possess a golden slumber,
Whiles hounds and horns and sweet melodious birds
Be unto us as is a nurse's song
Of lullaby to bring her babe asleep.

2.3.10–29

Anyone unfamiliar with Shakespeare's *Titus Andronicus* could be
excused for believing that this speech is from a play of romance,
tenderness and tranquility. A pastoral, perhaps, set in a Roman
'Forest of Arden'. However this lyrical sensuality, moving through
loving sexual excitement to a contented repose, gives no indication
of the true personality of the lovers, Aaron and Tamora. In fact, as
representatives of their sex, they are as villainous, monstrous,

cruel and heartless a pair as ever spat out an iambic pentameter. The play that they inhabit is hardly a pastoral.

Titus Andronicus, written around 1590 when Shakespeare was in his mid-twenties, has been variously described as 'a heap of rubbish rather than a structure', a 'barbaric pageant' and a 'horror comic'. T. S. Eliot called it 'one of the stupidest and most uninspiring plays ever written'. Other critics have seen it more favourably though. J. C. Maxwell wrote in his foreword to the Arden edition: 'one already sees Shakespeare in *Titus* planning on the grand scale and achieving a result that, however little it may appeal to us, is beyond the powers of any other dramatist writing at the time'. Peter Brook in his programme notes for the Stratford Memorial Theatre production in 1955 saw the play as 'an austere and grim Roman tragedy, horrifying indeed, but with a real primitive strength, achieving at times a barbaric dignity'. This Stratford revival, with Peter Brook's 'brilliantly imaginative' direction and Laurence Olivier's performance as Titus, has become a landmark in British theatre. It was not, however, their forthcoming collaboration on *Titus* that attracted attention in the summer of 1955, but rather that the play was being produced at all. It had only been revived once in the past 100 years and only three times since 1725. It had never been played at the Shakespeare Memorial Theatre – the only play in the First Folio so ignored – and there was astonishment when Brook proposed its revival. It was not always so unpopular. It was an immediate success at its first recorded performance in January 1594. Indeed in the late sixteenth and early seventeenth centuries *Titus* was *The Mousetrap* of its day. But public taste changed and there was revulsion at the grotesque, blood-letting plays of the kind typified by *Titus Andronicus*. Even so, it is remarkable that any play with William Shakespeare's name on it should have suffered theatrical obscurity for so long.

The great controversy over *Titus* really rages over who wrote it, for if the play was absent from England's stages for decades it was very much alive in the studies of Shakespeare scholars and literary detectives of all kinds. Now this was not part of the unending saga of the Marlowe, Bacon and Greene fanatics, but a steady and continuing examination of the text of *Titus* in the light of other playwrights' work in an attempt to ascribe the authorship accurately. Some saw absolutely no indication of Shakespeare's hand. 'Too disgusting to be the Bard's', said Nathan Field. Edward Ravenscroft, a minor Restoration playwright, stated in 1687 that he had been informed by 'some anciently conversant with the stage' that it was not Shakespeare's work 'but brought by a private author to be acted and Shakespeare only gave some master touches to one or two of the principal characters'. Dover Wilson points out, however, that Ravenscroft was not a very reliable person and was chiefly inspired by a desire to advertise his own 'improved' version. As late as 1929 a critic wrote 'of *Titus Andronicus* I need say nothing as scarcely anyone thinks Shakespeare wrote it.' But scholarly opinion was already shifting. Though there may have been an earlier play reworked and revised by Shakespeare, the bulk of the play is now believed to be his, except for the entire First Act which is generally attributed to George Peel, an established dramatist before Shakespeare began writing. The justifications for this attribution are too lengthy and complex for me to repeat here, but they involve minute comparisons of the *Titus* text with both Peel's other work and Shakespeare's early plays and poems. It still intrigues me that one modern Shakespearean academic, having examined the scholarly evidence, writes that he can never quite believe that it is Shakespeare's work 'while actually reading Act One'. Clearly what he is saying is that it does not 'feel' like Shakespeare. If the academic can have such a subjective response to the play's language, how does the actor respond when all his imaginative and technical skills are bent towards inhabiting a character and giving him a coherent and vibrant life?

I know from acting Titus at Stratford in 1982 that performing Act One was like being a handicapped runner in a race. The language, images and rhythms were weights holding one back. But, as we moved through Act Two, the play tightened and gathered pace. The language began to soar and the actor could take off and fly in the marvellous Act Three. Here is an example of Act One:

> TITUS: And here in sight of Rome, to Saturnine,
> King and commander of our commonweal,
> The wide world's Emperor, do I consecrate
> My sword, my chariot, and my prisoners;
> Presents well worthy Rome's imperious lord;
> Receive them then, the tribute that . . . .

I.I.246–51

And so on and so on and so on. There's lots more where that came from. Titus has very few lines in Act Two, but in the first speech of Act Three he is on his knees in the public street pleading for his sons' lives:

For these, Tribunes, in the dust I write
My heart's deep languor and my soul's sad tears.
Let my tears stanch the earth's dry appetite;
My sons' sweet blood will make it shame and blush.
O earth, I will befriend thee more with rain
That shall distil from these two ancient urns,
Than youthful April shall with all his show'rs.
In summer's drought I'll drop upon thee still;
In winter with warm tears I'll melt the snow
And keep eternal spring-time on thy face,
So thou refuse to drink my dear sons' blood.   3.1.12–22

Now this is still early Shakespeare and the actor has those 'two ancient urns' to cope with, but here is character, feeling, situation, need and poetry. Game, set and match to the scholars.

Titus Andronicus is a revenge play but, curiously, there are two revenge plots: one against Titus and one by him. Titus is a Roman general returning home in triumph after a victory against the Goths. At his chariot wheels he brings in chains the Queen of the Goths, Tamora, her three sons and a black slave, Aaron, whom we later learn is Tamora's lover. Titus's return follows the recent death of the Emperor:

Hail, Rome, victorious in thy mourning weeds!
Lo, as the bark that hath discharg'd her fraught
Returns with precious lading to the bay
From whence at first she weigh'd her anchorage,
Cometh Andronicus, bound with laurel boughs,
To re-salute his country with his tears,
Tears of true joy for his return to Rome.
Thou great defender of this Capitol,
Stand gracious to the rites that we intend!
Romans, of five and twenty valiant sons,
Half of the number that King Priam had,
Behold the poor remains, alive and dead!
These that survive let Rome reward with love;
These that I bring unto their latest home,
With burial amongst their ancestors.

1.1.70–84

However, before this happens, Titus sacrifices Tamora's eldest son, Alarbus, 't'appease their groaning shadows that are gone'. This is distressing to the Queen, but her pleas are not heeded and in an aside she and her remaining sons vow revenge on Titus. This incident provides the actor playing Lucius, Titus's son, with one of the most lip-smacking speeches in Shakespeare:

> See, lord and father, how we have perform'd
> Our Roman rites: Alarbus' limbs are lopp'd,
> And entrails feed the sacrificing fire,
> Whose smoke like incense doth perfume the sky.

I.I.142–5

Luckily for the audience, this is one horror that happens off stage! The dead Emperor's two sons are contending for the throne, but the Tribunes' and the peoples' choice is Titus. He refuses and puts his vote behind the Emperor's eldest son, Saturninus. In gratitude, Saturninus offers to make Titus's daughter, Lavinia, his Empress. Titus agrees but his sons claim tht she is already betrothed to Saturninus's brother, Bassianus, whom they support for Emperor, and who now takes her away. One of Titus's sons, Mutius, guards their escape, but Titus himself, humiliated and enraged, kills him. Saturninus announces that he has changed his mind and is now determined to marry Tamora, whom he has spotted for the first time only a few lines earlier. A general reconciliation takes place nevertheless and Act One ends with the two couples going up to the Temple to be married.

The Goths' revenge on Titus for sacrificing Tamora's son begins at once. The Queen's two remaining sons, Chiron and Demetrius, with Aaron's encouragement plot to rape Lavinia. They achieve this, assisted by their mother, the very next day during a hunting party, prefacing the deed with the murder of Lavinia's husband, Bassianus. Then, to prevent her accusations, the boys cut out Lavinia's tongue and chop off her hands. Aaron fixes the evidence so that two of Titus's three remaining sons are accused of Bassianus's murder. They are taken to execution and, for an attempt to free them, the third and eldest son, Lucius, is banished for life. At this point Titus's brother, Marcus, brings him face to face with his mutilated daughter. Aaron then arrives and announces that the Emperor has agreed to spare the lives of Titus's two sons if either Lucius, Titus or Marcus will 'chop off your hand and sent it to the King'. The three disagree about whose hand it should be and, while Lucius and Marcus are looking for an axe, Titus bids Aaron cut off his right hand. This is, of course, all a trick and it is not the sons who are returned but their two severed heads plus Titus's hand. Hammer blows of horror have fallen on Titus's head, but with this last one it seems that grief, pain and despair have hollowed him of all feeling. He is a man in a waking nightmare who can only murmur 'when will this fearful slumber have an end?'. For me this is one of Shakespeare's greatest moments. It's all him and so typical of his marvellous craft to find, at the height of a character's suffering, the simple phrase that locks tragedy into the everyday, human experience. For me, this line ranks with Lear's 'pray you undo this button' and Ophelia's 'I hope all will be well'.

This is also the moment of Titus's vow and the rest of the play is taken up with the acting out of his revenge. I won't reveal its extraordinary climax except to say that there are some magnificent moments of bizarre drama, breathtaking comedy and much fine language to come. Laurence Olivier has described Titus as 'a punishing role'. It is certainly that, though not because of its length. It is a 'suffering role' in which the character is a victim rather than a motivator for much of the time and that is what makes it exhausting. For the bulk of the play he is saying 'oh please don't do that to me. Oh, you've done it and it's all dreadful. It can't be any worse. Oh, yes it is. Now this has happened and it's very much worse'. All this is trying and relentless and it makes it hard for the actor to find variety and freshness, line by line. Titus's speeches can easily turn into one long complaint. The other difficulty with Titus is that he is old so that, like Lear, his stamina is limited and his capacity to take punishment is low. Therefore, unlike Macbeth or Othello, he is quickly pushed to his physical limits and he dredges energy from non-existent resources. Now, if the actor is not watchful, he can exhaust his resources too. When I was rehearsing in Stratford in 1982 John Barton, the director, warned me that the great pitfall for an actor in a role like Titus was to allow the emotion to take over. He constantly advised me to 'stay cool within the part'. I know that this was good counsel, but it is hard to achieve in acting terms, particularly when you have just had your hand chopped off and your children are being dismembered all around you. It is easier to achieve in some passages than others. Titus says, just after he has been shown his mutilated daughter,

It was my dear, and he that wounded her,
Hath hurt me more than had he kill'd me dead;
For now I stand as one upon a rock,
Environ'd with a wilderness of sea,
Who marks the waxing tide grow wave by wave,
Expecting ever when some envious surge
Will in his brinish bowels swallow him.

3.1.91–7

The shock of the sight of his daugher numbs Titus and it is as if for these passages he is standing outside himself, watching the events as if they were happening to a third person. There is a sense of detachment in this language and Barton's 'coolness' can at least be attempted. But, in the very next speech, talking to Lavinia, how can you stay detached with language like this?

> Shall thy good uncle and thy brother Lucius
> And thou and I sit round about some fountain,
> Looking all downwards to behold our cheeks
> How they are stain'd, like meadows yet not dry
> With miry slime left on them by a flood?
> And in the fountain shall we gaze so long,
> Till the fresh taste be taken from that clearness,
> And made a brine-pit with out bitter tears?
> Or shall we cut away our hands like thine?
> Or shall we bite our tongues, and in dumb shows
> Pass the remainder of our hateful days?
> What shall we do? Let us that have our tongues
> Plot some device of further misery
> To make us wonder'd at in time to come.
>
> 3.1.122–35

And yet, a little later on in the same scene, Shakespeare combines wonderfully the detachment with the overflowing emotion as Titus rejects Marcus's pleas to be more stoical in the face of his woes:

> If there were reason for these miseries,
> Then into limits could I bind my woes.
> When heaven doth weep, doth not the earth o'erflow?
> If the winds rage, doth not the sea wax mad,
> Threat'ning the welkin with his big-swol'n face?
> And wilt thou have a reason for this coil?
> I am the sea; hark how her sighs do blow.
> She is the weeping welkin, I the earth;
> Then must my sea be moved with her sighs;
> Then must my earth with her continual tears
> Become a deluge, overflow'd and drown'd;
> For why my bowels cannot hide her woes,
> But like a drunkard must I vomit them.   3.1.220–32

The other difficulty in playing Titus is getting the first act right. As I have said, the language is no help. There is plenty of what George IV found everywhere in Shakespeare: 'sad stuff'. But it is

Titus's actions that are hard to justify. He returns to Rome a conquering hero and at once, from a position of power, makes some stupid and quite potty mistakes. There is another close parallel here with Lear, whose division of his country and banishment of Cordelia begins the headlong tumble into calamity. So Titus's irrational behaviour, hubris and stubborness sets in motion the train of horrific events. He shows no compassion to his defeated enemy, Tamora. He refuses the crown – his only sensible act – but at once assumes the role of kingmaker and, of the two sons, he chooses the more unsuitable, an unstable hysteric. He kills his own son, refuses a proper burial and insults his few friends. Having been humiliated and then patronised by the Emperor, he then invites him to go hunting. All this has to be made sense of by the actor and the psychology got right, or no audience will tolerate him for the next two and a half hours. Who cares what happens to a cruel, stupid and reactionary old man? Titus is a soldier and a conservative. His life has been spent at the outposts of the Empire and for the last ten years he has been fighting the Goths. Twenty-one of his sons have died on the campaign – he has twenty-five to begin with or, as he says, 'half the number that King Priam had', which gives some indication of how he views himself. He anticipates general respect when he returns, but he is a child in the ways of Rome, politically naïve and expecting everyone to share his sense of military honour. He is out of step with the time and so one mistake leads to another. He is, in fact, unworldly, and for that we pity his vulnerability in this Rome – 'this wilderness of tigers' as he calls it when his eyes begin to open. I feel, however, that he can never become a truly tragic figure. Unlike Lear, who passes through madness to insight, Titus's sufferings only lead him to ultimate revenge. Retribution and retaliation become his philosophy. He is, nevertheless, conceived on a grand scale and anticipates, in part, the giants that were to come.

I also played Leontes in *The Winter's Tale* in that 1982 season at Stratford and it was fascinating coping with the quite different problems of very early and very late Shakespeare. The metronomic regularity of the verse of the early play, stiff and often artificial, contrasted with the complex, elusive but carefully structured rhythms of the later one. Shakespeare abandons one story half way through *The Winter's Tale*, takes up another and then thrillingly unites them at the end. *Titus* follows a simple and unbroken narrative line. We are at the heart of *The Winter's Tale* within 150 lines, whereas in *Titus* it takes three and a half acts. *Titus* is heavy with rhetoric, whilst *The Winter's Tale* springs with spontaneous speech. I was also rehearsing *Henry IV* before that season was out and there, almost at the mid-point of Shakespeare's writing life, one could look back at where he had been and forward to where he was to go. It was thus an extraordinary experience to rehearse *Henry IV* in the morning, perform a matinee of *Titus Andronicus* and an evening of *The Winter's Tale*. If there is one quality that separates *The Winter's Tale* and *Titus* it is characterisation and language. Before Shakespeare, no playwright had individualised a character so finely through the very words the character speaks and few have approached him since. Nobody else talks like Shylock, Hotspur or Othello. They are the words. Only one character, however, stands out unforgettably from the rest in this aspect in *Titus Andronicus*, splashing the ear with vivid, idiosyncratic words and phrases. Aaron, the play's principal villain, has a richness and an energy of language, wit and self-knowledge that elevates him above a mere horror story monster and excitingly anticipates such creations as Iago, Enobarbus and Mercutio.

In Aaron's first speech it is as though Shakespeare wants him to lift the play out of George Peel's hands and out of the dust of Rome's streets and give it an elevation from which tragedy can then topple it:

Now climbeth Tamora Olympus' top,
Safe out of Fortune's shot, and sits aloft,
Secure of thunder's crack or lightning flash,
Advanc'd above pale envy's threat'ning reach.
As when the golden sun salutes the morn,
And, having gilt the ocean with his beams,
Gallops the zodiac in his glistering coach
And overlooks the highest-peering hills,
So Tamora.
Upon her wit doth earthly honour wait,
And virtue stoops and trembles at her frown.
Then, Aaron, arm thy heart and fit thy thoughts
To mount aloft with thy imperial mistress,
And mount her pitch whom thou in triumph long
Hast prisoner held, fett'red in amorous chains,
And faster bound to Aaron's charming eyes
Than is Prometheus tied to Caucasus.
Away with slavish weeds and servile thoughts!
I will be bright and shine in pearl and gold,
To wait upon this new made emperess.

To wait, said I? To wanton with this queen,
This goddess, this Semiramis, this nymph,
This siren that will charm Rome's Saturnine,
And see his shipwreck and his commonweal's.   2.1.1–24

He encounters Tamora's two stupid, psychopathic sons, Chiron
and Demetrius, immediately after this speech. His language at
once takes on characteristics of the boys' personalities. He feeds
them words they want to hear:

The forest walks are wide and spacious,
And many unfrequented plots there are
Fitted by kind for rape and villainy.
Single you thither then this dainty doe,
And strike her home by force if not by words.

2.1.114–8

In the scene where Aaron chops off Titus's hand his speech
expresses only urgency and concern for the life of Titus's sons,
though in his asides he shares with the audience his glee at his own
villainy, Aaron is all evil, but Shakespeare ensures that he will
never lose the sympathy of the audience entirely for two reasons.
First, there is his wit and, secondly, there is his love for his child,
illicitly conceived on Tamora and threatened with murder by her
two sons. When captured at last, his account of his crimes is both
appalling and comic:

Even now I curse the day – and yet, I think,
Few come within the compass of my curse –
Wherein I did not some notorious ill:
As kill a man, or else devise his death;
Ravish a maid, or plot the way to do it;
Accuse some innocent, and forswear myself;
Set deadly enmity between two friends;
Make poor men's cattle break their necks;
Set fire on barns and hay-stacks in the night,
And bid the owners quench them with their tears.
Oft have I digg'd up dead men from their graves,
And set them upright at their dear friends' door
Even when their sorrows almost was forgot,
And on their skins, as on the bark of trees,
Have with my knife carved in Roman Letters
'Let not your sorrow die, though I am dead'.
Tut, I have done a thousand dreadful things
As willingly as one would kill a fly;

And nothing grieves me heartily indeed
But that I cannot do ten thousand more.

5.1.125-44

Dover Wilson wrote that *Titus Andronicus* 'seems to jolt and bump
along like some broken-down cart, laden with bleeding corpses
from an Elizabethan scaffold and driven by an executioner from
Bedlam dressed in cap and bells'. It is a brilliant image for the play,
but *Titus* reminds us constantly that that cart in time would
become the mighty engine of plays like *Macbeth* and *King Lear*.

GENEALOGICAL TABLE

This is a simplified table, showing the succession from Edward III to Henry VIII and those characters who are important in *Henry VI, Parts 1, 2 & 3* and *Richard III*. The dates refer to lives and not to reigns.

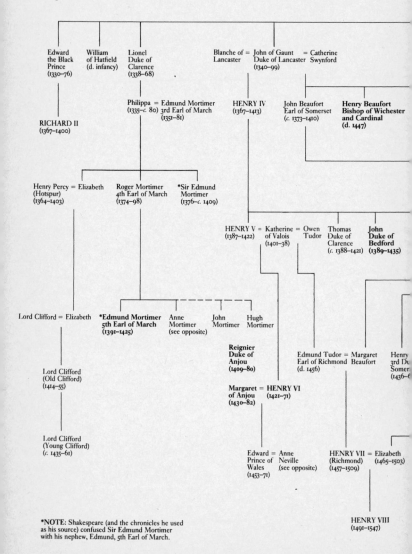

*NOTE: Shakespeare (and the chronicles he used as his source) confused Sir Edmund Mortimer with his nephew, Edmund, 5th Earl of March.

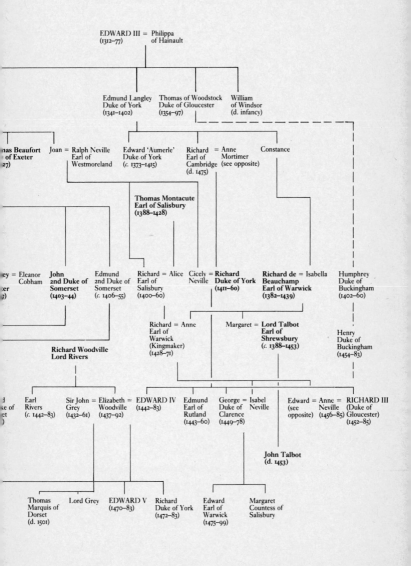

EDWARD III = Philippa
(1312–77)   of Hainault

Edmund Langley   Thomas of Woodstock   William
Duke of York   Duke of Gloucester   of Windsor
(1341–1402)   (1354–97)   (d. infancy)

…as Beaufort   Joan = Ralph Neville   Edward 'Aumerle'   Richard   = Anne   Constance
… of Exeter   Earl of   Duke of York   Earl of   Mortimer
…27)   Westmoreland   (c. 1373–1415)   Cambridge   (see opposite)
                                                                     (d. 1415)

                                             Thomas Montacute
                                             Earl of Salisbury
                                             (1388–1428)

…ey = Eleanor   John   Edmund   Richard = Alice   Cicely   Richard   Richard de   = Isabella   Humphrey
       Cobham   2nd Duke of   2nd Duke of   Earl of   Neville   Duke of York   Beauchamp   Duke of
…er   Somerset   Somerset   Salisbury   (1411–60)   Earl of Warwick   Buckingham
…)   (1403–44)   (c. 1406–55)   (1400–60)   (1382–1439)   (1402–60)

                                             Richard = Anne   Margaret = Lord Talbot   Henry
                                             Earl of   Earl of   Duke of
                                             Warwick   Shrewsbury   Buckingham
                               Richard Woodville   (Kingmaker)   (c. 1388–1453)   (1454–83)
                               Lord Rivers   (1428–71)

…d   Earl   Sir John = Elizabeth = EDWARD IV   Edmund   George = Isabel   Edward = Anne = RICHARD III
…e of Rivers   Grey   Woodville   (1442–83)   Earl of   Duke of Neville   (see   Neville (Duke of
…et   (c. 1442–83) (1432–61) (1437–92)   Rutland   Clarence   opposite)(1456–85) Gloucester)
…)   (1443–60)   (1449–78)   (1452–85)

                                                                                 John Talbot
                                                                                 (d. 1453)

        Thomas   Lord Grey   EDWARD V   Richard   Edward   Margaret
        Marquis of   (1470–83)   Duke of York   Earl of   Countess of
        Dorset   (1472–83)   Warwick   Salisbury
        (d. 1501)   (1475–99)

FURTHER READING

The following list of books is highly selective and, like the other views expressed in this volume, very much a matter of personal choice. It aims to provide a mixture of biography, background studies and criticisms:

C. L. BARBER *Shakespeare's festive comedy: a study of dramatic form in relation to social custom* (Princeton University Press, 1972, paperback)

JOHN BARTON *Playing Shakespeare* (Methuen, 1984, paperback)

MURIEL BRADBROOK *Shakespeare: the poet in his world* (Weidenfeld and Nicolson, 1978; Methuen, 1980, paperback)

JULIA BRIGGS *This stage-play world: English literature and its background 1580–1625* (Oxford University Press, 1983, cased and paperback)

NICHOLAS BROOKE *Shakespeare's early tragedies* (Methuen, 1968, o.p.)

ANTHONY BURGESS *Shakespeare* (Cape, 1970, o.p; Penguin, 1970) and *Nothing like the sun* (Hamlyn, 1982, n.e. paperback)

RICHARD DAVID *Shakespeare in the theatre* (Cambridge University Press, 1978; 1981 paperback)

NORTHROP FRYE *A natural perspective: the development of Shakespearean comedy and romance* (Harcourt, Brace & World, Inc, 1965 paperback)

ANDREW GURR *The Shakespearean stage 1574–1642* (Cambridge University Press, n.e. cased and paperback 1980)

ALFRED HARBAGE *Shakespeare's audience* (Columbia University Press, 1941 paperback; Magnolia, MA: Peter Smith, n.i. 1983)

MICHAEL HATTAWAY *Elizabethan popular theatre: plays in perform-ance* (Routledge and Kegan Paul, 1982; 1985 paperback)

TERENCE HAWKES *Shakespeare's talking animals: language and drama in society* (Edward Arnold, 1973, o.p.)

EMRYS JONES *The origins of Shakespeare* (Oxford University Press, 1977)

J. J. JORGENS *Shakespeare on film* (Indiana University Press, 1977, cased and paperback)

JAN KOTT *Shakespeare our contemporary* (Methuen, 1967 paperback)

MICHAEL LONG *The unnatural scene: a study in Shakespearean tragedy* (Methuen, 1976, o.p.)

ALLARDYCE NICOLL (ED) *Shakespeare in his own age* (Cambridge University Press, 1976 paperback)

ANNE RIGHTER *Shakespeare and the idea of the play* (Chatto and Windus, 1962, o.p.)

A. P. ROSSITER *Angel with horns and other Shakespeare lectures* (Longman, 1961, o.p.)

PETER SACCIO *Shakespeare's English Kings: history, chronicle and drama* (Galaxy Books, Oxford University Press, New York, 1982)

SAMUEL SCHOENBAWM *William Shakespeare: a documentary life* (Oxford University Press, 1979 compact edn., cased and paperback)

JOHN WILDERS *The lost garden: a view of Shakespeare's English and Roman history plays* (Macmillan, 1978, paperback)

JOHN DOVER WILSON *Life in Shakespeare's England* (Cambridge University Press, 1911, o.p; Penguin, 1944, o.p.)

JOYCE YOUINGS *Pelican social history of Britain: Sixteenth-century England* (Penguin, 1984).

It is often better to find out something about a particular play from the various anthologies and series available before going to the more specialised studies:

BBC TV Shakespeare Editions of the Plays
These contain a short discussion of the play by John Wilders, as well as an account by Henry Fenwick of some of the ideas which informed the production.

Edward Arnold Studies in English Literature
This series of short introductions now covers most of Shakespeare's plays and contains some of the best writing about them.

Penguin Shakespeare Library Anthologies
Anthologies of criticism on tragedies, histories and comedies.

Penguin Masterstudies
A new series designed to help students working at an advanced level.

Edward Arnold Stratford-upon-Avon Studies
A number of volumes of critical essays on Shakespeare as well as on Elizabethan and Jacobean theatre. Arranged thematically or chronologically.

Macmillan Casebook series
Anthologies of critical opinions on most of the plays.

Macmillan Text and Performance series
Critical introductions followed by considerations of theatricality.

Shakespeare Survey (Cambridge University Press)
Annual publication of essays, grouped around a particular theme or play, together with book and theatre reviews. Some of these essays are also collected in book form, for instance K. Muir and S. Wells (eds), *Aspects of 'King Lear'* (Cambridge University Press, 1982, cased and paperback). *Shakespeare Survey* (39) will consider Shakespeare on film and television.

British Council: Writers and their work (Profile Books)
Short introductions to groups of plays.

Useful reference books include two edited by Stanley Wells:
Shakespeare: an illustrated dictionary (Kaye and Ward, 1978; Oxford University Press, 1978, paperback)
Shakespeare: select bibliographical guides (Oxford University Press, 1974)

Many of the editions of the plays contain good introductions as well as suggestions for further reading. Besides the BBC TV editions, those published in paperback and aimed at a wide audience include:

The Arden Shakespeare (Methuen)
The New Penguin Shakespeare (Penguin)
The New Shakespeare and The New Cambridge Shakespeare
(Cambridge University Press)
The New Swan Shakespeare: Advanced Series (Longman)
The Oxford Shakespeare (Oxford University Press)
The Signet Classic Shakespeare (New American Library)